Effective Software Test Automation:

Developing an Automated Software Testing Tool

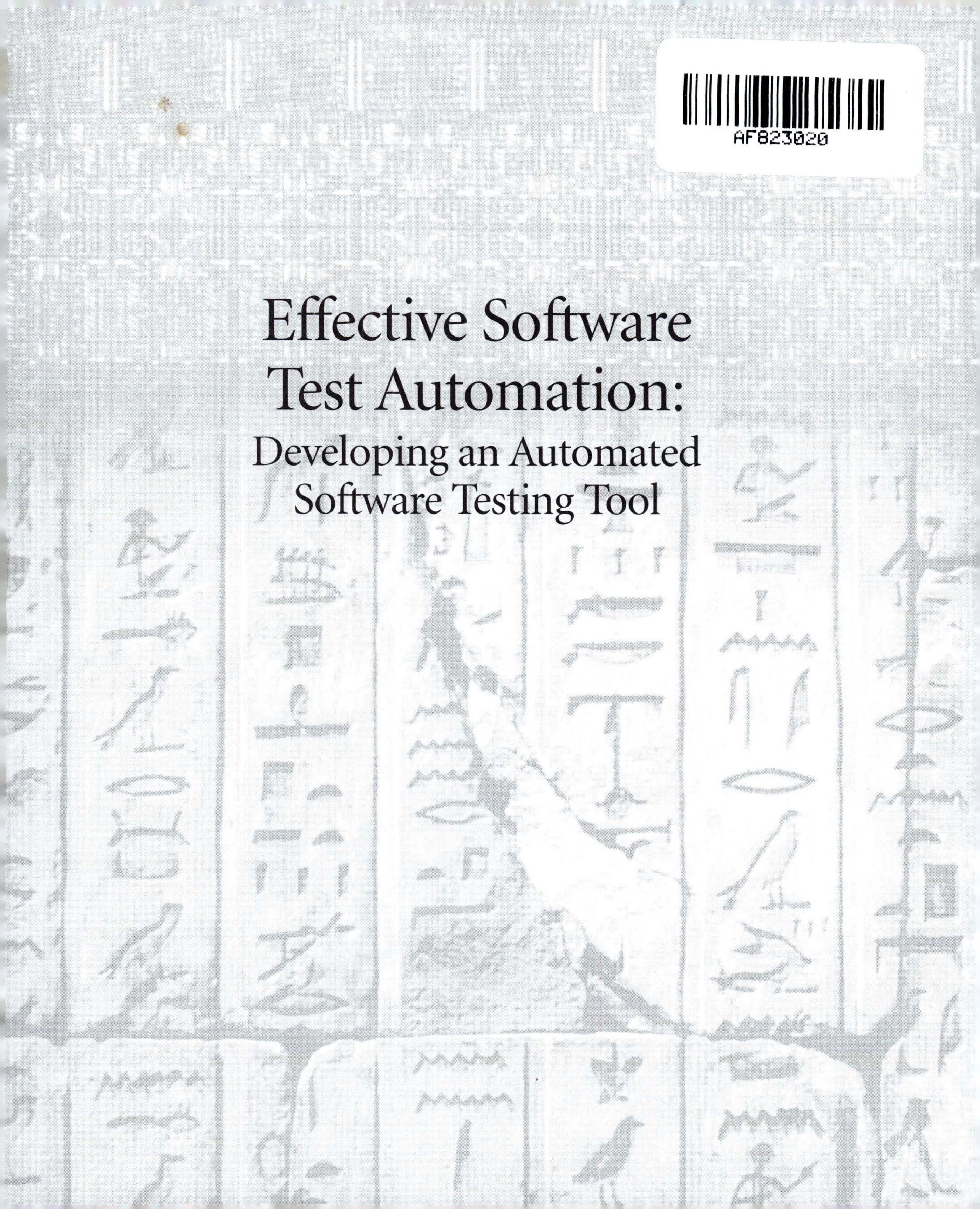

Effective Software Test Automation:

Developing an Automated Software Testing Tool

Kanglin Li and Mengqi Wu

SYBEX

San Francisco · London

Associate Publisher: Joel Fugazzotto
Acquisitions and Developmental Editor: Tom Cirtin
Production Editor: Erica Yee
Technical Editor: Acey Bunch
Copyeditor: Judy Flynn
Compositor: Maureen Forys, Happenstance Type-O-Rama
Graphic Illustrator: Jeff Wilson, Happenstance Type-O-Rama
Proofreaders: Laurie O'Connell, Nancy Riddiough
Indexer: Ted Laux
Cover Designer: Ingalls + Associates
Cover Illustrator/Photographer: Rob Atkins, The Image Bank

Library of Congress Card Number: 2003115585

ISBN: 0-7821-4320-2

Manufactured in the United States of America

10 9 8 7 6 5 4 3 2 1

SOFTWARE LICENSE AGREEMENT: TERMS AND CONDITIONS

The media and/or any online materials accompanying this book that are available now or in the future contain programs and/or text files (the "Software") to be used in connection with the book. SYBEX hereby grants to you a license to use the Software, subject to the terms that follow. Your purchase, acceptance, or use of the Software will constitute your acceptance of such terms.

The Software compilation is the property of SYBEX unless otherwise indicated and is protected by copyright to SYBEX or other copyright owner(s) as indicated in the media files (the "Owner(s)"). You are hereby granted a single-user license to use the Software for your personal, noncommercial use only. You may not reproduce, sell, distribute, publish, circulate, or commercially exploit the Software, or any portion thereof, without the written consent of SYBEX and the specific copyright owner(s) of any component software included on this media.

In the event that the Software or components include specific license requirements or end-user agreements, statements of condition, disclaimers, limitations or warranties ("End-User License"), those End-User Licenses supersede the terms and conditions herein as to that particular Software component. Your purchase, acceptance, or use of the Software will constitute your acceptance of such End-User Licenses.

By purchase, use or acceptance of the Software you further agree to comply with all export laws and regulations of the United States as such laws and regulations may exist from time to time.

Reusable Code in This Book

The author(s) created reusable code in this publication expressly for reuse by readers. Sybex grants readers limited permission to reuse the code found in this publication, its accompanying CD-ROM or available for download from our website so long as the author(s) are attributed in any application containing the reusable code and the code itself is never distributed, posted online by electronic transmission, sold, or commercially exploited as a stand-alone product.

Software Support

Components of the supplemental Software and any offers associated with them may be supported by the specific Owner(s) of that material, but they are not supported by SYBEX. Information regarding any available support may be obtained from the Owner(s) using the information provided in the appropriate read.me files or listed elsewhere on the media.

Should the manufacturer(s) or other Owner(s) cease to offer support or decline to honor any offer, SYBEX bears no responsibility. This notice concerning support for the Software is provided for your information only. SYBEX is not the agent or principal of the Owner(s), and SYBEX is in no way responsible for providing any support for the Software, nor is it liable or responsible for any support provided, or not provided, by the Owner(s).

Warranty

SYBEX warrants the enclosed media to be free of physical defects for a period of ninety (90) days after purchase. The Software is not available from SYBEX in any other form or media than that enclosed herein or posted to www.sybex.com. If you discover a defect in the media during this warranty period, you may obtain a replacement of identical format at no charge by sending the defective media, postage prepaid, with proof of purchase to:

SYBEX Inc.
Product Support Department
1151 Marina Village Parkway
Alameda, CA 94501
Web: `http://www.sybex.com`

After the 90-day period, you can obtain replacement media of identical format by sending us the defective disk, proof of purchase, and a check or money order for $10, payable to SYBEX.

Disclaimer

SYBEX makes no warranty or representation, either expressed or implied, with respect to the Software or its contents, quality, performance, merchantability, or fitness for a particular purpose. In no event will SYBEX, its distributors, or dealers be liable to you or any other party for direct, indirect, special, incidental, consequential, or other damages arising out of the use of or inability to use the Software or its contents even if advised of the possibility of such damage. In the event that the Software includes an online update feature, SYBEX further disclaims any obligation to provide this feature for any specific duration other than the initial posting.

The exclusion of implied warranties is not permitted by some states. Therefore, the above exclusion may not apply to you. This warranty provides you with specific legal rights; there may be other rights that you may have that vary from state to state. The pricing of the book with the Software by SYBEX reflects the allocation of risk and limitations on liability contained in this agreement of Terms and Conditions.

Shareware Distribution

This Software may contain various programs that are distributed as shareware. Copyright laws apply to both shareware and ordinary commercial software, and the copyright Owner(s) retains all rights. If you try a shareware program and continue using it, you are expected to register it. Individual programs differ on details of trial periods, registration, and payment. Please observe the requirements stated in appropriate files.

Copy Protection

The Software in whole or in part may or may not be copy-protected or encrypted. However, in all cases, reselling or redistributing these files without authorization is expressly forbidden except as specifically provided for by the Owner(s) therein.

I dedicate this book to my father and my mother, Li Zuoxi and OuYang Meifang, who have worked hard and are still working to bring us up. They now live in Leiyang, China, a beautiful and small city where the first people who knew how to make paper in the world lived 1900 years ago. To my sisters, Li Liangyu and Li Xingyu; my brother, Li Chungui; and their spouses, Deng Yousheng, Luo Meilong, and Liu Wang. To my nephews, Deng Hao, Luo Yuanzhao; and Li Chuteng. Finally, to my wife, Mengqi Wu, who made a contribution to this book. She is a system engineer at Lucent Technologies and is also the coauthor.

I also dedicate this work to the coworkers who lost their jobs during the economic hard times.

—Kanglin Li
Des Moines, IA

Acknowledgements

I hope you find this book a valuable reference for software development, especially for software test automation, of which the goal is to reduce defects and costs and enhance the quality and profitability of software products.

I extend my first thank to Tom Cirtin, the acquisitions and developmental editor who made this book available to you. He has worked diligently with wisdom, enthusiasm, and inspiration. He is the best. I also thank Jordan Gold.

Other members of the Sybex team include Acey J. Bunch, Judy Flynn, Erica Yee, and others. They have done a great job of technical editing, copyediting, and production editing with suggestions and comments. I want to thank them all for their good and hard work.

I also express my appreciation to my former coworkers at Agilent Technologies, Inc. for the good times we shared and the good work we did: Susan Powell, Kenneth Ward, Kevin Keirn, Chuck Heller, Pat Kennedy, Greg Kuziej, Phil Driggers, Jun Liu, Ting Wu, Jing-Dong Zhang, Dave Willis, Alicia, Jerry Metz, Mike Hawes, and Jayson Jackman. At this point, I also want to thank Marcie and Bob Hervey and Steve and Molly Child and their families for their friendship.

Special gratitude is extended to Mr. Ray Gonzalas, a software engineer from National Security Agency. He was one of the first people who read the original manuscript, word for word, for this book. He made valuable comments, numerous corrections, and constructive suggestions. The current rendition of this book reflects his hard work. Special thanks also goes to Lena Berrios. Another among the manuscript's first reviewers, she did a lot of editing to polish the language and improve the writing style. I worried that, as a professional librarian and linguist, she might be a bit bored reading a computer book. Fortunately, she told me she learned from it and encouraged me to finish this project.

Sincere thanks are extended to my graduate advisors, Dr. Aziz Amoozegar at North Carolina State University and Dr. M.R. Reddy at North Carolina A&T State University, who taught me how to think and how to write.

Finally I'd like to express my indebtedness to Dr. Gregory Tassey from the National Institute of Standards and Technology, who gave me the permission to use the facts and data of his published study.

Contents at a Glance

Contents

Introduction

There are many books about software testing management. When they discuss software test automation, they introduce third-party testing tools. This book describes techniques for developing a fully automated software testing tool. You can use this tool to generate test scripts for continuous unit testing, integration testing, and regression testing.

Software defects are common and cause economic losses from time to time. Today, software organizations invest more time and resources in analyzing and testing software as a unit rather than as independent entities. Software engineers have observed that writing testing code is as expensive and time consuming as developing the product itself. To ensure software quality, organizations encourage software developers and testers to achieve objectives such as these:

- Locating the source of defects faster and more precisely
- Detecting bugs earlier in the software development life cycle
- Removing more defects before the product is released

Improved testing tools can reduce the cost of software development and increase the quality of software. An automated testing tool must have the following characteristics:

- Accurate functionality, reliability, interoperability, and compliance
- An interface that is user friendly and easy to learn and operate
- Enhanced fault tolerance and automatic error recoverability
- Efficient algorithm for time and resource management
- Stable and mature final products that can be maintained and upgraded
- Easy portability with regard to installation, uninstallation, adaptability, and security

I have used many of the commercial software test tools. Their developers declare that they have the capability to conduct various types of software tests and meet the requirements of an organization. But they have limitations. For example, some of them require users to record a series of mouse clicks and keystrokes. Others require users to write test scripts in a specified script language or to generate a test script automatically to test only one function (member) of a software module. Furthermore, the test scripts produced by these tools and methods need to be edited and debugged before they can be executed to perform the desired tests. Automatic generation of the testing data is beyond the reach of these tools, and integration testing involves extensive manual stubbing and guesswork.

Software test engineers would like to see a fully automated software test tool on the market, one that is capable of completing testing tasks from generating test scripts and composing the testing cases to presenting the results and fixing the bugs. But the tool vendors are not able to keep up with the complexity and technology advancements in today's software projects. In addition, software products can include features that incorporate a company's trade secrets, which the commercial testing tools won't have the capability of testing. Engineers are often in the position of having to develop their own tools to cover the gaps. This book presents a way to develop and enhance a testing tool development with full automation.

When I was trained to use commercial tools, the trainers from the manufacturers presented hundreds of testing features. Software test engineers do appreciate these features, and they are important in improving the quality of software. But the tedious and time-consuming processes of editing and debugging the generated test scripts sometimes prevent a thorough software test. Thus, software products are delivered to end users with costly errors. These costs are shared by virtually all businesses in the United States that depend on software for their development, production, distribution, and after-sales supports and services. To address these current inadequacies, this book will introduce an automated method to minimize the data editing steps, generate a test script to test the entire application, and free you from having to edit and debug the test script manually. The final product simply accepts an application under test and delivers the test results.

Who This Book Is For

Software engineers have long relied on the tools and infrastructures supplied by the current software testing tool vendors. Some engineers tell successful stories. But more engineers experience frustrations. The automation is not enough, the test is not efficient, and the test script generation and data composition methods need to be improved. One expert's solution to software test automation is to develop testing tools instead of purchasing commercial tools developed with the current inadequate infrastructure. This book is written for people who are involved in software engineering and want to automate the software testing process for their organizations. With the methods introduced by this book, software engineers should gain a good understanding of the limited automation provided by the available testing tools and how to improve the current test infrastructure and conduct a fully automated software test.

This book is for software engineers who want more effective ways to perform software tests. The automated test tool introduced in this book can serve as an independent software test tool as well as an adjunct to the commercial tools.

I assume you are a moderately experienced software developer and a test engineer in the process of conducting software test for your organization. The explanations and examples in this book can be easily understood and followed by any intermediate- to advanced-level programmer interested in expanding their knowledge in both software development and software testing.

Knowledge of the fundamentals of software testing is essential for software test engineers. Examining a combination of programming and testing issues leads to a solid solution to software test automation. This book's content includes sound programming techniques with examples in C#. Then it gradually progresses to the development of a fully automated test tool. Although the sample code is in C# using the Microsoft Windows platform, the concept can be used with other languages and platforms.

As economists have reported, software failures result in a substantial economic loss to the United States each year. Approximately half of the losses occur within the software manufacturing industry. If you are a senior managerial administrator of a software organization, you are most likely interested in an improved software test method. The other half of the loss comes out of the pockets of the software end users. If your business or institution consists of software end users, you probably maintain teams to support the software purchased from the contract vendors. Being aware of testing methods will assist you with efficient software application in your organization.

How This Book Is Organized

In order to present ideas well, the first two chapters introduce the techniques of software testing and programming languages. Chapter 2 also lists advantages and disadvantages of the current testing tools and defines the objectives to overcoming the disadvantages. Chapters 3 through 6 focus on .NET programming related to the development of the AutomatedTest tool. During the fundamental discussions, as the knowledge becomes available and the time is appropriate, progress will be made on the AutomatedTest tool project. After the requisite background is covered, Chapters 7 through 11 continue to the completion of the AutomatedTest tool, using the programming techniques from chapters 3 through 6. At this point, the AutomatedTest tool will be able to generate test script to conduct unit testing, integration testing, and regression testing It will also report defects found. At last, Chapter 12 concludes this book with examples of testing some real life software.

The book is organized as follows:

Chapter 1, "Software Testing: An Overview," describes the techniques built into .NET that can make it possible to test software dynamically and illustrates how to integrate these techniques into an automated software test process.

Chapter 2, "Current Testing Infrastructure vs. the Proposed Testing Methods," presents a brief review of some of the automated testing tools on the market and the main points of the testing methods proposed in this book. The available tools have been proved by studies to be inadequate. The purpose of this chapter is to demonstrate the power of the new test method, of adding more testing capabilities to a testing tool, and of creating a fully automated test for new and complex software projects. The available tools test software in various environments (for example, Java, Unix, Linux, and Windows). Thus, the methods introduced are not limited to Microsoft platforms and products. They can be extended to other development environments.

Chapter 3, ".NET Namespaces and Classes for Software Testing," deals with the starting points of an automated testing task.

Chapter 4, ".NET Reflection for Test Automation," introduces the .NET Reflection namespace. The Reflection namespace can reflect the software under test as a prism reflects the sunlight.

Chapter 5, "Spreadsheets and XML for Test Data Stores," introduces a method to store testing cases inside an XML document at coding time. It also discusses how to program an MS Excel worksheet in the test script to store the test information and present test results.

Chapter 6, ".NET CodeDom Namespace," describes the method for using the .NET CodeDom namespace to generate test scripts based on the information revealed by the Reflection namespace.

Chapter 7, "Generating Test Scripts," implements the method using the .NET CodeDom to write test scripts based on classes, methods, and parameters dynamically. This method is able to generate one test script to test all members of an assembly. The advantage of generating one test script for an assembly is that the test script can return a complete and full object of the class under test after the execution. The returned object can be reused for integration testing or for testing a method passing parameters by objects.

Chapter 8, "Integration Testing," explores a method that will automatically test parameters passed by objects and conduct integration testing. Instead of using the available stubbing or mock objects methods, this book introduces a bottom-up approach to reuse the previously generated test script to automate integration testing.

Chapter 9, "Verification, Validation, and Presentation," describes the processes of the automatic test verification, validation, and result presentation. It also introduces a method showing how to use this tool to test software that is still in development, at its earliest available design. The result of the verification, validation, and bugs found are presented with a spreadsheet.

Chapter 10, "Finalizing the AutomatedTest Tool," wraps up the test tool development and shows how to improve the appearance of the graphical user interface.

Chapter 11, "Updating the AutomatedTest Tool for Testing the Windows Registry," shows you how to update the AutomatedTest tool for testing against the Windows system Registry. Thus, the readers can add more testing capabilities to this tool for more specific requirements.

Chapter 12, "Testing the AutomatedTest Tool," concludes the book by using the AutomatedTest tool to solve real-world software testing problems. This chapter also illustrates how to test the AutomatedTest project itself using methods introduced in this book.

About the Examples

The examples start with the programming precepts of C#. The goal is to use the predefined methods of a programming language to complete an AutomatedTest tool project. There are three kinds of example code in the chapters:

- Simple examples to demonstrate using C#
- Example projects to be tested by the AutomatedTest tool
- Sample code of the AutomatedTest tool project

The code examples in the first category most often appear in Chapters 3 through Chapter 6. Thereafter, Chapters 7 through 11 are totally dedicated to automating the test project. The sample code of these chapters is in the third category. There are only three examples of the second category, simulating a real assembly under test. They are implemented in Chapters 4, 8, and 11 immediately before the coding of the AutomatedTest tool begins. At the end of each chapter, one of the examples is submitted to the newly coded test tool.

In this book, the demonstration examples are managed assemblies. However, Chapter 5 briefly introduces interoperability between unmanaged and managed assemblies. When there is a need to test an unmanaged COM component, a simple conversion can turn an existing COM into a managed assembly, which can be tested by the AutomatedTest tool.

In Chapter 3 and thereafter, some code is added to the project in each chapter. At the end of each chapter, the sample code can be compiled to produce an executable assembly, and the testing tool achieves different degrees of automation until a fully automated test tool is developed by the end of the book.

The code in Chapter 4 enables the AutomatedTest tool to reflect an assembly under test. Chapter 5 implements XML documentation and an MS Excel worksheet for the testing case data stores. Chapter 6 introduces many fundamentals about CodeDom, which is used to generate test scripts automatically. Sample programs demonstrate how to use CodeDom to generate programs, but code is not added to the AutomatedTest tool in this chapter.

In Chapter 7, we'll resume coding the AutomatedTest tool and making this tool capable of generating a test script for a given assembly. After the addition of the code in Chapter 8, the tool will have the capability of testing parameters passed by objects and conduct integration testing. Chapter 9 covers the important test topics of verification, validation, and result presentation. After this chapter, you can use the tool to generate a fully functional test script. However, you still need to issue a line command to run and to deploy the test script. Chapter 10 guides you in adding the last batch of code (which builds and deploys the assembly from the test script) so that you achieve a fully automated test tool. At this point, the user can feed an assembly to the tool and get the test results with the classes, methods, and properties tested.

Finally, Chapter 11 discusses how to upgrade the tool with more capabilities. An example is given on how to add methods to generate code testing against the Windows Registry.

Where to Find the Source Code

The sample and project code for each chapter can be downloaded from `www.sybex.com` by searching this book using the title, the author, or the ISBN number, 4320. This saves the readers from having to type in the code. It also includes a complete compiled version of the project, which allows the readers to put the AutomatedTest into immediate practices for their software project.

To execute the `AutomatedTest.exe` file, you can copy it to a computer system. The minimum requirements for a computer system are as follows:

- Windows 95/98/2000/NT/XP
- Preinstalled .NET framework
- Preinstalled MS Excel
- 20MB of free hard disk space

Although the sample code in this book is developed under Microsoft Visual Studio .NET 2003 Integrated Development Environment (IDE), there are other open source .NET IDEs available for free download:

Eclipsing .NET IBM released Eclipse .NET to the opensource community. This product works with Windows XP/2000/NT/98/95. You can download the components for Eclipse .NET at `www.eclipse.org`. After downloading eclipse-SDK-2.1.2-win32.zip, you install it in conjuction with Microsoft .NET SDK, which you can also download for free at `http://msdn.microsoft.com/netframework/technologyinfo/howtoget/default.aspx`. Then, get the open source C# plug-in through the Eclipse .NET IDE. (For more detailed information about downloading and installing these programs, go to `www.sys-con.com/webservices/articleprint.cfm?id=360`.)

`#develop` (short for SharpDevelop) This is another open source IDE for C# and VB.NET on Microsoft's .NET platform. You can download #develop from `www.icsharpcode.net/OpenSource/SD/Default.aspx`.

DotGNU Portable .NET This open source tool includes a C# compiler, assembler and runtime engineer. The initial platform was GNU/Linux. It also works on Windows, Solaris, NetBSD, FreeBSD, and MacOS X. You can download this product from `www.southern-storm.com.au/portable_net.html`.

Chapter 1

Software Testing: An Overview

Any software product, no matter how accomplished by today's testing technologies, has bugs. Some bugs are detected and removed at the time of coding. Others are found and fixed during formal testing as software modules are integrated into a system. However, all software manufacturers know that bugs remain in the software and that some of them have to be fixed later (Beizer 1990). Testing is a necessary prerequisite for the successful implementation of a software product, but with the testing technologies currently available, it is often regarded as being difficult, tedious, time consuming, and inadequate. It is reported that bugs in the final products cost the United States economy $59.5 billion per year (Tassey 2002).

Testing accounts for 25% to 50% of the total budget in many software development projects. A test team usually consists of engineers that act as manual testers, tool users, and tool developers. Both the budget and the personnel are important because a product under development should be tested as thoroughly as possible.

Today, there are many testing tools on the market. However, they are considered to be fairly primitive with regard to the quality required (Tassey 2002). They can test software with some degrees of automation so that the test engineers can devote more time to solving problems in high-risk areas, but their automation is limited to simple reverse engineering and recording test script by mouse clicks or keystrokes. Test engineers expect more powerful and flexible testing tools with more automatic features to catch up with the rapid evolution of the software technology.

The goal of this book is to show you how to develop a testing tool, the AutomatedTest tool, to test a complex software product thoroughly with minimum human interaction. In addition to learning how to develop the testing tool, you'll gain the knowledge you need to implement the tool. For a controlled and gradual improvement of the automatic testing process, the discussion of the development of this tool contains comprehensive descriptions of Reflection, Code Document Object Model (CodeDom), late binding, Extensible Markup Language (XML), and MS Excel API programming. By the end of this book, you'll be able to use the tool to automatically test classes, methods, parameters, objects, and the Windows Registry based on the testing needs of a given assembly.

There are many computer operating systems and development languages serving today's software industry, such as Java, C++, Visual Basic, C#, Linux, Unix, and Windows. Some software engineers prefer one over the others, and some work with more than one.

NOTE Although this book's examples are written in C#, it does not imply an endorsement of Microsoft products or criticism of the other development environments and platforms. In fact, the methodology introduced in this book can be extended to other development environments and platforms. Java and .NET provide highly object-oriented environments to complete the testing tool projects. As you study the sample code in this book, you will learn the concepts of namespaces, data types, .NET Reflection, and .NET CodeDom with regard to software test automation.

In the .NET world, compiled physical applications, such as the files with `.exe` and `.dll` extensions, are often referred to as assemblies. An assembly could contain a single or multiple modules, such as namespaces and classes. Within such a hierarchy, fields, methods, properties, and events supported by the classes are the target of test units. This book covers the necessity, knowledge and techniques to complete the AutomatedTest project which at last will be capable of writing and executing code to test all the aspects of an assembly automatically. The discussion of the development of the AutomatedTest tool is based on automatically testing a real-world assembly. Example code for the tool is derived from actual test projects. They can be reused and referenced from tester to tester and from project to project. This tool offers features to conduct an investigation on the assembly under test by collecting testing information from the assembly and writing a test script to test it. . These testing tasks are accomplished dynamically and are not difficult, tedious, or time consuming to the test engineers after this development.

This chapter begins with a discussion of the basic software test concepts, the purpose of software test, the selection of a programming language and how they apply to automation. It also includes a discussion on how to effectively use these concepts to improve the current infrastructure of the software testing.

Purpose of Software Testing

Currently, total sales of software products have reached $180 billion a year in the United States. Due to the bug-bearing features, catastrophes caused by software products have happened from time to time.

In April 1999, a software defect caused the failure of the Cape Canaveral launch of a $1.2 billion military satellite. This has perhaps been the most expensive software failure in the history of the software industry. It subsequently triggered a complete military and industry review of the U.S. space launch programs, including software integration and testing processes.

You may still remember the loss of the NASA Mars Climate Orbiter in space in October 1999. That was due to the failure of a part of the software to translate English units of measurement into metric units. In 2002, I developed a module for an optical test instrument that validated there would be no mixture of such measurement units. If the Mars Climate Orbiter had developed such a module, the spacecraft would have been in orbit to this day.

This book is for everyone who is interested in software quality, including senior administrators, software project managers, software developers, software testers and software end users. When starting a new project, software organizations comply with development models. Software end users, developers, test engineers, and higher-level administrators are all involved in defining the requirements, specifications, and testing strategies. In most of the models, software testing is planned at the beginning of the process and conducted parallel to the development life cycles. One cannot test a product before understanding it. Testing a new product under development is always a learning experience for the test engineers. The time and effort involved depends on the complexity of the product and the experience of the test engineers. To a great extent, one of the benefits of using an automated tool is to prevent the test engineers from spending too much time learning a new product. Engineers are then able to focus on more complicated and high-risk problems.

Software testing is the process of exercising an application to detect errors and to verify that it satisfies the specified requirements. During the software development life cycle, software developers and test engineers are working both to find bugs and to ensure product quality. The delivered software product must include all required functions and be compatible with the customers' hardware.

For a long time, software testing has been conducted manually; that is, a human tester runs the application using predefined processes. Since the beginning of the software industry, software engineers have made great efforts to automate the software testing process. Many successful companies have manufactured software test tools that are now on the market. Today, there are many commercial software tools that can be used to find bugs so that they can be fixed prior to the product release. As mentioned earlier, these tools possess some automation (performing reverse engineering and writing the test scripts), but the following deficiencies are often present:

- The test scripts often need debugging.
- None of them can complete an entire test process independently.
- They implement processes that may not be consistent with the organization's software design.
- The reverse engineering process is separated from the test script generation.

In many cases, generating or recording a test script for each member within an assembly is an exhaustive job for the test engineers. Making up and documenting the testing data with the current tools is a 100% purely manual task. Therefore, the capabilities of these tools with regard to automation are limited.

With the automated software testing tool developed in this book, testers do not need to write test script by hand or by recording test scenarios. The software testing process will work with the least amount of human interaction. This tool is designed to be reusable and meet the testing needs of most software products. In other words, you are going to learn how to make reusable modules to test other code.

Expectations of Automated Software Testing

With a fully automated tool, software testing can be expected to save time, observe standards, and enhance product quality.

Software testing has always been important for the software industry. It is usually common to train the testing engineers and have them learn the testing techniques at the beginning of a project. As the experience and skill levels increase in the team, the coverage of the automated software testing increases. Remember, testing a newly developed product is always a learning experience for a software tester. Deep knowledge of a project makes full automation possible.

Technically, many testing tasks can be automated. However, the decision of whether to automate the testing tasks for an organization is a management issue as well as a technical one. The analysis should include the following:

- *In today's society, software projects are complex and intend to solve complicated problems.* Commercial software testing tool manufacturers usually need time to learn about a particular problem and to catch up with the technologies. In order to meet the time frame for a project, a testing team should develop an automated testing tool that is complementary to the commercial testing tools.
- *Sometimes, test engineers need to determine whether to incorporate automated testing into existing projects or into a new one.* At the beginning, the testing process always involves manual testing. Test engineers use this as a learning process. As the project progresses, test engineers become more knowledgeable about the product and potential problems become more foreseeable. Automated testing tools then can be added to deal with the possible problems. Eventually, this tool greatly benefits the future projects in an organization.
- *Organizations employ the Extreme Programming (XP) practice for risk-prone projects with unstable requirements.* They don't emphasize detailed requirements documentation. Instead, their code is constantly being modified and updated. Test scripts are part of the source code control along with the program code. Thus, automated testing is critical to the XP practices so that the test scripts can be modified and rerun for each of the frequent development iterations.
- *Occasionally an organization may not be interested in the commercial software testing tools.* In order to manage quality assurance, developing an automated testing tool significantly enhances the development project.

The life cycle of the software development model also affects the extent of an automated testing process:

- *Usually, modification occurs frequently at the beginning of a project.* Your goal is to develop a tool to generate test scripts automatically, which would reflect the changes and significantly enhance testing efficiency with unstable products.

- *Commercially available testing tools are said to be capable of testing graphical user interface (GUI) components.* Most of the time, users need to record a series of mouse clicks and keystrokes. Testing data of the recorded test script are usually hard coded. Sometimes, the recorded test scripts need to be revised and debugged before they can perform the testing. Thus, using and reusing these tools on an unstable product would be a nightmare. An automated testing tool should be capable of recognizing and verifying the GUI components by itself and generating a data driven test script.
- *As the technologies advance, programming becomes easier.* The development life cycle becomes shorter, giving the testers less time to test the products. An automated software test tool should relieve some of that pressure so testers have more time to identify high-risk areas of the project.

Automated Testing and XP Practice

Kent Beck created Extreme Programming (XP) in his book *Extreme Programming Explained: Embrace Change* (Addison-Wesley, 1999). By his definition, XP is a lightweight technique that focuses on coding for a risk-prone software project. It avoids the detailed specification and regards every task as a simple one. In order to accomplish a complex problem, it relies on frequent iterations and communications between developers, testers, and customers.

The first priority of managing an XP project is to make sure that in the end, all the needs of the customer are satisfied. However, XP members believe that it is not necessary for customers to foresee the needs of a product. Software developers are not fortunetellers and do not need to specify all requirements before coding. It is more useful to provide customers with a simple workable product as early as possible. Then, customers can explore the product and add or change their requirements. Developers will eventually achieve the goal through constantly revising the code, automatic testing, and continuous integration of the product.

Automated testing is a key to the success of using XP practice. Tests are needed when new code is added and when a method or a line of code is modified or deleted. The code is usually under constant change and evolving, and sometimes developers aren't aware of all the changes taking place. Only through frequent testing can programmers realize that the changes of the code are validated.

Due to constant changes in requirements, specifications, and the code, the tests should be automated so that none of the changes break the system. Unlike the code created in other development models, the XP code is in a liquid state. It can be redesigned, refactored, deleted, and completely redone. Later, the tests will make sure that the system still works. XP needs an iterative testing for the public interface of classes and components. The implementation of the system is under drastic change while the automated tests validate that the system still fulfills the contract of the interfaces. Only after a new or modified feature is validated by tests can it be integrated. Everything that can potentially break must be tested. The AutomatedTest project in this book will help XP teams automate the testing.

Software Test Engineers

This book focuses on the development of a tool for automated software testing. The implementation incorporates the tester's attitude of "test to break." As an automated tool, it is able to "use" a product from the perspective of an end user, has the "desire" for quality, and has "attention" in details. It is a user-friendly tool for both technical and nontechnical personnel. Many times, a tester is considered to be a good programmer also. This tool is capable of writing test scripts as well as an experienced tester who has a deep understanding of the software development process. Eventually, it reduces the learning curve so that the testers can focus on high-risk areas. If your team employs the XP practice, you will find this AutomatedTest tool extremely useful.

Today, it is common that testers and developers work closely together for one project. One testing tool may not be sufficient for solving all the problems that may appear. If you are a project manager, it will be more efficient for you to have both manual testers and automated testers on your team.

With effective communication, the automated and manual testing sections will complement each other and enhance each other's capabilities. Thus, a manager may want team members who are skillful in both manual and automated testing techniques. A quality product will benefit from a testing team with members who have different kinds of testing experiences. For example, some may have experience with the tools available on the market. Some may be good at using manual testing to test more complicated and high-risk areas of a product. Others might have significant programming experiences using C#, Visual Basic, C/C++, Java, or other languages to develop tools.

How to Automate Software Testing

The software industry has seen many great works on software testing. Textbooks have documented how to make testing plans and testing strategies and how to conduct automated software testing with the tools that are available on the market. Test engineers have benefited a lot from the accumulated knowledge, and software organizations have encouraged their testing teams to observe these documents.

The high-level development languages, such as Java, C#, and Visual Basic .NET, are object-oriented languages that aim at enabling programmers to quickly build a wide range of applications. The goal of these languages is to shorten the software development life cycles by providing the Common Language Runtime (CLR), the Java Virtual Machine (JVM), cross-language and cross-platform support, and automatic memory management. They also handle other low-level plumbing issues, such as type safety, available low-level libraries, array bounds checking, and so on. Thus, developers actually spend their time and resources on their application and business logic. Traditional testing methods cannot meet the speed of technological advancement. To meet the new time frame, there must be better and faster ways to test software products. Automated testing is receiving a lot of attention due to technological advancement as well as the ever increasing complexity of software products.

A .NET assembly organizes a software product in the structure of namespaces, class types, and class members. Assemblies are built by the Microsoft intermediate language assembler (MSIL). Then, the Microsoft disassembler can reverse-engineer the assemblies. We'll take advantage of.NET to develop a tool that should be capable of recognizing the classes and members in an assembly (a DLL or EXE file) and automatically write a test script for testing each method of this component. Thus, the automated software test tool developed in this book is capable of the following:

- Learning the assembly under test dynamically
- Conducting tedious or repetitive tasks dynamically
- Generating test scripts and running the scripts in batches in a scheduled manner
- Testing interfaces of COM objects and other software components with a specified data set
- Accessing a database to verify the testing results
- Accessing the Windows Registry to verify the testing results.

According to the developers of Microsoft Visual Studio .NET, the .NET Reflection namespace is able to reflect a given assembly. The .NET CodeDom namespace can write the test script dynamically. Late binding can invoke a method. The test data and test results will be presented using XML and MS Excel worksheets. Thus, making use of the .NET Reflection, .NET CodeDom, XML programming, and MS Excel API programming, the automated testing process can be viewed with six steps as shown in Figure 1.1. By the definition of regression testing, code is under constant testing and under constant change during the development life cycle. When bugs are detected and fixed, the regression testing will confirm that the fix is accurate and doesn't cause side effects. Thus, the iteration in Figure 1.1 is accomplished by regression testing.

Think of the relationship between the .NET Reflection namespace and the assembly under test as being similar to the relationship between a prism and sunlight. A prism reflects the sunlight into its spectrum of wavelengths; similarly, the .NET Reflection namespace disassembles an assembly into class, property, and method members. Thus, it automatically accomplishes the information gathering process. This process is similar to test engineers spending time learning the product. Thanks to the Reflection namespace, the test engineers can devote their time to identifying other risks.

FIGURE 1.1
Six steps of the automated software testing

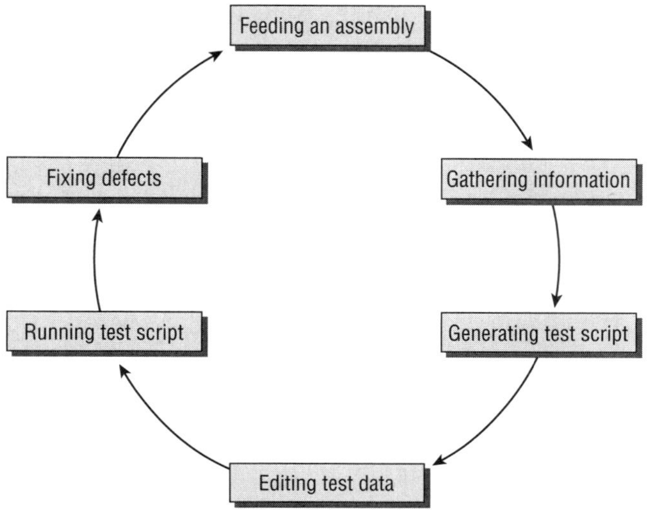

After the information is gathered, the .NET CodeDom, which is a new area of technology to software developers, becomes involved. Chapter 6 in this book is devoted to discussing the .NET CodeDom features in detail. Ultimately, the development of the AutomatedTest tool employs this namespace to write the test script based on the information disassembled by the .NET Reflection namespace.

Software test engineers have used tools on the market that are capable of reverse-engineering a software product. However, it sometimes becomes tedious to instruct the tools to write a test script for each of the members within an assembly. It is especially true when the assembly under test has hundreds of members. With the combination of the .NET Reflection and the .NET CodeDom, the AutomatedTest tool combines the information gathering and script writing processes with minimum interaction from a human tester.

To enable the data editing capability, the testing tool developed in this book can use an XML document or an MS Excel worksheet for data stores. XML has been widely accepted by many industrial standards. Enabling XML data storing enhances the software test automation. It also can be applied across different development environments and platforms.

The Excel worksheet is used to store testing data because of its popularity across the MS Windows platforms. The programmable MS Excel API offers great flexibility for testers to organize the test data. Then, the same MS Excel API programming techniques are incorporated into writing the test script, which tests the assembly against the testing cases and posts the test results.

In the Microsoft Visual Studio .NET integrated development environment (IDE), assemblies are built using the MSIL assembler. In order to run the test script, the test engineer can programmatically invoke the test with *late binding*—an ability to discover underlying types, methods, and properties of a given object and invoke the methods at runtime. Employing the late binding technique makes the automated testing tool more efficient. Therefore, you obtain a fully automated test tool with the assistance of the MS .NET programming environment.

Commercially available tools are not capable of testing a product thoroughly. When a new testing feature is requested, a testing tool manufacturer might promise that the tool would include this feature in the next release. To cope with the diversity of software, the tool developed in this book has enough "brain cells" to learn new lessons. By the end of this book, you will be able to upgrade this tool programmatically.

Test engineers have experienced the features of capturing screens and recording scenarios by using the tools on the market, which conduct unit tests, advanced stress tests, and load capability tests. The AutomatedTest tool doesn't require reverse engineering or recording actions. In its earlier stages, you can use this tool as a complement to the available testing tools and to the test engineers' skills and experiences. However, as the AutomatedTest tool project progresses, the tool will eventually address as many testing issues as possible.

Therefore, by using this fully automated testing tool, test engineers will be relieved from reverse-engineering, writing tedious scripts, and creating data stores. They can spend more time on tackling the high-risk areas of software. Furthermore, programming in the MS .NET environment provides test engineers with the advantage of developing a tool within the organization's time frame and budget. This applies to many other development environments and languages, such as Eclipsing .NET, DotGNU Portable .NET, Java, Visual Basic 6.0, C++, C# and Visual Basic .NET.

Software Testing and Programming Languages

It has already been mentioned that there are a lot of testing tools available on the market, and testing organizations have used the tools and achieved great success. Some popular testing tools write test scripts in Visual Basic 6.0 and execute the script in Visual Studio IDE. There is also literature that introduces how to write test scripts in Visual Basic 6.0 by hand. Some other tools are written in Java, such as JUnit, and JProbe. And there are tools to write test scripts for software products run on Unix, Linux, and other platforms. The sample code of this book will use C# of the Microsoft Visual Studio .NET environment as the programming language for both the tool and the test script.

The automation targets are mostly focused on problems from certain well-defined areas. That is because these problems and areas have experienced software failures in the past. Testing tools often write test scripts with a few repetitive code patterns to test different methods within a class.

For example, Listings 1.1–1.4 are excerpts from a test script generated in Chapter 8. These examples will help you understand how to test a few commonly encountered testing situations programmatically. At this point, compare the difference between these listings rather than trying to start a project using them.

Listing 1.1 Code to Test the *objAdvancedCalc.Square()* Method

```
shtRow = 12;
mName = "Square";
range = xSheet.get_Range("C12", "C12");
double length_12 = double.Parse(range.Value2.ToString());

try
{
  xResult.Cells.set_Item(12, 4, objAdvancedCalc.Square(length_12));
  TestPass(xResult, shtRow, mName);
}
catch (System.Exception err)
{
  TestFail(xResult, shtRow, mName, err.Message);
}

xResult.Cells.set_Item(shtRow, 6, "length = " + length_12);
range = xSheet.get_Range("D12", "D12");

if (range.Value2 != null)
{
  xResult.Cells.set_Item(shtRow, 5, range.Value2.ToString());
}
```

Listing 1.2 Code to Test the *objAdvancedCalc.SimpleCalc()* Method

```
shtRow = 14;
mName = "SimpleCalc";
range = xSheet.get_Range("C14", "C14");

Assembly appDomain_14 = Assembly.LoadFrom
➥(@"C:\Temp\LowLevelObj\Bin\Debug\TestLowLevelObj.dll");

Type TestClass_14 =
➥appDomain_14.GetType("LowLevelObjTest.TestLowLevelObj");

object objInst_14 = Activator.CreateInstance(TestClass_14);
MethodInfo mi_14 = TestClass_14.GetMethod("StartTest");

LowLevelObj.SimpleMath lvlMath_14 =
➥(LowLevelObj.SimpleMath) mi_14.Invoke(objInst_14, null);

range = xSheet.get_Range("D14", "D14");
```

```
LowLevelObj.Math_ENUM operation_14 = LowLevelObj.Math_ENUM.Add;

range = xSheet.get_Range("E14", "E14");
int Result_14 = int.Parse(range.Value2.ToString());

try
{
  objAdvancedCalc.SimpleCalc(lvlMath_14, operation_14, ref Result_14);
  TestPass(xResult, shtRow, mName);
}
catch (System.Exception err)
{
  TestFail(xResult, shtRow, mName, err.Message);
}

xResult.Cells.set_Item(shtRow, 6, "lvlMath = " + lvlMath_14);
xResult.Cells.set_Item(shtRow, 7, "operation = " + operation_14);
xResult.Cells.set_Item(shtRow, 8, "Result = " + Result_14);
```

Listing 1.3 Code to Test the *objAdvancedCalc.Sum()* Method

```
shtRow = 15;
mName = "Sum";
range = xSheet.get_Range("C15", "C15");

double[] anArray_15 = new double[range.Value2.ToString().Split(',').Length];
foreach (string z in range.Value2.ToString().Split(','))
{
  anArray_15[tempArrayIndex] = double.Parse(z); tempArrayIndex++;
};

tempArrayIndex = 0;

try
{
  xResult.Cells.set_Item(15, 4, objAdvancedCalc.Sum(anArray_15));
  TestPass(xResult, shtRow, mName);
}
catch (System.Exception err)
{
  TestFail(xResult, shtRow, mName, err.Message);
}

xResult.Cells.set_Item(shtRow, 6, "anArray = " + anArray_15);

range = xSheet.get_Range("D15", "D15");

if (range.Value2 != null)
{
  xResult.Cells.set_Item(shtRow, 5, range.Value2.ToString());
}
```

Listing 1.4 Code to Test the *objAdvancedCalc.GetType()* Method

```
shtRow = 16;
mName = "GetType";

try
{
  xResult.Cells.set_Item(16, 4, objAdvancedCalc.GetType());
  TestPass(xResult, shtRow, mName);
}
catch (System.Exception err)
{
  TestFail(xResult, shtRow, mName, err.Message);
}

range = xSheet.get_Range("C16", "C16");
if (range.Value2 != null)
{
  xResult.Cells.set_Item(shtRow, 5, range.Value2.ToString());
}
```

The four segments of code test different members of an assembly and solve different requirements. In general, they repeat a similar coding pattern approximately as follows:

1. Set up the necessary parameter(s)
2. Execute the method under test and catch the errors
3. Present the result of the execution

The methods under test behave differently. Methods tested in Listings 1.1, 1.2, and 1.3 all take parameters. The code segment in Listing 1.1, test method `objAdvancedCalc.Square()`, passes the parameter by value. The code in Listing 1.2, testing method `objAdvancedCalc.SimpleCalc()`, passes the first parameter by object, which is usually done by stubbing or by using the mock-objects method with other testing tools. However, this segment reuses an existing test script, which is introduced in Chapter 8. The advantage of reusing a test script is obvious. The code in Listing 1.3 tests a method, `objAdvancedCalc.Sum()`, by passing an array parameter. The code is totally different from that in the other listings in order to handle the items in an array. The code segment in Listing 1.4, testing method `objAdvancedCalc.GetType()`, takes no parameter, which is the simplest case. Each of the code segments in Listings 1.1, 1.3, and 1.4 returns a value. Testers are interested in seeing whether the actual return value matches the desired return value. Thus, the resulting presentation will display the return values after the execution. The method under test in Listing 1.2 does not return a value. One of the parameters is passed by reference, and the status of this parameter is altered during the execution. The presentation has to inform testers of these changes.

These are a few examples of different testing scenarios. An automated testing tool will be implemented to test all aspects of a real-world software product.

It might seem easy to code this pattern manually when there are not many members under test. But it is time consuming to code this way for an assembly with a large collection of classes and members. Also, it takes human testers longer to gain insight on each method in order to code with accuracy. On the other hand, it is hard for a tool to code the subtle difference between methods the first time. Debugging is always needed for test scripts written by a human. With the AutomatedTest tool, the test process will become fast for the repetitive jobs and debugging will not be needed.

We all know the boundary condition for testing cases, but we often spend a lot of time implementing it to compose the testing cases. This book introduces a couple of automated methods for composing the testing cases with ease, saving the testers time to investigate high-risk areas and to spend more time on other manual testing jobs. As you update the automation capacity for your institution, the solution for problems that arise repeatedly will eventually be automated. Only new problems will be tested manually and become automated later.

No matter what language they use to write test scripts, testers must have knowledge in testing and have skills in programming. The methods illustrated in this book can be extended to the languages and platforms you prefer.

In fact, C# was created for software developing, not for software testing. It is understandable that some C# experts use third-party software testing tools for their software projects. You may wonder how a programming language could ever be used to develop a testing tool. This is the area that will be explored in this book.

In the past, Visual Basic and Java have been used more often than other languages to write test scripts. For example, Rational's testing tool uses a reverse-engineering method and generates scripts in Visual Basic. The book *Visual Basic for Testers* (Sweeney 2001) introduces some techniques of writing test script, but it doesn't cover techniques for script automation. Java developers use JUnit as a testing tool. Using a programming language such as C# as a testing tool is a brand-new concept to many readers. This book will not only teach you how to write a test script for a particular assembly, it will also teach you how to develop a general tool to write test script dynamically. Thereafter, different organizations and different functional software projects can employ this method for their software development. To recap, the method will focus on solving the following problems:

- How to use predefined functions of a language (in this case, C#) that return relevant information about the assemblies under test
- How to create a front end with basic controls to view test information and results
- How to make and store testing cases in a database (in this case, MS Excel and XML documents) to drive the automatic generation of a test script.

- How to create a presentation showing the information of a component under test (in this case, using an Excel worksheet)
- How to implement a mechanism to generate test scripts for testing a class, a property, and a method (in this case, using the .NET CodeDom).
- How to enable the test scripts to test parameters passed by value, by references, and by objects
- How to enable the test scripts to test against the Windows system registry
- How to present the test results so that the developers will have as much information as possible to fix a defect responsible for the test failure

Using C# for Automation

The previous sections have discussed the possibilities of automated testing. This book is also an evolutionary result of software test techniques. Not all types of tests can be automated, so test engineers will still be necessary. But this book attempts to broaden the area of test automation by giving test engineers the knowledge to use automation techniques. As more test areas are automated, software test engineers will have more time to plan their test strategies and manage their budget and other resources efficiently. Test areas will be planned with more confidence and defects fixed on schedule. Especially, the high-risk areas will be tested manually and adequately. Developers, testers, and users will find new confidence in the production of products whose quality is dramatically improved.

Currently available testing tools may lack the capability to test the products developed with .NET platform and C#. Test engineers with desire for automation have to develop their own tools to accomplish their tasks.

Engineers know that C# is an advanced programming language. Although it is not designed to be a testing tool, it happens to have many methods that can be used in the testing process.

For example the .NET Reflection namespace can reflect an assembly as a prism reflects the sunlight. The .NET CodeDOM namespace can write code for the script. On the other hand, C# is a completely object-oriented programming language. The tool developed with C# will be easily reusable, portable, and maintainable. The COM interoperability enables the function to test COM/DCOM developed in other development environments.

However, when the test engineers need to use C# features to present the test results, a new form of the presentation may seem unfamiliar to the end users. In this case, using a broadly accepted method will enhance the usability of the new test method. With advanced programming techniques, one is able to reach the goal. For example, this book shows you how to program an XML mechanism and an MS Excel worksheet as the visual presentation of the automated test results. At first, an MS Excel worksheet presents the information of a component under test and provides space to store testing data. Later, the MS Excel API programmed in the test script presents the test result, provides references for the regression testing, and gives information for correcting the defects.

Test Scripts

A test script simulates an end user to run the application using a prescribed scenario so that a software product can be tested automatically. Traditionally, an automatic test script is written by a tester to test the methods of an assembly. When the test engineers write the automated test scripts, they must take time to define and analyze the requirements. As one or more of these values change during the software development process, the testers have to revise or rewrite the test scripts. This process will be repeated until the product is stable. Then the scripts may be interactively run to perform unit testing, integration testing, or regression testing. During the whole process, the task of the testing team is to improve and debug the test scripts and to meet the ever-changing testing requirements.

To reduce the tedious and time-consuming manual script-writing process, the automated testing tool is capable of detecting changes to the software definition automatically. If changes are made to the definition of the software, the tool will write a new test script accordingly. If the specification of the software is stable throughout the development life cycle, the test script can be rerun throughout the development life cycle for unit, integration, and regression testing.

The rules for developing a good software product apply to developing a good test script. In order to generate an efficient test script, the tool should have the mechanisms to reflect the detailed information of the project under test. A test script generated by the tool should possess the following features:

Reusability It requires great efforts to develop a testing tool. Software engineers will be more willing to make these efforts if they can meet the requirements of one project and reuse the tool for future projects. Because this book follows the management of a conventional software development to automatically generate reusable test scripts, it uses C# as a highly object-oriented language. The reusable tool and test script explore an assembly under test through namespaces, classes, methods, and properties. A test script for one testing case can be used to test another testing case. Finally, the tool itself can be reused and updated from project to project.

Readability Standard naming conventions must be used for variables and constants in the generated test script so the tester can review the code. The test script will precisely test the features of a software assembly. If there are some special needs for a software product, you can choose to update the AutomatedTest tool or revise the generated scripts. For example, if these special needs happen frequently, it is worthwhile to update the AutomatedTest tool. It makes software testing easier for the future projects. If the new requirements are not typical, the test engineer may decide not to update the tool but instead to modify the test script. In this case, a readable test script will be easier to modify.

Maintainability It is common knowledge that different software organizations use different software engineering practices. Requirements and designs are different from product to product, although they may share many common features. There are enough features in the AutomatedTest tool to cover most software products. When new features are expected in future projects, the AutomatedTest tool can be updated. An example of updating this tool to test the Windows Registry is presented in Chapter 11.

Portability Test engineers have the motivation to develop tools that can be used by their colleagues. With a simple installation process, the AutomatedTest tool is capable of performing the required testing tasks on different computer systems. Thus, other testers—as well as developers and IT and product learning personnel—can run the testing tool to detect bugs and defects.

As you work through the book, keep in mind that all successful software project rules apply to the development of the testing tool. No engineer writes perfect code. A test engineer is passionate about finding defects in code written by the others. This testing tool is able to generate an executable test script without debugging, which is a big time-saver. However, one must allow enough time to debug and test the AutomatedTest tool during and even after the tool development. Otherwise, it may introduce its own bugs into the software under test.

Summary

Recent findings by scientists and economists suggest that the infrastructure of current software testing is inadequate . Today, testers are encouraged to develop testing tools for an organization. This book introduces some new methods that are used to develop an automated testing tool. The methods and tool development will rectify the deficiencies of current testing tools as follows:

- You can use the methods introduced in this book to develop a testing tool in your preferred language and to develop one that fits the culture and business practices of your organization.
- The discussion of the methods and the tool is general and independent of other testing tools. You can add your own code to make this tool generate test scripts that compatible and interoperable with your current testing tools and methods.
- You can include this testing method in the source code control. Thus, the development and test team can update and share the testing cases and scripts easily.

- This tool will generate one test script to conduct a thorough test for an assembly or a class. It looks for what to test by itself. Therefore, testers can devote their time to exploring the high-risk areas of the products.
- A fully automated testing tool requires less time to learn and solves complex problems effectively. Thus, personnel from different departments can be involved in testing and find as many defects as possible at the early stages of development.
- The automation this tool provides eliminates the need for reverse engineering and a capture/replay procedure to write a test script. An automatically generated data store drives the test script generation. One script completes thorough unit testing for an assembly.
- The integration testing uses complete and real objects from the thorough assembly tests. Thus, it avoids the pitfalls of stub and mock objects.
- You can always upgrade this tool with new capabilities to keep up with the testing challenges in your organization.

It is important to observe software development management practices in order to successfully develop a testing tool. Chapter 2 will briefly review the current test tools that are available on the market. Starting from Chapter 3, the context of the book will include discussions of the technical fundamentals for software test and tool development. When there is enough background knowledge, code will be added to the AutomatedTest project in each chapter. In addition, three other sample projects will be developed in chapters 4, 8 and 11 to test and demonstrate the capabilities of the tool under development.

Chapter 2

Current Testing Infrastructure vs. the Proposed Testing Methods

Software has become an intrinsic part of business over the last decade. Virtually every business in every sector in the United States depends on it to aid in the development, production, marketing, and support of its products and services. By 2000, total sales of software reached $180 billion annually. The number of software engineers and programmers is approximately 1,282,000. Reducing the cost of software development and improving software quality are important objectives of the U.S. software industry.

These figures are based on a study by Dr. Gregory Tassey conducted under the auspices of the Research Triangle Institute and the National Institute of Standards and Technology (Tassey 2003). The same study also reported that the software industry suffered an economic loss because of an inadequate infrastructure for software testing. Software failures cause about $59.5 billion worth of loss to the economy annually, which accounts for almost one percent of the nation's gross domestic product. New testing tools and methods are needed immediately. According to his estimate, reducing one-third of the bugs in today's software will save the nation's economy $22.2 billion.

There is a wide variety of software testing tools on today's market. The manufacturers of these tools include Rational Software from IBM, Mercury Interactives, Segue Software. There are tools from other vendors and also some open source test tools such as Ant, JUnit, and JProbe.

As a software test engineer, I have appreciated the great capabilities of these testing tools, although they are not as automatic and effective as they could be. This chapter includes a brief discussion of some of their features. The common limitations of commercial tools include that they fail to keep up with the technology advancements and are hard to adapt to new design processes in the software industry. In this chapter, I'll propose methods for an improved test infrastructure to overcome these limitations.

Let's discuss some of the tools and their features for software test automation first.

Types of Software Testing

Manufacturers have developed tools to cover a wide range of testing tasks. However, utilizing these tools will not address the increasing complexities of software applications. Today, software organizations are incorporating multitier architectures, object-oriented design and programming, different kinds of interfaces, client-server and distributed applications, data communications, and huge relational databases, which all contribute to the exponential growth in software complexity. Test tool developers are unable to duplicate these complexities before a project progresses, making it often difficult or impossible for them to resolve the problems they present in advance. In addition, innovation from software engineers continues to improve the technology and add complexity to software projects. The tool developers can not predict these improvements, and so they must be considered on an individual basis to determine how to test.

For these reasons, it's imperative that each software organization develops its own tool to solve its unique testing issues. In order to assure quality products within an aggressive time schedule, the organization must develop an effective test approach with a scope in focus.

Determining a testing scope is critical to the success of a software project. Due to the short time frame and the intensive human interactions associated with the available software testing tools, it can become difficult to test all components of an application under development. It is always desirable to test the software thoroughly, but that's not always possible due to time and budget constraints. If the testing tools are capable of carrying out testing jobs and composing testing cases with full automation, human testers will have enough time to focus on high-risk areas.

Without a fully automated testing tool, test engineers usually determine critical requirements and high-risk areas by analyzing the requirements that are most important to the customers and the areas within the application that receive the most user focus. Decisions are often made to do no testing at all in noncritical areas, which can cause problems and even disasters in the future and turn these noncritical areas into critical ones. Thus, the scope of a fully automated testing tool should be every line of the code, and the code should be tested continuously day and night until most of the defects are found and the product is released.

After the testing scope is determined, you usually need to plan the testing phases, including the types and timing of tests to be performed in both the pre- and postrelease stages. Commercially available software testing tools are used to perform the following types of testing in a complete cycle:

Unit testing This type of testing tests individual application objects or methods in an isolated environment. It verifies the smallest unit of the application to ensure the correct structure and the defined operations. Unit testing is the most efficient and effective means to detect defects or bugs. The testing tools are capable of creating unit test scripts.

Integration testing This testing is to evaluate proper functioning of the integrated modules (objects, methods) that make up a subsystem. The focus of integration testing is on cross-functional tests rather than on unit tests within one module. Available testing tools usually provide gateways to create stubs and mock objects for this test.

System testing System testing should be executed as soon as an integrated set of modules has been assembled to form the application. System testing verifies the product by testing the application in the integrated system environment.

Regression testing Regression testing ensures that code modification, bug correction, and any postproduction activities have not introduced any additional bugs into the previously tested code. This test often reuses the test scripts created for unit and integration testing. Software testing tools offer harnesses to manage these test scripts and schedule the regression testing.

Usability testing Usability testing ensures that the presentation, data flow, and general ergonomics of the application meet the requirements of the intended users. This testing phase is critical to attract and keep customers. Usually, manual testing methods are inevitable for this purpose.

Stress testing Stress testing makes sure that the features of the software and hardware continue to function correctly under a predesigned set and volume of test scenarios. The purpose of stress testing is to ensure that the system can hold and operate efficiently under different load conditions. Thus, the possible hardware platforms, operating systems, and other applications used by the customers should be considered for this testing phase.

Performance testing Performance testing measures the response times of the systems to complete a task and the efficiency of the algorithms under varied conditions. Therefore, performance testing also takes into consideration the possible hardware platforms, operating systems, and other applications used by the customers.

Automated Testing Tools in the Marketplace

Based on the priorities set in the scoping phase, engineers need to determine which set of test types and which testing tools to use. To select the proper testing tool, keep in mind that, by nature, humans use comparison as an evaluation technique. Testers compare the capabilities and effectiveness of different tools. Sometimes they may decide to develop their own tool or test manually. The minimum requirement of a testing tool is the capability for unit and integration testing. In the following sections, I'll discuss without bias some of the sources for testing tools. The list of tool vendors is incomplete, is purely for reference, and is not an implied endorsement of any company or product. The discussion describes the solutions offered by some of the tool vendors (most of the descriptions are based on their advertisements and web pages).

DevPartner Studio from Compuware Corporation

Compuware test tool developers intend to make their tools automatically detect, diagnose, and facilitate resolution of software errors and performance problems. The NuMega DevPartner Studio 6.1 includes the following components:

BoundsChecker Tests for memory and resource leak detection of Visual C++ applications.

JCheck Used for thread and event analysis in Java applications.

SoftIce Used for debugging application problems within the Windows environment.

CodeReview Checks Visual Basic code for known coding problems.

SmartCheck Provides improved error handling within VB applications.

TrueTime Provides performance analysis of the applications.

FailSafe Tests for debugging errors.

NuMega TrueCoverage Reports how much code your test script executes for products written in Visual Basic and Visual C++ and for Java applications, which provides insight into whether the tests are executing the different portions of the program's code. This test ensures that the test script actually tests the code needing to be tested.

Please refer to `www.numega.com/products/vc/vc.html` for more information.

Insure++ from Parasoft

Insure++ is an automatic testing tool for runtime error detection for C/C++. Sometimes errors in C/C++ code aren't evident during testing, and sometimes problems such as memory corruption may cause code to crash on one machine and run perfectly on another. Insure++ tries to reveal the hidden defects in the code under test. It was specifically designed to help developers and QA personnel find and fix the difficult runtime errors that other testing techniques fail to uncover. More information about Insure++ can be viewed through `www.parasoft.com/insure/home.htm`

Mercury Interactive

Mercury Interactive provides products to test custom, packaged, and Internet applications. The suite of tools includes the following components:

TestDirector This tool provides test planning, execution, and defect-tracking functionalities. It can organize tests in hierarchical folders to help you plan and track them. The tool can track both manual and automated tests. It allows user-defined fields to be added, and it can be used with a variety of database management systems (Oracle, Sybase, MS SQL Server, and MS Access). TestDirector integrates with Mercury's capture/playback tool (WinRunner) and volume/stress tool (LoadRunner). It provides a good set of standardized reports but few custom reports features. This is a Windows-based tool.

WinRunner This is a Mercury's capture/playback tool for Windows applications, Web applications, and applications accessed through a terminal emulation (e.g., 3270, 5250). It is context sensitive when recording (i.e., objects can move and the tool can still find them, meaning it is not always hard-coded). The tool uses a proprietary scripting language and integrates well with ERP systems such as PeopleSoft. As mentioned, it integrates with TestDirector as well as the volume/stress tool (LoadRunner). It has many advanced features, such as the capability to read data from a file and exclude regions on a screen.

XRunner This is a Mercury's capture/playback tool for Unix applications. It is the same basic tool as WinRunner but for a Unix environment only. It integrates with LoadRunner but not TestDirector.

LoadRunner This tool is a volume/stress testing tool for both Windows and Unix environments. It integrates with WinRunner, TestDirector, and XRunner (as previously mentioned). This tool can simulate thousands of users and can create scenarios that benchmark performance of different vendors' components, such as servers, databases, and network components. It provides detailed reports that pinpoint locations of system bottlenecks.

For more information on Mercury Interactive tools, please refer to `www.mercuryinteractive.com`.

ObjectTester by ObjectSoftware, Inc.

ObjectCoverage is a tool to generate test scripts for unit testing at the implementation stage. With this tool, unit testing is defined as the lowest form of testing performed on developed units of software.

In C++ language, the smallest developed unit of software is a class, that is, a data structure and a set of operations that help in accessing and mutating the data structure. Software design defines classes as basic building blocks. These building blocks interact with each other to form the basis of an object-oriented application. Within a class, there are functions and data, which are encapsulated within the scope of a class and are not visible to the outside world. An object of the class can access these functions and data.

The ObjectTester tests the public functions coded in C++ within the class under test. After a user codes the ObjectTester in makefile, it creates a test script as follows:

1. Creates an instance of the class under test.
2. The instance invokes its methods with proper arguments (the arguments required for a method are created first and then the method is invoked).
3. If an argument to a method is an object of a class, then proper construction for that object is performed.
4. The created instance is destroyed at the end of the script generation.

The products from ObjectSoftware also include ObjectCoverage. For more information about ObjectSoftware products, please refer to `www.obsoft.com`.

Rational Software from IBM

Recently, Rational Software has become a branch of IBM. It is a full life cycle tool vendor that supports requirements management, visual modeling, testing, configuration, and change control. It has acquired various vendors' products over the years, such as VisualTest, SQA, Pure Atria, and Performance Awareness.

Rational Software developed a bundle of its testing tools with a collective name of SQA Suite. The bundle includes the following components:

Rational Test RealTime Typical users of Rational Test RealTime are embedded software developers working in integrated development environment (IDE) or with embedded targets. This rational tool supports the ability to test software products developed in C, C++, Ada, or Java. When its new version was released in 2002, the company declared that Rational Test RealTime would provide automated testing and runtime observation capabilities for embedded software running in a simulator, an emulator, or directly on other platforms. Its wizard-driven features include memory leak detection, performance profiling, code coverage analysis, unit testing, and scenario testing. This tool also supports Java-specific runtime analysis and makes use of JUnit for Java applications.

SQA Robot Software developers use Rational SQA Robot for functional and regression testing, and collecting performance data. It creates and runs test cases using instructions from users. It also uses capture/playback mechanism to create tests scripts, which can be edited and debugged. The test scripts are portable between different Windows versions.

SQA Repository This provides a database of information about tests and results. The database is accessible over the Internet.

SQA WebEntry This tool lets users query and modify the repository over the Internet.

SQA Manager This is a test harness and defect-tracking tool. It helps manage a QA team, including notifying team members of defects via e-mail messages.

SQA Process This is a formal methodology for testing client-server applications; for example, the tester gets the software, a written guide, and a few days with a consultant to help set up a QA strategy for an organization.

SQA LoadTest This is a volume/stress testing tool. It helps test performance with heavy loads by simulating multiple users running the same test case with different data each time.

Rational PureCoverage This tool measures program coverage for C and C++ programming environments by function, block, or line. It contains a customizable graphical user interface and can be updated dynamically as tests are running.

Visual Test Rational Visual Test is not a part of the tool bundle. It was first developed by Microsoft and then acquired by Rational Software. It uses TestBasic language to code test cases and suites for GUI tests. The user interface allows users to develop test programs and manage test suites. Users can write test programs by hand or use the Scenario Recorder to record test sessions with a manner of capture/playback. The test program recorded by the Scenario Recorder often requires editing and debugging in order to fulfill the desired tasks.

For more information, please refer to `www.rational.com`.

Segue Software

Segue's test was designed for a readiness management solution. It provides a decision support system for managing quality and reliability through the project life cycle. Segue software offers integrated tools and services. The software includes a console, workflow and drill-down reports, and services and processes to help organizations make sound product launch decisions.

The Segue Software tools include features to help testers do the following:

- Plan, document, and manage testing activities
- Maintain communication between QA and development groups.
- Identify a product's strengths and weaknesses throughout the project life cycle

Segue Software's Silk family of e-business testing products automate several threads of the testing process, including unit and regression testing (SilkTest), load and performance testing (SilkPerformer), and scenario testing (SilkRealizer).

Segue Software also developed an automated version of SilkPlan aimed at quality assurance testers and developers streamlining and automating the application testing process. Its features include integrated defect tracking, unattended test execution, and a centralized scripts repository and reports generator.

Additional products in the Silk line include SilkMonitor, SilkObserver, SilkMeter, and SilkRadar. For more information, visit the Segue Software's website at `www.segue.com`.

TestWorks from Software Research, Inc.

This is an integrated suite of testing tools that provides management of test suites with coverage analysis. The test scripts for TestWorks are obtained by capture/playback for both text- and GUI-based applications. It has a Unix version to generate test cases from templates provided by the user. It is capable of source code analysis to measure complexity and identify bugs or possible trouble areas. For more information about TestWorks, please refer to `www.soft.com/Products/index.html`.

Open Source Testing Tools

Most likely, the open source testing tools are for Java developers. There are several products available:

Ant First, it is becoming the emerging standard for build automation in Java. It allows developers to write tests in an XML build script. This script uses Java classes to perform testing. When it is used across platforms, the script needs modification. Ant is capable of accomplishing the basic tasks of a build tool; for example, compilation, archive creation, and class path management. It also automates test, report, and other miscellaneous useful tasks, such as source code control interaction, FTP, and property file editing. After the script is written and debugged with Ant, a Java application can be retrieved from source code control, built, customized to its intended environment (production versus integration, for instance), tested, and deployed to a remote server.

JUnit This is the often used tool for Java unit testing. It is a testing framework that allows developers to run repeatable tests by specifying the way the code is intended to work. JUnit is also a regression testing framework. It is used by the developer who implements and debugs unit test scripts in Java and measures the effect of code changes of the application. JUnit is open-source software, released under IBM's Common Public License Version 0.5 and hosted on SourceForge.

JProbe Suite This provides performance profiling, memory debugging, code coverage, and thread analysis capabilities in an integrated suite, designed specifically for Java developers. It identifies areas of code that have the highest potential for scalability and performance issues. It reports what is causing problems and where the problematical line of source code is. These products paint a graphical picture of running the program, from memory usage to calling relationships.

Cactus This provides container testing services for servlets, JavaServer Pages (JSP) custom tags, and servlet filters. It offers testing on connection pools, Enterprise JavaBeans (EJB), and JSP. But the early version of it did not include any services specifically designed to facilitate this type of testing.

To do the test, Cactus provides objects called redirectors, which serve as entry points to the container. These objects execute testing cases written for Cactus and provide access to container objects such as HttpServletRequest, PageContext, and FilterChain. There is one proxy per directly supported API: one for servlets, one for filters, and one for custom tags. Developers are still working on more of those. If the users want to test components that are indirectly supported, they can choose the most appropriate redirector (usually Servlet-Redirector) to gain access to the container.

Cactus also integrates with the JUnit framework and tries to begin a transparent, to the developer, conversation between the redirector and the user. As usual, users need to learn the Cactus base class, Cactus objects, and Cactus test cases to write test scripts for Cactus. Cactus documentation recommends that you learn how to program mock objects to make object stubs for integration testing.

HttpUnit This is another open-source testing tool; it concentrates on functional testing, or black-box testing, for web developers. HttpUnit tries to detect problems arising from each possible permutation of the product instead of testing smaller units of code segments.

For more details on these tools, please refer to the following resources:

`www.diasparsoftware.com/articles/JUnit/jUnitStarterGuide.html`

`sourceforge.net/projects/httpunit/`

`www.mockobjects.com`

`jakarta.apache.org/commons/cactus/index.html`

Comparing Testing Tools

There are so many automated testing tools on the market. I have discussed only a few of them. A significant number of products cover various stages of the software testing life cycle. However, they share a similar passive philosophy for the generation of test scripts or programs; that is, following a pattern of specifying a product under test, specifying a method under test, and editing and debugging the test script generated, all by a human tester. The test script or program is written with three means: by the tester, by the testing tool using reverse engineering, and by capturing/replaying a test scenario. Whichever way the test script is written, debugging is a possible last step. After reading the reviews of testing tools in this chapter, you may notice that a specific standardized test technology (such as reference data and metric) that is readily available for commercial software appears to be lacking. These testing tools require customization and contain inconsistencies because development of testing tools lags behind new software product release (ITToolbox 1999). All of the tools, including the famous Mercury Interactive WinRunner, open source JUnit, and Rational Test RealTime, take risks to meet a short time-to-market thorough test, technology advancement, new design process adoption and third party software inclusion. The current tools all fall in the following categories of the economic impact of an inadequate infrastructure for software testing (Tassey, 2002):

- Lack of the ability to conduct a thorough test
- Lack of the ability for integration and interoperability testing
- Lack of a mechanism for the automated generation of test scripts

- Lack of a rigorous test for determining when a product is good enough to release
- Lack of readily available performance metrics and test measuring procedures.

To address these gaps, experts urge software development organizations to develop their own automated software test tools (Dustin 2002). This book introduces a test method and tool to provide full automation and generate flawless test scripts. In the rest of this chapter, I will summarize the potential features of this method to improve the current software testing infrastructure.

The Proposed Software Testing Tool

As it has been observed, there is a great need for reliable test technology. The existing testing tools often lag behind the development of software applications (ITToolbox 1999). Testers have frequently complained that many of the testing tools are confusing and sometimes are misleading to the firm that uses them. They often can not perform the testing jobs the tool vendors declare they can perform. They are more like computer-added software testing tools instead of fully automated testing tools. In the following sections, I'll present the main improvements of the proposed testing method and some advantages you can gain by developing a testing tool for your own organization.

Improvement of Unit Testing

The available testing tools can generate unit test scripts by reverse engineering. However, testers must identify which unit or method to test. Such a test script tests only one method at a time. When a class contains numerous methods, the volume of test scripts can make the testing clumsy and require intensive labor. The advantage of automation disappears. It is almost impossible to test all the methods with these unit test scripts.

This book introduces a tool that actively looks for all methods of an assembly to test. After the tester feeds an assembly to this tool, it generates one test script to test all the constructors, methods, and properties, including methods inherited from the base class. Thus, it strives for a thorough test.

Developers often implement overloaded constructors and methods to increase the flexibility of their applications. Ambiguous testing cases must be avoided. When the tools require the testers to specifically select a method to test, testers don't need to worry about whether the method is overloaded or not. But this AutomatedTest tool receives an assembly to test. It knows how to test each method with different sets of parameters when it is overloaded. For example, the HighLevelObj project developed in Chapter 8 has a `Triangle()` method that is overloaded three times to compute the areas of an equilateral, an isosceles, and a scalene triangle, such as:

```
Triangle(double length)
Triangle(double length1, double length2)
Triangle(double length1, double length2, double length3)
```

Each requires its own set of parameters. The AutomatedTest tool will actively find these overloads, create corresponding data values. Then, it will match the data with the parameter requirements and use the data to drive the test script generation.

Automated Generation of Testing Data

Testers have experienced the difficulty in composing testing cases by using the available tools. In order to assign proper values to the parameters, testers are required to spend time and study every module of the application under test. This is one of the main obstacles for software test automation today. The AutomatedTest tool will be able to automatically generate testing values based on the nature of each parameter. It can also use testing cases stored in an XML document specified by the developer at the coding time. Thus, it saves testers time and the testing data can be accurate. Testers can focus on solving problems in high-risk areas.

When using the existing testing tools, testers have to declare arrays for parameters passed by array during the time the generated test script is being debugged. The proposed tool employs an easy approach to solving this problem. Debugging will not be a necessary step.

In addition, the generated testing cases can be edited and modified. When the testing cases are modified, the data store provides instructions for valid values. Otherwise, the testers can assign invalid values to parameters in order to test the error handling capability of an application. Multiple and different testing cases can be supplied to one test script at the same time. Thus, it can test many testing cases and data paths within a short period of time and find the most bugs.

A Unique Approach for Integration Testing

There is an inadequate infrastructure for integration and interoperability testing. In today's software testing tool markets, it is a convention that testing tools allow testers to insert object stubs or mock objects to test methods passing parameters by objects. If a tool has the capability of generating stubs automatically, it is considered an effective tool. The AutomatedTest tool will provide a friendly interface for automatic or customized object stubbing.

In addition, the tool will use a unique approach for such a purpose. It reuses an object returned from a previously generated test script. Because the proposed testing tool automatically generates one single test script to test all constructors, invokes all methods and assigns values to all properties, a successful execution of this test script builds a complete and real object of the class under test. During integration testing, the previously tested class is considered to be a lower-level class, which acts as a server. The client is considered to be a higher-level class. When an object of a lower-level class is encountered in testing a higher-level class, the previously built test script will be invoked and provide this object by late binding. Thus, this method of integration testing avoids objects stubbing and mock objects. The reuse of the previously built unit test script makes the integration testing more realistic. It will add power to detect bugs and ensure interoperability between various class objects.

Ability to Be Updated with New Testing Capabilities

Testers have observed that testing tools often lag behind the new software development projects of their organization. Capabilities might be added, but new issues appear as new projects are tested and testers are forced to again wait until a new release. In addition, a lot of new projects include components that may be an organization's trade secret. When the software is tested, the commercial tools most likely lack the capabilities to produce a thorough test unless your organization shares these secrets with the tool vendors. These are reasons why more and more experts believe software developers should develop their own automated testing tools.

This book introduces programming methods to test software for your institution. It will also introduce a method to update the testing tool dynamically with new capabilities. For example, in Chapters 3 through 10, a complete AutomatedTest tool with many features will be built. Chapter 11 introduces a method on how to update this tool to test new features, such as testing the Windows Registry when the application under test needs to access or mutate it.

Updating the tool with new capabilities is not limited to adding features to test the Windows Registry. You can add new testing functionalities to this tool by using a similar approach. For example, by the end of this book, the testing tool will be able to conduct unit testing, integration testing, regression testing, performance testing, error handling testing, and system testing. In the future, you can add functions for recovery testing, security testing, and other types of testing depending on the requirement of your organization. (Automated GUI testing is a topic for another book.)

Writing Test Script Based on Data

The current testing tools often generate test scripts based on a reverse-engineering process or on a capture/playback method (Kit 1995, Marick 1998). For instance, the capture/playback tools capture users' keystrokes, mouse activity, and display output. The captured information, including the output that has been validated by the tester, form a baseline for future testing of product changes. The tool can then automatically play back the previously captured tests whenever needed and validate the results by comparing them to the previous saved baseline. This method is popular and considered effective. It frees the testers from having to manually rerun tests over and over again when fixes, enhancements, or other changes are made to the product. The playback part of these tools is easy. However, after fixes, enhancements, and changes are made to the product, the captured scenarios may become obsolete. The captured test script needs to be modified by an experienced test tool user, or a new test script needs to be captured by repeating the keystrokes and mouse activities. Those factors can intimidate test tool users.

The AutomatedTest tool will not use the capture/playback approach to write test scripts. In contrast to these passive testing tools, the AutomatedTest tool uses a method that actively searches through the whole assembly under test and finds all members to test. Then, it prepares a data store with appropriate testing cases for all members. Based on the members found and the testing cases composed, a test script is generated. Finally, it compiles the test script into an executable assembly (`.exe`) or a dynamic link library (`.dll`) or both. The executable is able to be run and rerun independently. The data store can be copied and modified. The execution of the test script can test against one or multiple copies of the test data stores. On the other hand, the DLL assembly can be invoked for later integration testing by late binding.

Thus, by clicking a few buttons, a tester is able to do the following:

1. Feed a product under test to the tool.
2. Examine the test results.
3. Report the detected defects through a defect tracking system.

Every single test script tests all functional units of a module and can be reused for integration testing and regression testing. The integrated modules can be further integrated into the targeted application system. Then, the unit testing scripts can be pooled with a test harness. As the integration grows, testing is conducted by reinvoking the previously built test scripts against the changes. If the regression testing fails due to the desired modifications, the test script becomes obsolete. In this case, a new test script and data store can be generated by simply feeding the testing tool with the newly built assembly. When the entire system is integrated, each module should have been tested successfully at least once. Thereafter, if more testing is needed to meet the quality control requirements, sufficient regression testing will be continued with little effort.

Summary

The requirement for much quicker development and testing cycles has led to the creation of sophisticated quality tools that automate testing for many of the testing types. This chapter listed some of the commercially available software testing tools.

When these tools are used for software testing projects, instructions are needed for the test tools to write a test script. Testing each method within a class requires that the tool write and generate a test script which is a tedious, time-consuming and error-prone process. The tester needs to compose test cases arbitrarily. Finally, the test scripts need to be modified and debugged. Automation is mainly limited to the test executions and defect reports.

This book introduces an active method for software testing and shows you how to achieve fully automated testing. Rather than waiting for instructions, the AutomatedTest tool looks for what needs to be tested in the code. The ultimate goal is to dramatically shorten the time required to achieve a higher-quality software application.

CHAPTER 3

.NET Namespaces and Classes for Software Testing

Microsoft Visual Studio .NET has been developed to include the languages Visual C# .NET, Visual Basic .NET, Visual J# .NET, and Visual C++ .NET. With .NET-aware applications, by specifying the namespace and types of a component, software engineers can develop a program in one language and then reference it in other languages. A C# class designed by you could use code written by other developers, and other developers could use code written by you in their programs. The developers may use Visual C# .NET, Visual Basic .NET, C++, Visual Basic 6.0, or other languages to develop various COM components. The .NET Framework enables cross-platform execution and cross-platform interoperability.

The namespace solves the problems that occur when developers accidentally use the same name for their classes. Although this book is not meant to teach you how to program, it will be helpful for you to have a good understanding of the programming hierarchies, so I'll address those in this chapter. For example, you use *TestForm* to name one of your classes in the testing tool project. Later, when you use this class, you may create objects:

```
TestForm testForm = new TestForm();
```

Eventually, you are going to package the testing tool into a .NET assembly and distribute it for others to use, or someone might obtain this assembly and want to integrate it into their application. They may also integrate another assembly from other testing group, and that assembly could also contains a class called `TestForm`. When they create a new `TestForm` object in their application code, they'll need to know which class is used to create the object. Is it the one in your test tool or the one that belongs to the other assembly?

C# uses the concept of namespace to solve this dilemma. Namespaces organize classes under a named group. Under the same namespace, multiple classes can be declared. The namespace name can be used to help distinguish between two classes with the same name.

With regard to the development of the AutomatedTest tool, your mission in this chapter is to understand the fundamentals of the namespaces and classes in an assembly. Once you have a good idea about them, you'll know the importance of discovering them programmatically. Then you'll be prepared to begin the development of the automatic testing tool.

Throughout the book, the sample C# source code will be listed. There are three types of source code for different purposes. One is the code for the samples designed to present the fundamentals of C# programming. The second is for samples to build assemblies that will be tested using the AutomatedTest tool. The last is the code for the AutomatedTest project itself, which is developed with the knowledge of the first type of code and is used to test the second type of code. Some chapters may have all three types of the code. Others may have only one or two types.

Discovering the Namespace of a Product

To implement a C# project, the first thing a developer needs to do is to declare a meaningful namespace. To test a given assembly, the first thing a test engineer needs to do is to discover the namespace of the assembly. It is true that the Microsoft Visual Studio .NET integrated development environment (IDE) always gives a namespace to a project by default. In the real world, developers often change the default name of the namespace to fit their project.

In a C# program, the name of the namespace is given after a `namespace` identifier (a keyword). Classes to be included in the namespace must be declared within the namespace's curly brackets. For example, we are going to give the namespace name `TestTools.AutomatedTest` to the testing tool project. The code can be written as in Listing 3.1.

Listing 3.1 A Nest Namespace Declaration

```
namespace TestTools.AutomatedTest
{
    class TestForm
    {
   ...
    }

   class StubForm
   {
   ...
   }
   ...
}
```

In this example, the namespace `TestTools.AutomatedTest` has two parts separated with a dot (.), which is for convenience in case you need to develop more than one test tool. The namespace `AutomatedTest` is said to be nested within the `TestTools` namespace. Thus, the namespace `TestTools` includes different tools in general. The `AutomatedTest` part targets the automated testing market. If you are interested in having a semi-automated tool within the `TestTools` namespace, you can declare it as `TestTools.SemiAutomatedTest`.

Within namespaces, developers can declare classes. The code in Listing 3.1 declares two classes, `TestForm` and `StubForm`, within the `AutomatedTest` namespace. Later, if another developer also writes a class called `TestForm`, as long as they use a different name for the namespace, the two classes with the same name can coexist in one application. This feature helps test engineers a lot because they can specify a namespace to find the correct classes to test.

The nest namespace structure can also be declared as in Listing 3.2. The outcomes of code in Listings 3.1 and 3.2 are identical.

Listing 3.2 Another Way to Write a Nest Namespace

```
namespace TestTools
{
    namespace AutomatedTest
    {
       class TestForm
       {
         ...
       }

      class StubForm
      {
         ...
      }
      ...
   }
}
```

But remember, developers do not have to use a nested namespace if they do not plan to offer more than one distinct product under one namespace. For example, if they decide to use only the second part for the namespace, the code in Listing 3.1 can be rewritten as in Listing 3.3.

Listing 3.3 A Simple Namespace Declaration

```
Namespace AutomatedTest
{
    class TestForm
    {
       ...
    }

   class StubForm
   {
       ...
   }
   ...
}
```

Besides classes, some other types of declarations can be found in a namespace:

Structure A value type similar to a lightweight class that can have parameterized constructors and members. Code for a default constructor is not needed and inheritance is not allowed in a C# structure.

Interface A collection of abstract methods, properties, and event definitions. An interface cannot be directly created, but must be converted from a class or structure that implements an interface by adhering to its definitions.

Enumerator A programming type that allows developers to group name/value pairs under a specified name called the enumerator list. Every enumerator has an underlying type, which can be any integral type except char.

Delegate A .NET type equivalent to a reference type that refers to a static method or to an instance method. It is used for one instance to pass a method as a parameter.

For the AutomatedTest project, this book will guide you in completing the code to test classes and interfaces. You can add your own methods to test the rest of the possible types.

Discovering the Namespace in Multiple Source Files

C# is an object-oriented programming language. In object-oriented programming, the software developers write short code to implement a method—that is, as few lines of code in a method as possible. When a file containing the namespace is too big, the developers may separate the file into multiple source code files. All of the files start with the same name as the namespace. But the names of the classes are different. When the project is built, the .NET compiler combines all the classes into the same namespace and assembly.

For example, when you implement the AutomatedTest project in this book, you are going to make two Windows forms, a TestForm and a StubForm, and they will be created with the `TestForm` and `StubForm` class types, respectively. Each of them will appear in a separate source file but bear the same namespace. Thus, you'll have at lease two source files in the project: `TestForm.cs` and `StubForm.cs`. The code skeletons in Listing 3.1 will be divided into these two files, shown in Listings 3.4 and 3.5, respectively.

Listing 3.4 C# Code Skeleton of the *TestForm.cs* File

```
namespace TestTools.AutomatedTest
{
    class TestForm
    {
      .
      .
      .
    }
}
```

The second source file contains the declaration of the StubForm class and uses the same namespace as shown in Listing 3.5.

Listing 3.5 **C# Code Skeleton of the *StubForm.cs* File**

```
namespace TestTools.AutomatedTest
{
   class StubForm
   {
      .
      .
      .
    }
}
```

Of course, there will be more than two classes in the TestTools.AutomatedTest namespace. The examples are used to illustrate how developers may separate classes into multiple source files carrying the same namespace. When the two source files are built, the .NET compiler builds more than one class into an assembly with a single namespace. When you develop the AutomatedTest tool in the later chapters, you need to keep these things in mind in order to conduct a thorough test for a given assembly.

Testing Classes and Namespaces

After the declaration of a namespace, developers declare classes within the namespace. These classes can be reused within the namespace or in the other namespaces. When a class is used inside a different namespace, the developers can refer to it by prefixing the class name with the name of its namespace. For example, if you want to use the TestForm class in Listing 3.3, your code must be like the following:

```
AutomatedTest.TestForm myTestForm = new AutomatedTest.TestForm();
```

This code creates a AutomatedTest.TestForm object.

If you want to use the TestForm class in Listing 3.1 or Listing 3.2, the code must be as follows:

```
TestTools.AutomatedTest.TestForm myTestForm = new
➥TestTools.AutomatedTest.TestForm();
```

Using this syntax helps distinguish between classes and namespaces. When you test an assembly, this line of code is in the test script to test the default constructor. In C# programming, when a variable is declared from a primitive data type, such as a string or a number, the initialization is not done by a constructor. Instead, objects created from the other data types are initialized via the invocation of the constructors. A C# class can define any number of constructors, each of which takes a unique set of arguments. As you know, every C# class is endowed with a default constructor. A default constructor in C# doesn't take any arguments. It ensures that all state data, such as field variables of the class, are set to their default values. The keyword `new` allocates appropriate computing resources for creating an instance of the class.

The discovery and declaration of namespaces and classes are the first step for a software test procedure. Now is a good time for you to create some C# projects as warm-up exercises to give you a full understanding of namespaces and classes. If you still need more information about namespaces and classes, you can refer to the C# books listed in the bibliography at the end of this book.

For this book, your task is to develop a program to test other software products. Now that you know the basics about the namespace and class in C# programming, you can implement the testing tool project. To start the AutomatedTest tool project, you will follow the same procedure a software developer follows to manage a software development project. However, the context of this book focuses only on the stages of implementation, testing, and maintaining.

To start the implementation, the first step is to create the AutomatedTest project. The next section guides you step by step through creating the project. Then you can declare the namespace and its classes. In the rest of the book, you will add classes, and class members into the project until you achieve a fully automated software testing tool.

Creating the AutomatedTest Tool Project

You will begin the development of the AutomatedTest tool in this section. The code in this section only declares a namespace and a class for the AutomatedTest tool. The namespace and class will be empty except for the code generated by the Microsoft Visual Studio .NET IDE.

The following exercise is based on the assumption that you have Microsoft Visual Studio .NET 2003 IDE (C#) and MS Excel 2000/XP installed on your computer system. To start a project and declare the `TestTool.AutomatedTest` namespace and the `TestForm` class, follow these steps:

1. Create a new folder under `C:\` and name it `SourceCode`. This folder will be used to organize all the example code of this book based on chapters. Then, create a subfolder named `Chapter03` under `C:\SourceCode`.
2. Start the Microsoft Visual Studio .NET IDE from the Programs menu.
3. Click File ➢ New ➢ Project. Figure 3.1 shows the New Project window.

NOTE Your screen might appear differently depending upon the components (languages) that you have installed.

FIGURE 3.1
Create a new Windows application project with C#.

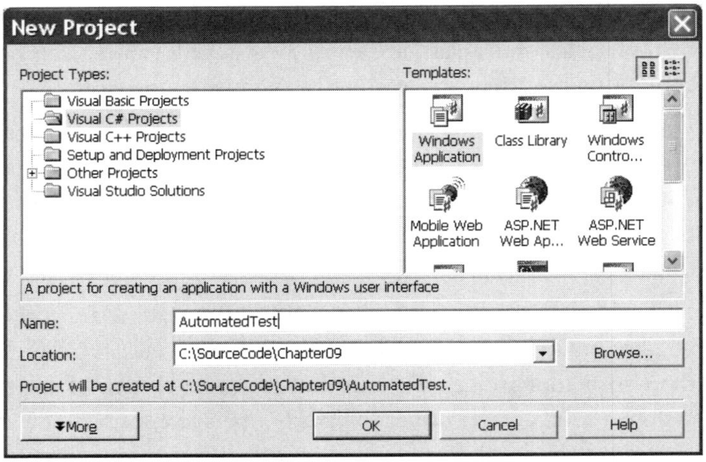

4. In the Project Types list, select Visual C# Projects. In the Templates list, select Windows Application.
5. In the Name field, type **AutomatedTest**.
6. For the Location, click the Browse button and locate the `C:\SourceCode\Chapter03` folder.
7. Click the OK button. Your AutomatedTest project is created with a default form. The form is named Form1 and appears in the design editor.
8. In the Solution Explorer, right-click `Form1.cs`. A menu appears.
9. Click Properties. In the File Name field, rename it **TestForm.cs**.
10. Right click on TestForm in the design editor and choose Properties from the pop-up menu. The form properties appear on the right panel (the location of the properties may be different if you have a custom setup of the IDE).
11. For the Text property, change Form1 to Automated Software Test.
12. For the (Name) property, change Form1 to TestForm.
13. In the Solution Explorer, right-click `TestForm.cs` and choose View Code. The C# IDE has already generated some code for this project. The namespace name is by default `AutomatedTest`, the name given to the project in step 6. Listing 3.6 is the C# code generated by the Microsoft Visual Studio .NET IDE.
14. Prefix the name of the namespace with `TestTools`. The namespace becomes `TestTools.AutomatedTest`. The class name is already `TestForm` (changed in step 12).

You can begin to build this project now. If there are compiling errors, the possible cause is that some of the lines still contain the text *Form1*. Replacing all occurrences of *Form1* with *TestForm* will fix this problem.

Listing 3.6 The C# IDE-Generated Code for the *TestForm.cs* File

```
using System;
using System.Drawing;
using System.Collections;
using System.ComponentModel;
using System.Windows.Forms;
using System.Data;

namespace AutomatedTest
{
    /// <summary>
    /// Summary description for Form1.
    /// </summary>
    public class TestForm : System.Windows.Forms.Form
    {
        /// <summary>
     /// Required designer variable.
     /// </summary>
     private System.ComponentModel.Container components = null;

     public TestForm()
     {
         //
      // Required for Windows Form Designer support
      //
      InitializeComponent();

      //
      // TODO: Add any constructor code after InitializeComponent call
      //
     }

     /// <summary>
     /// Clean up any resources being used.
     /// </summary>
     protected override void Dispose( bool disposing )
     {
      if( disposing )
      {
        if (components != null)
        {
         components.Dispose();
        }
      }
      base.Dispose( disposing );
```

```
        }

        #region Windows Form Designer generated code
        /// <summary>
        /// Required method for Designer support - do not modify
        /// the contents of this method with the code editor.
        /// </summary>
        private void InitializeComponent()
        {
            //
         // Form1
         //
         this.AutoScaleBaseSize = new System.Drawing.Size(5, 13);
         this.ClientSize = new System.Drawing.Size(336, 290);
         this.Name = "Form1";
         this.Text = "Automated Software Test";

        }
        #endregion

        /// <summary>
        /// The main entry point for the application.
        /// </summary>
        [STAThread]
        static void Main()
        {
         Application.Run(new TestForm());
        }
       }
   }
```

The Microsoft Visual Studio .NET IDE generates the code lines and comments. A line prefixed with three slashes (///) in a C# program is an XML comment, which will be built into an XML help file and be visible to future users. A line prefixed with two slashes (//) is a comment line similar to that in a C++ or a Java program, which is visible only to the programmer. In this project, we will delete the Microsoft Visual Studio .NET IDE generated comments at this point. But in Chapter 4, you'll see how to incorporate testing cases into the XML comments at coding. After the above steps are done and the comments are removed, the `TestForm.cs` file looks like Listing 3.7.

Listing 3.7 New Code for *TestForm.cs* without Comments

```
using System;
using System.Drawing;
using System.Collections;
using System.ComponentModel;
using System.Windows.Forms;
```

```
using System.Data;

namespace TestTools.AutomatedTest
{
       public class TestForm : System.Windows.Forms.Form
       {
    private System.ComponentModel.Container components = null;

    public TestForm()
    {
       InitializeComponent();
    }

    protected override void Dispose( bool disposing )
    {
    if( disposing )
    {
      if (components != null)
      {
      components.Dispose();
      }
    }
    base.Dispose( disposing );
    }


    private void InitializeComponent()
    {

       this.AutoScaleBaseSize = new System.Drawing.Size(5, 13);
       this.ClientSize = new System.Drawing.Size(336, 290);
       this.Name = "TestForm";
       this.Text = "Automated Software Test";

    }


    [STAThread]
    static void Main()
    {
       Application.Run(new TestForm());
    }
  }
}
```

Now the AutomatedTest project has a fully qualified namespace, `TestTools.AutomatedTest`, and one class, `TestForm`, which inherits a base class, `System.Windows.Forms.Form`. Inside the `TestForm` class, the Microsoft Visual Studio .NET IDE has generated a default constructor:

```
public class TestForm : System.Windows.Forms.Form
```

```
{
  ...
  public TestForm()
  {
    ...
  }
  ...
}
```

Then, the `protected override void Dispose(bool disposing)` method is inherited from the `System.Windows.Forms.Form` class, which destroys the form when the `TestForm` exiting event occurs.

The `private void InitializeComponent()` method adds Windows form controls to the form.

NOTE At this point, the code within this method sets values to only four of the properties of the `TestForm` class, which is referred to by the C# keyword `this`. However, in later chapters, more window form controls will be added to this form.

Finally, `static void Main()` is the entry point method of the test tool project. The statement `Application.Run(new TestForm())` in the `static void Main()` method creates a new instance of the `TestForm` and starts it.

You have seen how to prefix the class type with the namespace to create a class object. However, when the class is referred to within its own class domain or namespace domain, the namespace prefix can be omitted. On many occasions, programmers would like to use the keyword `this` to refer to the class by itself.

Now you can run this project. The form looks similar to Figure 3.2.

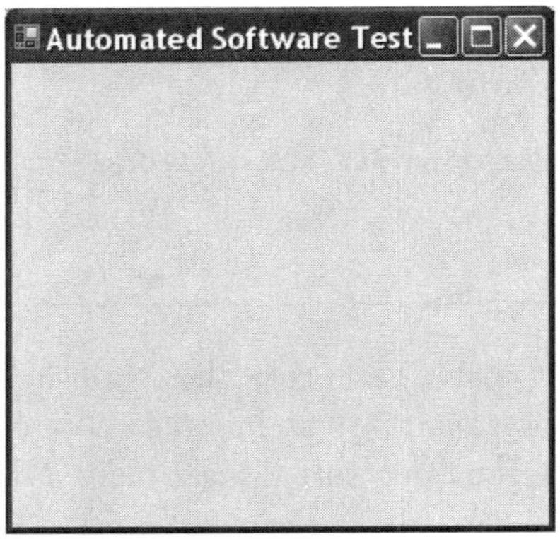

FIGURE 3.2 The empty form of the AutomatedTest project.

As you can see, it's blank so you can't do anything with it yet. However, you have learned the importance of namespaces and classes for the C# program. When you are ready to test this project, you know how to start the investigation of the `TestTools.AutomatedTest` namespace and the `TestForm` class. You have also experienced how easy it is to use the Microsoft Visual Studio .NET IDE to make a Windows application. In later chapters, you will add more code to enable the AutomatedTest project to perform software testing tasks. Most of the code will be added between the curly brackets of the `TestForm` class.

At this point in the chapter, we'll move away from the development of the testing tool and introduce you to some more C# fundamentals.

C# Keywords: *using* and *namespace*

We have discussed how to create new namespaces. This section focuses on how to use existing namespaces. You may have noticed that there are some code lines in the beginning of Listings 3.6 and 3.7 that start with the keyword `using` followed by a namespace, which is an existing namespace. You can use the C# keyword `using` in a variety of ways to make it work with the namespaces more easily and save yourself a great deal of typing. For example, in the previous sections, we used the following statement to create a new object for the `TestForm` class:

```
TestTools.AutomatedTest.TestForm myTestForm = new
➥TestTools.AutomatedTest.TestForm();
```

A `using` statement can be used in a program as follows:

```
using TestTools.AutomatedTest;
```

With the `using` keyword, the statement to create a `TestForm` object becomes shorter:

```
TestForm myTestForm = new TestForm();
```

In real-world programming, a spelled-out fully qualified class name that includes the namespace identifier can get a bit too long, especially if the namespace identifier is also fully qualified and long.The keyword `using` saves you from this.

There is also another way to use the `using` keyword. In C#, it provides a shortcut by defining an aliased name for the fully qualified class identifier, and you can use the alias name instead of the fully qualified class identifier once the alias is established.

You can alias a name with a statement having the following formula:

- The `using` keyword
- The alias name
- An equals sign

- The fully qualified class name with the namespace identifier
- A statement-terminating semicolon

Using this formula, the following statement creates an alias for the TestForm class:

```
using ShortForm = TestTools.AutomatedTest.TestForm;
```

When the TestForm class is referenced in the code, you can write ShortForm to replace TestTools.AutomatedTest.TestForm. For example, you can write a Main() method to create a TestForm instance with the fully qualified identifier:

```
static void Main()
{

  Application.Run(new TestTools.AutoMatedTest.TestForm());

}
```

With the alias created by the using statement in a program, the preceding method can be rewritten as follows:

```
static void Main()
{

  Application.Run(new ShortForm());

}
```

Note that the using statements must appear in the source code before or immediately after the namespaces are declared. If the using statements appear after class declarations, you receive the following error message from the C# compiler:

```
error CS1519: Invalid token 'using' in class, struct,
   or interface member declaration.
```

Declaring *namespace* Directives with the Keyword *using*

You have seen two ways to use the using keyword in a C# program. You can see that when you write programs, prefixing every class name with its full namespace can get tedious, especially if you need to do it many times. Fortunately, the use of the using keyword helps reduce the coding time.

Using the using keyword with a namespace identifier tells the C# compiler that you want to refer to classes in a specified namespace without prefixing the class names with the namespace identifiers. The .NET System namespace defines numerous C# core classes, which deal with all the primitive data types, mathematical manipulations, garbage collections, and so on. Therefore, there is a using directive in almost all C# IDE–generated projects:

```
using System;
```

A `using` statement in a C# program is called a namespace directive. Namespace directives tell the C# compiler that the code will use classes from the namespace and that the classes won't be prefixed with the namespace name during coding. As the previous example demonstrates, with the `using System` directive, you can simplify a line of code statement.

The C# compiler does the work to find the definition of each class in one of the namespaces referenced in the namespace directives. For example, the following namespace directives are defined in the beginning of the AutomatedTest project in Listing 3.7:

```
using System;
using System.Drawing;
using System.Collections;
using System.ComponentModel;
using System.Windows.Forms;
using System.Data;
```

When you write code to use a class from any of the above namespaces, you do not have to prefix the class name with its namespace.

So far, we have explored the method to create and use namespace directives. Many namespaces are predefined in the Microsoft Visual Studio .NET platform. There are numerous classes and methods in the namespaces. Some of them will be used very often in this project. Others may not be used here, but they will be used in other projects.

It is a tedious job for a developer to figure out what namespaces, classes, and methods have already been defined by the Microsoft Visual Studio .NET platform. Therefore, the next section includes a review of some namespaces you might encounter in the testing tool project or in developing other projects.

Primitive .NET Data Type and C# Representation

In the preceding section, I mentioned the primitive Microsoft Visual Studio .NET data types within the `System` namespace. In this section, you'll see how you can use regular expressions in place of the Microsoft Visual Studio .NET System data types when you write C# code. For example, the `System` namespace has a data type `System.Int32`. But a C# developer would rather write `int` in the C# program instead of writing `System.Int32`:

```
int myInteger;
```

The AutomatedTest tool will also use the regular expression of the `System` data type in the test script generated. Table 3.1 lists the `System` data types and their equivalent C# expressions. The data representation ranges are listed for respective data types so it will help you make sure the automated testing tool can determine boundary conditions for testing cases

TABLE 3.1 The Primitive System Data Types and Their C# Expressions

Primitive .NET Data Type	C# Representation	Representation Range
`System.Byte`	`byte`	0 to 255
`System.SByte`	`sbyte`	–128 to 127
`System.Int16`	`short`	–32,768 to 32,767
`System.Int32`	`int`	–2,147,483,648 to 2,147,483,647
`System.Int64`	`long`	–9,223,372,036,854,775,808 to 9,223,372,036,854,775,807
`System.UInt16`	`ushort`	0 to 65,535
`System.UInt32`	`uint`	0 to 4,294,967,295
`System.UInt64`	`ulong`	0 to 18,446,744,073,709,551,615
`System.Single`	`float`	1.5×10^{-45} to 3.4×10^{38}
`System.Double`	`double`	5.0×10^{-325} to 1.7×10^{308}
`System.Object`	`object`	Useful for any class; often needs boxing and unboxing
`System.Char`	`char`	U+0000 to U+ffff
`System.String`	`string`	Dependent on system memory
`System.Decimal`	`decimal`	10^{0} to 10^{28}
`System.Boolean`	`bool`	true or false

You can see in Table 3.1 that Microsoft Visual Studio .NET refers to data types with the classes in the `System` namespace. The C# representation is similar to the representation in C++. The test script generated later by the automated testing tool will use the C# representation for easy code review.

Predefined .NET Namespaces for Automated Testing

The .NET Framework contains classes in a variety of predefined namespaces that you will use in your C# code for the AutomatedTest project. When this tool is used for software test projects, it should have the capability of discovering these and other namespaces used by the projects under test. These namespaces are often referred to as dependencies. Table 3.2 describes a few of the predefined namespaces. They will be used in the AutomatedTest tool and the other sample projects in future chapters, so it's worthwhile to discuss them in detail here.

TABLE 3.2 A Quick Review of the .NET `System` Namespaces

Namespace	Function
`System`	Contains classes that possess basic functionality, such as data type conversions, mathematical operations, program invocation, garbage collection, and process environment management. The `System` namespace is the largest one provided with .NET.
`System.CodeDom`	Contains classes that include the elements of a source code document. In this book, it's used to generate test scripts dynamically.
`System.Collections`	Contains classes that define collections of objects, such as lists, queues, sorted list, arrays, ArrayList, hash tables, and dictionaries. The testing tool and the test script use this namespace to store data temporarily.
`System.ComponentModel`	Contains classes that create runtime and design-time components and controls.
`System.Data`	Contains classes that defines the ADO.NET data access architecture. The ADO.NET architecture enables you to build components that can manage data from multiple data sources in either disconnected or connected mode.
`System.Diagnostics`	Contains classes that can be used to debug .NET applications, to trace the execution of your code, to monitor performance of your application using performance counters and reading and writing to event logs, and to start and stop processes.
`System.Drawing`	Contains classes that add graphics device interface (GDI) drawing functionality.
`System.IO`	Contains classes that can read from and write to data streams and disk files with specifications of synchronous and asynchronous input/output.
`System.Net`	Contains classes that provide a class wrapper around the many network protocols available today and handle DNS, HTTP, and FTP requests. If your interest is Web testing, you will find many of the types in this namespace useful.
`System.Reflection`	Contains classes that provide a view of the types, methods with parameters, properties, and fields available to a .NET application. You can even programmatically create and invoke types at runtime.
`System.Resources`	provides classes that help developers create, store, and manage culture aware resources within a localization application.
`System.Runtime.InteropServices`	Provides functionalities for "unmanaged code."
`System.Text`	Contains classes that can be used to work with ASCII, Unicode, UTF-7, and UTF-8 character encodings.

TABLE 3.2 CONTINUED A Quick Review of the .NET `System` Namespaces

Namespace	Function
`System.Threading`	Contains classes that enable multiple operating system threads in the .NET applications, thereby creating a true multithreaded application.
`System.Timers`	Contains classes to fire an event on a timed interval or on a more complex time schedule.
`System.Web`	Contains classes to implement the Hypertext Transfer Protocol (HTTP).
`System.Windows.Forms`	Contains classes to build full-featured Windows applications with features such as dialog boxes, menus, and buttons.
`System.XML`	Contains classes to process XML data. Provides support for XML 1.0, XML namespaces, XML schemas, XPath, XSL and XSLT, DOM Level 2, and SOAP 1.1.

NOTE Table 3.2 lists 18 .NET namespaces. This is not a complete list; it is meant to just give you a feel for how much has been done by the .NET Framework developers. If you are interested in more information, you can refer to the Microsoft Visual Studio .NET Framework SDK documentation for a complete list of namespaces and classes (`http://msdn.microsoft.com`). Table 3.2 lists only the namespaces necessary to the AutomatedTest project and the other sample code in this book. The CodeDom and Reflection namespaces are the core of automation, `System.Reflection` gathers the test information, and `System.CodeDom` generates the test scripts.

Retrieving Type Classes under Test

In the previous sections, you saw how to develop and use namespaces and classes. You also learned about various namespaces predefined in Microsoft Visual Studio .NET IDE. It is important to have a good understanding of them in order to test a software product and develop a testing tool. As a software tester, it is more interesting to discover what's in a software application under test. The rest of this chapter will guide you in exploring the `Type` class of the Microsoft Visual Studio .NET Framework, which is used to enable the testing tool to programmatically recognize namespaces and classes. The Microsoft Visual Studio .NET Reflection namespace has been mentioned many times so far and now you will begin to understand how it will be used in programs.

To investigate the type classes of a given assembly, examples in the following sections will make reference to the `System.Reflection` namespace. You will get a feeling for how the `Type` class acts as a window into the `Reflection` API and enables the access to the metadata. The abstract class `System.Type` represents a type in the Common Type System (CTS). The Common Type System is what enables you to examine objects across all languages in the .NET family. Because each object uses the same framework, runtime, and type system in the .NET Framework, object and type information is easily obtainable by the Reflection namespace.

Another asset of the `Type` class is the capability to create objects programmatically and use them at runtime. This is a main feature we are going to use in the testing tool project. In the following sections, a few of the .NET namespaces will be used in the examples. This will make you familiar with the .NET namespaces and know how to explore the .NET namespaces within a given component under test.

The `System.Type` class provides several methods to retrieve type information from objects. The following sections describe three different ways:

- Retrieve type information by type name.
- Retrieve type information by process name.
- Retrieve type information by a specified assembly name.

Although these three implementations perform essentially the same task, each is useful under a specific situation. Depending on the circumstance of your application, you might need to use only one of the methods to gather the type information for testing purposes.

Retrieving Types by Name

A lot of Microsoft Visual Studio .NET documentation has introduced `ILDAsm.exe` as a disassembling tool for you to get insight into a given assembly. When you use the `ILDAsm.exe`, you launch this program from a Visual Studio .NET command prompt or through clicking the Start ➢ Run menu. But in order for the testing tool to conduct a survey on a given assembly, it needs to implement a mechanism to discover the assembly information dynamically. For a given assembly, when you need to view the information of a certain class, you simply specify the name of a type. The C# program can query almost all aspects of the object by using the Reflection namespace. For example, you can get information to find out whether the object is a class, what its base system type is, and many other properties.

To give you a feeling about using the `Type` class for software testing, we'll start with a console application to retrieve the type information of a given object. The project name is QueryByName in the accompanying source code. The C# code is shown in Listing 3.8. This program reveals three properties of the `System.Reflection.Assembly` class type.

Listing 3.8 Querying *System.Reflection.Assembly* Type Information by Name

```
using System;

namespace QueryByName
{

   class TypeName
   {

      [STAThread]
      static void Main(string[] args)
      {
         Type t = Type.GetType("System.Reflection.Assembly");
         Console.WriteLine("Name : {0}",t.Name);
         Console.WriteLine("Underlying System Type :
{0}",t.UnderlyingSystemType);
         Console.WriteLine("Is Class : {0}",t.IsClass);
      }
   }
}
```

`GetType()` is a static method in the `Type` class and is overloaded three times by the Microsoft Visual Studio .NET platform. In this case, it receives a string of a type name as its parameter. The second overload receives two parameters. The first parameter has the same meaning as the previous overload. The second parameter is a Boolean parameter that specifies whether to throw or ignore the `TypeLoadException` if an error occurs. The third overload also uses the two parameters the previous overloads used. However, it needs a third Boolean parameter to indicate whether it is case sensitive with respect to the first string parameter. After the `GetType()` method is invoked, it returns a `Type` instance of the received string argument. In this case, the instance is represented by the variable `t`. Then, the static `Console.WriteLine()` method prints a few properties of the `Assembly` class; that is, `Name`, `UnderlyingSystemType`, and `IsClass`.

After the project is implemented and saved, you can build it and run it by pressing F5 within the Microsoft Visual Studio .NET IDE or by opening a Visual Studio .NET command prompt and issuing a DOS command from the folder where `QueryByName.cs` is located. In this case, the `QueryByName.cs` file is saved in the `C:\SourceCode\Chapter03\QueryByName\` folder. Here is the DOS command:

```
csc QueryByName.cs
```

When you bring up a regular DOS command prompt for the csc compiling command, you need to set up the correct environment variables for the Microsoft Visual Studio .NET platform. Chapter 11 will introduce a few ways to set up environment variables. If you have built this project with the Microsoft Visual Studio .NET IDE, the `QueryByName.exe` executable is saved in the `C:\SourceCode\Chapter03\QueryByName\Bin\Debug` folder. If you used the DOS command to compile the `QueryByName.cs` file, the executable is saved directly under the `C:\SourceCode\Chapter03\QueryByName` folder. You can run the executable by navigating to the respective folder and issuing a command such as this from a DOS command prompt:

```
QueryByName.exe
```

After the execution of the `QueryByName.exe` executable, values of three properties of the `Assembly` class are retrieved by the respective `Type` class properties. For example, the `System.Reflection.Assembly` class has the class name `Assembly`, as shown in Figure 3.3. Its fully qualified identifier is `System.Reflection.Assembly`, and it is truly a class.

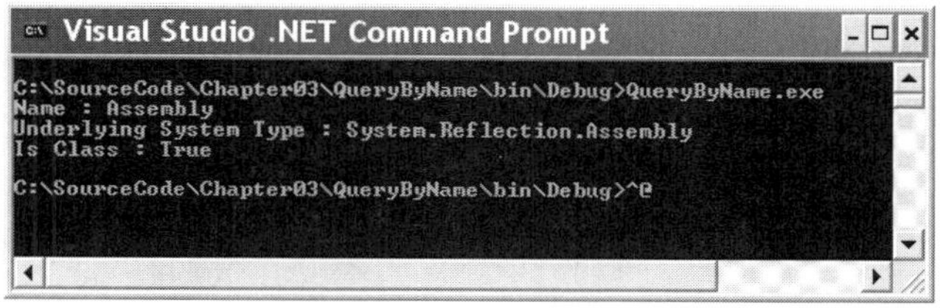

FIGURE 3.3 Querying Assembly type information by its name.

NOTE Pressing F5 from the Microsoft Visual Studio .NET IDE builds the active project and runs the executable. When the project is a console application, the execution brings up a DOS console window and closes the console window after the execution. To view the execution results, you can start a DOS or a Visual Studio .NET command prompt. You start a Visual Studio .NET command prompt by clicking Start ➤ Programs ➤ Microsoft Visual Studio.NET ➤ Visual Studio .NET Tools ➤ Visual Studio .NET Command Prompt. From the command prompt, issue an executable command (`QueryByName.exe` in this case). The result is similar to Figure 3.3.

These are all read-only properties accessed through the `System.Type` instance, `t`. The useful properties of the `System.Type` class, which will provide information for test script generations, are listed in Table 3.3.

TABLE 3.3 Properties of the `System.Type` Class

Property	Description
`Assembly`	Gets the `System.Reflection.Assembly` that the type is declared in. A read-only property.
`AssemblyQualifiedName`	Reads the fully qualified name of the `System.Type`, including the name of the assembly from which the type was loaded.
`Attributes`	Gets the attributes associated with the type.

TABLE 3.3 CONTINUED Properties of the System.Type Class

Property	Description
BaseType	Retrieves the type from which the current type directly inherits.
DeclaringType	Overridden. Gets the class that declares this member.
DefaultBinder	Gets the default binder used by the system.
FullName	Returns the fully qualified name of the type, including the namespace of the type.
GUID	Extracts the GUID associated with the type.
HasElementType	Returns the value indicating whether the current type encompasses or refers to another type; that is, whether the current type is an array or a pointer or is passed by reference.
IsAbstract	Gets the value to indicate whether the type is abstract and must be overridden.
IsAnsiClass	Retrieves a Boolean value to indicate whether the string format attribute AnsiClass is selected for the type.
IsArray	Indicates whether the type is an array.
IsAutoClass	Indicates whether the string format attribute AutoClass is selected for the type.
IsAutoLayout	Indicates whether the class layout attribute AutoLayout is selected for the type.
IsByRef	Indicates whether the type is passed by reference.
IsClass	Indicates whether the type is a class or other data type, such as a value type or an interface.
IsCOMObject	Indicates whether the type is a COM object.
IsContextful	Indicates whether the type can be hosted in a context.
IsEnum	Indicates whether the current type represents an enumeration.
IsExplicitLayout	Indicates whether the class layout attribute ExplicitLayout is selected for the type.
IsImport	Indicates whether the type was imported from another class.
IsInterface	Indicates whether the type is an interface; that is, not a class or other data type.
IsLayoutSequential	Indicates whether the class layout attribute SequentialLayout is selected for the type.
IsMarshalByRef	Indicate whether the type is marshaled by reference.

TABLE 3.3 CONTINUED Properties of the System.Type Class

Property	Description
IsNestedAssembly	Indicates whether the type is nested and visible only within its own assembly.
IsNestedFamANDAssem	Indicates whether the type is nested and visible only to classes that belong to both its own family and its own assembly.
IsNestedFamily	Indicates whether the type is nested and visible only within its own family.
IsNestedFamORAssem	Indicates whether the type is nested and visible only to classes that belong to either its own family or its own assembly.
IsNestedPrivate	Indicates whether the type is nested and declared private.
IsNestedPublic	Indicates whether a class is nested and declared public.
IsNotPublic	Indicates whether the top-level type is not declared public.
IsPointer	Indicates whether the type is a pointer type.
IsPrimitive	Indicates whether the type is one of the primitive types.
IsPublic	Indicates whether the top-level type is declared public.
IsSealed	Indicates whether the type is declared sealed.
IsSerializable	Indicates whether the type is serializable. An object of a serializable type can be persistent via serialization.
IsSpecialName	Indicates whether the type has a name that requires special handling.
IsUnicodeClass	Indicates whether the string format attribute UnicodeClass is selected for the type.
IsValueType	Indicates whether the type is a value type.
MemberType	Overridden. Gets a bitmask indicating the member type.
Module	Gets the module (the DLL) in which the current type is defined.
Name	Gets the name of this member.
Namespace	Gets the namespace of the type.
ReflectedType	Overridden. Gets the class object that was used to obtain this member.
TypeHandle	Extracts the handle for the current type.
TypeInitializer	Returns the initializer for the type.
UnderlyingSystemType	Gets the type provided by the common language runtime that represents this type.

You might be wondering how this information will be useful to you. It will be repeatedly used in the testing tool project. Once the AutomatedTest tool knows the class type, it knows how to create objects for the class and access the properties of the class under test. Then it generates legal C# statements and puts code into a test script. Without the type information, the testing tool does not know what to test. As a class name is examined by the `Reflection` classes further, the testing tool can gather the underlying type for each piece of information needed for the test script. Remember, the Reflection namespace makes the automated testing process possible and will be used later in the development of the AutomatedTest tool.

Retrieving Types by Instance

You have seen how to retrieve type information by name when you know the type's name. However, as a software tester, you often spend a lot of time learning a namespace and its classes. When `GetType()` is used differently, you can also use an instance of an object to examine the type information. Let's make a new C# console application project with the name of QueryByInstance and use it to discover the type information of an instance. Listing 3.9 shows the code to process this task.

Listing 3.9 Querying Type Information Using the Instance of an Object

```
using System;

namespace QueryByInstance
{
   class TypeInstance
   {
      [STAThread]
      static void Main(string[] args)
      {
         string myVar = "Retrieving types by instance";
         Type t = myVar.GetType();
         Console.WriteLine("Name : {0}",t.Name);
         Console.WriteLine("Underlying System Type :
{0}",t.UnderlyingSystemType);
         Console.WriteLine("Is Class : {0}",t.IsClass);
      }
   }
}
```

You see the difference of calling the `GetType()` method in this and the previous example. The execution of this `GetType()` method is not the same as calling a static method and it doesn't take any parameters. The goal of this example is to examine the type information of the variable `myVar`, which is a string variable. Rather than specifying that you want to view type information of the `System.String` class, you create an instance of a string variable `myVar`. Then you call the

GetType() method. Finally, the Console.WriteLine() method is called the same way as before and prints the type properties of Name, UnderlyingSystemType, and IsClass.

Build the project and run it. The information obtained for the String type is shown in Figure 3.4.

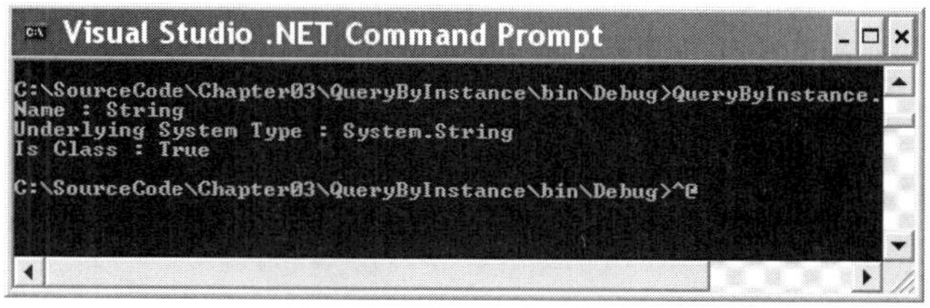

FIGURE 3.4 Querying System.String type information by specifying the instance

The class name of the variable myVar is String. Its fully qualified identifier is System.String. It is truly a class. Comparing this with the previous example, you're obtaining the same information, but the difference is that you don't have to know the name of the type before the fact. You simply call the GetType() method and assign it to a Type object, which you query for the name, underlying system type, and any other interesting properties.

Retrieving Types from a Given Assembly

This method is the most interesting one for developing the AutomatedTest tool. Most of the time, test engineers will be asked to test an assembly instead of a class or a created object. Because they don't know what is inside the assembly, test engineers spend a lot of time, and thus a good portion of the budget for the project, doing manual testing. However, using the technique introduced here to retrieve type information from a given assembly enables the tester to get the job done quickly. Note that the given assembly could be an executable (*.exe file) or a dynamic link library (*.dll file).

Let's make another C# console application project, QueryAssembly, to demonstrate this usage. Listing 3.10 contains the code necessary to examine the type information of the executable itself.

Listing 3.10 Examining a Currently Running Process for Type Information

```
using System;
using System.Reflection;
using System.Diagnostics;

class AssemblyType
{
   public static void Main(string[] args)
   {
```

```
            Process p = Process.GetCurrentProcess();
            string assemblyName = p.ProcessName + ".exe";
            Console.WriteLine("Examining : {0}", assemblyName);
            Assembly a = Assembly.LoadFrom(assemblyName);

            Type[] types = a.GetTypes();
            foreach(Type t in types)
            {
               Console.WriteLine("\nType : {0}", t.FullName);

               Console.WriteLine("Base class : {0}",t.BaseType.FullName);
            }
        }
    }
```

With the use of two more using statements, this example introduces two new namespaces, System.Diagnostic and System.Reflection. In the System.Diagnostic namespace, the Process class is used to examine the currently running processes. The static Process.GetCurrentProcess() method retrieves the name of the process invoked by the entry point method. Then the ProcessName property returns a string name of the invoked process (QueryAssembly.exe in this case). The Process class has many other methods and properties. The ProcessName property provides the dynamic functionality that ensures that the code will work no matter what the name of the application is.

After the process name is discovered, the System.Reflection namespace is used. The invocation of the static Assembly.LoadFrom() method loads the assembly with a name retrieved by the ProcessName property. Finally, the foreach loop enumerates the types defined in the process. The Console.WriteLine() method prints the properties of FullName and its base class for each enumerated type. You are getting closer and closer to an automated testing tool.

After you finished typing in the code in Listing 3.10, you can build it and run it. Figure 3.5 shows the output of this application. This time, the application finds that the current process is from an executable file, QueryAssembly.exe. It has an instance of the AssemblyType class, and it has a base class of System.Object.

FIGURE 3.5
Process information obtained with the Reflection API

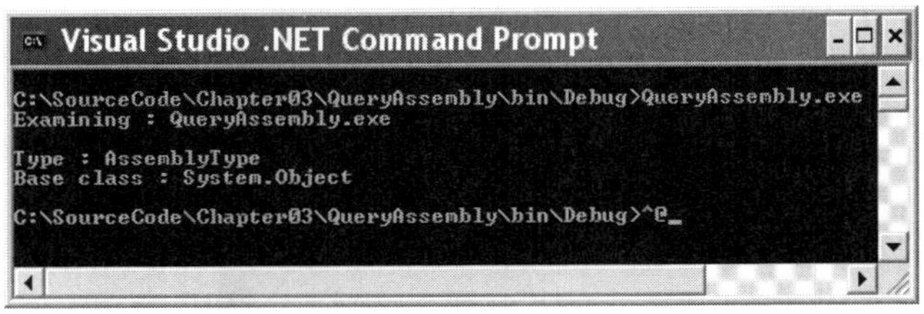

This is a simple assembly. It can be manually achieved easily, too. But in the real world of testing a software product, an assembly is often much more complicated. The point of this example is to show you how to use the Reflection namespace in your AutomatedTest tool and how to use the type enumeration when a tester is unaware of the given assembly. However, this section only covers a small portion of the `System.Reflection` namespace. Chapter 4 will discuss the use of `System.Reflection` in detail from various aspects.

Retrieving the type information from a given assembly enables you to examine the current running process and the actual application itself and to display all internal classes and their types dynamically.

To reinforce what you learned in this chapter, you can add a few more dummy classes to this project and see how much detail can be revealed dynamically.

Summary

The C# namespace wraps classes, structures, interfaces, enumerators, and delegates. Other declarations can not be placed directly under a namespace. Namespaces help distinguish the classes and structures from other classes and structures that have the same name.

A fully qualified class or structure name includes the name of its namespace or namespaces. To refer to a class or a structure in a C# program, the code must qualify the data type name by prefixing it with the name of the namespace and a period.

The C# `using` keyword is useful for working with namespaces. It can be used to provide a shortened, aliased name for a particular class in a particular namespace. It can also be used as a namespace directive, which tells the C# compiler that the code will be referencing classes in a specific namespace and that the code will not be prefixing the classes with its namespace identifier. For the development of AutomatedTest tool project, you will use the `System.Reflection` namespace and `System.Type` class to discover the dependencies referred by the `using` statements of an application under test programmatically.

You can code your own namespaces and use namespaces developed by others using the techniques outlined in this chapter. The .NET Framework ships with a variety of class-populated namespaces, helping programmers code everything from Windows applications to XML processors and security programs. Namespaces in the Microsoft Visual Studio .NET Framework also provide classes that you can use to build C# code using advanced techniques, such as multithreaded software and Reflection.

Testing is made easier by knowing what is actually in an assembly under test. This chapter included three examples that used the `System.Type` class to explore a given application and find information about the namespaces and classes it contains. The `System.Type` class provides numerous properties to retrieve useful information related to testing classes. The purpose of this chapter was to familiarize you with the importance of examining the classes within a known assembly. In the next chapter, we will focus more on the combination of the `System.Reflection` and `System.Type` namespaces to examine a given assembly for its classes, constructors, interfaces, enumerators, properties, methods, and parameters. Obtaining the insight into a given assembly by the `System.Reflection` namespace helps write test scripts programmatically.

Chapter 4

.NET Reflection for Test Automation

In Chapter 3, you saw how to use the .NET Reflection namespace to obtain information from a given assembly. A single assembly may contain multiple namespaces. A namespace may contain multiple classes. The Microsoft Visual Studio.NET IDE already provides a tool, `ILDasm.exe`, to disassemble an assembly into the underlying code, type metadata, and assembly manifest. You need a channel for the AutomatedTest tool to do the design-time investigation of a .NET assembly. Instead of executing `ILDasm.exe`, the AutomatedTest tool uses classes defined within the `System.Reflection` namespace to programmatically obtain the same information.

In this chapter, you will incorporate the `System.Reflection` namespace into the testing tool project, enable the project to find the target to test, and write code into a test script based on the characteristics of the target. After a discussion about manipulating the namespace and examining an assembly at runtime, this chapter will also includes a discussion of how a .NET client uses the late binding technique to invoke a given class and its methods, which is an important aspect of .NET/COM interoperability. The techniques to test classic COM will be discussed as well.

The Basics of Reflection

If you happen to be a VB 6.0 programmer, you may have referenced TypeLib information in your projects to discover information about a dynamic link library (DLL). Now you are in the .NET era. You use the Reflection namespace for the runtime type discovery. Like a prism reflecting the sunlight into a wavelength spectrum, the Reflection namespace has classes and methods to differentiate a given assembly into its types and members. Therefore, it sees through the assembly under test for the AutomatedTest tool.

`System.Reflection` namespace provides help to load an assembly at runtime and discover the same sort of information the `ILDasm.exe` discovers. Then it obtains a list of all types contained within a given module, including the methods, fields, properties, enumerators, and events defined. It can also programmatically discover the set of interfaces supported by a given class (or structure), the parameters of a method, as well as other related details (base class, namespace information, and so forth). This is the very information a tester must know accurately in detail, and it requires a lot of consideration at the beginning of a testing task.

There is a reason the `System.Type` class was discussed in the previous chapter. In order to obtain information from a given assembly, the `System.Reflection` namespace is often used together with the `System.Type` class. As you will see, the `System.Type` class contains a number of methods that are able to extract valuable information about the current type you are testing. The `System.Reflection` namespace also contains numerous related types to facilitate late binding and dynamic loading of assemblies.

System.Type Class

Yes, the `Type` class again. You learned some things about the `Type` class in the preceding chapter. Many of the items defined within the `System.Reflection` namespace make use of the abstract `System.Type` class. The `System.Type` class hosts a number of methods used to discover the details behind a given item. The list of the complete set of members is quite long. However, this section presents some most frequently used properties and methods of the `System.Type` class.

The following are properties of the `System.Type` class to discover a number of basic properties about the type of interest (e.g., each of them returns a value `true` or `false` based on whether the type is an abstract class, an array, a class, and so forth):

`IsAbstract`

`IsArray`

`IsClass`

`IsCOMObject`

`IsEnum`

`IsInterface`

`IsPrimitive`

`IsNestedPublic`

`IsNestedPrivate`

The following are methods to obtain an array representing the items (interfaces, methods, properties, and so forth) of interest:

`GetConstructors()`

`GetEvents()`

`GetFields()`

`GetInterfaces()`

`GetMethods()`

`GetMembers()`

`GetNestedTypes()`

`GetProperties()`

Each of these method returns a related array (e.g., `GetFields()` returns a `FieldInfo` array, `GetMethods()` returns a `MethodInfo` array, and so on). Remember, each of these methods also has a singular form (e.g., `GetField()`, `GetMethod()`, `GetProperty()` and so on) that retrieves a specific item by name rather than an array of all related items.

Finally, there are these:

`FindMembers()` Returns an array of filtered `MemberInfo` types based on search criteria

`GetType()` Returns a type instance for a given string name

`InvokeMember()` Allows late binding to a given item

When you review the listed properties and methods, you may have noticed they are useful for the AutomatedTest tool project. The following sections illustrate how to integrate the `System.Type` class into C# programs. Your goal is to make progress in implementing the testing tool project.

Discovering Type Information of a Variable

Programmatically, you can use a few different ways to code C# to find out the type class of a variable or an object instance. However, you are not supposed to use the keyword `new` to directly create a `System.Type` object because the `System.Type` class is an abstract class. Let's begin with the first way to use the `GetType()` method defined within the `System.Object` to discover the type instance of an object.The following code assigns the type name of the `myForm` variable to the `t` variable:

```
// Find out the Type using the TestForm instance.
TestForm myForm = new TestForm();
Type t = myForm.GetType();
```

The second way to perform the same task is to use the static `GetType()` method defined within the `System.Type` class. Be sure to specify the textual name of the item of interest for this investigation:

```
// Get a Type using the static Type.GetType() method.
Type t = null;
t = Type.GetType("TestForm");
```

This code converts the string `"TestForm"` to a `Type` variable, `t`.

You can also obtain an instance of type using the `typeof()` method, which requires a parameter of the real type name:

```
// Get the Type using typeof.
Type t = null;
t = typeof(TestForm);
```

The code also assigns a type value to the `t` variable.

These three methods perform the same task. The static `Type.GetType()` and the method `typeof()` do not need to first create an object instance in order to extract the type information of the object. The `System.Reflection` can supply the type names needed by the `GetType()` and typeof() methods. Depending on the development stage of the AutomatedTest tool, you will be instructed to use these methods alternatively. The combination of the System.Reflection namespace and the System.Type class members is a perfect fit for the AutomatedTest process.

So that you can become more familiar with the Reflection namespace and the Type class, you'll develop a sample .NET assembly in the next section. This assembly will be used to demonstrate the capabilities of the System.Reflection and the System.Type class.

NOTE The AutomatedTest tool will continuously test this sample assembly as new features are added throughout this book.

Creating a Sample Class for Testing

In this section, you'll begin to develop a low-level class that performs simple math calculations. In this chapter, the calculator will be used to demonstrate how to use the combination of the System.Reflection namespace and System.Type class to explore an assembly under test. The AutomatedTest tool will test this calculator with gradually increasing degrees of automation throughout the rest of the book.

In this chapter, you'll create a simple calculator project named LowLevelObj. You will build a HighLevelObj project that will pass a parameter as the LowLevelObj object in Chapter 8, in which a method to conduct integration testing is introduced.Follow these steps to build the simple calculator:

1. Start the Microsoft Visual Studio.NET IDE.
2. Choose File ➢ New ➢ Project.
3. Select C# Projects in the left pane.
4. Select Class Library in the right pane.
5. Type in **LowLevelObj** for the project name, which is also the namespace by default.
6. Enter **C:\SourceCode\Chapter04** for the location.
7. Click OK.

After the project is created, you implement the SimpleMath.cs file with a class, SimpleMath and two enumerators, Math_ENUM and Power_ENUM. Then, you implement some methods and properties within the SimpleMath class to perform the basic arithmetic operations.

The construction of the Math_ENUM enumeration is to create a set of symbolic math operators to represent addition, subtraction, multiplication, and division. By the definition of the C# language, each of the symbols is equivalent to a numerical value starting from 0 and incrementing by 1 consecutively. The implementation of the Math_ENUM starts with a public modifier and a keyword enum. Then use a verb to symbolize each of the math operators. The symbols are separated with a comma and each occupies one line. The complete implementation of the Math_Enum looks like the following code snippet:

```
public enum Math_ENUM
{
   Add,
   Subtract,
   Multiply,
   Divide
}
```

You can continue the same pattern to complete the Power_ENUM implementation. This time the symbols represent the power operations for square, cube, and square root.

These two enumerations will be used in the SimpleMath class and also can be used in other programs. In order to implement the SimpleMath class, you can start the class declaration as follows:

```
public class SimpleMath
{
}
```

This declaration also carries a public modifier for public visibility. A keyword, class, indicates that SimpleMath is declared as a class. The constructors, fields, properties, and methods will all be implemented within the curly brackets. For example, this class first implements five fields. For the purpose of testing whether the AutomatedTest project can test the fields of a given class, these fields are declared public.

```
public double Result;
public Math_ENUM lastSimpleOperation;
public Power_ENUM lastPowerOperation;
public int FirstNum;
public int SecondNum;
```

Each field declaration starts with a new line and ends with a semicolon.

Then, implement the two constructors. One of them is the default constructor. You simply start it with a keyword, public, and the class name SimpleMath with a pair of parentheses. Finish it with a pair of curly brackets:

```
public SimpleMath()
{
}
```

Next, overload a constructor with two integer parameters to initialize two of the fields. It looks like this:

```
public SimpleMath(int num1, int num2)
{
   FirstNum = num1;
   SecondNum = num2;
}
```

Thus, when a programmer creates an object from the `SimpleMath` with a default constructor, the values of the `FirstNum` and `SecondNum` fields are initialized to be zero. The overloaded constructor will initialize these two fields with integer values inside the parentheses.

We also implement this class with two `public` read-only properties. The property `LastSimpleOperation` contains only a keyword, `get`, to return the value of the `lastSimpleOperation` field. The `return` statement is included within a pair of curly brackets. Notice that the name of the property starts with an uppercase *L* and the name of the field starts with lowercase *l* because C# is a case-sensitive language. The final code of this property is similar to the following:

```
public Math_ENUM LastSimpleOperation
{
   get {return lastSimpleOperation;}
}
```

You can use this method to complete the `LastPowOperation` property.

The rest of the job involves implementing two public methods, `SimpleCalc()` and `PowerCalc()`. The `SimpleCalc()` method takes two numerical parameters and one `Math_ENUM` parameter. It performs addition, subtraction, multiplication, and division of the two numerical parameters. The return type of this method is `double`. A keyword, `switch`, is used to make the `operation` decision with regard to the value of the third parameter. Finally, it assigns the value of the third parameter to the `lastSimpleOperation` field and returns the final value of the `Result` field. The code snippet is as follows:

```
public double SimpleCalc(int x, int y, Math_ENUM operation)
{
   switch (operation)
   {
      case Math_ENUM.Add:
         Add(x, y);
         break;
      case Math_ENUM.Subtract:
         Subtract(x, y);
         break;
      case Math_ENUM.Multiply:
         Multiply(x, y);
         break;
      case Math_ENUM.Divide:
         Divide(x, y);
         break;
   }
   lastSimpleOperation = operation;
   return Result;
}
```

The implementation of the PowerCalc()method is similar. The difference is that it takes only one numerical parameter and one Power_ENUM parameter, and conducts power calculations. These two methods call seven private methods, each representing one mathematical operation.

For example, the Add() method is implemented with two numerical parameters for simple calculation:

```
private void Add(int x, int y)
{
   Result = x + y;
}
```

The Square() method is implemented with only one parameter for power calculation:

```
private void Square(int x)
{
   Result = x*x;
}
```

They simply assign the outcome of the mathematical operation to the Result field. You can complete the rest of the private methods—Subtract(), Multiply(), Divide(), Cubic() and SquareRoot()—using the coding patterns we just used.

The C# language allows programmers to add XML comments at code time. The AutomatedTest project will be implemented in the next chapter to use the testing cases stored in an XML document. Therefore, the last task to complete this class is to add some XML comments with testing data for the SimpleMath class.

I recommend inserting the XML documentation comments after all the members of the class are completely coded. The XML comments are added only for the public members and types. To do this, you simply place the cursor immediately before the declaration of a member or a type (a class or an enumeration). Then type in three slashes, ///. The Microsoft Visual Studio .NET IDE automatically generates an XML skeleton with appropriate XML tags and attributes. For example, if you type in three slashes when the cursor is at the top of the SimpleCalc() declaration, the generated XML skeleton looks like this:

```
/// <summary>
///
/// </summary>
/// <param name="x"></param>
/// <param name="y"></param>
/// <param name="operation"></param>
/// <returns></returns>
```

All the generated XML tags start with a <summary> tag, and followed by none, one, or more than one <param> tags with attributes for the names of the required parameters. If the return type of a method is not void, it creates a <returns> tag. Otherwise, there is not a <returns> tag.

With the C# language, you must complete the XML comments by adding the descriptions for all the XML tags between each pair of > and < symbols. In order to make use of the XML comments for testing data store, for the <param> and <return> tags, you can append a text `e.g.,` followed by a value for the corresponding parameter and the expected return. In this case, after the descriptions and testing data values are added, the XML comments for the `SimpleCalc()` method looks similar to this:

```
/// <summary>
/// Conduct a simple math operation
/// </summary>
/// <param name="x">assign an integer, e.g., 245</param>
/// <param name="y">assign an integer, e.g., 45</param>
/// <param name="operation">assign an value of Math_ENUM, e.g., Subtract</param>
/// <returns>Returns a double result, e.g., 200</returns>
```

Besides the description for each tag, the addition assigned values to each of the required parameters and the expected result of the <returns> tag. The parameter `"x"` has a value of `245`, `"y"` `45` and `"operation" Subtract`, respectively. The value `Subtract` is the abbreviation of `Math_ENUM.Subtract`, which will be recognized by the AutomatedTest tool later. The <returns> tag has an assignment of the expected value `200`, which is the result of 245 – 45.

Using this explanation, you can complete the XML comments for the other public members and types. Listing 4.1 shows the complete implementation of the `SimpleMath` class.

Listing 4.1 Code for the *SimpleMath.cs* Example with Testing Data in the XML Documentation Comments

```
using System;

namespace LowLevelObj
{
   public enum Math_ENUM
   {
      Add,
      Subtract,
      Multiply,
      Divide
   }

   public enum Power_ENUM
   {
      Square,
      Cubic,
      SquareRoot
   }

   /// <summary>
```

```
/// A class for simple calculations
/// </summary>
public class SimpleMath
{
   public double Result;
   public Math_ENUM lastSimpleOperation;
   public Power_ENUM lastPowerOperation;
   public int FirstNum;
   public int SecondNum;

   public SimpleMath()
   {
   }



   /// <summary>
   /// Initiate a SimpleMath object
   /// </summary>
   /// <param name="num1">assign an integer, e.g., 23</param>
   /// <param name="num2">assign an integer, e.g., 47</param>
   public SimpleMath(int num1, int num2)
   {
      FirstNum = num1;
      SecondNum = num2;
   }

   /// <summary>
   /// Read only property
   /// </summary>
   public Math_ENUM LastSimpleOperation
   {
      get {return lastSimpleOperation;}
   }

   /// <summary>
   /// Read only property
   /// </summary>
   public Power_ENUM LastPowOperation
   {
      get {return lastPowerOperation;}
   }

   /// <summary>
   /// Conduct a simple math operation
   /// </summary>
   /// <param name="x">assign an integer, e.g., 245</param>
   /// <param name="y">assign an integer, e.g., 45</param>
   /// <param name="operation">assign an value
➥of Math_ENUM, e.g., Subtract</param>
   /// <returns>Returns a double result, e.g., 200</returns>
```

```
public double SimpleCalc(int x, int y, Math_ENUM operation)
{
   switch (operation)
   {
      case Math_ENUM.Add:
         Add(x, y);
         break;
      case Math_ENUM.Subtract:
         Subtract(x, y);
         break;
      case Math_ENUM.Multiply:
         Multiply(x, y);
         break;
      case Math_ENUM.Divide:
         Divide(x, y);
         break;
   }
   lastSimpleOperation = operation;
   return Result;
}

private void Add(int x, int y)
{
   Result = x + y;
}

private void Subtract(int x, int y)
{
   Result = x - y;
}

private void Multiply(int x, int y)
{
   Result = x * y;
}

private void Divide(int x, int y)
{
   Result = x / y;
}

/// <summary>
/// Conduct a power operation
/// </summary>
/// <param name="x">assign an integer, e.g., 37</param>
/// <param name="operation">Assign an arithmetic
➥operation, e.g., Cubic</param>
/// <returns>Returns an integer, e.g., 50653</returns>
public double PowerCalc(int x, Power_ENUM operation)
{
   switch (operation)
```

```
            {
               case Power_ENUM.Square:
                  Square(x);
                  break;
               case Power_ENUM.Cubic:
                  Cubic(x);
                  break;
               case Power_ENUM.SquareRoot:
                  SquareRoot(x);
                  break;
            }
            lastPowerOperation = operation;
            return Result;
         }

         private void Square(int x)
         {
            Result = x*x;
         }

         private void Cubic(int x)
         {
            Result = x*x*x;
         }

         private void SquareRoot(int x)
         {
            Result = Math.Sqrt((double)x);
         }
      }
   }
```

This implementation is straightforward. After you add the XML comments, you need to complete the following steps to enable the XML document generation from the Microsoft Visual Studio .NET IDE:

1. In the Solution Explorer, right-click the LowLevelObj project name and choose Properties from the pop-up menu. The property page appears.
2. In the LowLevelObj property page, click Configuration Properties on the left.
3. Find the XML Documentation File field on the right and type in a filename: **`LowLevelObj.xml`**.
4. Click the OK button to return to the Microsoft Visual Studio .NET IDE.
5. Press Ctrl+Shift+B. `LowLevelObj.dll` and `LowLevelObj.xml` are built in the `C:\SourceCode\Chapter04\LowLevelObj\bin\Debug\` folder.

Because XML comments are not added for the public enumerations, the public fields, and the public default constructor in Listing 4.1, you will receive some warning messages such as the following after the successful compilation:

```
c:\sourcecode\chapter04\lowlevelobj\simplemath.cs(15,3):
 warning CS1591: Missing XML comment for publicly visible type
or member 'LowLevelObj.Power_ENUM.Cubic'
```

Because we are not interested in assigning testing data values to them, you can ignore these warning messages. Not assigning too many testing data values also keeps the code list and the XML document short for easy reviewing. To view the generated XML document, you can navigate to the `..\Bin\Debug\` folder, right-click the `LowLevelObj.xml` file, and choose to open it with Internet Explorer or another browser. Listing 4.2 shows this XML document.

Listing 4.2 The *LowLevelObj.xml* Document Generated by the Microsoft Visual Studio .NET IDE with Testing Data Values from Code Time

```
<?xml version="1.0"?>
<doc>
   <assembly>
   <name>LowLevelObj</name>
   </assembly>
   <members>
      <member name="T:LowLevelObj.SimpleMath">
         <summary>
         A class for simple calculations
         </summary>
      </member>
      <member name="M:LowLevelObj.SimpleMath.#ctor(System.Int32,System.Int32)">
         <summary>
         Initiate a SimpleMath object
         </summary>
         <param name="num1">assign an integer, e.g., 23</param>
         <param name="num2">assign an integer, e.g., 47</param>
      </member>
      <member name="M:LowLevelObj.SimpleMath.SimpleCalc(
➥System.Int32,System.Int32,LowLevelObj.Math_ENUM)">
         <summary>
         Conduct a simple math operation
         </summary>
         <param name="x">assign an integer, e.g., 245</param>
         <param name="y">assign an integer, e.g., 45</param>
         <param name="operation">assign an value of Math_ENUM,
➥e.g., Subtract</param>
         <returns>Returns a double result, e.g., 200</returns>
      </member>
      <member name="M:LowLevelObj.SimpleMath.PowerCalc(
➥System.Int32, LowLevelObj.Power_ENUM)">
         <summary>
```

```
            Conduct a power operation
            </summary>
            <param name="x">assign an integer, e.g., 37</param>
            <param name="operation">Assign an arithmetic operation,
➥e.g., Cubic</param>
            <returns>Returns an integer, e.g., 50653</returns>
        </member>
        <member name="P:LowLevelObj.SimpleMath.LastSimpleOperation">
            <summary>
            Read only property
            </summary>
        </member>
        <member name="P:LowLevelObj.SimpleMath.LastPowOperation">
            <summary>
            Read only property
            </summary>
        </member>
    </members>
</doc>
```

At this point, you've seen how an XML test data store is created. It has been frequently observed that the commercial testing tools generate test scripts with hard-coded data values. Hard-coding data values can cause problems for reusability and maintainability. The test scripts fail to execute when any change occurs to the project. In the next chapter, I will discuss the method of using the `LowLevelObj.xml` to build a data-driven AutomatedTest tool. In addition to the XML data-driven test scripts, I will also introduce a method to generate test scripts with data stored in a spreadsheet.

Now you are ready to use the `System.Reflection` namespace and the `System.Type` class to discover the methods, properties, enumerations, and fields for the given `LowLevelObj.dll` assembly.

Gathering Test Information Using the *System.Type* Class

In the previous section, you developed a `LowLevelObj.SimpleMath` class. Now you are going to write a program to discover the information of this class. This section guides you through completing a C# console application to achieve this purpose.

Use the steps you used earlier to create a CalcDiscovery project, but in step 4, select Console Application instead of Class Library. After the Microsoft Visual Studio .NET IDE generates the skeleton code, add a `LowLevelObj.dll` reference to the project. To add the `LowLevelObj.dll` as a reference, do the following:

1. Choose Project ➢ Add Reference.
2. Navigate to `C:\SourceCode\Chapter04\LowLevelObj\bin\Debug\`.

3. Select `LowLeveObj.dll`.
4. Click the OK button.

The project is created and ready for you to code. Add the following `using` statements to the beginning of the `CalcDiscovery.cs`:

```
using System;
using System.Reflection;
using LowLevelObj;
```

TIP As discussed in Chapter 3, the keyword `using` followed by a namespace will save you from having to type a fully qualified class name for object initialization.

During the programming, the `CalcDiscovery` class defines a number of static methods that look more or less similar. The first method is `ListMethods()`, which extracts information about all of the methods from the `SimpleMath` class using a `Type` object. This is accomplished by calling `Type.GetMethods()` to return an array of `MethodInfo` types:

```
// discover all method names from SimpleMath.
public static void ListMethods(SimpleMath myCalc)
{
   Console.WriteLine("==== Methods of SimpleMath ====");

   Type t = myCalc.GetType();
   MethodInfo[] mi = t.GetMethods();
   foreach(MethodInfo m in mi)
   {
      Console.WriteLine("Method: {0}", m.Name);
      Console.WriteLine("Return type: " + m.ReturnType);
   }
   Console.WriteLine("====================\n");

}
```

The `ListMethods()` method needs a parameter passed by a `LowLevelObj.SimpleMath` object. Through the `Type` variable, `t`, `GetMethods()`collects all the methods of the `LowLevelObj.dll` assembly into the `MethodInfo` array, `mi`. Then the `foreach` loop enumerates the names and return the types of the methods. After the execution, this method should print the names of the public methods of the `SimpleMath` class on the console screen, similar to the following:

```
Method: SimpleCalc
Return type: System.DoubleMethod: PowerCalc
Return type: System.Double
...
=========================
```

You have finished finding the methods. Now you'll want to find the fields of the SimpleMath class. The implementation of the ListFields() method is similar to the implementation of ListMethods(); it calls the Type.GetFields() method to result in a FieldInfo array:

```
// Discover all fields from SimpleMath.
public static void ListFields(SimpleMath myCalc)
{
   Console.WriteLine("===== Fields of SimpleMath =====");;

   Type t = myCalc.GetType();
   FieldInfo[] fi = t.GetFields();
   foreach(FieldInfo field in fi)
      Console.WriteLine("Field: {0}", field.Name);

   Console.WriteLine("===================\n");

}
```

The code of the ListMethods() and the ListFields() methods resemble each other except that one enumerates a MethodInfo array and the other enumerates a FieldInfo array.

Next, you need to implement a ListStatistics() method. This method reveals some brand marks for the type class of interest, in this example, SimpleMath:

```
// Reveal some statistics about SimpleMath class.
public static void ListStatistics(SimpleMath myCalc)
{
   Console.WriteLine("===== Statistics about SimpleMath =====");
   Type t = myCalc.GetType();

   Console.WriteLine("Full name is: {0}", t.FullName);
   Console.WriteLine("Base is: {0}", t.BaseType);
   Console.WriteLine("Is it abstract? {0}", t.IsAbstract);
   Console.WriteLine("Is it a COM object? {0}", t.IsCOMObject);
   Console.WriteLine("Is it sealed? {0}", t.IsSealed);
   Console.WriteLine("Is it a class? {0}", t.IsClass);
   Console.WriteLine("===================\n");

}
```

You need one more method to discover the available properties within a class under test. The ListProperties() method is the last method for this project for the purpose of discovering information of the members of the SimpleMath class:

```
// Gather all properties information from the SimpleMath class.
public static void ListProperties(SimpleMath myCalc)
{
   Console.WriteLine("===== Properties of SimpleMath =====");
```

```
        Type t = myCalc.GetType();
        PropertyInfo[] pi = t.GetProperties();
        foreach(PropertyInfo prop in pi)
           Console.WriteLine("Prop: {0}", prop.Name);

        Console.WriteLine("===================\n");

}
```

The algorithm of this method is similar to the implementation of the previous two methods. The difference is that it calls the `GetProperties()` method of the `Type` class to find other properties.

Finally, you need to implement an entry point method, the `Main()` method, of the `CalcDiscovery` class by simply calling each of the static methods implemented earlier, which are listed here:

```
using System;
using System.Reflection;
using LowLevelObj;

namespace Discovery
{
   class CalcDiscovery
   {

// insert the above static methods here...

      [STAThread]
      static void Main(string[] args)
      {
         SimpleMath myCalc = new SimpleMath();
         ListMethods(myCalc);
         ListFields(myCalc);
         ListStatistics(myCalc);
         ListProperties(myCalc);
      }
   }
}
```

You probably remember the method to retrieve type information by instance in Chapter 3; you'll find that this project uses the same approach to programmatically find the methods, fields, properties, and some statistics within a given assembly.

After building the project, test run the executable from folder `C:\SourceCode\Chapter04\CalcDiscovery\bin\Debug\CalcDiscovery.exe`. Your results should be similar to that in Figure 4.1.

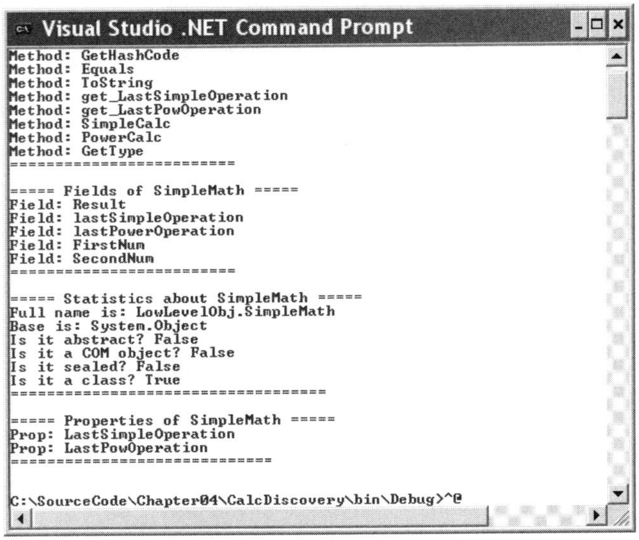

FIGURE 4.1 Test run results of the CalcDiscovery reflection.

Review the content in Figure 4.1. You can scroll this command prompt window to see the entire results. If you have done software testing manually or by using other testing tools, you can see how easy it is to use these methods introduced in this section to find out all the useful information to test an assembly. You may want to know what else the `System.Reflection` can do to automate a testing process. In the next section, you'll see how to discover the parameter information within a method.

Enumerating Method Parameters

To write a complete and useful test script automatically with the AutomatedTest tool, it's not enough to find out types, fields, properties, and method members. You must also know the parameters within a method in detail and assign proper values to the parameters to call the method. To illustrate this, you will add more code to the CalcDiscovery project to find the method parameters of the `SimpleMath` class.

First, you create a `private static void GetMethodParams()` method as follows:

```
private static void GetMethodParams(MethodInfo mi)
{
   ParameterInfo[] myParams = mi.GetParameters();
Console.WriteLine("Method has " + myParams.Length + " parameters");
   // Show some info for param.
   foreach(ParameterInfo pi in myParams)
   {
```

```
            Console.Write("Parameter position: {0}", pi.Position);
            Console.Write(" Parameter name: {0}", pi.Name);
            Console.Write(" Parameter type: {0}\n", pi.ParameterType);

        }
    }
```

To declare the `GetMethodParams()` method, you need a parameter passed by a `MethodInfo` object. The `GetParameters()` method of the `MethodInfo` class returns a `ParameterInfo` array of the parameters within a given method. The first `Console.WriteLine()` statement shows how many parameters a method needs. The `foreach` statement starts enumerating the method parameters. Within the `foreach` loop, the first `Console.Write()` statement extracts the position of the parameter. The second statement returns the name of the parameter, and the third, the parameter type. With this kind of information, the AutomatedTest tool will be able to write a code-based test script to invoke a method accurately.

Next, nest the `GetMethodParams()` method inside the `ListMethods()` method as shown here. The new addition is shown in bold:

```
public static void ListMethods(SimpleMath myCalc)
{
   Console.WriteLine("===== Methods of SimpleMath =====");
   Type t = myCalc.GetType();
   MethodInfo[] mi = t.GetMethods();
   foreach(MethodInfo m in mi)
   {
      Console.WriteLine("Method: {0}", m.Name);
      GetMethodParams(m);
   }
   Console.WriteLine("=========================\n");

}
```

After the modification, when this method enumerates the names of the methods in the `SimpleMath` class, it first prints the name of the method. Then it gets information for required parameters and returns the type of each method by calling the `GetMethodParameter()` method.

After you build it without any error messages, you can run the `CalcDiscovery.exe` from a command prompt window. The output is shown in Figure 4.2.

You may want to examine the output to make sure the information printed in the console screen is what you have implemented for the `SimpleMath` class. The `Type` class lists the return types and parameter types by their .NET system names instead of the conventional type names you write in the C# program. For example, `System.Double` is equivalent to `double`.

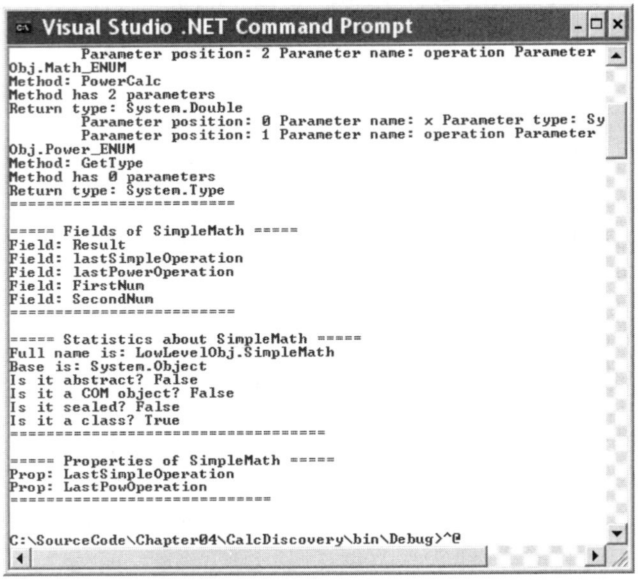

FIGURE 4.2
Method parameter information of the SimpleMath class

Testing Software with the .NET Reflection Namespace

The `System.Reflection` namespace defines a number of related type classes. Similar to the other namespaces for software testing purpose, some of them are more interesting than others. Table 4.1 lists a few of the core items; some of them were used in the previous sections.

TABLE 4.1 Some Important Classes in the `System.Reflection` Namespace

`System.Reflection` Type	MEANING
`Assembly`	This class (in addition to numerous related types) contains a number of methods that allow you to load, investigate, and manipulate an assembly.
`AssemblyName`	This class allows you to discover numerous details behind an assembly's identity (version information, culture information, and so forth).
`EventInfo`	This class holds information for a given event.
`FieldInfo`	This class holds information for a given field.
`MemberInfo`	This is the abstract base class that defines common behaviors for the `EventInfo`, `FieldInfo`, `MethodInfo`, and `PropertyInfo` types.
`MethodInfo`	This class contains information for a given method.

TABLE 4.1 CONTINUED Some Important Classes in the `System.Reflection` Namespace

`System.Reflection` **Type**	**MEANING**
`Module`	This class allows you to access a given module within a multi-file assembly.
`ParameterInfo`	This class holds information for a given parameter.
`PropertyInfo`	This class holds information for a given property.

The appropriate use of the classes listed in Table 4.1 will surely expand the horizon of the AutomatedTest tool. The next section will demonstrate how the `Assembly` class is used.

Loading an Assembly

Earlier in this chapter, you saw how to find out the type class in a namespace or an assembly to explore the test information. In the real testing world, testers want to test a given assembly and let the testing tool to find out all the namespaces and type classes. As shown in Table 4.1, you can use the `Assembly` class for this purpose. With the implementation of the static `Load()` methods, the `Assembly` class is able to dynamically load an assembly and invoke class members at runtime (late binding), as well as discover numerous characteristics about the assembly.

In Chapter 3, you created an AutomatedTest project, but it could do nothing for you yet. Now you can add the methods to make it capable of loading an assembly and discovering the types for testing. (Remember that only at the end of this book will the AutomatedTest project be complete with all the functions.) In order to keep the source code organized as you accumulate knowledge throughout the book, I recommend that you make a new folder, `C:\SourceCode\Chapter04`, and copy the AutomatedTest project from `C:\SourceCode\Chapter03` to `C:\SourceCode\Chapter04`. Then use the following steps to create a Windows form and add an `OpenFileDialog`, some other controls, and the code:

1. Start the Microsoft Visual Studio .NET IDE and open the AutomatedTest project from the `C:\SourceCode\Chapter04\AutomatedTest` folder.
2. From the Solution Explorer, right-click on the Project name and choose Add ➢ Add Windows Form to make a new Windows dialog form. The Add New Item - AutomatedTest dialog box appears.
3. In the Name Field, type **TypeUnderTest** as a new class name. TypeUnderTest is also the filename for the source code of the new class by default. Because the class name and the filename do not have to be the same, you can rename them if you want. Click the Open button. An empty form appears in the design area.

4. Add a Label control from the tool box to the form, and make changes to the following properties:

   Name: lblTypeAvailable

   Text: Select data types to test from the available list:

   Modifiers: public

   TextAlign: MiddleLeft

5. Add a CheckedListBox and name it chckListType

6. Add a CheckBox with these properties:

   Name: Checkbox1

   Text: Select All

7. Add a Button with the following properties:

   Name: btnOK

   Text: OK

8. Add another Button with the following properties:

   Name: btnCancel

   Text: Cancel

If you specify the TypeUnderTest form to be the startup object and then build the project and run it, this form should start up on the screen. The CheckedListBox should be empty at this moment, similar to Figure 4.3. After the code is implemented and methods are in full function, the TypeUnderTest form will use the CheckedListBox to list the available classes within the assembly under test. After you view the form, remember to set the startup object back to the TestForm object.

FIGURE 4.3
A new form for listing available classes of an assembly under test

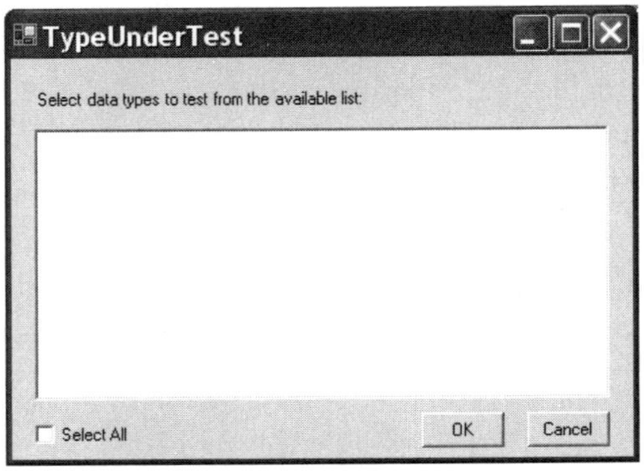

A Windows Form as a Startup Object

To make a Windows form a startup object for a project in the Microsoft Visual Studio .NET IDE, you can follow these steps:

1. Right-click on the project name in the Solution Explorer and choose Properties. The property page for the project appears.
2. Locate the Startup Object field and type in the name of the Windows form you want to use as a startup. For example, for the TypeUnderTest form, you would type **TestTools.AutomatedTest.TypeUnderTest**.
3. Click the OK button to return to the Microsoft Visual Studio .NET IDE. Press F5 to build and run the project. If the compiler returns an error message, such as `TestTools.AutomatedTest.TypeUnderTest does not have a suitable main method`, the specified startup form needs a `Main()` method implementation. In this case, the `Main()` method can be written into the `TypeUnderTest` class as follows:

```
[STAThread]
static void Main()
{
   Application.Run(new TypeUnderTest());
}
```

After creating and viewing the controls for the TypeUnderTest form, you can resume adding more controls to the TestForm:

1. Click the TestForm design editor.
2. Add an OpenFileDialog object by double-clicking it in the toolbox. Accept the default properties.
3. Add a Button to the TestForm and change its properties as follows:

   Name: btnStart

   Text: Start

The TestForm is similar to the one in Figure 4.4. We'll stop the form construction now and start to add code for assembly loading. In the next chapters, you will continue to make more GUI components for the TestForm.

FIGURE 4.4
TestForm with a Start button for the AutomatedTest project

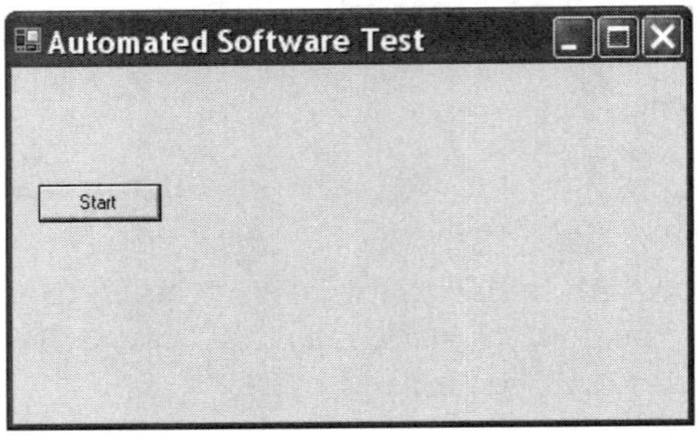

Right-click the TypeUnderTest design form and choose View Code. The C# IDE has generated some code for the `TypeUnderTest.cs` file. You are going to add some methods to this form. First, add a private field and a public property to get the state of the dialog form. These determine whether the tester clicks the OK button or the Cancel button on the TypeUnderTest form:

```
private DialogResult m_typeState;
public DialogResult TypeState
{
   get
   {
      return m_typeState;
   }
}
```

That was easy enough. With only a keyword, `get`, used in the `TypeState` property, this is a read-only property. Thus, the users can access but not alter the value for the `TypeState` property.

With the TypeUnderTest form open in the design editor, double-click the OK button. The C# IDE generates the event handling code and navigates you to the place to add code. The `btnOK_Click()` event is implemented as follows:

```
private void btnOK_Click(object sender, System.EventArgs e)
{
   m_typeState = DialogResult.OK;
   this.Hide();
}
```

When the OK button is clicked, the `m_typeState` gets the value `DialogResult.OK` and the TypeUnderTest form becomes invisible. Code the Cancel button in a manner similar to how the OK button was coded. The code for the `btnCancel_Click()` event looks like this:

```
private void btnCancel_Click(object sender, System.EventArgs e)
{
   m_typeState = DialogResult.Cancel;
   this.Hide();
}
```

Therefore, when the Cancel button is clicked, it assigns a `DialogResult.Cancel` value to the `m_typeState` and makes the form invisible.

At last, add an event handler for the checkBox1 control by double-clicking it on the form and adding the following code:

```
private void checkBox1_CheckedChanged(object sender, System.EventArgs e)
{
   if (checkBox1.Checked)
   {
      for (int i = 0; i<chckListType.Items.Count; i++)
         chckListType.SetItemChecked(i, true);
   }
   else
   {
      for (int i = 0; i<chckListType.Items.Count; i++)
         chckListType.SetItemChecked(i, false);
   }
}
```

As the text of the Checkbox1, Select All, promises, the action is coded in the first part of the `if` statement. When the check box is checked, all the types in the check list box will be selected. The coding is now complete for the TypeUnderTest form.

The code for the `TypeUnderTest.cs` file is similar to Listing 4.3. Listing the implemented code is to make sure your code will compile without error. Note that the code and comments generated by the Microsoft Visual Studio .NET IDE are omitted in Listing 4.3 to conserve space.

Listing 4.3 Added Code Lines of the *TypeUnderTest.cs* File

```
using System;
using System.Drawing;
using System.Collections;
using System.ComponentModel;
using System.Windows.Forms;

namespace TestTools.AutomatedTest
{
   public class TypeUnderTest : System.Windows.Forms.Form
   {
      public System.Windows.Forms.CheckedListBox chckListType;
      private System.Windows.Forms.Label lblTypeAvailable;
      private System.Windows.Forms.Button btnOK;
      private System.Windows.Forms.Button btnCancel;
      private System.Windows.Forms.CheckBox checkBox1;
      private System.ComponentModel.Container components = null;

...
```

```
        private DialogResult m_typeState;
        public DialogResult TypeState
        {
           get
           {
              return m_typeState;
           }
        }

        private void btnOK_Click(object sender, System.EventArgs e)
        {
           m_typeState = DialogResult.OK;
           this.Hide();
        }

        private void btnCancel_Click(object sender, System.EventArgs e)
        {
           m_typeState = DialogResult.Cancel;
           this.Hide();
        }

        private void checkBox1_CheckedChanged(object sender, System.EventArgs e)
        {
           if (checkBox1.Checked)
           {
              for (int i = 0; i<chckListType.Items.Count; i++)
                 chckListType.SetItemChecked(i, true);
           }
           else
           {
              for (int i = 0; i<chckListType.Items.Count; i++)
                 chckListType.SetItemChecked(i, false);
           }
        }
     }
  }
```

The `Assembly.Load()` method is not used in the TypeUnderTest form. It will be used in the `TestForm.cs` file because most of the testing actions occur there. Let's start the implementation for the `TestForm.cs`:

1. Click the TestForm in the design editor. The TestForm editor is activated.
2. Double-click the Start button.

You are in the place to start coding the Start button event handler, `btnStart_Click()`. Add the following two method calls at the cursor:

```
GetAssemblyName();
GetTypesOfAssemblyUnderTest();
```

These are the two methods you will implement next. Since you need to use `System.Reflection` in the AutomatedTest tool project, you need to add a `using System.Reflection` statement at the beginning of the `TestForm.cs` file:

```
using System;
using System.Drawing;
using System.Collections;
using System.ComponentModel;
using System.Windows.Forms;
using System.Data;
using System.Reflection;
```

Then, the method `GetAssemblyName()`uses the open file dialog box and specifies an assembly to test. After the assembly is specified by the open file dialog box, this method assigns the filename of the assembly to a string field, `AssemblyNameToTest`:

```
private string AssemblyNameToTest;
private void GetAssemblyName()
{
   openFileDialog1.Title="DLL under test";
   openFileDialog1.Filter ="DLL files (*.dll)|*.dll|Executable files
➥(*.exe)|*.exe|All files (*.*)|*.*";
   if (openFileDialog1.ShowDialog() == DialogResult.OK)
   {
      AssemblyNameToTest = openFileDialog1.FileName;
   }
   else
   {
      AssemblyNameToTest = "";
   }
}
```

As you would expect, you want to test `.dll` and `.exe` assemblies. The Filter property of the `openFileDialog1` object uses these two file extensions to filter the filenames from a folder. The `ShowDialog()` method returns a `DialogResult` value. If the OK button is clicked, it assigns the selected filename to the `AssemblyNameToTest` variable.

Loading Type Classes from an Assembly

From here on, you are going to use the Reflection namespace. That is why this is a new section even though you'll continue the task from the preceding section.

The method `GetTypesOfAssemblyUnderTest()` will populate the available types from a given assembly into the TypeUnderTest form:

```
private void GetTypesOfAssemblyUnderTest()
{
   if (AssemblyNameToTest.Length <= 0)
```

```
        {
           return;
        }
        TypeUnderTest typeDUT = new TypeUnderTest();
        try
        {
           Assembly asm = Assembly.LoadFrom(AssemblyNameToTest);
           Type[] tys = asm.GetTypes();
           foreach (Type ty in tys)
           {
              typeDUT.chckListType.Items.Add(ty.Name);
           }
        }
        catch(Exception ex)
        {
           MessageBox.Show(ex.Message);
           return;
        }
       typeDUT.lblTypeAvailable.Text = "Available types for the selected
   ➥Assembly:\n" + AssemblyNameToTest;


        typeDUT.ShowDialog();
    }
```

The first if statement checks to see whether an assembly name is selected. If there is no assembly selected, the method stops execution. Otherwise, it initializes a new instance, `typeDUT`, of the TypeUnderTest class. The `try` statement loads a valid assembly by invoking a static `Assembly.LoadFrom()` method, which requires the filename of the assembly. The `GetTypes()` method extracts all the types of the assembly. Then it uses the types to populate the check list box with a `foreach` loop (type enumeration). If the assembly is not valid, the `catch` statement pops up an error message and terminates this method call. After the `try-catch` statement, the program assigns the filename of the assembly under examination to a public label instance, `typeDUT.lblTypeAvailable`, in the TypeUnderTest form. At last, the invocation of the `typeDUT.ShowDiallog()` method brings up the instance of TypeUnderTest form. So you can compare your code, the full list of the `TestForm.sc` file now is shown in Listing 4.4.

Listing 4.4 The Full List of *TestForm.cs* with C# IDE-Generated Lines Omitted

```
using System;
using System.Drawing;
using System.Collections;
using System.ComponentModel;
using System.Windows.Forms;
using System.Data;
```

```
using System.Reflection;

namespace TestTools.AutomatedTest
{
   public class TestForm : System.Windows.Forms.Form
   {
      private System.Windows.Forms.Button btnStart;
      private System.Windows.Forms.OpenFileDialog openFileDialog1;
      private System.ComponentModel.Container components = null;

      ...
      ...
      static void Main()
      {
         Application.Run(new TestForm());
      }

        private void btnStart_Click(object sender,System.EventArgs e)
      {
         GetAssemblyName();
         GetTypesOfAssemblyUnderTest();
      }

      private string AssemblyNameToTest;

      private void GetAssemblyName()
      {
         openFileDialog1.Title="DLL under test";
         openFileDialog1.Filter ="DLL files (*.dll)|*.dll|Executable
➥files (*.exe)|*.exe|All files (*.*)|*.*";
         if (openFileDialog1.ShowDialog() == DialogResult.OK)
         {
            AssemblyNameToTest = openFileDialog1.FileName;
         }
         else
         {
            AssemblyNameToTest = "";
         }
      }

      private void GetTypesOfAssemblyUnderTest()
      {
         if (AssemblyNameToTest.Length <= 0)
         {
            return;
         }
         TypeUnderTest typeDUT = new TypeUnderTest();
         try
         {
            Assembly asm = Assembly.LoadFrom(AssemblyNameToTest);
            Type[] tys = asm.GetTypes();
```

```
                foreach (Type ty in tys)
                {
                    typeDUT.chckListType.Items.Add(ty.Name);
                }

            }
            catch(Exception ex)
            {
                MessageBox.Show(ex.Message);
                return;
            }
            typeDUT.lblTypeAvailable.Text = "Available types for the selected
➥ Assembly:\n" + AssemblyNameToTest;

            typeDUT.ShowDialog();

        }
    }
}
```

Build the project and test-run it by pressing F5 from the Microsoft Visual Studio .NET IDE. The AutomatedTest form appears. Do the following to explore the `LowLevelObj.dll` assembly:

1. Click the Start button.
2. Navigate to `C:\SourceCode\Chapter04\LowLevelObj\bin\Debug`.
3. Select `LowLevelObj.dll` and click the Open button. The TypeUnderTest form appears with the names of the `SimpleMath` class and the enumerators (Figure 4.5).

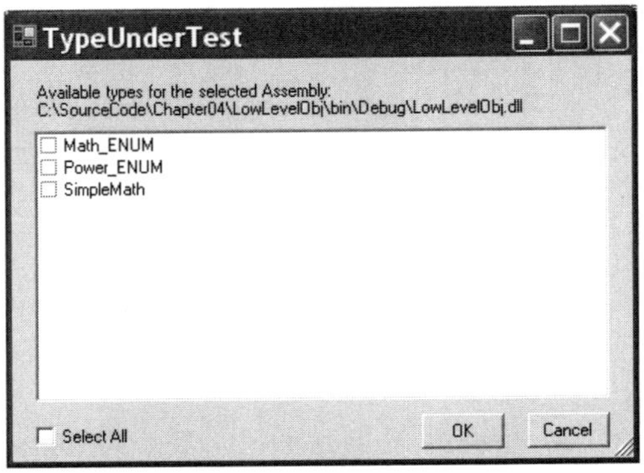

FIGURE 4.5
The discovery of the `SimpleMath` class by the AutomatedTest project

NOTE If you prefer to build the project with a line command from a command prompt, you can issue a `csc /out:AutomatedTest.exe TestForm.cs TypeUnderTest.cs` command from inside the `C:\SourceCode\Chapter04\AutomatedTest\` folder. This line command will become more complex as we continue to add references and classes into the project. I suggest you build this project from the Microsoft Visual Studio .NET IDE. In addition, a `Devenv.exe` command is introduced to programmatically build a project with full automation in Chapter 10.

The `SimpleMath` class is a small assembly. The types within it include two enumerators and one class. To get an idea of the possible complicated testing tasks you may run into, click the Cancel button and do some more experiments on a big assembly with this tool:

1. Click the Start button.
2. Navigate to `C:\WINDOWS\Microsoft.NET\Framework\v1.1.4322` (or to a similar location if your version of the Microsoft Visual Studio .NET IDE is different).
3. Select `Mscorlib.dll` and click Open button. The TypeUnderTest form appears as it does in Figure 4.6. You can see quite a few types available in the `mscorlib.dll` assembly. It is worthwhile to stop here for a moment to examine the names of the types in this assembly. Many of them are often used in the C# programming practices and have been used by you in the projects in this book. For example, `System.String`, `System.Int32`, `Sytesm.Type` and `System.Math` are used in all C# projects.

You can now enjoy the benefits of a fully automated testing tool. Sometimes you may be not asked to test all of the types in an assembly with one run. The check list box gives you the ability to select only the types you're interested in testing. It is useful, especially when a given assembly has a long list of types. Of course, if you want to test all of the types with one test script, you can check the Select All check box. The advantage of testing an application with one test script is obvious. It makes the library of test scripts simple and management easy.

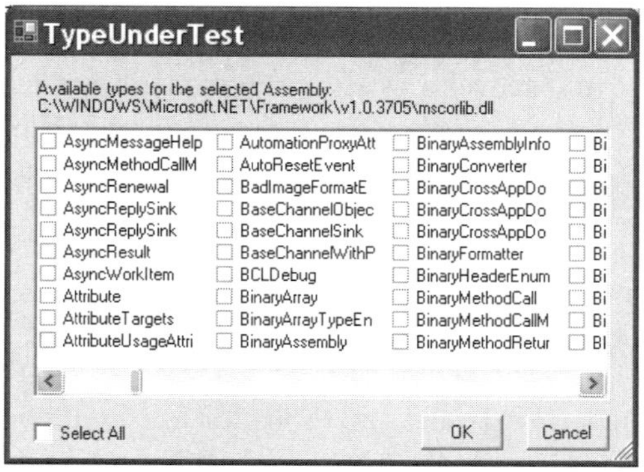

FIGURE 4.6
Loaded types from the `mscorlib.dll` assembly

If you want to reinforce what you learned in the previous sections, you can continue to discover the constructors, methods, properties, and so on of these types within the other .NET-developed assemblies. Getting familiarized with these assemblies is useful for software developers, although the goal of this book is to build a fully automated tool to test any given assembly.

Note that there is also a static `Assembly.Load()` method, which passes in a friendly name of the assembly you are interested in loading into memory. As you may notice, this method, as well as the `Assembly.LoadFrom()` method, has been overloaded a number of times to provide the flexibility for you to load an assembly. One variation to be aware of is that the textual information sent into the `Assembly.Load()` method may contain additional string segments beyond the friendly name. Specifically, you may choose to specify a version number, public key value, locale, and strong name. A friendly name is the class name you use to start a variable declaration.

Collectively, the set of items identifying an assembly with .NET is called the *display name*. The format of a display name is a comma-delimited string that begins with the friendly name followed by optional qualifiers (that may appear in any order).

At this point, I have described how to use the `foreach` keyword to do a few enumerations for a given assembly:

- Enumerating types in a referenced assembly
- Enumerating class methods
- Enumerating class properties
- Enumerating class fields
- Enumerating method parameters

The AutomatedTest project has implemented only the type enumeration so far. The others will be used as the project progresses and to write test scripts programmatically. These methods discover the essential information a test engineer needs to learn before starting to test a given assembly. This is a costly overhead for any testing organization. With help from the `System.Reflection` classes and methods, the AutomatedTest tool dramatically reduces these overhead costs.

Now you understand how to use some of the core items defined within the `System.Reflection` namespace to discover a wealth of information at runtime. The AutomatedTest has been enabled to discover the types in a given assembly. This is the starting point for any type of software testing. The next section discusses dynamic invocation, which will help you construct the AutomatedTest tool.

Dynamic Testing Invocation (Late Binding)

Besides the `Assembly` class methods for runtime type discovery, the `System.Reflection` namespace covers additional functionalities. Reflection provides the ability to use late binding.

Using the late binding technique can enable the AutomatedTest tool to resolve the existence of (and name of) a given type and its members at runtime (rather than compile time). Once the presence of a type has been determined, the AutomatedTest tool is able to dynamically invoke any of the methods, access properties, and manipulate the fields of a given entity. Keep in mind that the AutomatedTest tool is meant to dynamically generate a test script, compile it into a .NET assembly, and invoke the test process. Thus, the software testing process becomes fully automated.

Let's examine how to dynamically invoke a method in the `SimpleMath` class by using the `System.Activator` class.

First, the `System.Activator` class is the key to late binding. `Activator.CreateInstance()` is the method that is able to create an instance of a type at runtime. This method has been overloaded many times in order to provide flexibility. One variation of the `CreateInstance()` method takes a valid `Type` object.

Let's create a new C# console project, LateBinding, to demonstrate this method. After the Microsoft Visual Studio .NET IDE opens the code editor, you type in the code in Listing 4.5 to create a `SimpleMath` instance.

Listing 4.5 Code Lines of the *LateBinding.cs* File

```
using System;
using System.Reflection;

namespace LateBinding
{
  public class LateBind
  {
    public static void Main(string[] args)
    {
      // Use Assembly class to load SimpleMath.
      Assembly asm = null;
      try
      {
        asm = Assembly.LoadFrom(@
➥"C:\SourceCode\Chapter04\LowLevelObj\bin\Debug\LowLevelObj.dll");
      }
      catch(Exception e)
      {
        Console.WriteLine(e.Message);
      }

      // Get the SimpleMath type.
      Type myCalc = asm.GetType("LowLevelObj.SimpleMath");

      // Create the SimpleMath instance.
```

```
            object obj = Activator.CreateInstance(myCalc);

            // Get info for SimpleCalc.
            MethodInfo mi = myCalc.GetMethod("SimpleCalc");

            // Now a method with parameters.
            object[] paramArray = new object[3];
            paramArray[0] = 3;                  // parameter x
            paramArray[1] = 4;                  // parameter y
            paramArray[2] = asm.GetType("Math_ENUM");// parameter operation
            // Invoke method
            double x = (double)mi.Invoke(obj, paramArray);

            Console.WriteLine("Late Binding Result: {0}", x);
        }
    }
}
```

The `Assembly.LoadFrom()` method loads the `SimpleMath.dll` into the memory. When this method is called, the full path of the `LowlevelObj.dll` is passed as a parameter.

A file path in a Windows system contains at least one backslash, \, which is often referred to as an escape character in C# as well as in C++ and Java. An escape character could be a backslash, a tab, a quotation mark, or some other nonprintable character. So that a method can take a string parameter with escape characters, the escape characters are prefixed with a backslash; for example, although a pathname normally takes one backslash, two are needed. The first is the prefix, and the second is the real one. However, the code in the Listing 4.5 doesn't use this method of introducing a backslash to the pathname. Instead, it uses a @-quoted string literal notation, which in C# is called a *verbatim string*. Using verbatim string, it bypasses the backslash cryptic escape character format.

If the loading is successful, the `Type` object, `myCalc`, stores the type of the `SimpleMath` class by invoking the `GetType()` method. Then the `obj` variable is created to point to a `SimpleMath` instance in memory that has been created indirectly using the `Activator` class.

Now, you want conduct a simple calculation calling the `SimpleCalc()` method of the `SimpleMath class`. As you know, the `SimpleCalc()` method needs three arguments: two numbers, and an operator. In order to meet these requirements, the first step is to obtain a `MethodInfo` type for the `SimpleCalc()` method using `Type.GetMethod()` from a `MethodInfo` class. Then use an `object` array variable to manufacture the required parameters, such as in the code from Listing 4.5:

```
object[] paramArray = new object[3];
paramArray[0] = 3;                  // parameter x
paramArray[1] = 4;                  // parameter y
paramArray[2] = asm.GetType("Math_ENUM");// parameter operation
```

In the parameter array, the first two values are integer numbers. The third parameter, operation, is assigned by invoking another `GetType()` method to obtain the `Math_ENUM`. The default is the value at the first position of the enumerator, that is, the `Math_ENUM.Add`. This causes the invocation of the `SimpleCalc()` method to add the first two parameters, 3 + 4. Later chapters will introduce methods to test enumerators with automation.

Finally, the invocation of the `Invoke()` method from the `MethodInfo` class concludes the late binding by consuming the `obj` instance and the parameter array. The `Console.WriteLine()` is responsible for printing the result, `x`, of the calculation.

At this point, you can build the project from the Microsoft Visual Studio .NET IDE and test-run it from a command prompt window. The result is shown in Figure 4.7.

FIGURE 4.7
Result of 3 + 4 = 7 by late binding

The screen shows the late binding result, 7, as the result of 3 + 4. Thus, you learned how to late-bind and invoke a method. This will be useful for software test automation.

Summary

As mentioned, .NET `System.Reflection` namespace is to an assembly what a prism is to sunlight. A prism dissolves sunlight into a wavelength spectrum. The .NET Reflection dissolves an assembly into its types, methods, and properties. So far, you have seen a few interesting aspects of the the `System.Reflection` namespace within a robust object-orient environment. You have also implemented the AutomatedTest project to obtain the types of a given assembly. When you program using .NET, the major reflection services revolve around the `System.Type` class and the `System.Reflection` namespace.

As you have experienced, reflection is the process of exploring information of an assembly at runtime in order to understand the "who, what, where, why, and how" of a given assembly, which are all of interest to a software test engineer.

You have experienced the difficulties of composing testing values using commercial testing tools. Some tools hard-code testing cases in their test scripts. The hard-coded values render the script invalid when the project is under development. In Chapter 5, I will discuss the MS Excel API and XML programming with C#. We will use these techniques in the AutomatedTest project for collecting test information, driving script generation, and presenting the results.

Chapter 5

Spreadsheets and XML for Test Data Stores

The AutomatedTest project needs a space to store data for testing the components. The data includes names of the classes within an assembly, the constructors, the names of the other members within the classes, and the values for the parameters of the methods and constructors. Testers have to compose the data stores manually using open source and commercially available testing tools.

When testing software manually, a test engineer stores the data in many proprietary data formats. A commercial testing tool usually provides a unique data store method that requires special training. For both commercial and the open source testing tools, testing data is often hard-coded in the test script.

There are many spreadsheet or database programs suitable for storing the testing data for the AutomatedTest tool. For example, XML documents have become a standard for many organizations for data store and data exchange. Within the Microsoft Visual Studio .NET IDE, C# allows developers to add XML documentation comments, and then it generates an XML help document. It is easy and effective for developers to set up a testing case when coding a method with XML comments. The AutomatedTest tool will be able to read data stored within the XML document. Using this method, the tester will never need to worry about guessing when composing testing data.

The purpose of this book is to introduce a general test method for different development environments. An MS Excel spreadsheet and an XML document will be used for demonstration purpose. Later, you can extend these methods to adopt other data store methods suitable for your organization. The objective is to enable a data-driven test script generation.

Working with MS Excel Objects in C#

To program in C# with the MS Excel application programming interface (API), you can use the Interoperability services, which can convert unmanaged COM applications, such as MS Word or Excel, so they can be used with the managed .NET assemblies. This section introduces a method to use the unmanaged MS Excel component for a test data store.

As it is known, MS Excel is the spreadsheet component of Microsoft Office. The majority of the MS Excel functionality is achieved through automation via the Microsoft Excel 9/10 Object Library. Microsoft Office 2000 offers Excel 9, and Microsoft Office XP offers Excel 10. In this section, I will discuss the Excel Application object, Workbook object, Worksheet object, and Range object. Then we'll continue the AutomatedTest project with Excel API programming to store testing data.

There are numerous classes and other data types in the `Excel.dll` assembly. `ILDasm.exe` is an intermediate language disassembler to investigate managed assemblies. When you add a reference of Microsoft Excel Object Library to a .NET project, the Microsoft Visual Studio

.NET IDE will convert the unmanaged Microsoft Excel Object Library to a managed `Interop.Excel.dll` assembly. Using `ILDasm.exe` to open the `Interop.Excel.dll`, you find all of the data types of the `Interop.Excel.dll` assembly, including the Excel Application, Workbook, Worksheet, and Range. The assembly conversion and the reference addition will be discussed in detail in the section called "*Opening an MS Excel Application*", later in this chapter. The ILDasm view of the Excel assembly is shown in Figure 5.1. Actually, the AutomatedTest project has been programmed in Chapter 4 to reveal the same information as the ILDasm does. After reviewing the properties and methods of the instances of the Excel Application, Workbook, Worksheet and Range, you can use most of the popular languages, such as C# and Visual Basic, for Excel API programming. Using the MS Excel API, you can accomplish most tasks you could accomplish using MS Excel with a mouse and keyboard.

In the next sections, I'll discuss the objects provided by the MS Excel application and the associated properties, methods, and events. You will find some examples to help you learn how these objects are used in C# programming to customize an application.

The Object Model of Excel

MS Excel objects are organized in their own hierarchical object model. The Application object is the highest in the hierarchy. It can include a collection of workbooks, worksheets, charts, and other windows. A workbook contains a few worksheets. A worksheet is composed of numerous ranges and cells arranged in columns and rows.

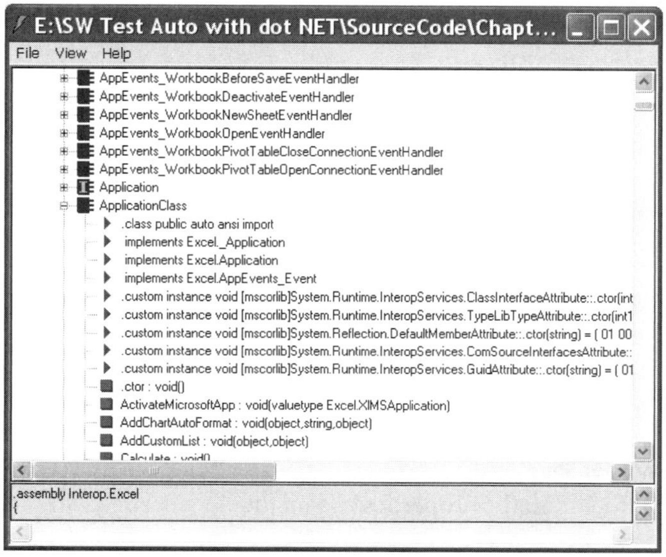

FIGURE 5.1
The ILDasm.exe view of the MS Excel 10.0 Object Library

The Excel Application Object

MS Excel is the application object in this case. The common properties of the Excel objects include `ActivePrinter`, `Caption`, `Visible`, and `WindowState`. Some methods of the object are `CheckSpelling`, `Help`, and `Quit`. When you start work with an Excel spreadsheet, you initialize an Excel application first.

Opening an MS Excel Application

Different from the usual way to open an application, by choosing Start ➤ Programs, MS Excel can be opened programmatically with C# code:

```
Excel.Application xApp = new Excel.Application();
```

This piece of code creates an Excel Application object. You can then create a workbook by coding as follows:

```
Excel.Workbook xBook = xApp.Workbooks.Add(1);
```

This piece of code also adds the workbook to the application. `Workbooks` becomes the property of the application, and `Add()` is a method implemented with the `Workbooks` interface.

You can not directly work with the workbook or the application with data modification. To make Excel store information, you need to add a spreadsheet to the Workbook object. (Hereafter, *worksheet* will be used to refer to a spreadsheet.) The following code syntax adds a worksheet to a workbook. A worksheet is the place for holding information for an Excel application:

```
Excel.Worksheet xSheet = (Excel.Worksheet)xBook.ActiveSheet;
```

At this point, although the objects are created, they are all invisible. To make them visible, set the `Visible` property of the application to be true:

```
xApp.Visible = true;
```

Usually after opening an application, you need to use a keyboard or a mouse to get the application to do something. However, the purpose of this section is to get Excel to do things without direct human interaction. Thus, you need to know how to use the methods and how to manipulate the properties of the Excel application with C# coding. Here's a brief review of some of the properties that accept or deliver data for a worksheet:

`ActiveCell` This property returns a Range object of the cell currently in focus. Methods associated with the Range object are available with the `ActiveCell` property. For example, you can find the row number of the active cell with this code:

```
int rowNum = Application.ActiveCell.Row;
```

`ActiveSheet` This property returns a Range object representing the sheet that is currently in focus. All the properties and methods associated with the Range object are accessible from this property. To find the name of an active sheet, you can code as follows (where `shtName` is a string variable that stores the name of a sheet):

```
string shtName = Application.ActiveSheet.Name;
```

`ActiveWorkbook` This property returns a Range object representing the workbook that is currently in focus. For example, you can find the path of a workbook with this a line of code (where `filePath` is a string variable that stores the file location of the specified workbook):

```
string filePath = Application.ActiveWorkbook.Path;
Range cellRange = Application.ActiveSheet.Cells(3, 4);
```

`Cells` This property returns a Range object representing a collection of all the cells in the active worksheet. Each single cell has a coordinate reference paired with column and row indexes. For example, the following line makes the `cellRange` variable point at the cell at the third row and fourth column of a worksheet, which is often referred to D3:

`Sheets` When a workbook is added to the application, the workbook refers to a collection of sheets. The `Sheets` property returns a collection of `Sheets` objects in the active workbook. All the properties and methods associated with the `Sheets` collection are available with this property. For example, use the following syntax to find out the number of sheets in the active workbook (where `sheetNum` is an integer variable and `Count` is a property of the Sheets collection):

```
int sheetNum = Application.Sheets.Count;
```

`WorksheetFunction` There are numerous predefined functions with this property, including `Average()`, `BetaDist()`, `Ceiling()`, `Clean()`, `Degrees()`, `ExponDist()`, `Max()`, `Min()`, `Pi()`, `Round()`, `SubTotal()`, and `Sum()`. For example, to find the value of pi, use the following code:

```
double pi = Application.WorksheetFunction.Pi();
```

These are the main properties used to form the Excel application hierarchy. To apply these for future test data stores, we'll start a new project to use what you have learned to create an Excel worksheet programmatically and set some values to it:

1. Start the Microsoft Visual Studio .NET.
2. Choose File ➤ New ➤ Project.
3. Select Visual C# Project from the Project Types list in the left pane and Console Application from the Templates list on the right.
4. Enter **StartExcel** in the Name field, make sure `C:\SourceCode\Chapter05` is in the Location field, and click OK to go to the code editor.
5. Add an Excel reference to this project by choosing Project ➤ Add Reference from the main menu.

6. Select the COM tab and navigate to Microsoft Excel 9/10 Object Library. Click on it to highlight it and click the Select button to add it to the Selected Components list. Click the OK button to return to the code editor. At this time, if you navigate to the `C:\SourceCode\Chapter05\StartExcel\Bin\Debug` folder, you should find an Interop.Excel.dll assembly which is converted from the unmanaged Microsoft Excel Object Library.
7. Add the code in Listing 5.1 to the `StartExcel.cs` file.

Listing 5.1 Code List of the *StartExcel.cs* Project

```
using System;
using Excel;
namespace StartExcel
{
  class ExcelApplication
  {
    [STAThread]
    static void Main(string[] args)
    {
      //Create an application object
      Excel.Application xApp= new Excel.Application();

      //Create a workbook object
      Excel.Workbook xBook = xApp.Workbooks.Add(1);

      //Assign the active worksheet of the workbook
//object to a worksheet object
    Excel.Worksheet xSheet=(Excel.Worksheet)xBook.ActiveSheet;
      xApp.Visible=true;
xBook.SaveAs(@"C:\Temp\StartExcelTest.xls", XlFileFormat.xlWorkbookNormal,
➥ "", "", false, false, 0, "", 0, "", "", "");
      xSheet.Cells.set_Item(1,1, "ActiveBook Path");
      xSheet.Cells.set_Item(2,1, "ActiveSheet Name");
      xSheet.Cells.set_Item(3,1, "Sheets Count");
      xSheet.Cells.set_Item(4,1, "Average of Numbers");
      xSheet.Cells.set_Item(5,1, "ActiveCell Coordinate (Row, Column)");

      xSheet.Cells.set_Item(1,2, xBook.Path);
      xSheet.Cells.set_Item(2,2, xSheet.Name);
      xSheet.Cells.set_Item(3,2, xApp.Sheets.Count);
      xSheet.Cells.set_Item(4,2, xApp.WorksheetFunction.Pi());
      xSheet.Cells.set_Item(5,2, xApp.ActiveCell.Row + ", " +
➥xApp.ActiveCell.Column);
      xSheet.Columns.AutoFit();
    }
  }
}
```

The initialization of an Excel instance in this example is achieved by the `new Excel.Application()` statement. Just as you can open many Excel applications manually, you can open as many Excel instances as you need programmatically. The Excel object is a member of the Windows collection, representing all the open Excel windows. In the future, you may be interested in programming MS Word as you did Excel. The programming method is similar.

After a workbook is added to the `Excel.Application` instance and a worksheet instance is set to point at the active worksheet of the workbook, remember to set the `visible` property of the application to `true`. Then, you use a few statements of `Cells.set_Item()` to assign some values to the specific cells. Within the `Cells.set_Item()` method, there are three parameters. The first parameter is an integer referring to the row the cell is in. The second parameter is an integer referring to the column. The third is the value to be assigned to the cell.

The last statement, `xSheet.Columns.AutoFit()`, makes enough space in the Excel sheet to show all the contents contained within a cell. `Worksheet.Columns` also has many other properties and methods to manipulate columns. Similarly, `Worksheet.Rows` has properties and methods to manipulate rows. We will investigate more methods of these properties in later sections and chapters because the testing data will be directly stored in cells, which are defined with column and row references. Now you can run this project, which opens an Excel application with the data you specified, as shown in Figure 5.2. You can insert other code in the StartExcel example for practice.

The next few sections give more details about the StartExcel project. More useful information is also presented to prepare the AutomatedTest project. You'll use the information presented in these sections at the end of this chapter and in later chapters to complete the AutomatedTest project.

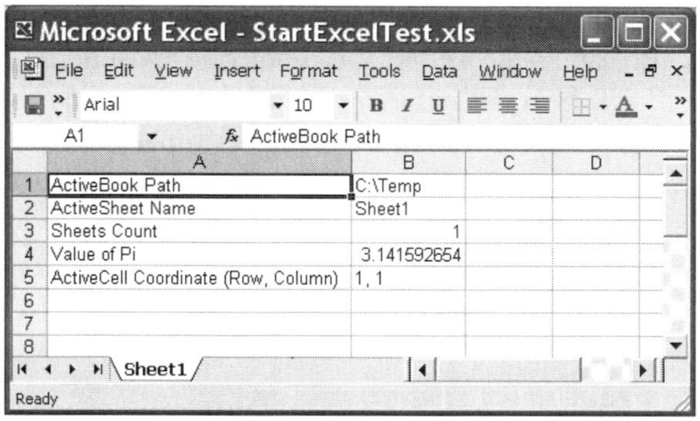

FIGURE 5.2
An Excel sheet with data opened by the StartExcel project

Creating a Workbook Object

The Workbook object was created by the Application.Workbooks.Add() statement. This object is a member of the Workbooks collection for the open workbooks. Each workbook in the collection is distinguished by its respective index number, which is the number given as a parameter passed in the Add() method. To manipulate the properties of this object, you need to refer to it by prefixing its name or the index number by placing the workbook object before the method, separated by a period, as in xBook.SaveAs(). For example, the code in the StartExcel.cs file uses the object name to invoke a SaveAs() method:

```
xBook.SaveAs(@"C:\Temp\StartExcelTest.xls",
➥ Excel.XlFileFormat.xlWorkbookNormal, "", "",
➥ false, false, 0, "", 0, "", "", "");
```

The SaveAs() method of the MS Excel XP was declared as follows:

```
public abstract new void SaveAs(System.Object Filename,
➥    System.Object FileFormat, System.Object Password,
   System.Object WriteResPassword, System.Object ReadOnlyRecommended,
➥    System.Object CreateBackup, Excel.XlSaveAsAccessMode AccessMode,
➥    System.Object ConflictResolution, System.Object AddToMru,
➥    System.Object TextCodepage, System.Object TextVisualLayout,
➥    System.Object Local);
```

This requires 12 parameters. A filename and a file format are the first two. The file format can be a value of the Excel.XlFileFormat enumeration, such as xlWorkbookNormal (a normal Excel workbook), xlTextMSDOS (plain text), xlCSV (comma-separated values), xlHtml (HTML), or xlXMLSpreadsheet (XML). The rest are the password, a read-only recommendation, the backup option, and the other attributes. However, in older versions of Excel (for example Excel 2000), the SaveAs() method took only the first 11 parameters. The last one, System.Object Local, was omitted.

You also can create a new Workbook object using the ActiveWorkbook property of the application. To refer to an active workbook, you can code the following to make the xBook object point at the active workbook of an Excel application:

```
Workbook xBook = Application.ActiveWorkbook;
```

Otherwise, you can open an existing workbook using the Application.Workbooks.Open() method by passing the filename as a parameter, such as:

```
Workbook xBook = Application.Workbooks.Open(@"C:\Temp\StartExcelTest.xls");
```

Workbook Properties

After the initialization of a workbook, you can invoke and manipulate its various methods and properties. The Workbook object has properties including `HasPassword`, `Name`, `Path`, and `Sheets`:

`HasPassword` Returns a value of `true` or `false` to find out whether the specified workbook has a password. For example, the fourth parameter of the `SaveAs()` method specifies a password. If a password is assigned to a workbook, the Excel application will prompt the correct password before opening the workbook. For the StartExcel project, the password is empty. The `HasPassword` returns `false` in this case.

`Name` The name of the specified workbook. For the preceding example, the code `ActiveWorkbook.Name` can retrieve the name for the xBook object. The Excel application assigns a default value to a new workbook, such as Book*xx*, where *xx* is a number to distinguish one workbook from the others.

`Path` The physical location of the specified workbook. In the previous example, to retrieve the path of the xBook object you would use `xBook.Path`, which returns a value `C:\Temp`. This value represents the folder name where the workbook is saved by the invocation of the `SaveAs()` method.

`Sheets` Returns a Sheets collection that includes all the sheets in the specified workbook. As a result, all the properties and methods of the Sheets collection are also applicable to this property. The previous example counts the number of sheets by assigning the value of the `xApp.Sheets.Count` to cell B3, which is 1, as shown in Figure 5.2.

Workbook Methods

You can directly manipulate a workbook by mutating values of the properties. Methods often provide more powerful functions for the data management of a workbook. The following sections will help you become familiar with some methods of the Workbook object: `Activate()`, `Add()`, `Close()`, `Open()`, `PrintOut()`, and `Protect()`.

Activate()

The `Activate()`method activates a specified workbook. For example, to activate an existing workbook, `C:\Program Files\Microsoft Office\Office10\Samples\SAMPLES.XLS`, you would use the following code:

```
Workbooks(@"C:\Program Files\Microsoft Office\
➥Office10\Samples\SAMPLES.XLS ").Activate();
```

Add()

The `Add()` method creates a new workbook. The following code is used in the StartExcel project:

```
Excel.Workbook xBook = xApp.Workbooks.Add(1);
```

This causes the addition of the `xbook` object to the `xApp` object. In this case, the parameter has a value of 1. It can also take the following values to create different objects:

- `Excel.XlWBATemplate.xlWBATChart` creates a workbook with a single chart sheet.
- `Excel.XlWBATemplate.xlWBATExcel4MacroSheet` creates a workbook with a single Excel 4 macro sheet.
- `Excel.XlWBATemplate.xlWBATExcel4IntlMacroSheet` creates a workbook with an Excel 4 international macro sheet.
- `Excel.XlWBATemplate.xlWBATWorksheet` creates a workbook with a single worksheet.

For example, to create a workbook with a single worksheet, use the following code:

```
Workbooks.Add(Excel.XlWBATemplate.xlWBATWorksheet);
```

This format of the possible values reflects the construction of any Excel enumerator. For example, in this case, the name of the XlWBATemplate enumerator is within the Excel namespace. You can start an `ILDasm.exe` session to discover all other Excel enumerators and their possible values. However, the AutomatedTest tool will be able to recognize all the possible values of any enumerator automatically. Thus, it can assign a proper data type to a parameter under test when writing a test script. You also have the option to assign an invalid value to test an enumerator parameter based on your testing requirements.

Close()

The `Close()` method closes a specified workbook. The syntax is as follows:

```
Workbook.Close(SaveChanges, FileName, RouteWorkbook);
```

Here are the parameters:

- `SaveChanges` requires one of the following values:
  - `True` saves changes before closing the workbook.
  - `False` discards changes before closing the workbook.
  - `Omitted` shows a message box asking whether you want to save the changes before closing the workbook.
- `FileName` requires a filename for the workbook.

- `RouteWorkbook` requires one of the following values:
  - `True` sends the workbook to the next recipient.
  - `False` does not send the workbook.
  - `Omitted` shows a message box asking whether you want to send the workbook to the next recipient.

For example, if you want to close the test sheet of the StartExcel project, you can add the following code at the end of the `StartExcel.cs` file, where the name is C:\Temp\StartExcelClose.xls, and the workbook must not to be routed:

```
xBook.Close(true, @"C:\Temp\StartExcelClose", false);
```

Open()

The `Open()` method opens an existing workbook. It accepts a parameter to specify the complete path of the existing workbook. The following syntax would open `C:\Program Files\Microsoft Office\Office10\Samples\SAMPLES.XLS`:

```
Workbook.Open(@"C:\Program Files\Microsoft Office\
➥Office10\Samples\SAMPLES.XLS ");
```

PrintOut()

The `PrintOut()` method prints the workbook. Here is the syntax:

```
Workbook.PrintOut(From, To, Copies, Preview,
➥ActivePrinter, PrintToFile, Collate, PrToFileName);
```

The parameters have the following meanings:

`From` Specifies the first page to be printed.

`To` Specifies the last page to be printed.

`Copies` Specifies the number of copies to be printed.

`Preview` Indicates the desire to view the print preview. The value is `true` or `false`.

`ActivePrinter` Specifies the printer to be used. You can find these values from the Windows system Registry following the key and path, as in HKEY_CURRENT_USER\Software\Microsoft\Windows NT\CurrentVersion\PrinterPorts. Chapter 11 introduces methods to conduct software test against the Windows system registry.

`PrintToFile` Specifies whether the workbook should be printed as a PostScript file or through a printer. The value is `true` or `false`. People often convert a PostScript file to a PDF file format.

`Collate` Specifies whether the print copies should be collated. The value is `true` or `false`.

PrToFileName Indicates a filename of the PostScript file to which the workbook is saved. This option is applicable only if the `PrintToFile` parameter is set to `true`.

Thus, for example, to use a preinstalled printer to print three copies of pages 1 to 2 of the `C:\Temp\StartExcelTest.xls` workbook for the sample code in Listing 5.1, you can add this code:

```
xBook.PrintOut (1, 2, 3, false, "HP LaserJet III on Ne00:",
➥   false, false, null);
```

After this code is invoked, you can find the hard copies at your designated HP LaserJet III printer.

Protect()

The `Protect()` method is used to set a password to protect a specified workbook. The syntax is as follows:

```
Workbook.Protect(Password, Structure, Windows);
```

The parameters have the following meanings:

Password Specifies the password for the workbook. The password is case sensitive.

Structure Specifies whether the structure of the workbook should be protected. If it is set to `true`, the structure of the workbook is protected; otherwise, the structure is not protected.

Windows Specifies whether the workbook window should be protected. If it is set to `true`, the workbook window is protected; otherwise, the workbook window is not protected. For example, here is the code to protect an active workbook:

```
ActiveWorkbook.Protect("password", null, null);
```

Workbook Events

From the Workbook object, the following events can be handled:

Activate() When the workbook gets focus, this event occurs. A workbook receives focus after any of the following actions:

- Manually opening an existing workbook by choosing File ➢ Open
- Manually selecting a workbook from a list of the open workbooks
- Programmatically executing a `Workbook.Activate()` method
- Programmatically executing a `Workbook.Open()` method

BeforePrint() This event occurs after the Print command is issued and before the Print dialog box is shown.

`BeforeSave()` This event occurs after the Save or Save As command is issued and before the Save As dialog box is displayed.

`BeforeClose()` This event occurs just before a workbook is closed—for example, when you choose Close or Exit from the File menu or when the `Close()` method of the Workbook object is executed. The event handler for this event executes before the workbook is closed and the Save As dialog box is displayed.

`Deactivate()` This event occurs when a workbook loses focus.

`NewSheet()` When a new sheet is added to the workbook, this event is triggered.

`Open()` This event occurs when a workbook is opened.

There are other properties, methods, and event handlers for a Workbook object. However, these are the ones most often used.

Creating a Worksheet Object

The Worksheet object is controllable entirely by programming. It is a member of Worksheets collection, which represents all the sheets in a workbook. For example, you can change the value, the color, the column, and the row properties. In MS Excel, you can reference a particular worksheet by its ordinal number in the workbook collection:

```
Worksheets(1);
```

Or you can reference it by the name of the worksheet:

```
Worksheets("Sheet1");
```

As with the name of a workbook, when a worksheet is added to a workbook, the Excel application assigns a default name such as Sheet*xx*, where *xx* represent a unique number.

In MS Excel, moving a worksheet's position automatically changes its index number in the worksheet collection. The leftmost worksheet has an index of 0 and the rightmost one has the largest index number. To avoid confusion, the safer course is to start by giving each worksheet a unique name. In later code, you can refer to a worksheet by always calling its name, not its index. In the next sections, I discuss the most useful of the properties, methods, and event handlers of a Worksheet object.

Worksheet Properties

The Worksheet object supports the following properties:

`Name` Assigns a name to or gets the name of a worksheet. To assign a name to a worksheet, you would use this code:

```
ActiveWorksheet.Name = "FirstSheet";
```

And here's the code to get the name of the worksheet (where `shtName` is a string variable):

```
string shtName = ActiveWorksheet.Name;
```

`StandardHeight` Returns the standard height of all the rows in the specified worksheet.

`StandardWidth` Returns the standard width of all the columns in the specified worksheet.

`Visible` Specifies whether a worksheet is visible or hidden. The value is `true` or `false`.

`UsedRange` Returns a Range object that represents the used range in the specified worksheet. The used range is the range that contains data in a worksheet.

Worksheet Methods

The Worksheet object can perform the following actions:

`CheckSpelling()` Checks the spelling of the text in the worksheet. The C# code is as follows:

```
Worksheet.CheckSpelling(CustomDictionary, IgnoreUppercase,
   AlwaysSuggest, SpellLang);
```

`CheckSpelling()` has the following parameters:

- `CustomDictionary` is an additional file used by Excel in case a word is not found in the main dictionary.
- `IgnoreUppercase` has a value of `true` or `false` to indicate whether all capital letters of a word should be checked.
- `AlwaysSuggest` has a value of `true` or `false` to indicate if Excel automatically suggests an alternate for the misspelled words.
- `SpellLang` specifies the language of the dictionary to be used.

`Copy()` Makes a copy of the specified worksheet. The C# code is as follows:

```
Worksheet.Copy(Before or After);
```

`Copy()` has the following parameters:

- `Before` indicates the worksheet before which the copied worksheet has to be placed.
- `After` indicates the worksheet after which the copied worksheet has to be placed.

`Delete()` Removes a worksheet from a Workbook object. Executing the following C# code removes the active worksheet:

```
ActiveSheet.Delete();
```

`Move()` Moves a worksheet that is referred by the Worksheet object. The C# code is as follows:

```
Worksheet.Move(Before, After);
```

It has the following parameters:

- `Before` specifies the worksheet before which the moved worksheet is to be placed.
- `After` specifies the worksheet after which the moved worksheet is to be placed.

`Protect()` Protects a worksheet by password. Here is the C# code:

```
Worksheet.Protect(Password, DrawingObjects, Contents, Scenarios,
➥UserInterfaceOnly, AllowFormattingCells, AllowFormattingColumns,
➥AllowFormattingRows, AllowInsertingColumns, AllowInsertingRows,
➥AllowInsertingHyperlinks, AllowDeletingColumns, AllowDeletingRows,
➥AllowSorting, AllowFiltering, AllowUsingPivotTables);
```

Here are the parameters:

- `Password` sets the password with a string variable.
- `DrawingObjects` has a `true` or `false` value to determine if the drawing objects in the worksheet are protected
- `Contents` has a value of `true` or `false` to determine if the cell contents in the worksheet are protected.
- `Scenarios` has the value of `true` of `false` to determine if the scenarios in the worksheet are protected.
- `UserInterfaceOnly` has a value of `true` or `false` to determine if the user interface or both the user interface and the macros in the worksheet are protected.
- `AllowFormattingCells`, `AllowFormattingColumns`, `AllowFormattingRows`, `AllowInsertingColumns`, `AllowInsertingRows`, `AllowInsertingHyperlinks`, `AllowDeletingColumns`, `AllowDeletingRows`, `AllowSorting`, `AllowFiltering`, and `AllowUsingPivotTable` all have set values to determine whether the columns, rows, and cells of a worksheet can be manipulated.

`Unprotect()` Removes the protection password applied to the specified worksheet with a C# code:

```
Worksheet.Unprotect(Password);
```

Thus, you need to remember the password given by the `Protect()` method. Otherwise, the worksheet will not be opened.

Worksheet Events

The Worksheet object supports the following events:

Activate() This event is fired when a worksheet is activated. It happens when you click any where on an open worksheet or when the `Worksheet.Activate()` method is executed in a program.

Change() Changing any value in the cells of the worksheet causes this event to happen.

Deactivate() This event happens when a worksheet loses focus. A worksheet loses focus when you click on another worksheet or when the `Worksheet.Deactivate()` method is executed.

SelectionChange() Selecting controls of the worksheet causes this event to happen.

Creating a Range Object

As you know, the worksheet is the area in which data is placed. The Range object in Excel is a section of the worksheet. It consists of one of more cells specified by some key strokes, a series of mouse clicks, or lines of C# code. There are a few different ways to specify a range with C# code:

get_Range() Returns a Range object that represents one cell or a series of cells. The code is as follows (where `Name` represents the name of the range):

```
Worksheet.get_Range(Name);
```

For example, A1:C4 specifies the range of cells from A1 to C4 in a rectangle. Here's another way of coding the get_Range() method:

```
Worksheet.get_Range(Cell1, Cell2);
```

`Cell1` represents the upper-left corner of the range and `Cell2` represents the lower-right corner. `Cell1` and `Cell2` can be cell addresses. Range objects representing a single cell, or complete rows or columns. For example, the range A1 to C4 can be specified in the following way:

```
Worksheet.get_Range("A1", "C4");
```

Cells() Returns a single cell as a Range object. Both the Worksheet and the Range object can prefix it. Here is code:

```
Worksheet.Cells(RowIndex, ColumnIndex);
```

Or you can use this:

```
Range.Cells(RowIndex, ColumnIndex);
```

`RowIndex` is the row number of the cell and `ColumnIndex` is the column number of the cell.

`Rows()` Returns a complete row of a Range object. Both the `Worksheet` and the Range object support the `Rows()` method. You can use either one of the following lines of code (where `Index` is the row number):

```
Worksheet.Rows(Index);
Range.Rows(Index);
```

`Columns()` Returns a complete column of a Range object. Similar to the `Rows()` method, it perform actions with Worksheet and Range objects. Use either of the following (where `Index` is the column number):

```
Worksheet.Columns(Index);
Range.Columns(Index);
```

Range Properties

The Range object has a number of properties:

`Address` Gets the address of the specified text. The following code retrieves the address of a range:

```
string addr = Range.Address;
```

`Column` Gets the number of the first column in the specified range.

`Count` Gets the number of cells in the specified range.

`Formula` Sets or gets the formula for the specified range or a single cell. For example, this code sets the formula for the cell A6:

```
Range cellSum = Worksheet.get_Range("A6", "A6");
cellSum.Formula = "=SUM(A1:A5)";
```

In this code, `cellSum` is a Range object of a single cell, A6, and `"=Sum(A1:A5)"` is the formula that sums the values in the cells A1 through A5. When you enter a formula, you enclose the entire formula between an opening and closing parentheses. The formula must start with an equal sign, =.

Because Formula is a write and read property, you can assign value to and access the content of it. To get the formula of A6, you would use the following code (where `mySum` is a string variable):

```
string mySum = cellSum.Formula;
```

Cells in the worksheet returns string values and numbers. If a cell contains the value `true` or `false`, it returns a Boolean value. This property of a Range object will be used often in the AutomatedTest project to automatically recognize data types for parameters so that accurate test scripts will be written.

`NumberFormat` Sets or gets the numeric format for the specified range. For example, to set the numeric format of the cells to 00.00, use the following code, which shows two decimal places for a float number:

```
Range mySum;
mySum.NumberFormat = "00.00";
```

`Row` Gets the number of the first row in the specified range.

`Value` Sets or gets the value in the specified range or a single cell.

Range Methods

We use the Excel in the AutomatedTest project because we need data in the worksheet. The Range object supports a number of methods for alternating data values in cells:

`Copy()` Copies the values in a range to another location. For example, to copy a value from C3 to C8, you would use the following C# code:

```
Worksheet xSheet;
Range Source = xSheet.get_Range("C3", "C3");
Range Destination = xSheet.get_Range("C8", "C8");
Source.Copy(Destination);
```

`Cut()` Cuts the values in cells of a Range object and places them in a specified destination. You can program to paste them to a new range. The C# code syntax is as follows:

```
Worksheet.get_Range(Source).Cut(Destination);
```

`Source` and `Destination` represents the locations where the values should be copied from and pasted to. For example, executing the following code cuts the values in cells A2 through A5 and then pastes them to C2 through C5:

```
Range Source = xSheet.get_Range("A2", "A5");
Range Destination = xSheet.get_Range("C2", "C5");
Souce.Cut(Destination);
```

`DataSeries()` Assigns a data series in the specified range. It is equivalent to choosing Edit ➢ Fill ➢ Series in Excel. Here is the syntax:

```
Worksheet.get_Range(range).DataSeries(RowCol, Type, Date,
   Step, Stop, Trend);
```

It takes the following parameters:

- RowCol instructs the program to fill the cell with the series in rows or columns. Values are Excel.XlRowCol.xlColumns for columns and `Excel.XlRowCol.xlRows` for rows.
- Type instructs the program to fill the cells with the values in a certain incremental function. The following are the possible values:
- `Excel.XlDataSeriesType.xlAutoFill` to fill the selected cells with the same value that appears in the first cell counting from top and left
- `Excel.XlDataSeriesType.xlChronological` to fill a series of selected cells with date values incremented by the number of days of a Day, a WeekDay, a Month or a Year
- `Excel.XlDataSeriesType.xlDataSeriesLinear` to fill the selected cells with a linear function
- `Excel.XlDataSeriesType.xlGrowth` to fill the selected cells with a growth trend function.
- `Date` specifies a data type for Excel.XlDataSeriesType.xlChronological. The following are the possible values:
- `Excel.XlDataSeriesDate.xlDay` for the increment number of days in a day
- `Excel.XlDataSeriesDate.xlMonth` for the increment number of days in a month
- `Excel.XlDataSeriesDate.xlYear` for the increment number of days in a year
- `Excel.XlDataSeriesDate.xlWeekday` for the increment of a day of a week, but skipping Saturdays and Sundays.
- Step gives the number of units by which the values is incremented. For example, for the series 1, 5, 9, 13 …, the step is 4.
- Stop specifies the last value to be assigned to the cells.
- Trend gives the trend to fill the data series. Set this parameter to `true` for both the linear trend and the growth trend. Set it to false for standard series.

`FillDown()` Copies the format and value of the topmost row and pastes the same to all the cells in the specified range.

`FillUp()` Copies the format and value of the last row and pastes the same to all the cells in the specified range.

`FillRight()` Copies the format and value of the leftmost column and pastes the same to all the cells in the specified range.

`FillLeft()` Copies the format and value of the extreme right column and pastes the same to all the cells in the specified range.

`Insert()` Inserts cells in the specified range. The syntax requires one parameter, `Shift`:

```
Range.Insert(Shift);
```

This parameter indicates the direction to accommodate the inserted cell. There are two possible values:

```
Excel.XlInsertShiftDirection.xlShifToRight
Excel.XlInsertShiftDirection.xlShiftDown
```

That completes the review of basic programming techniques for an MS Excel worksheet. Next, we will add data store capabilities to the AutomatedTest project.

Building a Data Store for Automated Software Testing

In the previous sections, I discussed the Excel Application, Workbook, Worksheet, and Range objects with regard to C# programming. There are a lot more properties, methods, and events in Excel that deserve attention, but to build an automated test tool, we need to use only a portion of the Excel functionality. The next step is to add an Excel data store to the AutomatedTest project.

First, you need to copy the AutomatedTest project from the `C:\SourceCode\Chapter04` folder to `C:\SourceCode\Chapter05`. The source code of the project can be downloaded from this book's website (`www.sybex.com`). Then, open this project from Microsoft Visual Studio .NET IDE. Remember to add to the project a reference to the Microsoft Excel Object Library. In the next sections, you'll need to implement the following methods:

`PassSelectedTypesUT()` To gather the selected types of interest to the tester.

`InitMethodInventory()` To do a method inventory of the types of interest with the assistance of the following helper methods:

> **`CreateExcelSheet()`** To initialize an Excel instance with a Workbook object and a Worksheet object. It also manipulates some properties of the worksheet with the test data store.
>
> **`AddExpectedValue()`** To add a value to be tested against when a method returns a value. If a method does not have a return value, a void method in C#, no expected value will be added by this method.
>
> **`GrabCells()`** To alternate values of the cell according to the nature of the parameter type and the methods under test.

NOTE The provided source code was developed with `Excel.dll` from version 1.4 preregistered on my PC. If your C# compiler in the Microsoft Visual Studio .NET IDE complains that the type or namespace name Excel could not be found when you load and compile a project from the downloaded source code, the cause could be the variation of the Excel minor version. You can check the status of all the references by expanding the `References` node in Solution Explorer. A yellow exclamation mark indicates a bad reference. In order to compile this project, you can remove the bad reference and add the reference back by right-clicking References and choosing Add Reference. From the Add Reference dialog box, choose the COM tab, find and select the Microsoft Excel Object Library. At last, click OK to complete the reference addition. This can also solve other compiling issues with regard to bad references.

Making a Utility Class

Before you start implementing these methods, a common class should be added to the project to house some often needed static utilities. To add this class, do the following:

1. In the Solution Explorer, right-click the AutomatedTest project.
2. Choose Add ➢ Add Class.
3. In the Name field, type **TestUtility** for the class name.
4. Click the Open button to go to the code editor.

With `TestUtility.cs` open in the code editor, change the class name to TestUtility. Then add the two methods in Listing 5.2 and Listing 5.3.

Listing 5.2 Implementation of the *ConvCHAR()* Method

```
public static string ConvCHAR(int pPosition)
{
  string PreChar="";
  if (pPosition > 26)
  {
    pPosition -= 26;
    PreChar="A";
  }
  byte aByte = byte.Parse((pPosition + 64).ToString());
  byte[] bytes1 = { aByte, 0x42, 0x43 };
  byte[] bytes2 = { 0x98, 0xe3 };
  char[] chars = new char[3];
  Decoder d = Encoding.UTF8.GetDecoder();
  int charLen = d.GetChars(bytes1, 0, bytes1.Length, chars, 0);

  // The value of charLen should be 2 now.
  charLen += d.GetChars(bytes2, 0, bytes2.Length, chars, charLen);
  foreach(char c in chars)
  {
```

```
        Console.Write("U+" + ((ushort)c).ToString() + "  ");

        return PreChar + c.ToString();
    }
    return "Need an entry";
}
```

The static ConvCHAR() method in Listing 5.2 will be used to convert an integer to an ASCII character. Table 5.1 shows the integers and their corresponding ASCII characters.

TABLE 5.1 Code page for the ASCII characters.

Decimal	Letter	Decimal	Letter	Decimal	Letter
65	A	74	J	83	S
66	B	75	K	84	T
67	C	76	L	85	U
68	D	77	M	86	V
69	E	78	N	87	W
70	F	79	O	88	X
71	G	80	P	89	Y
72	H	81	Q	90	Z
73	I	82	R		

In an Excel worksheet, row index is expressed by an integer, column index by a letter or letters. The ConvCHAR() method takes an integer parameter, pPosition. It converts the parameter position in a method in correspondence to a column letter(s) in the Excel worksheet. The actual return type is a string. Because we often deal with the first 26 letters in an Excel sheet, the method is named with a character.

A static method can be invoked directly without initializing an object of the TestUtility class. But you need to prefix the method with its class name. When this method is executed, for example, it converts the number 1 to *A* or the number 26 to *Z:*

```
TestUtility.ConvCHAR(1); or TestUtility.ConvCHAR(26);
```

In the code list, number 64 is added to each parameter position to assure that the first returned character is *A*. In case, the worksheet extends beyond the first 26 letters, it can convert an integer value to a string of more than one character, such as it converts a column index 27 to an ASCII symbol AA, 28 to AB and so on.

Listing 5.3 implements another static utility method, `SysToCSPros()`, which converts the .NET `System` data type to the regular C# representation as shown in Table 3.1 in Chapter 3.

Listing 5.3 Implementation of the *SysToCSPros()* Method

```
public static string SysToCSPro(string s)
{
  string x="";
  if (s.StartsWith("System.Boolean"))
    x="bool";
  else if (s.StartsWith("System.Int16"))
    x="short";
  else if (s.StartsWith("System.SByte"))
    x="sbyte";
  else if (s.StartsWith("System.Byte"))
    x="byte";
  else if (s.StartsWith("System.UI16"))
    x="ushort";
  else if (s.StartsWith("System.Int32"))
    x="int";
  else if (s.StartsWith("System.Int64"))
    x="long";
  else if (s.StartsWith("System.Char"))
    x="char";
  else if (s.StartsWith("System.Single"))
    x="float";
  else if (s.StartsWith("System.Double"))
    x="double";
  else if (s.StartsWith("System.Decimal"))
    x="decimal";
  else if (s.StartsWith("System.String"))
    x="string";
  else if (s.StartsWith("System.Object"))
    x="object";
  else if (s.StartsWith("System.UInt32"))
    x="uint";
  else if (s.StartsWith("System.UInt64"))
    x="ulong";
  else
    x=s;

  if (s.EndsWith("[]"))
    x=x + "[]";
  return x;
}
```

You have observed the difference between the .NET `System` data type and the C# regular representation. When you use the `GetType()` method to determine the type of a variable, it returns the type with the form of `System.xxx`, which is different from the conventional expression in C#.

For later review of the test script, you'll implement a `SysToCSPro()` method to get the conventional C# representation. For example, when a `System.Int32` is returned by the `GetType()` method, a string `"int"` will be returned by the `SysToCSPro()` method. C# programmers are more familiar with the keyword `int` than with `System.Int32` for reviewing purpose. Throughout the code, `if` statements are used. The last `if` statement deals with array variables marked with a pair of square brackets, [ ]. The purpose is to make sure that the array declaration will be kept after the conversion and correct declaration is coded in the test script.

Save the `TestUtility.cs` file. Open or activate the `TestForm.cs` file in the code editor. You are ready to add to it methods for using an Excel sheet for data store.

Collecting Test Information of Types

The `GetTypesOfAssemblyUnderTest()` method implemented in Chapter 4 will be modified by adding the `PassSelectedTypesUT()` method call as the last line of the code. As the method name indicates, this method passes the selected class type under test from the TypeUnderTest form to the `TestForm` class. Listing 5.4 lists the code.

Listing 5.4 Implementation of the *PassSelectedTypesUT()* Method of the *TestForm.cs*

```
private string m_typesDUT;
private void PassSelectedTypesUT(TypeUnderTest typeDUT)
{
  if (typeDUT.TypeState == DialogResult.OK)
  {
    m_typesDUT = "";
    for (int i = 0; i<typeDUT.chckListType.Items.Count; i++)
    {
      if (typeDUT.chckListType.GetItemChecked(i))
        m_typesDUT = m_typesDUT + typeDUT.chckListType.GetItemText(
➥typeDUT.chckListType.Items[i]) + " ";
    }
  }
  else
  {
    m_typesDUT = "";
  }
}
```

The declaration of this method needs a parameter passed by a `TypeUnderTest` object, `typeDUT`. In Listing 5.4, the first line adds a private string field, m_typesDUT, which is used to hold the names of types under test from the check box list of the TypeUnderTest form. When the OK button is clicked in the form, the `if` statement within the `for` loop examines the checked type of interest in the test. Finally, it assigns the names of the types as a string value to the `m_typesDUT` field.

The GetTypesOfAssemblyUnderTest() method created in Chapter 4 is modified by adding a line of code at the end to invoke the PassSelectedTypesUT() method, as shown in Listing 5.5 with bold text.

Listing 5.5 Modified *GetTypesOfAssemblyUnderTest()* Method Calling the *PassSelectedTypesUT()* Method

```
private void GetTypesOfAssemblyUnderTest()
{
  if (AssemblyNameToTest.Length <= 0)
  {
    return;
  }
  ...
  typeDUT.lblTypeAvailable.Text = "Available types for the selected Assembly:

  typeDUT.ShowDialog();

  PassSelectedTypesUT(typeDUT);
}
```

Creating an Excel Application

The previous sections have discussed usages of the Excel application programming technology. In this section, you will see how to add an Excel application programmatically to the AutomatedTest project and do the real testing.

The PassSelectedTypesUT() method gets a string variable storing the names of the types to be tested. Although it doesn't contain any Excel application code, it provides what is needed to start an Excel worksheet.

After the discussion in the previous sections, you should find that coding a method to create an Excel worksheet is straightforward. The code is listed in Listing 5.6.

Listing 5.6 Using the *CreateExcelSheet()* Method to Create an Excel Application

```
Excel.Application xApp;
Excel.Workbook xBook;
Excel.Worksheet xSheet;

private void CreateExcelSheet()
{
  xApp= new Excel.Application();
  xBook = xApp.Workbooks.Add(1);
  xSheet=(Excel.Worksheet)xBook.ActiveSheet;
  xSheet.Cells.set_Item(1,1, "CLASS NAME");
```

```
    xSheet.Cells.set_Item(1,2, "METHOD NAME");
    xSheet.Cells.set_Item(1,3, "PARAMETERS TYPES AND NAMES");
    Excel.Range range;
    range = xSheet.get_Range("A1", "Z1");
    range.Interior.ColorIndex=8;
    range.Columns.AutoFit();
    range.Font.Bold=true;
    xApp.Visible=true;
  }
```

Before you actually start to code the method, three fields are created as objects of the `Excel.Application`, `Excel.Workbook`, and `Excel.Worksheet`. After a new Excel instance is created, a new workbook is added to the Excel application. Finally, a worksheet is added into the Workbook object. Then most of the activities happen on the worksheet. For example, callings of the `set_Item()` method assign values to the headers of the data store.

After the data store headers are set up, a `get_Range()` method creates a Range object and returns it to a range variable. Then some properties of this object are altered by invoking different methods or properties. For example, the first property assigning a value to the `ColorIndex` property of the Range object adds some visual effects to the worksheet, which helps with readability. The last three lines of code adjust the width of the columns according to the length of the headers and change the font of the headers to bold. Finally, the following code line makes the Excel application visible:

```
xApp.Visible=true;
```

Setting this value to `false` will hide the Excel application.

Testing against Expected Return Values

When you use the `System.Reflection` namespace to explore a class, it finds where a method returns a value or an object, or is void. If the method returns a value or an object, you want test whether an actual return matches an expected return.

Next, you are going to prepare a space to store a specified value as the expected return value to be tested against. During the testing of a targeted method, if the actual return value matches the specified value expected, the test passes. Otherwise, the test fails. Listing 5.7 lists the implementation of the `AddExpectedValue()` method.

Listing 5.7 **Implementation of the *AddExpectedValue()* Method**

```
private void AddExpectedValue(Excel.Worksheet xs, int shtRow, MethodInfo mi)
{
  Excel.Range range = null;
  int parCount=0;
  try
  {
```

```
        foreach (ParameterInfo pi in mi.GetParameters())
        {
          parCount++;
        }
        string ColChar = TestUtility.ConvCHAR(parCount + 3);

        range =xs.get_Range(ColChar + shtRow, ColChar + shtRow);
        range.AddComment("Expect to return a " + mi.ReturnType.ToString());
        range.Interior.ColorIndex = 43;
        range.Font.ColorIndex = 3;
        range.Font.Bold = true;
      }
      catch{}
    }
```

The required parameters of the `AddExpectedValue()` method include a Worksheet object, an integer indicating the row number of the Excel sheet, and the name of the method under test within a given type class. The `foreach` loop counts how many parameters in the method in order to add a hint comment to the expected return column after the parameters are all enumerated. The expected value is placed in the column position and row position indicated by `ColChar` and `shtRow`, respectively.

The `range.AddComment()` method adds a comment to the Range object (a single cell in this case). The comment tells the tester what to do with this parameter. When the range is activated later, the user can view the passed text, which is convenient when the tester needs to make modifications on the worksheet. The last three lines of the code use Range properties of `Interior.ColorIndex`, `Font.ColorIndex`, and `Font.Bold` to alternate the properties of the targeted range object. The conventional visual effects will help the testers when reviewing the test data store.

Implementing Data Stores

This section is important for building the data store. The `GrabCells()` method gathers most of the information used to test a method of interest. This method is interesting, rich in features, and can do many things for the data and the testing.

Listing 5.8 Implementation of the *GrabCells()* Method to Make a Data Store with the Excel Sheet

```
private void GrabCells(Excel.Worksheet xs, int shtRow,
➥   int shtCol, string setText, ParameterInfo p)
{
  string ColChar = TestUtility.ConvCHAR(shtCol);
  Excel.Range range = null;

  range =xs.get_Range(ColChar + shtRow, ColChar + shtRow);
```

```
  if (null != p)
  {
    range.Value2 = TestUtility.SysToCSPro(p.ParameterType.ToString())
➥+ " " + setText;
  }
  else
    range.Value2 = setText;
  if (p != null)
  {
    //Assign a numeric value to a parameter
    AssignAutoValuesToParams(p, range);
  }

  //range.Columns.AutoFit();
  try
  {
    if (p == null)
    {
      range.Font.ColorIndex = 3;
    }
    else if (p != null)
    {
       range.AddComment(TestUtility.SysToCSPro(p.ParameterType.ToString())
➥+ " " + setText);
    }
    if (p != null)
    {
      if (p.ParameterType.ToString().IndexOf("&")>0)
      {
        if (p.IsOut)
          range.Interior.ColorIndex = 8;
//set color to an out parameter cell
        else
          range.Interior.ColorIndex = 6;
//set color to a ref parameter cell

      }
    }
  }
  catch{}

  //added for enum
  string formulaStr = null;
  string[] tempShort = null;
  bool defaultEnumIsSet = false;

  if (p != null)
  {
    if (p.ParameterType.IsEnum)
    {
      FieldInfo[] enumMembers = p.ParameterType.GetFields();
      foreach (FieldInfo fs in enumMembers)
```

```
        {
          tempShort = fs.ToString().Trim().Split(' ');
          if (tempShort[tempShort.Length - 1] != "value__")
          {
            formulaStr = formulaStr + tempShort[tempShort.Length - 1] + ",";
            if (!defaultEnumIsSet)
            {
              defaultEnumIsSet = true;
              range.Value2 =tempShort[tempShort.Length - 1];
            }
          }
        }
        defaultEnumIsSet = false;
        formulaStr = formulaStr + "xxxx";
        formulaStr = formulaStr.Replace(" ", ".");
        formulaStr = formulaStr.Replace(",xxxx", "");

        try
        {
          range.Validation.Delete();
          range.Validation.Add(Excel.XlDVType.xlValidateList,
➥Excel.XlDVAlertStyle.xlValidAlertStop,
➥Excel.XlFormatConditionOperator.xlBetween, formulaStr, "");
    range.Validation.ShowError=false;
        }
        catch{}
      }
    }
  }
```

At first glance, this implementation seems lengthy. However, it is not difficult to understand. What follows is a discussion of the functionality of each piece of the code.

The declaration takes five parameters:

```
private void GrabCells(Excel.Worksheet xs, int shtRow, int shtCol, string
setText, ParameterInfo p)
```

They are the Worksheet object, `xs`; the integer numbers of the row, `shtRow`; and the column indexes, `shtCol`, indicating where to place the parameter; a string variable, `setText`, to be assigned to a worksheet cell; and the last parameter, `ParameterInfo` variable, `p`, which holds information for the parameter under test.

The column index is converted to a character; thus it can be used in the Excel application. The Range object is declared to represent the cell with the row and column indexes passed. This range object contains only one cell:

```
string ColChar = TestUtility.ConvCHAR(shtCol);
Excel.Range range = null;

range =xs.get_Range(ColChar + shtRow, ColChar + shtRow);
```

```
if (null != p)
{
  range.Value2 = TestUtility.SysToCSPro(p.ParameterType.ToString())
➥+ " " + setText;
}
else
  range.Value2 = setText;
```

Then the code checks the value of the passed parameter `p` with an `if` statement. If the value is not `null`, it assigns the range with a string value of the parameter type. Otherwise, it places the content of the `setText` variable into the respective range.

To enable the AutomatedTest tool to compose a data store with automatic assignments to the values of the parameters, another `if` statement is used to check the same p parameter. The purpose of separating this `if` statement from the previous one is to make the discussion easy and to focus on only one problem at a time:

```
if (p != null)
{
    //Assign a numeric value to a parameter
  AssignAutoValuesToParams(p, range);
}
```

This `if` statement checks the existence of a parameter again. Then it calls an `AssignAutoValuesToParams()` helper method to assign appropriate values to it. This helper method is listed in Listing 5.9.

Listing 5.9 **Code of the *AssignAutoValuesToParams()* Helper Method**

```
private void AssignAutoValuesToParams(ParameterInfo p, Excel.Range range)
{
  Random rndAssign = new Random(); //added for random assignment

  if (p.ParameterType.ToString().IndexOf("Boolean")>0)
    range.Value2= "true";

  if (p.ParameterType.ToString().IndexOf("Boolean")>0 &&
➥p.ParameterType.ToString().IndexOf("&") > 0)
    range.Value2 = "false";

  if (isNumberType(TestUtility.SysToCSPro(p.ParameterType.ToString())))
{
    if (p.ParameterType.ToString().IndexOf("Double")>0 ||
➥p.ParameterType.ToString().IndexOf("Decimal")>0)
      range.Value2= (double)(rndAssign.Next()/1000000);
    else
      range.Value2= (int)rndAssign.Next()/1000000;
  }
}
```

One of the motivations of developing this tool is to simplify the process of composing test data stores. Currently, the testing methods on the market require the tester to generate a test script to test a method and compose a test data store for each test script. When you use these tools to make a data store, the job is totally manual and you have to follow some rules.

For the AutomatedTest tool, you have achieved most of the automation by enumerating classes, methods, and parameters. You have also enabled the testing tool to create an MS Excel worksheet for the data stores automatically. Now, you have also enabled the AutomatedTest tool to assign values to the data store.

The `AssignAutoValuesToParams()` helper method in Listing 5.9 accepts a `ParameterInfo` and an Excel Range variable. It starts with a `Random` variable declaration. Then it checks whether the `ParameterInfo` variable, `p`, is a Boolean type. The first `if` statement assigns a default `true` value to the targeted cell of a Boolean parameter. The second `if` statement initiates a `false` value to the targeted cell for the Boolean parameter that is passed by reference or is an `out` parameter.

At last, the third `if` statement checks whether the parameter is numeric by calling an `isNumberType()` helper method (Listing 5.10). Then it assigns a random number to a numeric parameter. If the parameter type is `Double` or `Decimal`, it assigns a number with decimal points. Otherwise, the assignment truncates the decimal points for a long, short, or integer parameter. Notice that 1000000 is a factor used to generate some decimal points for a double or a decimal variable and reduce the scale of a random number for the numeric variables. If your test project requires different numeric magnitude, you can alter this factor. In the future, you can modify this auto-assignment with more capabilities, such as boundary conditions and invalid assignments.

Listing 5.10 Implementation of the *isNumberType()* Helper Method to Differentiate Parameters into Numeric and Nonnumeric Types

```
private bool isNumberType(string typeStr)
{
  if (typeStr.StartsWith("int") ||
    typeStr.StartsWith("double") ||
    typeStr.StartsWith("long") ||
    typeStr.StartsWith("short") ||
    typeStr.StartsWith("uint")  ||
    typeStr.StartsWith("float") ||
    typeStr.StartsWith("decimal") ||
    typeStr.StartsWith("ulong") ||
    typeStr.StartsWith("ushort"))
  {
     return true;
  }

  return false;
}
```

Numeric data types are primitive data types. The `isNumberType()` helper method uses an `if` statement to check the parameter passed by a string variable. If it finds the identification of a numeric parameter, it returns a `true` value. Otherwise, it returns a `false` value.

After the code segments for the implementation of the `AssignAutoValuesToParams()` and `isNumberType()` methods, the `GrabCells()` method in Listing 5.8 continues with code to employ visual effects to tell whether a parameter is a `ref` or an `out` parameter. A `try-catch` statement confines all this actions. For example, suppose you want a greenish background color for `ref` parameters and magenta color for `out` parameters. You also want to insert a comment into the cell for each parameter. This comment will include the information of the parameter type and name, which will provide a convenient way for users to modify a testing case with accuracy. When the mouse pointer is over a parameter cell, the comment for that cell pops up. The following code segment is extracted from Listing 5.8:

```
...
try
{
  if (p == null)
    range.Font.ColorIndex = 3;
  else if (p != null)
  {
    range.AddComment(TestUtility.SysToCSPro(p.ParameterType.ToString())
➥+ " " + setText);
  }
  if (p != null)
    if (p.ParameterType.ToString().IndexOf("&")>0)
    {
      if (p.IsOut)
//set color to an out parameter cell
        range.Interior.ColorIndex = 8;
      else
//set color to a ref parameter cell
        range.Interior.ColorIndex = 6;

    }
}
catch{}
...
```

This is the first `try` statement. The main purpose of it is to add a comment in the targeted cell so that the test engineer can see the parameter type when placing the mouse over the cell. The other statements alternate the `Interior.ColorIndex` property of the cell based on whether the parameter is passed by value, passed by reference, or is an `out` parameter.

The next code segment handles enumerator variables:

```
...
string formulaStr = null;
string[] tempShort = null;
bool defaultEnumIsSet = false;

if (p != null)
{
  if (p.ParameterType.IsEnum)
  {
    FieldInfo[] enumMembers = p.ParameterType.GetFields();
    foreach (FieldInfo fs in enumMembers)
    {
      tempShort = fs.ToString().Trim().Split(' ');
      if (tempShort[tempShort.Length - 1] != "value__")
      {
        formulaStr = formulaStr + tempShort[tempShort.Length - 1] + ",";
        if (!defaultEnumIsSet)
        {
          defaultEnumIsSet = true;
          range.Value2 =tempShort[tempShort.Length - 1];
        }
      }
    }
    defaultEnumIsSet = false;
    formulaStr = formulaStr + "xxxx";
    formulaStr = formulaStr.Replace(" ", ".");
    formulaStr = formulaStr.Replace(",xxxx", "");
    try
    {
      range.Validation.Delete();
      range.Validation.Add(Excel.XlDVType.xlValidateList,
➥Excel.XlDVAlertStyle.xlValidAlertStop,
➥Excel.XlFormatConditionOperator.xlBetween, formulaStr, "");
range.Validation.ShowError=false;
    }
    catch{}
  }
}
...
```

This code segment checks whether or not the parameter type is an enumerator. If it is an enumerator, the `foreach` statement finds all the possible constants of this enumerator. These constant values are all added to a string and separated by a comma. The `xxxx` string is added to the end of the string so that the comma at the end of the string can be removed. Of course you can use other coding techniques to achieve this. But I think this is an easy way.

The final goal of this piece of code is to add the possible values of an enumerator to the targeted cell as an Excel validation. This is done by the last `try-catch` statement. Here, you can experience the `Validation` property of the Range object. When the test engineers edit the data store by clicking the cell, the cell drops down a list of all the possible values of the enumerator. This makes it easy to edit the data store and prevents the engineers from typing incorrectly when a valid value is needed for the entry.

On the other hand, test engineers are prepared to test the software under adverse conditions. The `ShowError` property of the `Validation` property is turned off by the following statement:

```
range.Validation.ShowError=false;
```

If there is a need for testing a parameter against an invalid testing case, this parameter cell accepts entries other than the values in the list.

Completing the Method Inventory for the Types under Testing

Finally, you need to implement the `InitMethodInventory()` method (Listing 5.11). This method calls the helper methods implemented previously. Then the method itself is eventually executed by the Start button click event, `btnStart_Click()`, of the TestForm.

Listing 5.11 The *InitMethodInventory()* method of the TestForm.cs

```
private Assembly DUTAsm;
private string XlsFilenameToSave;
private int TotalMethodRows;

private void InitMethodInventory()
{
  //this will be modified later
  XlsFilenameToSave = @"C:emp\SoftTestDataStore.xls";
  int i=2;
  if (m_typesDUT.Length>1)
  {
    //open the Excel sheet
    CreateExcelSheet();

    //load the DLL
    try
    {
      DUTAsm = Assembly.LoadFrom(AssemblyNameToTest);
    }
    catch(Exception err)
    {
      MessageBox.Show(err.Message);
    }

    Type[] types = null;
    types = DUTAsm.GetTypes();
```

```
      foreach (Type t in types)
      {
        if (m_typesDUT.IndexOf(t.Name)>-1)
        {
          ConstructorInfo[] cis = t.GetConstructors();
          foreach (ConstructorInfo ci in cis)
          {
            GrabCells(xSheet, i, 1, t.Name, null);
            GrabCells(xSheet, i, 2, t.Name, null);
            ParameterInfo[] ps = ci.GetParameters();
            foreach (ParameterInfo p in ps)
            {
          GrabCells(xSheet, i, p.Position + 3, p.Name, p);
            }
            i++;
          }

          MethodInfo[] ms = t.GetMethods();

          foreach (MethodInfo m in ms)
          {
            GrabCells(xSheet, i, 1, t.Name, null);
            GrabCells(xSheet, i, 2, m.Name, null);
            ParameterInfo[] ps = m.GetParameters();
            foreach (ParameterInfo p in ps)
            {
          GrabCells(xSheet, i, p.Position + 3, p.Name, p);
            }
        if (m.ReturnType.ToString() == "System.Void")
            {
            }
            else
            {
              AddExpectedValue(xSheet, i, m);
            }
            i++;
          }
        }
      }

      try
      {
        xBook.SaveAs(XlsFilenameToSave, Excel.xlNormal,
 "", "", false, false, 0, "", 0, "", "", "");
      }
      catch(Exception err){MessageBox.Show(err.Message);}
    }
    TotalMethodRows = i;
  }
```

Here are the explanations of the code. First you add three private fields, which are an Assembly object, DUTAsm, to represent the Assembly under test, a string object, XlsFilenameToSave, as a filename to save the datasheet, and a integer object, TotalMethodRows, for the total count of methods within the assembly:

```
private Assembly DUTAsm;
private string XlsFilenameToSave;
private int TotalMethodRows;
```

Then, you declare the InitMethodInventory() method, which takes no parameter and returns a void type.

After the method declaration, a statement assigns a filename for the data store.:

```
XlsFilenameToSave = @"C:emp\SoftTestDataStore.xls"
```

This assignment is a temporary code line for now. You will investigate this name in more detail later, so that the AutomatedTest tool assigns a name based on the assembly under test. Next, the first if statement checks whether any Type class is selected to test from the TypeUnderTest form. If at least one Type class is selected, the execution continues. Otherwise, the execution stops.

To continue the execution of the InitMethodInventory() method, the code first calls the CreateExcelSheet() method to create an Excel application. Then, it loads the assembly with a static Assembly.Loadfrom() method invocation by the specified name of the assembly under test. The code segment follows:

```
...
CreateExcelSheet();

//load the DLL
try
{
   DUTAsm = Assembly.LoadFrom(AssemblyNameToTest);
}
catch(Exception err)
{
   MessageBox.Show(err.Message);
}
...
```

Next, a Type array variable, types, is declared to hold the type collection of the Assembly under test.

```
...
Type[] types = null;
types = DUTAsm.GetTypes();
...
```

After the types array is declared, a foreach statement and an if statement examine whether or not to test each of the available types within the assembly, as shown in the following code.

If the Type class is selected to test, it first enumerates the ConstructorInfo array to discover the constructors and list the names of the constructors in the Excel worksheet:

```
...
ConstructorInfo[] cis = t.GetConstructors();
foreach (ConstructorInfo ci in cis)
{
  GrabCells(xSheet, i, 1, t.Name, null);
  GrabCells(xSheet, i, 2, t.Name, null);
  ParameterInfo[] ps = ci.GetParameters();
  foreach (ParameterInfo p in ps)
  {
    GrabCells(xSheet, i, p.Position + 3, p.Name, p);
  }
  i++;
}
...
```

The nested foreach loop enumerates the parameters for the constructor. The GrabCells() method is used here to enter information to the Excel sheet. A variable, i, represents the count of constructors, and is also used to refer to the row number index for the Excel sheet. The value of variable i keeps on incrementing as the constructor enumeration progresses.

After the constructor information is collected in the data store, the InitMethodInventory() method continues to declare a MethodInfo array to collect all the methods within a type class under test. It calls the GrabCells() helper method to enter the type class name and the method name in the Excel worksheet one by one:

```
...
MethodInfo[] ms = t.GetMethods();

foreach (MethodInfo m in ms)
{
  GrabCells(xSheet, i, 1, t.Name, null);
  GrabCells(xSheet, i, 2, m.Name, null);
  ParameterInfo[] ps = m.GetParameters();
  foreach (ParameterInfo p in ps)
  {
    GrabCells(xSheet, i, p.Position + 3, p.Name, p);
  }
  if (m.ReturnType.ToString() == "System.Void")
  {
  }
  else
  {
    AddExpectedValue(xSheet, i, m);
  }
```

```
    i++;
  }
  ...
```

Similar to the constructor enumeration, the nested `foreach` loop enumerates the parameters of the method and enters information of each of the parameters into the Excel worksheet. Finally, it checks whether the method returns a value one by one. If it does, it adds a space to store an expected value to the worksheet by calling the following method:

```
AddExpectedValue(xSheet, i, m);
```

The integer variable `i` increments as the method enumeration progresses.

The last `try` statement uses the `SaveAs()` method of the Workbook object to save the Excel data store. After information of all methods of the type classes is entered into the data store, the method returns to the TestForm form, and the final iteration of variable i is assigned to the `TotalMethodRows` variable.

Now you are ready to build and to test-run the AutomatedTest project with new testing features. When you run it, the appearance of the AutomatedTest tool is still similar to Figure 4.4 because you've not made any new GUI constructions for the TestForm in this chapter.

Gathering Information for Test

The AutomatedTest project is now built. Let's examine the information it gathers for the software testing step by step. Click the Start button from the TestForm application. An open file dialog box appears like the one in Figure 5.3.

FIGURE 5.3
The open file dialog box to specify an assembly to test

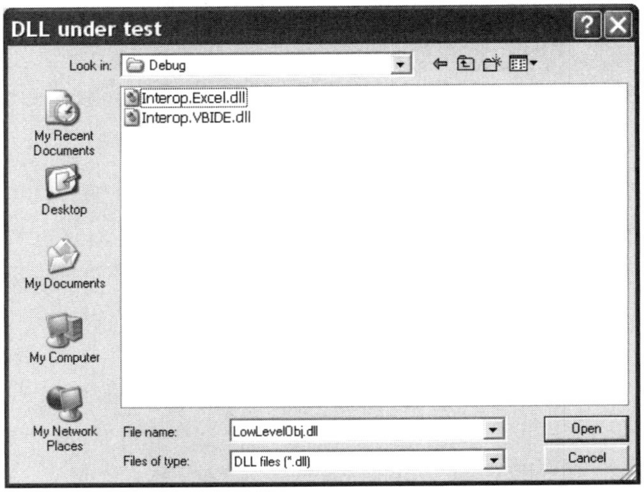

In the Files of Type field at the bottom of the dialog box, you can specify whether you want to test a DLL or an EXE assembly. If you see the same DLL files in your program as shown in Figure 5.3, select `Interop.Excel.dll` and click Open button. If not, navigate to `C:\SourceCode\Chapter05\AutomatedTest\Bin\Debug`.

At this point, you should have these two DLL files in this folder. These files were created by converting the Excel 9/10 Library Object from the legacy COM to the managed assembly when you added the reference in steps 5 and 6 in the section "Opening an MS Excel Application" earlier in this chapter.

If you have the need to test other existing COM components, you can achieve the managed assembly conversion by issuing a line command from the DOS command window. For example, you can convert the `Excel.dll` to `Interop.Excel.dll` by issuing the following command:

```
C:\>tlbimp Excel.dll /out:Interop.Excel.dll
```

Make sure the `Interop.Excel.dll` is selected in the open file dialog box. After you click the Open button, the TypeUnderTest form appears with numerous type classes of the Excel assembly, as shown in Figure 5.4. If you compare this list with the result opening the same assembly with `ILDasm.exe` (Figure 5.1), you will find that they contain the same information. The difference is that you will use the information shown in Figure 5.4 to generate a script to test the `Excel.dll` assembly. But the information revealed by the `ILDasm.exe` in Figure 5.1 can not directly serve this purpose.

You can play with this form by clicking the check boxes. You can select or deselect all classes to test. Or you can select only one or a few of the classes to test. This discussion will be based on selecting only one type to test because the Excel assembly has so many type classes. Also, notice that the check list is sorted in ascending order.

FIGURE 5.4
Type information of the Excel assembly

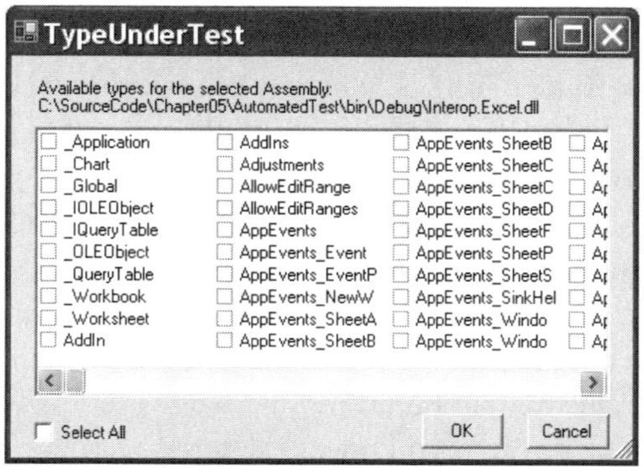

Use the scroll bar to navigate to the Range class, which you should be somewhat familiar with. Check the Range class check box and click the OK button. The specified Excel application opens. You can see the addition of the testing data store in progress. Don't click anywhere on the worksheet until it completely enters the information. Figure 5.5 shows the beginning portion of the information in the Excel worksheet.

FIGURE 5.5
The method inventory worksheet of the Range class in the Excel assembly

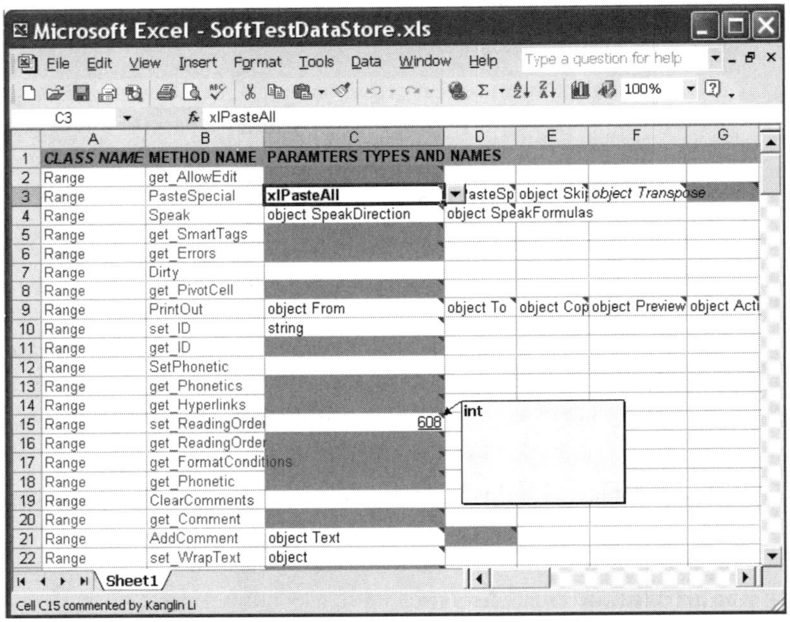

The exhaustive worksheet in Figure 5.5 lists 203 methods and properties for the Range class. The first column (column A) is the name of the type class, which is Range. Column B lists all the names of the methods. The rest of the columns list all the parameters a method takes, if it takes any. The green-colored cells indicate where a return value should be entered for testing this method. Some methods return void, thus a green-colored cell indicating an expected value is not needed for them. If you hover the mouse pointer over the red triangle of any parameter cell, including the cells for expected return values, a comment pops up to show the parameter type and the parameter name. Cell C15 shows a comment informing you that the `set_ReadingOrder` property requests an integer parameter. The AutomatedTest tool automatically assigns a value to it, in Figure 5.5, the value is 608. However, the assignment is random and different for each run. If you hover the mouse pointer over cell F3, the comment reads "object Transpose" for this parameter (Figure 5.6).

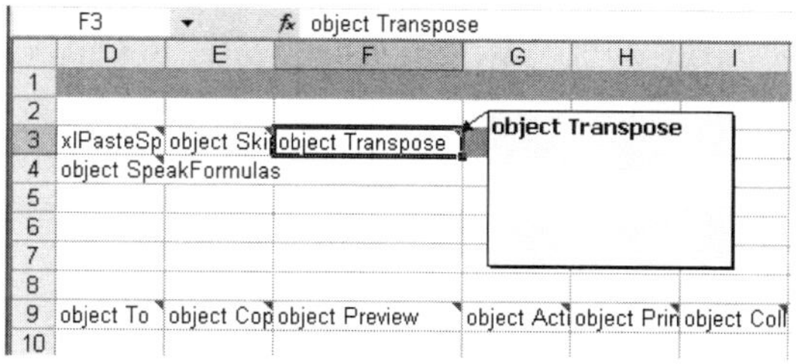

FIGURE 5.6
The parameter type and name shown by hovering the mouse pointer over a parameter cell

Of course, the AutomatedTest tool can do more than this. Click cell C3 to activate it. The parameter type in this cell is `Excel.XlPasteType`, the parameter name is `Paste`. An arrow appears at the right. Click the arrow and you'll see a list of values of the `Excel.XlPasteType` enumerator, as show in Figure 5.7. You can select any one of these for a testing case. The AutomatedTest tool assigns the first in the list to be the default. This feature offers the valid values of a parameter and ensures correct entry. If you want to test an invalid value of a parameter, this cell accepts any invalid entry via typing.

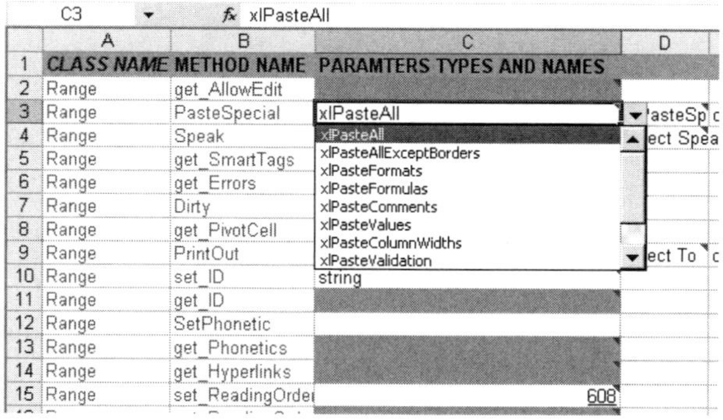

FIGURE 5.7
List of possible values of a parameter with an enumerator data type

You see the advantage of this tool to test a complex assembly like Excel. If a tester wants to accomplish this manually, they would need to spend a few hours or even days to collect the information and enter it into a spreadsheet with accuracy. Armed with this technique, test engineers are able to compose test data stores quickly. Because appropriate values are assigned to the parameters, the users of the AutomatedTest have the option to leave them as they are or to make alterations to them. If users choose to use the data value assigned by the tool, the test can be completed without a pause for data editing. Otherwise, the AutomatedTest will pause before the test script is generated. The user can edit the test data store. After the confirmation of the data editing, the AutomatedTest tool resumes the tasks of completing the test script and presents the test results.

Enabling XML Documentation for the Test Data Store

When you coded the LowLevelObj project in Chapter 4, you inserted XML documentation comments and built the corresponding `LowLevelObj.xml` document. This section will implement a few helper methods to make use of the testing data stored in that XML file. You will make this an optional feature of the AutomatedTest tool.

XML Programming

Assuming the AutomatedTest project is still open within the Microsoft Visual Studio .NET IDE, here are the steps to complete the project:

1. Add a CheckBox control to the TestForm in the design editor. Alter the properties of this control as follows:

   Name: chckXMLDataDoc

   Text: Enable XML Data

2. Switch to the code view of `TestForm.cs` and add the following `using` statements at the beginning of the file:

   ```
   using System.Xml;
   using System.Xml.XPath;
   using System.IO;
   ```

   - The `System.Xml` namespace will be used for creating an object to access XML documents.
   - The `System.Xml.XPath` namespace is for the navigation to a segment within the XML documents.
   - The `System.IO` namespace is always needed where an external file is involved in the project. In this section, it will be used to access the XML documentation.

3. Implement a `MakeUseXMLDataStore()` helper method as shown in Listing 5.12. This method is to extract the values of the parameters stored in an XML help document and place them into the Excel worksheet programmed previously. Thus, the randomly assigned values will be overwritten with the XML assignments, which should be more specific.

Listing 5.12 Code of the *MakeUseXMLDataStore()* Helper Method

```
private void MakeUseXMLDataStore()
{
  XmlDocument xmldoc = CreateXMLDocObj();

  //add code to read XML data into Excel data store
```

```
    for (int RowC = 2; RowC < TotalMethodRows; RowC++)
    {
      //Get the Column with data;
      int ColC = 0;
      Excel.Range colRange = xSheet.get_Range(TestUtility.ConvCHAR(1)
➥+ RowC, TestUtility.ConvCHAR(1) + RowC);
      while (colRange.Value2 != null || colRange.Comment != null)
      {
        ColC++;
        colRange = xSheet.get_Range(TestUtility.ConvCHAR(ColC) +
➥RowC, TestUtility.ConvCHAR(ColC) + RowC);
      }

  if (ColC > 3) //parameter starts from column 3
      {
        for (int ColCount = 3; ColCount < ColC; ColCount++)
        {
        ReadXMLTestDataIntoDataStore(xmldoc, RowC, ColCount);
        }
      }
    }
    try
    {
      xBook.Save();
    }
    catch()
    {
    }
  }
```

This method performs the following actions:

1. First, it creates an XmlDocument object.
2. Then, it uses a `for` loop to keep track the number of methods to be tested in the data store, including the ones overloaded.
3. Within the `for` loop, there are an `Excel.Range` object, a `while` loop, and an `if` statement. The `Excel.Range` object is to extract information from the previously created Excel worksheet and match the information with that in the XML document. The `while` loop is used to count the number of parameters a method requires. Within the `if` statement, a `for` loop is nested. The `if` statement checks to see whether a method needs parameter or not. Because the Excel worksheet starts filling parameter information from column 3 on, iteration of variable ColC greater than 3 indicates possible needs of parameters or returns. Finally, the nested `for` loop calls the `ReadXMLTestDataIntoDataStore()` helper method to retrieve the needed values of the parameters from the XML document one by one.

4. Implement a `CreateXMLDocObj()` helper method as shown in Listing 5.13. This method is to make sure there is an XML help document within the same folder as the assembly under test. When the XML help document is found, this method creates an `XmlReader` object and passes the information to an `XmlDocument` object.

Listing 5.13 Code of the *CreateXMLDocObj()* Helper Method to Return an *XmlDocument* Object

```
private XmlDocument CreateXMLDocObj()
{
  string[] pathFolderName = AssemblyNameToTest.Split('\\');
  string xmlRoot = AssemblyNameToTest.Replace(
➥pathFolderName[pathFolderName.Length - 1], "");
  DirectoryInfo xmlDir = null;
  try
  {
    xmlDir = new DirectoryInfo(xmlRoot);
  }
  catch(Exception e)
  {
    MessageBox.Show(e.Message + "

" No XML document is found.");
    return null;
  }
  FileInfo[] AllFiles = xmlDir.GetFiles();
  FileInfo xmlFile = null;
  foreach(FileInfo xmlF in AllFiles)
  {
    if (xmlF.Extension == ".xml")
    {
      xmlFile = xmlF;
      break;
    }
  }

  if (xmlFile != null)
  {
    XmlReader xmlRead = new XmlTextReader(File.OpenRead(xmlFile.FullName));
    XmlDocument xmlDoc = new XmlDocument();
    xmlDoc.Load(xmlRead);
    xmlRead.Close();

    return xmlDoc;
  }

  return null;
}
```

This method performs the following actions:

1. Creates a string array, `pathfolderName`, and a string variable, `xmlRoot`, based on the path and filename of the assembly under test.
2. Uses a `try-catch` statement to create a `DirectoryInfo` object, `xmlDir`, based on the string variable xmlRoot.
3. Uses a `foreach` loop to find the XML document within the `xmlDir` object.
4. Finally, creates an `XmlDocument` object to load the XML document using an `if` statement.
5. Implement a `ReadXMLTestDataIntoDataStore()` helper method. The code, listed in Listing 5.14, extracts a piece of data from the XML document and inserts it into the corresponding cell in the Excel worksheet.

Listing 5.14 Code of the *ReadXMLTestDataIntoDataStore()* Helper Method

```
private void ReadXMLTestDataIntoDataStore(XmlDocument xmlDoc, int RowC, int
ColC)
{
  XmlNodeList memNames = xmlDoc.GetElementsByTagName("member");

  Excel.Range xmlRange = xSheet.get_Range(TestUtility.ConvCHAR(ColC)
➥+ RowC, TestUtility.ConvCHAR(ColC) + RowC);

  for (int memCount = 0; memCount<memNames.Count; memCount++)
  {
    XmlAttributeCollection memAtt = memNames[memCount].Attributes;

    string classMem = (string) xSheet.get_Range(TestUtility.ConvCHAR(1)
➥+ RowC, TestUtility.ConvCHAR(1) + RowC).Value2;
    string methodMem = (string) xSheet.get_Range(TestUtility.ConvCHAR(2)
➥+ RowC, TestUtility.ConvCHAR(2) + RowC).Value2;

    if (memAtt[0].Value.IndexOf(classMem + "." + methodMem) >0 ||
➥memAtt[0].Value.IndexOf(classMem + ".#ctor(") >0)
    {
      XmlNodeList paramNodes = memNames[memCount].ChildNodes;

      for (int paramCount = 0; paramCount < paramNodes.Count; paramCount++)
      {
        if (paramNodes[paramCount].Name == "param")
        {
          XmlAttributeCollection paramAtt = paramNodes[paramCount].Attributes;

          string[] commentStr = null;
          try
          {
            commentStr = xmlRange.Comment.Shape.AlternativeText.Split(' ');
```

```
                }
                catch{}
                if (commentStr != null)
                {
                  if (paramAtt[0].Value == commentStr[commentStr.Length - 1])
                  {
          PlaceDataFromXmlDocToExcel(paramNodes[paramCount].InnerXml, xmlRange);
                    break;
                  }
                }
              }

              if (paramNodes[paramCount].Name == "returns")
              {
                if (xmlRange.Comment.Shape.AlternativeText.IndexOf(
      ➥"Expect to return a") >= 0)
                {
          PlaceDataFromXmlDocToExcel(paramNodes[paramCount].InnerXml, xmlRange);
                  break;
                }
              }
            }
          }
        }
      }
```

This method uses the following reasoning to fulfill its goal:

1. The XML document tags each method, property, or constructor inside a class as a member. The created `XMLNodeList` is a collection of the members. Each node of the members has an attribute. This attribute holds the name of the member.
2. The second statement creates an `Excel.Range` object. This object contains the information of a parameter of interest and its row and column coordinates in the Excel worksheet.
3. The first `for` loop uses the information contained by the `Excel.Range` object to probe the XML nodes by matching the parameter name in the Range object with the attributes of the XML nodes. If a value was found in a node of the XML document for the parameter of interest, the value is placed in the Excel worksheet by calling the `PlaceDataFromXmlDocToExcel()` helper method.
4. The nested `for` loop finds all the assigned values in the XML document for all the parameters and expected returns.
5. Implement a `PlaceDataFromXmlDocToExcel()` helper method as shown in Listing 5.15. When this method is called, the needed information is already identified within the XML document. The only task of this method is to make the value available for the execution of the software test in the Excel worksheet.

Listing 5.15 Code of the *PlaceDataFromXmlDocToExcel()* Helper Method.

```
private void PlaceDataFromXmlDocToExcel(string FromXMLText,
➥  Excel.Range xmlRange)
{
  string GotoCell = FromXMLText;
  int startData = GotoCell.IndexOf("e.g.,");

  try
  {
    GotoCell = GotoCell.Substring(startData);
    GotoCell = GotoCell.Replace("e.g.,", "").Trim();
  }
  catch
  {
  }


  xmlRange.Value2 = GotoCell;
}
```

In this method, the following takes place:

1. The declaration requires two parameters. One contains the data from the XML document, the other the position where the parameter is located in the Excel worksheet.
2. Then, using `"e.g.,"` as an identifier, the `try-catch` statement invokes the `Substring()` method to look for the position of the identifier, get the testing data on the right side of the identifier, and ignore the text to the left of it.
3. At last, it inserts the testing data into the Excel worksheet.

Locate the btnStart_Click() event in `TestForm.cs` coded previously and add the `MakeUseXMLDataStore()` method call at the end of this event with an `if` statement. This `if` statement checks whether the XML documentation option is checked or not. After the addition, the code of the `btnStart_Click()` event looks similar to the following, with the newly added lines in bold:

```
private void btnStart_Click(object sender, System.EventArgs e)
{
  GetAssemblyName();
  GetTypesOfAssemblyUnderTest();

  InitMethodInventory();

  if (chckXMLDataDoc.Checked)
  {
```

```
            MakeUseXMLDataStore();
        }
    }
```

Testing with the Data Stored in the XML Document

When you built the LowLevelObj project in Chapter 4, a `LowLevelObj.xml` file was created. To refresh your memory of what values were assigned to the parameters, let's examine the XML document by referring to Listing 4.2 in Chapter 4.

You recall that when you inserted the XML documentation comments in Chapter 4, you only worked with the `<summary>`, `<param>` and `<returns>` tags and added testing values for the `<param>` and `<returns>` tags. After you built the project, the compiler added the `<member>`, `<members>` and `<doc>` tags. For the `<member>` tag, it included an attribute of the member name. The text for each tag you inserted is intact.

Now, with the AutomatedTest project loaded in an open Microsoft Visual Studio .NET IDE, press F5 to build and run this project. When the AutomatedTest form appears, do the following:

1. Check the Enable XML Data check box on the form of the AutomatedTest tool.
2. Click the Start button to start a new test session as you did in the previous example. An open file dialog box appears.
3. From the open file dialog box, navigate to the `C:\SourceCode\Chapter04\LowLevelObj\bin\Debug` folder and select the `LowLevelObj.dll`.
4. Click the Open button. The TypeUnderTest form appears. From this form, select the check box beside the `SimpleMath`.
5. Click the OK button. An Excel worksheet appears and starts filling up with data. When the data is complete, the Excel worksheet has all the data values from the XML documents, as shown in Figure 5.8.

Comparing the values in Figure 5.8 with the values in the XML document of Listing 4.2 in Chapter 4, you can see that all the values in the comments of the LowLevelObj project of Chapter 4 are imported to the Excel worksheet. The values in this kind of worksheet will be directly used to generated test scripts for the software testing examples of the rest of the book.

Because the data for these testing cases are assigned at coding time, there will be no pause for data store editing. This method involves the software developers in the software testing and will make the testing case composition more efficient and accurate.

FIGURE 5.8
Testing data store with the data values passed from the XML document for testing the LowLevelObj.dll

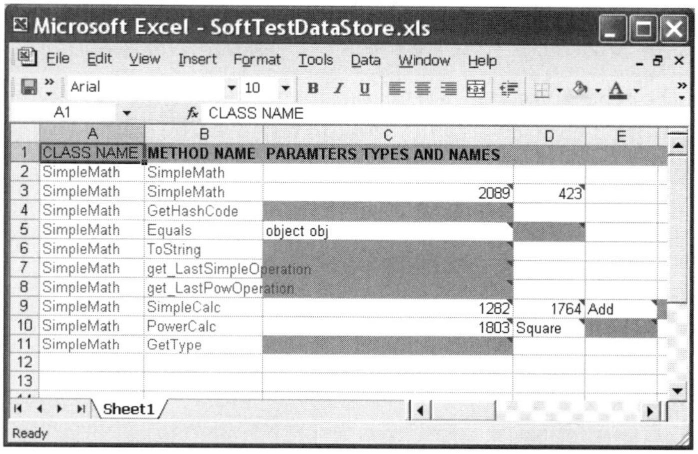

In later chapters, you will see more examples to demonstrate how to use these features for data stores and discover other features for complex testing tasks.

Summary

In this chapter you saw how you can use an Excel worksheet and an XML document to store testing data for the automated test tool.

You saw how you can create an automated test tool capable of opening and storing data in an Excel worksheet by programming the properties, methods, and events of an Excel Application object, Workbook objects, Worksheet objects, and Range objects. After the basic discussion of the Excel application, you made progress by actually coding the AutomatedTest project. Now the project is capable of collecting all of the necessary information for the test. The information includes the names and classes of the assembly under test, the methods within the classes, and the parameters and return types of the methods.

Then, you saw how to retrieve testing data from an XML document that was built from the inserted comments at coding time by developers. This provides an easy way for data editing and makes the most sense.

In the real software testing world, a software test engineer can make the use of any database or spreadsheet formats for data stores. The examples can be extended to other data storing mechanisms and other software development platforms.

The next chapter will start a new topic: the .NET CodeDom namespace, which has been seldom discussed in publications before. In this book, the CodeDom namespace will be used to write Visual C#.NET or VB .NET programs dynamically.

For the AutomatedTest project, you will use the CodeDom namespace to write the test scripts. These scripts will be able to test all of the methods of a given class using the information collected in the Excel worksheet defined in this chapter.

Chapter 6

.NET CodeDom Namespace

The main goal of the software testing is to write a test script to test all classes, methods, and properties of an assembly. The core of the AutomatedTest tool is the automatic mechanism performing the following tasks:

- Discovering the classes, methods, and properties within an assembly under test
- Defining testing cases based on the nature of the assembly
- Writing a test script to do the test
- Executing the test script
- Presenting the test results
- Reusing the test script assembly for later regression testing and integration testing

Thus, the AutomatedTest tool can guarantee a thorough test and find bugs effectively. In the previous chapters, you have seen how the AutomatedTest tool used the .NET Reflection namespace, the .NET `Type` class, MS Excel API programming, and XML documentation to complete the first task, collecting information about the classes, methods, and properties from the assembly under test. Next, you need to enable the AutomatedTest tool to write the test script. To do this, you'll need to learn about a new territory of programming techniques: using the `System.CodeDom` namespace.

CodeDom stands for the Code Document Object Model. It is capable of dynamically generating code on the fly for a tool builder. Test engineers repetitively build testing tools, which are used to generate test scripts dynamically. Thus, the CodeDom namespace provides test engineers with a new tool that can be used to generate the automatic test scripts.

This chapter will start with an introduction to the `System.CodeDom` namespace. You can then follow the examples to create a few projects that demonstrate how the `System.CodeDom` namespace is used to write code programmatically.

Dynamic CodeDom Programming

In this section, first you'll see how CodeDom namespace automatically generates a C# program. Then, I'll discuss how CodeDom namespace does it in depth and show you how to code your own applications with it.

First, let's start a new project, AutoGenerateCode. This project uses types and methods of the `System.CodeDom` and `System.CodeDom.Compiler` namespaces to generate a `StartExcel.cs` file, which will be identical to the one coded in Chapter 5. The only difference is that the one in Chapter 5 is written by a software programmer and the one in this chapter will be written by the CodeDom namespace. To begin, follow these steps:

1. Start a new project from the Microsoft Visual Studio .NET IDE.

2. Select C# Project from the list on the left pane, and select Console Application in the right pane.
3. Name the project AutoGenerateCode.
4. Type **`C:\SourceCode\Chapter06`** in the Location field.
5. Click OK. The code editor opens with an `AutoGenerateCode.cs` file.
6. Choose Project ➢ Add Reference to add a reference to the Microsoft Excel 9.0/10.0 Object Library.
7. Start coding. The code is shown in Listing 6.1.

Listing 6.1 Code of the *AutoGenerateCode.cs* File to Generate a C# Program Automatically

```
using System;
using System.CodeDom;
using System.CodeDom.Compiler;
using System.IO;
using System.Reflection;

namespace AutoGenerateCode
{
   class AutoClass
   {
      static CodeEntryPointMethod cm;
      static CodeDomProvider codeProvider;
      static ICodeGenerator cg;
      static CodeNamespace cnamespace;
      static CodeCompileUnit TestUnit;
      static CodeTypeDeclaration co;

      private static void initializeCodeDom()
      {
         TestUnit = new CodeCompileUnit();
         codeProvider = new Microsoft.CSharp.CSharpCodeProvider();
         cg = codeProvider.CreateGenerator();
         cnamespace = new CodeNamespace("StartExcel");
      }

      private static void AddUsingStatement()
      {
         cnamespace.Imports.Add(new CodeNamespaceImport("System"));
      }

      private static void AddNamespace()
      {
         TestUnit.Namespaces.Add(cnamespace);
      }
```

```
        private static void StartClass()
        {
            co = new CodeTypeDeclaration("ExcelApplication");
            co.Attributes = (System.CodeDom.MemberAttributes)TypeAttributes.Public;
        }

        private static void StartMainMethod()
        {
            cm = new CodeEntryPointMethod();
        }

        private static void MainMethodBody()
        {
            CodePropertyReferenceExpression pState = null;
            CodeExpression[] pCode = null;
            CodeFieldReferenceExpression cLeft=null;
            CodeFieldReferenceExpression cRight=null;

            cm.Statements.Add(new CodeParameterDeclarationExpression(
➥typeof(Excel.Application), "xApp = new Excel.Application()"));
            cm.Statements.Add(new CodeParameterDeclarationExpression(
➥typeof(Excel.Workbook), "xBook = xApp.Workbooks.Add(1)"));
            cm.Statements.Add(new CodeParameterDeclarationExpression(
➥typeof(Excel.Worksheet), "xSheet = (Excel.Worksheet)xBook.ActiveSheet"));

            cLeft=new CodeFieldReferenceExpression(null, "xApp.Visible");
            cRight=new CodeFieldReferenceExpression(null, " true");
            cm.Statements.Add(new CodeAssignStatement(cLeft, cRight));

            pCode = new CodeExpression[]{new CodeFieldReferenceExpression(
null, "@\"C:\Temp\StartExcelTest.xls\", -4143, \"\", \"\", false, false,
➥0, \"\", 0, \"\", \"\", \"\"")};
            cm.Statements.Add(new CodeMethodInvokeExpression(null,
➥"xBook.SaveAs", pCode));

            pCode = new CodeExpression[]{new CodeFieldReferenceExpression(null,
➥"1, 1, \"ActiveWorkbook Path\"")};
            cm.Statements.Add(new CodeMethodInvokeExpression(null,
➥"xSheet.Cells.set_Item", pCode));

            pCode = new CodeExpression[]{new CodeFieldReferenceExpression(null,
➥"2, 1, \"ActiveSheet Name\"")};
            cm.Statements.Add(new CodeMethodInvokeExpression(null,
➥"xSheet.Cells.set_Item", pCode));

            pCode = new CodeExpression[]{new CodeFieldReferenceExpression(null,
➥"3, 1, \"Sheet Count\"")};
            cm.Statements.Add(new CodeMethodInvokeExpression(null,
➥"xSheet.Cells.set_Item", pCode));

            pCode = new CodeExpression[]{new CodeFieldReferenceExpression(
➥null, "4, 1, \"Value of Pi\"")};
```

```
        cm.Statements.Add(new CodeMethodInvokeExpression(null,
➥"xSheet.Cells.set_Item", pCode));

        pCode = new CodeExpression[]{new CodeFieldReferenceExpression(
➥null, "5, 1, \"ActiveCell Coordinate (Row, Column)\"")};
        cm.Statements.Add(new CodeMethodInvokeExpression(null,
➥"xSheet.Cells.set_Item", pCode));

        pCode = new CodeExpression[]{new CodeFieldReferenceExpression(
➥null, "1, 2, xBook.Path")};
        cm.Statements.Add(new CodeMethodInvokeExpression(null,
➥"xSheet.Cells.set_Item", pCode));

        pCode = new CodeExpression[]{new CodeFieldReferenceExpression(
➥null, "2, 2, xSheet.Name")};
        cm.Statements.Add(new CodeMethodInvokeExpression(null,
➥"xSheet.Cells.set_Item", pCode));

        pCode = new CodeExpression[]{new CodeFieldReferenceExpression(
➥null, "3, 2, xApp.Sheets.Count")};
        cm.Statements.Add(new CodeMethodInvokeExpression(null,
➥"xSheet.Cells.set_Item", pCode));

        pCode = new CodeExpression[]{new CodeFieldReferenceExpression(
➥null, "4, 2, xApp.WorksheetFunction.Pi()")};
        cm.Statements.Add(new CodeMethodInvokeExpression(null,
➥"xSheet.Cells.set_Item", pCode));

        pCode = new CodeExpression[]{new CodeFieldReferenceExpression(
➥null, "5, 2, xApp.ActiveCell.Row + " + "\", \"" + " +
➥xApp.ActiveCell.Column")};
        cm.Statements.Add(new CodeMethodInvokeExpression(null,
➥"xSheet.Cells.set_Item", pCode));

        pState = new CodePropertyReferenceExpression(null, "xSheet");
        cm.Statements.Add(new CodeMethodInvokeExpression(pState,
➥"Columns.AutoFit"));
    }

    private static void WrapUpCode()
    {
        co.Members.Add(cm);
        cnamespace.Types.Add(co);

        TextWriter t = null;
        string targetFile = "StartExcel.cs";
        t = new StreamWriter (new FileStream (targetFile, FileMode.Create));

        cg.GenerateCodeFromNamespace(cnamespace, t, null);
        t.Close();
    }
```

```
        [STAThread]
        static void Main(string[] args)
        {
            initializeCodeDom();
            AddUsingStatement();
            AddNamespace();
            StartClass();
            StartMainMethod();
            MainMethodBody();
            WrapUpCode();
        }
    }
}
```

The AutoGenerateCode.cs file is certainly lengthy! This may be a limitation of CodeDom programming due to its conceptual representation of programming constructs. But the files can be reused, and it can write code so a software programmer doesn't have to. A popular use of the CodeDom namespace is for developing automatic source code generators. The goal of code generators is to minimize repetitive coding tasks and to minimize the number of human-generated lines of source code. When this program is executed, it is capable of writing another program within fractions of a second. If the programming process is repetitive, a lengthy program like this is worthwhile.

Because the CodeDom namespace can generate a program by itself, you can reuse it to generate more complicated test scripts programmatically. It will significantly save you time in the future. After you learn how to use it, you will not write test scripts any more.

To help you understand the CodeDom statements, the rest of this section includes an analysis of the code. Code segments will be abstracted from Listing 6.1 in sequence.

First, let's investigate the five using statements:

```
using System;
using System.CodeDom;
using System.CodeDom.Compiler;
using System.IO;
using System.Reflection;
...
```

The System namespace, which contains a lot of basic .NET data types and methods, is a must for any C# program. The System.CodeDom and System.CodeDom.Compiler namespaces are the ones we are most interested in for writing the AutomatedTest tool. The System.IO namespace provides the ability to input/output a file. In this case, a System.IO.TextWriter object is used to save the generated C# code as StartExcel.cs.The System.Reflection namespace, discussed in previous chapters, reflects a complex assembly into its basic units, such as classes, methods, properties, and parameters.

Next, you start to code a class declaration. After the class name, `AutoClass`, is declared, you declare the following fields. I use some short names for the fields in order to reduce the length of the code lines, such as `cg` for code generator, `co` for code type declaration, and `cm` for code method declaration:

```
...
static CodeDomProvider codeProvider;
static CodeCompileUnit TestUnit;
static ICodeGenerator cg;
static CodeNamespace cnamespace;
static CodeTypeDeclaration co;
static CodeEntryPointMethod cm;
...
```

These static fields are all related to the CodeDom namespace. The first three fields enable the secret power of the CodeDom namespace. You can instruct it to generate a program in C# or VB .NET with the `CodeDomProvider` class and ask it to compile the generated program from memory with the `CodeCompileUnit` and `ICodeGenerator`, respectively. Then you use the other three fields to declare a namespace, a class, and a method with `CodeNamespace`, `CodeTypeDeclaration`, and `CodeEntryPointMethod`, respectively, which are basic components of a console project.

Now, you implement the static `initializeCodeDom()` method:

```
private static void initializeCodeDom()
{
   TestUnit = new CodeCompileUnit();
   codeProvider = new Microsoft.CSharp.CSharpCodeProvider();
   cg = codeProvider.CreateGenerator();
   cnamespace = new CodeNamespace("StartExcel");
}
```

The only task of the `initializeCodeDom()` method is to initialize four of the CodeDom objects. The initialization of the CodeDom objects is similar to writing other C# code. For the `codeProvider` object, you have two options for its initialization. In this case, your code is as follows:

```
codeProvider = new Microsoft.CSharp.CSharpCodeProvider();
```

This explicitly enables the program to write C# code for the `StartExcel.cs` file.

If the `codeProvider` object is initialized as shown here, the resulting `StartExcel.cs` file will be written in VB .NET:

```
codeProvider = new Microsoft.VisualBasic.VBCodeProvider();
```

I encourage you to try both and see the different results.

The last statement assigns a name, `StartExcel`, to the namespace.

The next method is the `AddUsingStatement()` method, which is coded as follows:

```
private static void AddUsingStatement()
{
   cnamespace.Imports.Add(new CodeNamespaceImport("System"));
}
```

The targeted StartExcel program needs only one `using` statement, which makes this method easy and neat. The `AddUsingStatement()` method produces a line of C# code for the StartExcel.cs source code:

```
using System;
```

If the `VBCodeProvider` is chosen to generate the targeted code, this method generates a line of VB.NET code for the StartExcel.vb file:

```
imporpts System
```

Of course, you can make more `using` statements for other projects with similar syntax. Next is the `AddNamespace()` method:

```
private static void AddNamespace()
{
   TestUnit.Namespaces.Add(cnamespace);
}
```

The `AddNamespace()` method uses the `TestUnit` object with regard to the namespace addition, which produces the following line of code:

```
namespace StartExcel {
```

To add a class to the `StartExcel` namespace, the `StartClass()` method is coded as follows:

```
private static void StartClass()
{
   co = new CodeTypeDeclaration("ExcelApplication");
   co.Attributes = MemberAttributes.Public;
}
```

This method, `StartClass()`, starts coding the constructor of a class, which does only two things. The first line gives a name to the class, `ExcelApplication`. The second line defines this class as a `public` class. You can image what the resulting line of code looks like:

```
public class ExcelApplication {
}
```

Within the class, the `StartMainMethod()` method adds an entry point method to the `StartExcel` namespace:

```
private static void StartMainMethod()
{
   cm = new CodeEntryPointMethod();
}
```

By default, the `CodeEntryPointMethod()` constructor takes these steps to create an entry point method:

- Initializes the `CodeMemberMethod` object, `cm`
- Gives a method name, `Main`
- Defines the attributes, `public`
- Defines a return type, `void`

  No arguments are declared for this `Main()` method.

The next helper method generates the code statements for the entry point method as follows:

```
private static void MainMethodBody()
{
   CodePropertyReferenceExpression pState = null;
   CodeExpression[] pCode = null;
   CodeFieldReferenceExpression cLeft=null;
   CodeFieldReferenceExpression cRight=null;

   cm.Statements.Add(new CodeParameterDeclarationExpression(
➥typeof(Excel.Application), "xApp = new Excel.Application()"));
...
...
}
```

It is easy to create a namespace, class, and method by using classes and methods of the CodeDom namespace. However, the `MainMethodBody()` method uses various new types of the CodeDom namespace to add code to the method body. This method uses three classes of the CodeDom namespace to initialize various statements:

`CodePropertyReferenceExpression`

`CodeExpression`

`CodeFieldReferenceExpression`

Then, it uses `CodeMemberMethod.Statements.Add()` syntax to add the initialized statement to the specified method. For generating the 12 statements of the targeted StartExcel program, this coding pattern is repeated. For other complicated statements, such as `try-catch`, `if`, `for`, and `while` loops, CodeDom namespace provides other techniques, which are not needed for the discussion here. But you will learn about these techniques in the next chapters.

Next, a `WrapUpCode()` method is used to complete the code generation by the CodeDom namespace and save the generated code by using a `TextWriter` object and an `ICodeGenerator` object:

```
private static void WrapUpCode()
{
```

```
        co.Members.Add(cm);
        cnamespace.Types.Add(co);

        TextWriter t = null;
        string targetFile = "StartExcel.cs";
        t = new StreamWriter (new FileStream (targetFile, FileMode.Create));
        cg.GenerateCodeFromNamespace(cnamespace, t, null);
        t.Close();
    }
```

It is easy enough. This method adds the generated method to the class and then adds the class to the namespace. Finally, it uses the `System.CodeDom.ICodeGenerator` object together with the `System.IO.TextWriter` object to save the generated code to a specified filename. In this case the filename is `StartExcel.cs`, which is stored in the `TargetFile` variable. This file will be saved in the current directory together with the `AutoGenerateCode.exe` file.

At last, you code the `Main()` method to call the seven helper methods. The method invocation initializes the objects from the CodeDom namespace first. The other methods use those procedures within the CodeDom objects to add a `using` statement and create a namespace, a class, an entry point method, and some code statements until `StartExcel.cs` is completed:

```
static void Main(string[] args)
{
    initializeCodeDom();
    AddUsingStatement();
    AddNamespace();
    StartClass();
    StartMainMethod();
    MainMethodBody();
    WrapUpCode();
}
```

After you finish coding the project, you can build and run it by pressing F5. Then, by navigating to the `C:\SourceCode\Chapter06\AutoGenerateCode\bin\Debug` folder, you find that this project creates a new `StartExcel.cs` file, whose name is stored in the `TargetFile` variable in the code list. This file has the same content of that developed in Chapter 5 by hand. You may be curious and want to compare the generated code with the hand-written code in Listing 5.1. You can do so by following these steps:

1. Navigate to the `C:\SourceCode\Chapter06\AutoGenerateCode\Bin\Debug` folder.
2. Double-click the `StartExcel.cs` file. It opens in a Microsoft Visual Studio .NET IDE.

The content is shown in Listing 6.2.

Listing 6.2 The CodeDom-Generated *StartExcel.cs* File

```
namespace StartExcel {
    using System;


    public class ExcelApplication {

        public static void Main() {
            Excel.Application xApp = new Excel.Application();
            Excel.Workbook xBook = xApp.Workbooks.Add(1);
            Excel.Worksheet xSheet = (Excel.Worksheet)xBook.ActiveSheet;
            xApp.Visible =  true;
            xBook.SaveAs(@"C:\Temp\StartExcelTest.xls", -4143,
➥"", "", false, false, 0, "", 0, "", "", "");
            xSheet.Cells.set_Item(1, 1, "ActiveWorkbook Path");
            xSheet.Cells.set_Item(2, 1, "ActiveSheet Name");
            xSheet.Cells.set_Item(3, 1, "Sheet Count");
            xSheet.Cells.set_Item(4, 1, "Value of Pi");
            xSheet.Cells.set_Item(5, 1, "ActiveCell Coordinate (Row, Column)");
            xSheet.Cells.set_Item(1, 2, xBook.Path);
            xSheet.Cells.set_Item(2, 2, xSheet.Name);
            xSheet.Cells.set_Item(3, 2, xApp.Sheets.Count);
            xSheet.Cells.set_Item(4, 2, xApp.WorksheetFunction.Pi());
            xSheet.Cells.set_Item(5, 2, xApp.ActiveCell.Row + ", " +
➥xApp.ActiveCell.Column);
            xSheet.Columns.AutoFit();
        }
    }
}
```

You also can compare these two files using a comparing program, such as WinDiff, from the Start ➤ Run menu. To compile the `StartExcel.cs` file into a console application, you would open a Visual Studio .NET 2003 command prompt window. Then, change to the `C:\SourceCode\Chapter06\AutoGenerateCode\bin\Debug` folder and use the following command set (Figure 6.1):

```
csc /r:Interop.Excel.dll StartExcel.cs
```

Press return. This will build `StartExcel.exe`. Issue a `Dir` command from the DOS command window. You will see the newly generated `StartExcel.exe` assembly. The `StartExcel.exe` can be run from the command line (Figure 6.1).

Running `StartExcel.exe` from the command line, you'll see an Excel worksheet open with data that is identical to that in Figure 5.2.

Now you know how to use the CodeDom namespace to generate a simple project. The following sections describe the CodeDom namespace in more detail so that you can use more of the methods to write practical test scripts.

FIGURE 6.1
The StartExcel.exe is ready to run and create an Excel worksheet

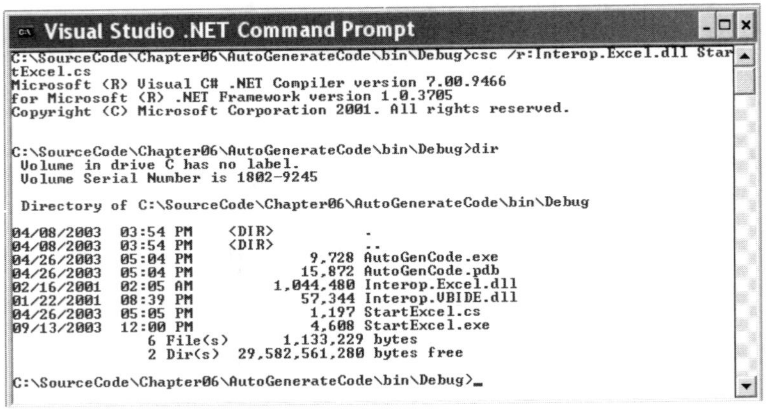

NOTE WinDiff is a tool installed with Microsoft Visual Studio 6. Unfortunately, this tool is not a part of Microsoft Visual Studio .NET.

NOTE At this point, the AutoGenerateCode project did not implement a late-binding method to build the StartExcel assembly dynamically. It generated the source code for the StartExcel program. To compile the CodeDom-generated StartExcel.cs program, you can open a Visual Studio .NET 2003 command prompt to invoke the C# compiler (`csc.exe`), which invokes a batch file from `C:\Program Files\Microsoft Visual Studio .NET\Common7\Tools\vsvars32.bat`. This batch file sets up a .NET compiling environment. However, you can open a regular command compiler if you have set your path variable to the `C:\WINNT\Microsoft.NET\Framework\v1.1.4322` folder or similar. Chapter 11 will discuss a few ways to alter environment variables.

The *System.CodeDom* Namespace

In general, the CodeDom namespace has the capability of building customized applications and outputting source code into multiple programming languages at runtime. The `System.CodeDom` namespace has a number of types that represent the structure of source code. These are independent of a current programming language. The most common languages that CodeDom namespace generates are C# and VB .NET. As with the AutoGenerateCode project, the code generated by the CodeDom namespace is in memory before the code generation statement is issued. Because the `System.CodeDom` namespace also provides types to compile the source code at runtime, it can make the software testing a completely automated process.

System.CodeDom namespace contains numerous types of programming techniques representing any possible .NET types (class, interface, structure, enumeration, or delegate). Within these types, the CodeDom namespace can create various members (properties, methods, and events). Within the member implementation, the CodeDom namespace can write various statements (foreach loops, while loops, if-else statements, and other object manipulation). I will focus on the aspects of the CodeDom namespace that are useful for the AutomatedTest project to generate C# source code. To make the coding easy, the test script to be generated by CodeDom will follow the skeleton for a C# console application, which is represented in Listing 6.3.

Listing 6.3 The Skeleton C# Code for the Test Scripts to Be Generated by the *CodeDom* namespace

```
namespace <TestNamespace>
{
    using System;
    <more using statements>

    public class <TestClassName>
    {
        private string <filedname>
        <more fields>

        public <TestClassname> (string <cstorParameter>)
        {
            <cstor Statements>
        }

        public void <TestMethod>
        {
            <Method Statements>
        }

        <More methods>
    }
    <More Classes>
}
```

Obviously, this layout has a simple structure and is easy to comprehend. The code strategy of the AutomatedTest project will follow this pattern to generate a test script for assemblies under test. The task in this chapter is to find out how to achieve all the code segments using System.CodeDom namespace. The next section lists the CodeDom methods that correspond to coding the namespace, class, constructors, methods, and other members.

Types of *System.CodeDom* Namespace

To accomplish the previous C# skeleton part by part, the first task is to programmatically declare a namespace. The `System.CodeDom` namespace provides several types to represent a .NET namespace. Table 6.1 lists the namespace types.

TABLE 6.1 Types Provided by CodeDom to Build a Namespace.

Type to Build Namespace	Description
`CodeNamespace`	Builds a single namespace declaration
`CodeNamespaceCollection`	Builds a collection of namespaces
`CodeNamespaceImport`	Builds a single namespace import statement
`CodeNamespaceImportCollection`	Builds a collection of namespace import statements

The `CodeNamespace` is the type often used in the AutomatedTest project. To achieve the declaration of a class in the skeleton, the `CodeTypeDeclaration` is used. Table 6.2 presents the types for declaring any possible type structures for programming, such as classes, structures, enumerations, interfaces, and delegates.

TABLE 6.2 Types of the CodeDom Namespace to Declare Type Structures

CodeDom Type to Build Types	Description
`CodeTypeDeclaration`	Declares a class, structure, enumeration, or interface. The underlying type definition corresponds to one of the properties such as `IsClass`, `IsInterface`, `IsStruct`, and `IsEnum`.
`CodeTypeDeclarationCollection`	Declares a type collection.
`CodeTypeDelegate`	Declares a delegate.

You are familiar with the hierarchy structure of a C# program. A namespace contains a number of types. A type contains a number of members (properties, methods, and events). The `System.CodeDom` namespace contains types to declare a number of members. Table 6.3 presents the type items to perform these functions.

In the experience of a software developer, most of the coding occurs inside method implementations. `System.CodeDom` namespace provides numerous types that can program various looping and decision constructs, code comments, and structured exception handling logic (`try`,

TABLE 6.3 Types of the CodeDom Namespace to Build Members

CodeDom Type to Build Member	Description
`CodeConstructor`	Makes a constructor for a type
`CodeEntryPoint`	Makes an entry point method of a program with default attributes (for example, `Main()`)
`CodeMemberEvent`	Makes an event declaration for a class
`CodeMemberField`	Declares code of a field within a class
`CodeMemberMethod`	Declares code of a method within a class
`CodeMemberProperty`	Declares code of a property declaration within a class
`CodeParameterDeclarationExpression`	Declares code for a parameter of a member
`CodeTypeConstructor`	Represents the static constructor for a class. A static constructor is called when the type is loaded.
`CodeTypeMember`	Uses an abstract base class to start a member within a type
`CodeTypeMemberCollection`	Declares a collection of members within a defined type
`MemberAttributes`	Declares attributes with identifiers that are used by `CodeTypeMember`

`catch`, `finally`, and `throw`). An exhaustive description of these many `System.CodeDom` types is beyond the scope of this book. Our next example, however, will cover a number of them.

The LastCodeDom Example

The CodeDom example you will now build is a console application (written in C#) named LastCodeDom. The program will perform a number of steps to generate a set of CodeDom segments. You will use many of the types and methods discussed earlier to declare a namespace, two classes, and one method for each class. By completing the example, you will learn how to use CodeDom methods to do the following:

- Display a console window for a target language prompt.
- Programmatically write an application including a namespace, data types, fields, properties, and methods.
- Programmatically construct code statement to invoke methods from an existing assembly. Most of the fun occurs here.
- Dynamically compile the assembly under construction.

- Dynamically execute the assembly after building.
- Display the results on the console screen.

The basic idea here is to let you have the opportunity to use the types of the `System.CodeDom` to program various code segments. The targeted source code is in Listing 6.4, and seems much simpler than the CodeDom example itself. However, you will extend what you learned from this example to the next chapters to complete the AutomatedTest project.

Listing 6.4 The Targeted C# Source Code to Be Generated by the *LastCodeDom* Example

```
// This program uses the LowLevelObj.SimpleMath class
namespace UseMyCalc {
    using System;
    using LowLevelObj;


    public class TestMyCalculator {

        private System.Double result;

        private Math_ENUM operation;

        public TestMyCalculator() {
        }

        private Math_ENUM p_Operation {
            get {
                return this.operation;
            }
            set {
                operation = value;
            }
        }

        public void UseMyCalculator(int x, int y) {
            if ((y == 0)) {
                Console.WriteLine("Caution, a number is divided by zero!!!");
            }
            SimpleMath myCalc = new SimpleMath();
            for (int i = 0; (i < 4); i = (i + 1)) {
                operation = (Math_ENUM)i;
                try {
                    result = myCalc.SimpleCalc(x, y, operation);
                }
                catch (System.Exception e) {
                    Console.WriteLine("Error: " + e.Message);
                }
```

```
                Console.WriteLine(x + "" + y + "" +
➥operation.ToString()+ ""  + result);
            }
        }
    }

    public class RunCodeDomCode {

        public static void Main() {
            TestMyCalculator TestMyCalc = new TestMyCalculator();
            TestMyCalc.UseMyCalculator(45, 10);
        }
    }
}
```

The main purpose of the code in Listing 6.4 is to execute the `SimpleCalc()` method of the `LowLevelObj.SimpleMath` class. If you are interested in exercising more of the CodeDom techniques, you can add more functionality to the program.

Making the *Main()* Method

The LastCodeDom example is a console application that is driven by a `Main()` method performing each aspect of the listed specification. As you did with the other software code you have developed, you start a new project by running the Microsoft Visual Studio .NET IDE. Name this one LastCodeDom and save it in the `C:\SourceCode\Chapter06` folder.

TIP At this point, I recommend that you copy `LowLevelObj.dll` from `C:\SourceCode\Chapter04\LowLevelObj\Bin\Debug` to the LastCodeDom project local folder, `C:\SourceCode\Chapter06\LastCodeDom\bin\Debug`, so you can debug and test-run this project during coding.

For the coding, you'll start with some `using` statements and the `namespace` definition. Listing 6.5 shows the `Main()` method with the namespace, class, and references declarations.

Listing 6.5 C# code of the *Main()* Method using the *System.CodeDom* for the *AutoMyCalculator* Class and the *LastCodeDom* Namespace

```
using System;
using System.CodeDom;
using System.CodeDom.Compiler;
using Microsoft.CSharp;
using Microsoft.VisualBasic;
using System.IO;
using System.Reflection;

namespace LastCodeDom
```

```
{
   class AutoMyCalculator
   {
      private static ICodeGenerator iCG;
      private static ICodeCompiler iCC;
      private static string CSorVB;
      private static string asmName;

      [STAThread]
      static void Main(string[] args)
      {
         // Request an input for desired language.
         Console.Write("Enter CS for C# or VB for VB.NET: ");
         CSorVB = Console.ReadLine();

         // Set up the language providers.
         switch(CSorVB.ToUpper())
         {
            case "cs":
            case "CS":
               PrepareCSharpFactory(ref CSorVB);
               break;
            case "vb":
            case "VB":
               PrepareVBNETFactory(ref CSorVB);
               break;
            default:
   Console.WriteLine("Usage:

               CSorVB = null;
               break;
         }


   //check if the entry is a valid language supported by CodeDom
         if(CSorVB != null)
         {
      // Write the code graph in memory into a physical file
            CreateFile(CSorVB, ref iCG);
            Console.WriteLine("Save completed.");

            // Now compile the code into a .NET DLL.
            Console.WriteLine("Compiling code...");
            CreateAssmply(iCC, CSorVB);

            // Now launch the application!
            RunAssembly();
            Console.WriteLine("End of the LastCodeDom");
         }
      }
   }
}
```

At the beginning of the class, two interface instances are declared, `ICodeGenerator` and `ICodeCompiler`. Then, the code declares a string variable, `CSorVB`, for the source code provider identifier, and another string variable, `asmName`, for the assembly name.

The purpose of the `Main()` entry point method is to call a few helper methods to do the following:

1. Read an input from the prompt.
2. Create a code provider object.
3. Prepare the code and save the code graph from memory to a physical file.
4. Build the code into an assembly.
5. Finally, execute the application.

In the first step, the input from the prompt is read to determine whether to create a `CSharpCodeProvider` object or a `VBCodeProvider` object. A `switch` statement is used to call either the `PrepareCSharpFactory()` helper method to make a C# provider or the `PrepareVBNETFactory()` helper method to make a VB .Net code provider.

If the user enters CS to specify C# as the source code target, the `PrepareCSharpFactory()` method is called. It prepares a `CSharpCodeProvider` object. This object sets up the interface references of `CreateGenerator` and `CreateCompiler`, respectively. The code for this method is in Listing 6.6.

Listing 6.6 Code for the *PrepareCSharpFactory()* Helper Method

```
private static void PrepareCSharpFactory(ref string CSorVB)
{
   CSorVB = "cs";
   CSharpCodeProvider cscp = new CSharpCodeProvider();
   iCG = cscp.CreateGenerator();
   iCC = cscp.CreateCompiler();
}
```

If the user enters VB for the source code target, the program calls the `PrepareVBNETFactory()` method to create a `VBCodeProvider` object and set up the respective interface references. The code for this method is in Listing 6.7.

Listing 6.7 Code for the Helper *PrepareVBNETFactory()* Method

```
private static void PrepareVBNETFactory(ref string CSorVB)
{
   CSorVB = "vb";
   VBCodeProvider vbcp = new VBCodeProvider();
   iCG = vbcp.CreateGenerator();
   iCC = vbcp.CreateCompiler();
}
```

Reviewing the code in these two helper methods, you can see that the code providers support two interfaces: `ICodeGenerator` and `ICodeCompiler`. The `ICodeGenerator` has methods to create code in memory from CodeDom. The method defines namespaces, types, code statements, and so forth. The `ICodeGenerator` is defined by .NET developers as follows:

```
// an interface to generate source code using CodeDom.
public interface System.CodeDom.Compiler.ICodeGenerator
{
  bool IsValidIdentifier(string value);
  bool Supports(GeneratorSupport supports);
  string CreateEscapedIdentifier(string value);
  string CreateValidIdentifier(string value);
  string GetTypeOutput(CodeTypeReference type);
  void GenerateCodeFromCompileUnit(CodeCompileUnit e, TextWriter w,
➥CodeGeneratorOptions o);
  void GenerateCodeFromExpression(CodeExpression e, TextWriter w,
➥CodeGeneratorOptions o);
  void GenerateCodeFromNamespace(CodeNamespace e,  TextWriter w,
➥CodeGeneratorOptions o);
  void GenerateCodeFromStatement(CodeStatement e, TextWriter w,
➥CodeGeneratorOptions o);
  void GenerateCodeFromType(CodeTypeDeclaration e, TextWriter w,
➥CodeGeneratorOptions o);
  void ValidateIdentifier(string value);
}
```

The other interface is the `ICodeCompiler`. It is defined by Microsoft developers as shown here, and it is used to compile a source code file into a .NET assembly:

```
// An interface to compile code into a .NET assembly.
public interface System.CodeDom.Compiler.ICodeCompiler
{
  CompilerResults CompileAssemblyFromDom(CompilerParameters options,
➥CodeCompileUnit compilationUnit);
  CompilerResults CompileAssemblyFromDomBatch(CompilerParameters options,
➥CodeCompileUnit[] compilationUnits);
  CompilerResults CompileAssemblyFromFile(CompilerParameters options,
➥string fileName);
  CompilerResults CompileAssemblyFromFileBatch(CompilerParameters options,
➥string[] fileNames);
  CompilerResults CompileAssemblyFromSource(CompilerParameters options,
➥string source);
  CompilerResults CompileAssemblyFromSourceBatch(CompilerParameters options,
➥string[] sources);
}
```

After the `Main()` method obtains a reference for each interface, an `if` statement is used to check whether the user enters a valid language target by checking the `CSorVB` variable. Then it calls the other helper methods to generate the code, build the assembly, and execute the application. In the next sections, I will examine each of the helper methods.

The *CreateFile()* Method

The `CreateFile()` method code, shown in Listing 6.8, generates a new `*.vb` or `*.cs` file and saves it in the current application directory. The `.vb` or `.cs` extension is determined by the passed parameter. The file naming strategy is similar to the first example; that is, a fixed name, `TestMyCalc.cs` or `TestMyCalc.vb`, will always be used for the resulting file. Then it calls the `CreateNamespace()` method to create the code and save the file. At last, it closes the file.

Listing 6.8 The *CreateFile()* Method

```
// Create the a text file for the source code.
private static void CreateFile(string CSorVB, ref ICodeGenerator iCG)
{
   string fileName = String.Format("TestMyCalc.{0}", CSorVB);
   TextWriter txtW = new StreamWriter (new FileStream(fileName,
➥FileMode.Create));

   CreateNamespace(iCG, txtW);
   txtW.Close();
}
```

CreateNamespace() Using CodeDom

The `CreateNamespace()` method uses various classes and methods of the CodeDom namespace. It creates two field members, two type classes, a property, a `UseMyCalculator()` method, and an entry point method for the target project. Thus, this is the method where most of the actions occur. The code segment of the CodeDom seems long (Listing 6.9). Sometimes it requires several lines to produce a simple statement. But it is useful and can be reused for software testing.

Listing 6.9 The Lengthy Code of the *CreateNamespace()* Method

```
private static void CreateNamespace(ICodeGenerator iCG, TextWriter w)
{
   // Add a comment at the beginning of the program.
   CodeCommentStatement c = new CodeCommentStatement(
➥"This program uses the LowLevelObj.SimpleMath class");
   iCG.GenerateCodeFromStatement(c, w, null);
```

```
// Declare the namespace.
CodeNamespace cnamespace =
   new CodeNamespace("UseMyCalc");

// Add reference to other namespaces.
cnamespace.Imports.Add(new CodeNamespaceImport ("System"));
cnamespace.Imports.Add(new CodeNamespaceImport ("LowLevelObj"));

// Insert the first Class.
CodeTypeDeclaration co = new CodeTypeDeclaration ("TestMyCalculator");
co.IsClass = true;
co.TypeAttributes = TypeAttributes.Public;
cnamespace.Types.Add(co);

// Add the default constructor.
CodeConstructor cstor = new CodeConstructor();
cstor.Attributes = MemberAttributes.Public;
co.Members.Add(cstor);

// add a double field.
CodeMemberField cf = new CodeMemberField("System.Double", "result");
cf.Attributes = MemberAttributes.Private;
co.Members.Add(cf);

//add a Math_ENUM field.
cf = new CodeMemberField("Math_ENUM", "operation");
cf.Attributes = MemberAttributes.Private;
co.Members.Add(cf);

// Add a p_Operation property.
CodeMemberProperty cp = new CodeMemberProperty();
cp.Name = "p_Operation";
cp.Attributes = MemberAttributes.Public | MemberAttributes.Final ;
cp.Type = new CodeTypeReference("Math_ENUM");

// Make a get statement.
cp.GetStatements.Add(new CodeMethodReturnStatement
   (new CodeFieldReferenceExpression(new
   CodeThisReferenceExpression(), "operation")));

// Make a set statement.
cp.SetStatements.Add(new CodeAssignStatement(
   new CodeArgumentReferenceExpression("operation"),
   new CodeArgumentReferenceExpression("value")));
co.Members.Add (cp);

// Make a UseMyCalculator() method.
CodeMemberMethod cm = new CodeMemberMethod();
cm.Name = "UseMyCalculator";
cm.Attributes = MemberAttributes.Public | MemberAttributes.Final ;
cm.Parameters.Add(new CodeParameterDeclarationExpression(
➥"System.Int32", "x"));
```

```
    cm.Parameters.Add(new CodeParameterDeclarationExpression(
➥"System.Int32", "y"));


    //Make an if statement
    CodeFieldReferenceExpression cLeft=new CodeFieldReferenceExpression(
➥null, "y");

    CodeFieldReferenceExpression cRight = new CodeFieldReferenceExpression(
➥null, "0");

    CodeExpression[] pCode = new CodeExpression[]{new
➥CodeFieldReferenceExpression(null,
"\"Caution, a number is divided by zero!!!\"")};

    CodeConditionStatement ifState = new CodeConditionStatement(new
➥CodeBinaryOperatorExpression(cLeft, CodeBinaryOperatorType.ValueEquality,
➥cRight), new CodeExpressionStatement(new CodeMethodInvokeExpression(null,
➥"Console.WriteLine", pCode)));
    cm.Statements.Add(ifState);

    //make a new object (SimpleMath myCalc = new SimpleMath();)
    CodeVariableDeclarationStatement DclNew = new
➥CodeVariableDeclarationStatement("SimpleMath", "myCalc",
       new CodeVariableReferenceExpression("new SimpleMath()"));
    cm.Statements.Add(DclNew);

    //the following segment Makes a for loop

    //Make a try-catch statment
    cLeft=new CodeFieldReferenceExpression(null, "result");
    cRight=new CodeFieldReferenceExpression(null,
➥"myCalc.SimpleCalc(x, y, operation)");

    CodeStatement[] trySt;
    CodeExpression[] passPar = new CodeExpression[]{new
➥CodeFieldReferenceExpression(null, "xResult, shtRow, mName")};

    trySt = new CodeStatement[] {new CodeAssignStatement(cLeft, cRight),
    };

    passPar = new CodeExpression[]{new CodeFieldReferenceExpression(null,
➥"\"Error: \" + e.Message")};

    CodeCatchClause catchCl = new CodeCatchClause("e", new
➥CodeTypeReference(typeof(Exception)), new CodeExpressionStatement(new
➥CodeMethodInvokeExpression(null, "Console.WriteLine", passPar)));

    CodeCatchClause[] catchSt = new CodeCatchClause[]{ catchCl
                                };
    //make an assignment <operation = i>
```

```
        cLeft=new CodeFieldReferenceExpression(null, "operation");
        if (CSorVB.ToUpper() == "CS")
            cRight=new CodeFieldReferenceExpression(null, "(Math_ENUM)i");
        else
            cRight=new CodeFieldReferenceExpression(null, "CType(i, Math_ENUM)");

    //Make a statement to invoke the Console.WriteLine method
        CodePropertyReferenceExpression pState =
            new CodePropertyReferenceExpression(null, "Console");

        if (CSorVB.ToUpper() == "CS")
        {

            pCode = new CodeExpression[]{new CodeFieldReferenceExpression(null,
➥"x + \"\t\" + y + \"\t\" + operation.ToString()+ \"\t\"  + result")};
        }
        else //Make a VB.NET code
        {
            pCode = new CodeExpression[]{new CodeFieldReferenceExpression(null,
➥"x & \" \" & y & \" \" & operation.ToString() & \" \" & result")};
        }

        //Wrap the above in the for loop
        CodeIterationStatement forLoop = new CodeIterationStatement(
            new CodeVariableDeclarationStatement("System.Int32", "i", new
➥CodePrimitiveExpression(0)),
            new CodeBinaryOperatorExpression(
            new CodeFieldReferenceExpression(null, "i"),
            CodeBinaryOperatorType.LessThan,
            new CodePrimitiveExpression(4)
            ),
            new CodeAssignStatement(
            new CodeFieldReferenceExpression(null, "i"),
            new CodeBinaryOperatorExpression(new CodeFieldReferenceExpression(
➥null, "i"),
            CodeBinaryOperatorType.Add,
            new CodePrimitiveExpression(1))
            ),
            new CodeStatement[]
        {
            new CodeAssignStatement(cLeft, cRight),
            new CodeTryCatchFinallyStatement(trySt, catchSt),
            new CodeExpressionStatement(new CodeMethodInvokeExpression(pState,
➥"WriteLine", pCode))
        }
            );
        cm.Statements.Add(forLoop);
        co.Members.Add(cm);

        //Make a RunCodeDomCode class
        co = new CodeTypeDeclaration("RunCodeDomCode");
```

```
      co.IsClass = true;
      co.TypeAttributes = TypeAttributes.Public;
      cnamespace.Types.Add(co);

      //Make an entry point Main method
      CodeEntryPointMethod entryCM = new CodeEntryPointMethod();

      //declare a new TestMyCalculator object
      DclNew = new CodeVariableDeclarationStatement("TestMyCalculator",
➥"TestMyCalc",
         new CodeVariableReferenceExpression("new TestMyCalculator()"));


      entryCM.Statements.Add(DclNew);
      //Make statement to involve a method
      pState =
         new CodePropertyReferenceExpression(null, "TestMyCalc");
         pCode = new CodeExpression[]{new CodeFieldReferenceExpression(
➥null, "45, 10")};
      entryCM.Statements.Add(new CodeMethodInvokeExpression(pState,
➥"UseMyCalculator", pCode));

      co.Members.Add(entryCM);

      // Finally, generate the code.
      iCG.GenerateCodeFromNamespace (cnamespace, w, null);
   }
```

The order in which you write the program by the CodeDom is similar to the order you might use to compose a C# program by hand. The first statement creates a comment. Then you begin to give a name for the namespace, `UseMyCalc`, and add two `using` statements for the needed references. Let's examine the code based on statements:

```
      // Add a comment at the beginning of the program.
         CodeCommentStatement c = new CodeCommentStatement(
➥"This program uses the LowLevelObj.SimpleMath class");
      iCG.GenerateCodeFromStatement(c, w, null);

      // Declare the namespace
      CodeNamespace cnamespace =
         new CodeNamespace("UseMyCalc");

      // Add statement for references to other namespaces.
      cnamespace.Imports.Add(new CodeNamespaceImport ("System"));
      cnamespace.Imports.Add(new CodeNamespaceImport ("LowLevelObj"));
```

After generating a comment, the code segments declare a namespace and add two `using` statements.

Then, the code initializes the building of the TestMyCalculator class. The isClass property of the CodeTypeDeclaration object is set to be true. The attribute of the CodeTypeDeclaration object is set to be public. Immediately, the CodeNamespace.Types.Add() method adds the class to the namespace using the following code:

```
// Make the first Class.
CodeTypeDeclaration co = new CodeTypeDeclaration ("TestMyCalculator");
co.IsClass = true;
co.TypeAttributes = TypeAttributes.Public;
cnamespace.Types.Add(co);
```

In this example, the TestMyCalculator class needs only a default constructor, two private fields, and a property. CodeDom code for these constructions is easy to understand:

```
// Make the default constructor.
   CodeConstructor cstor = new CodeConstructor();
   cstor.Attributes = MemberAttributes.Public;
   co.Members.Add(cstor);

   // Make a double field.
   CodeMemberField cf = new CodeMemberField("System.Double", "result");
   cf.Attributes = MemberAttributes.Private;
   co.Members.Add(cf);

   //add a Math_ENUM field
   cf = new CodeMemberField("Math_ENUM", "operation");
   cf.Attributes = MemberAttributes.Private;
   co.Members.Add(cf);

   // Make a p_Operation property.
   CodeMemberProperty cp = new CodeMemberProperty();
   cp.Name = "p_Operation";
   cp.Attributes = MemberAttributes.Public | MemberAttributes.Final ;
   cp.Type = new CodeTypeReference("Math_ENUM");

   //Make the get statement.
   cp.GetStatements.Add(new CodeMethodReturnStatement
      (new CodeFieldReferenceExpression(new
      CodeThisReferenceExpression(), "operation")));

   //Make the set statement.
   cp.SetStatements.Add(new CodeAssignStatement(
      new CodeArgumentReferenceExpression("operation"),
      new CodeArgumentReferenceExpression("value")));
   co.Members.Add (cp);
```

Look at the preceding code. After the definition of each member, an `Add()` method is called. For the property code generation, you need to make a `get` and a `set` statement before the `Add()` method is called.

Next, the code to build the `UseMyCalculator()` method needs some attention. The generated code is quite simple: it has an `if` statement, a `for` loop, a `try-catch` statement within the `for` loop, and a few other simple expressions. Thus, the code covers a broad range of CodeDom techniques. From this program, you will learn how to use the CodeDom classes in Table 6.4 to accomplish rather complex code.

TABLE 6.4 Summary of the Frequently Used Classes of the `System.CodeDom` Namespace

CLASS	DESCRIPTION
`CodeArgumentReferenceExpression`	Declares a reference to an argument.
`CodeAssignStatement`	Declares a simple assignment statement.
`CodeBinaryOperatorExpression`	Declares an expression that consists of a binary operation between two expressions.
`CodeCatchClause`	Declares a catch exception block.
`CodeCommentStatement`	Declares a statement consisting of a single comment.
`CodeCompileUnit`	Provides a top-level object to use for compilation.
`CodeConditionStatement`	Declares a conditional branch statement, typically represented as an `if` statement.
`CodeConstructor`	Declares the declaration of an instance constructor for a type.
`CodeEntryPointMethod`	Declares the entry point of an executable.
`CodeExpression`	Declares a code expression. This is a base class for other code expression objects and is never instantiated.
`CodeExpressionStatement`	Declares a statement that consists of a single expression.
`CodeFieldReferenceExpression`	Declares a reference to a field.
`CodeIterationStatement`	Declares a `for` statement, or a simple loop through a block of statements, using a test expression as a condition for continuing to loop.
`CodeMemberMethod`	Declares a declaration for a method of a class.
`CodeMemberProperty`	Declares a declaration for a property of a class.
`CodeMethodInvokeExpression`	Declares an expression that invokes a method.
`CodeMethodReturnStatement`	Declares a return statement.

TABLE 6.4 CONTINUED Summary of the Frequently Used Classes of the `System.CodeDom` Namespace

CLASS	DESCRIPTION
`CodeNamespace`	Declares a namespace declaration.
`CodeNamespaceImport`	Declares a namespace import directive that indicates a namespace to use.
`CodeParameterDeclarationExpression`	Declares a parameter declaration for a method, property, or constructor.
`CodePrimitiveExpression`	Declares a primitive data type value.
`CodePropertyReferenceExpression`	Declares a reference to a property.
`CodeSnippetExpression`	Declares a literal expression.
`CodeThisReferenceExpression`	Declares a reference to the current local class instance.
`CodeTryCatchFinallyStatement`	Declares a `try` block, with any number of catch clauses and, optionally, a `finally` block.
`CodeTypeDeclaration`	Declares a type declaration for a class, structure, interface, or enumeration.
`CodeTypeReference`	Declares a data type for CodeDom objects.
`CodeVariableDeclarationStatement`	Declares a declaration of a variable.
`CodeVariableReferenceExpression`	Declares an expression that references a local variable.

Each of these types represents a different code segment to be generated. For example, supposed you need to generate a code segment like the following:

```
Console.WriteLine(x + "" + y + "" + operation.ToString()+ ""  + result);
```

You need to use the `CodeMethodInvokeExpression` type that takes three parameters:

```
 CodePropertyReferenceExpression pState =
   new CodePropertyReferenceExpression(null, "Console");
      pCode = new CodeExpression[]{new CodeFieldReferenceExpression(null,
➥"x + \"\t\" + y + \"\t\" + operation.ToString()+ \"\t\"  + result")};
new CodeExpressionStatement(new CodeMethodInvokeExpression(pState, "WriteLine",
pCode));
```

The parameters have the following meanings:

- `pState` is the constructor argument, a new `CodePropertyReferenceExpression` object that represents the name of the type you wish to invoke
- `"WriteLine"` is the name of the method to be invoked
- `pCode` holds the parameters to be passed into the method

Another example is to use the `CodeCondition` type to build an `if` statement like the following:

```
if (y == 0) {
    Console.WriteLine("Caution, a number is divided by zero!!!");
}
```

The `if` statement reminds the user of not dividing a number by 0. Its corresponding CodeDom statements take a similar approach with the help of quite a few other CodeDom types:

```
...
//Make an if statement
CodeFieldReferenceExpression cLeft=new CodeFieldReferenceExpression(null, "y");
   CodeFieldReferenceExpression cRight = new CodeFieldReferenceExpression(
➥null, "0");
   CodeExpression[] pCode = new CodeExpression[]{new
➥CodeFieldReferenceExpression(null,
➥"\"Caution, a number is divided by zero!!!\"")};

   CodeConditionStatement ifState = new CodeConditionStatement(new
➥CodeBinaryOperatorExpression(cLeft, CodeBinaryOperatorType.ValueEquality,
➥cRight), new CodeExpressionStatement(new CodeMethodInvokeExpression(null,
➥"Console.WriteLine", pCode)));
   cm.Statements.Add(ifState);
...
```

These CodeDom types have the following meanings

- `cLeft = new CodeFieldReferenceExpression(null, "y")` and `cRight = new CodeFieldReferenceExpression(null, "0")` make a left, y, and a right, 0, element for the condition statement.
- The new initialization of `pCode` object is similar to the preceding code segment.
- `new CodeBinaryOperatorExpression(cLeft, CodeBinaryOperatorType.ValueEquality, cRight)`, servers as a parameter to initialize the `ifState` object, and uses the `cLeft` and `cRight` objects to write a line of C# code such as: `if y == 0`.
- `new CodeExpressionStatement(new CodeMethodInvokeExpression(null, "Console.WriteLine", pCode))` makes a true statement, that is, invokes the `Console.WriteLine()` method to write the contents stored by the `pCode` variable.

The constructor of the `CodeConditionStatement` has been overloaded three times. The example takes two parameters, one writes the condition statement, and the other writes the true statement. If you have a false statement, you add another CodeDom object as the third parameter. Then an `else`-statement will be added to the generated code. This example doesn't need an `else` statement. But, I believe, you can accomplish an `else` statement easily for an `if` statement when you need it. The third overload is the default constructor of the `CodeConditionStatement` class. You can use it to initialize a default object.

To invoke the `SimpleCalc()` method from the `SimpleMath` class of the `LowLevelObj` assembly, you need to instruct the CodeDom objects to write a statement that creates a new instance of the `LowLevelObj.SimpleMath` class. Let's look into the CodeDom statements:

```
    //make a new object (SimpleMath myCalc = new SimpleMath();)
    CodeVariableDeclarationStatement DclNew = new
➥CodeVariableDeclarationStatement("SimpleMath", "myCalc",
       new CodeVariableReferenceExpression("new SimpleMath()"));
    cm.Statements.Add(DclNew);
```

In these statements, it's important to know the following:

- The `CodeVariableDeclarationStatement` class takes three parameters for the class type, the assigned variable name, and invocation of the class constructor.
- The `cm.Statements.Add(DclNew)` statement adds this variable declaration into the method.

The rest of the code within the `UseMyCalculator()` method writes a `for` loop. The `for` loop has a loop assignment statement, a `try-catch` syntax, and a statement to write the `UseMyCalculator()` result to the console window. Let's look at the desired end code in C#:

```
for (int i = 0; (i < 4); i = (i + 1)) {
   operation = (Math_ENUM)i;
      try {
         result = myCalc.SimpleCalc(x, y, operation);
      }
      catch (System.Exception e) {
         Console.WriteLine("Error: " + e.Message);
      }
      Console.WriteLine(x + " " + y + " " + operation.ToString()
➥+ " " + result);
}
```

In the code of the LastCodeDom project, CodeDom statements are executed to create the assignment, the `try-catch`, and the method invocation expressions within the `for` loop .

For example, the assignment is created with the following CodeDom code to make a left and a right field reference expression:

```
...
//make an assignment <operation = i>
cLeft=new CodeFieldReferenceExpression(null, "operation");
if (CSorVB.ToUpper() == "CS")
   cRight=new CodeFieldReferenceExpression(null, "(Math_ENUM)i");
else
   cRight=new CodeFieldReferenceExpression(null, "CType(i, Math_ENUM)");
...
```

Later, a new `CodeAssignStatement(cLeft, cRight)` object as the first item of a `CodeStatement` array uses the new `cLeft` and `cRight` objects to make a line of code such as:

```
operation = (Math_ENUM)i;
```

Due to the different techniques of converting data types between C#.NET and VB .NET programming, an `if`-statement is implemented. The C# code creates an unboxing statement to convert variable `i` from an integer to a `Math_ENUM` data type. The VB .NET code uses a `CType()` method to do it.

Boxing and Unboxing

Boxing is used by a line of code to explicitly convert a value type to a type object or to any interface type implemented by this value type. It actually allocates an object instance and copies the value into the new object. For example, the following declaration initializes a value-type variable:

```
int i = 168;
```

A boxing operation can be applied on the variable `i`:

```
object box = i;   //Boxing
```

Unboxing is a programming method that explicitly converts an object from the type object to a value type or from an interface type to a value type that implements the interface. Continuing with the preceding example, unboxing can be applied on the box variable to convert it back to an integer object:

```
int j = (int)box;   // Unboxing
```

The corresponding `try-catch` CodeDom code is as follows:

```
...
//Make a try-catch statment
cLeft=new CodeFieldReferenceExpression(null, "result");
cRight=new CodeFieldReferenceExpression(null,
➥"myCalc.SimpleCalc(x, y, operation)");

CodeStatement[] trySt;
CodeExpression[] passPar = new CodeExpression[]{
➥new CodeFieldReferenceExpression(null, "xResult, shtRow, mName")};
trySt = new CodeStatement[] {new CodeAssignStatement(cLeft, cRight),
   };

passPar = new CodeExpression[]{new
➥CodeFieldReferenceExpression(null, "\"Error: \" + e.Message")};

CodeCatchClause catchCl = new CodeCatchClause("e",
➥new CodeTypeReference(typeof(Exception)), new CodeExpressionStatement(new
➥CodeMethodInvokeExpression(null, "Console.WriteLine", passPar)));
```

```
CodeCatchClause[] catchSt = new CodeCatchClause[]{ catchCl
    };
...
```

The following are the important parts to code a try-catch segment:

- The cLeft and cRight field reference expressions are for the try statement.
- The try statement is a code statement array. In this case, the length of the array is one (1) for the invocation of the SimpleCalc() method, which combines the cLeft and cRight expressions.
- The catch clause includes a new exception declaration and a method to write the error message to a console window.

Finally, the third expression is similar to the one you have coded for the if statement that writes on the console window. The difference is that this expression writes the result of the SimpleCalc() method execution instead of writing a simple error message.

After these three expressions are prepared, they will be added as statements into a for loop statement. The for loop CodeDom statement uses the following C# syntax:

```
//Wrap the above in the for loop
CodeIterationStatement forLoop = new CodeIterationStatement(
   new CodeVariableDeclarationStatement("System.Int32", "i",
new CodePrimitiveExpression(0)),
   new CodeBinaryOperatorExpression(
   new CodeFieldReferenceExpression(null, "i"),
      CodeBinaryOperatorType.LessThan,
      new CodePrimitiveExpression(4)
   ),
   new CodeAssignStatement(
      new CodeFieldReferenceExpression(null, "i"),
      new CodeBinaryOperatorExpression(new
CodeFieldReferenceExpression(null, "i"),

      CodeBinaryOperatorType.Add,
      new CodePrimitiveExpression(1))
   ),
   //end the initialization of the iteration
   new CodeStatement[]
   {
      new CodeAssignStatement(cLeft, cRight),
      new CodeTryCatchFinallyStatement(trySt, catchSt),
      new CodeExpressionStatement(new CodeMethodInvokeExpression(
pState, "WriteLine", pCode))
   }
      );
cm.Statements.Add(forLoop);
```

There are only two C# code statements in the preceding code snippet; each is separated from the rest of the code by a semicolon. The second statement is short and straightforward. But, the first one is rather complex and needs some explanation. To make it easy to analyze the code, you can divide the first statement into two parts. The first part starts from the `CodeIterationStatement forLoop` object declaration and ends at the comments before the `new CodeStatement[]` array, which starts the second part.

The first part has three subparts. First, it uses the `CodeVariableDeclarationStatement` class to declare an integer variable `i` and assigns `0` to `i` as the initial value. Second, it uses the `CodeBinaryOperatorExpression` class to set the test condition and make sure the value stored in variable `i` is less than 4. The last subpart enables the integer value stored in variable `i` to increase by one (1) for each iteration. Overall, the first part writes:

```
for (int i = 0; (i < 4); i = (i + 1))
```

The second part of the first statement includes the already declared statements of the assignment, the `try-catch` statement, and the method invocation statement. The end result is the following code segment in C#.NET language:

```
{
   operation = (Math_ENUM)i;
   try {
      result = myCalc.SimpleCalc(x, y, operation);
   }
   catch (System.Exception e) {
      Console.WriteLine("Error: " + e.Message);
   }
   Console.WriteLine(x + "" + y + "" + operation.ToString()
➥+ ""  + result);
}
```

The second statement, `cm.Statements.Add(forLoop)`, concludes the `UseMyCalculator()` method by simply adding the generated `for` loop into it. Then, the LastCodeDom project immediately executes a statement to complete the first class implementation:

```
co.Members.Add(cm);
```

The second class is prepared to build an EXE assembly, which has a simple entry point `Main` method to execute the `UseMyCalculator()` method of the first declared class. The CodeDom rational is similar to, but much more condensed than, the previous class and method.

After the second class is added to the namespace, the last statement in the `CreateNamespace()` method, `iCG.GenerateCodeFromNamespace(cnamespace, w, null);`, uses the code generator object of the CodeDom to generate the code for the specified namespace and saves it with a given filename, which is created in `CreateFile()` method in this case.

The *CreateAssembly ()* Method Makes Another Assembly

After the CreateNamespace() method is coded, you have almost completed this example. At this point, the C# code is automatically generated and saved. You should be able to use the csc.exe to compile the TestMyCalc.cs file and run the TestMyCalc.exe file. Or you can create a new C# console application by starting the Microsoft Visual Studio .NET IDE and adding the TestMyCalc.cs file to the project, building it, and running it. However, the CodeDom can build an assembly dynamically instead of using the csc.exe or building starting a new project. You should take advantage of this.

The CreateAssembly() method is going to make use of the created ICodeCompiler interface and build a .NET DLL assembly from the generated C# code. Listing 6.10 shows the code of this helper method.

Listing 6.10 Code of the *CreateAssembly()* Helper Method

```
private static void CreateAssmply(ICodeCompiler itfCC, string CSorVB)
{
   // Give a name to the assembly.
   asmName = String.Format("TestMyCalc{0}Asm", CSorVB.ToUpper());

   // Build the assembly.
   CompilerParameters parms = new CompilerParameters();
   parms.OutputAssembly = asmName + ".dll";

   parms.CompilerOptions = @"/t:library /r:C:\SourceCode\Chapter06\
➥LastCodeDom\Bin\Debug\LowLevelObj.dll";
   iCC.CompileAssemblyFromFile(parms,   String.Format("TestMyCalc.{0}",
CSorVB));
}
```

After you know how to use the CompileAssemblyFromFile() method from the interface, the code is more straightforward than before. It simply composes a string name for the assembly to be built. Then it assigns the correct arguments to the compiling parameters. Finally, the invocation of the CompileAssemblyFromFile() method accomplishes the entire task.

NOTE Notice that I have made this project a library assembly. If you remove the text /t:library from the parameter assignment of the CompileAssemblyFromFile() method, the method will compile this project into an executable assembly (.exe). I encourage you to try it and test-run the executable.

RunAssembly() Using Late Binding

Usually, after we develop a software application, we run it by issuing a command from a command window or double-clicking the executable. But test engineers who like to do things programmatically. Thus, you need to complete the final task to build the `RunAssembly()` helper method.

This method loads the auto-generated assembly into a new `AppDomain` and exercises the `TestMyCalculator` class using late binding. Let's code it and examine the code in Listing 6.11.

Listing 6.11 The Helper Method *RunAssembly()*

```
private static void RunAssembly()
{
   // Create an AppDomain to load the assembly.
   AppDomain appDomain = AppDomain.CreateDomain("TestMyCalculator");
   Assembly a = appDomain.Load(asmName);

   // Get the TestMyCalculator Class type.
   Type TestClass = a.GetType("UseMyCalc.TestMyCalculator");
   object obj = Activator.CreateInstance(TestClass);

   //Invoke the UseMyCalculator method
   MethodInfo mi = TestClass.GetMethod("UseMyCalculator");
   mi.Invoke(obj, new object[]{1234, 567});
}
```

In this method, the following occurs:

- The first two statements create an `AppDomain` object and an Assembly object using the assembly.
- Then, the `GetType()` method creates a `TestMyCalculator` object using the `Activator.CreateInstance()` method.
- Finally, the code invokes the `UseMyCalculator()` method. The project is completely coded. Next, you'll build it and run it.

Execution of the Auto-Generated Code

If you have entered both CS and VB to test the project previously, you should have in the `..\LastCodeDom\Bin\Debug` folder two source code files named `TestMyCalc.cs` and `TestMyCalc.vb`, respectively. Plus, you should have two assemblies named `TestMyCalcCSAsm.dll` and `TestMyCalcVBAsm.dll`, respectively. Figure 6.2 shows how Windows Explorer looks on my computer.

FIGURE 6.2
CodeDom-generated source code files and assemblies

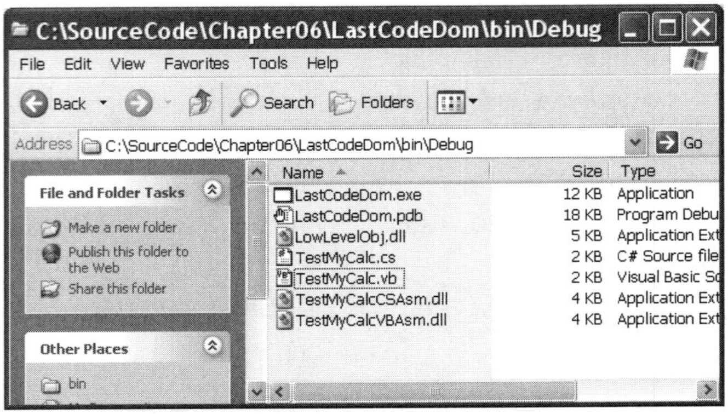

Now that the project is completed, you should build it and run it again to obtain the newest executable. I prefer to open a DOS command window for executing console applications:

1. Navigate to the folder `C:\SourceCode\Chapter06\LastCodeDom\bin\debug` using the change directory command.
2. Type **`LastCodeDom.exe`** and press Enter.
3. When the program prompts for target source code, type either **CS** or **VB** (not both) and press Enter. Within a millisecond or two, you have accomplished the following tasks:
   - Writing code for an application
   - Building an assembly
   - Running the assembly

If this is a software test task, your job is done and you are ready for the next adventure. Now your command window should look like the one shown in Figure 6.3.

FIGURE 6.3
The `LastCodeDom.exe` application in the console window.

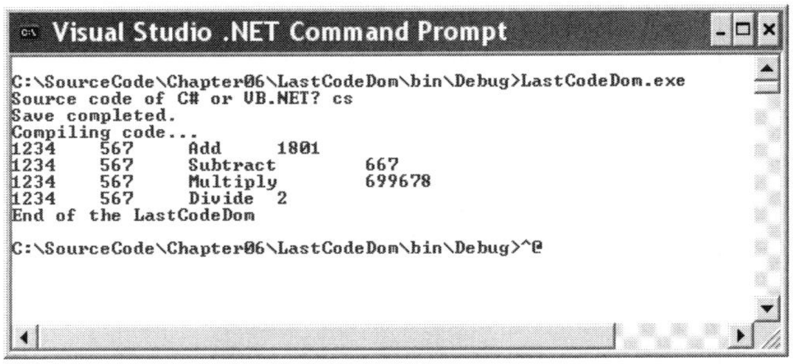

Running the `LastCodeDom.exe`, you invoked the `SimpleCalc()` method from the `LowLevelObj.SimpleMath` class, which obtained the results of the addition, subtraction, multiplication, and division of 1234 and 567.

Listing 6.12 shows the generated VB .NET source code (the C# code is shown in Listing 6.4).

Listing 6.12 The VB .NET Source Code Generated by the *LastCodeDom* Project

```
'This program uses the LowLevelObj.SimpleMath class
Imports System
Imports LowLevelObj

Namespace UseMyCalc

    Public Class TestMyCalculator

        Private result As Double

        Private operation As Math_ENUM

        Public Sub New()
            MyBase.New
        End Sub

        Public Property p_Operation As Math_ENUM
            Get
                Return Me.operation
            End Get
            Set
                operation = value
            End Set
        End Property

        Public Sub UseMyCalculator(ByVal x As Integer, ByVal y As Integer)
            If (y = 0) Then
                Console.WriteLine("Caution, a number is divided by zero!!!")
            End If
            Dim myCalc As SimpleMath = new SimpleMath()
            Dim i As Integer = 0
            Do While (i < 4)
                operation = CType(i, Math_ENUM)
                Try
                    result = myCalc.SimpleCalc(x, y, operation)
                Catch e As System.Exception
                    Console.WriteLine("Error: " + e.Message)
                End Try
                Console.WriteLine(x & " " & y & " " & operation.ToString() _
➥& " " & result)
                i = (i + 1)
            Loop
        End Sub
    End Class
```

```
        Public Class RunCodeDomCode

            Public Shared Sub Main()
                Dim TestMyCalc As TestMyCalculator = new TestMyCalculator()
                TestMyCalc.UseMyCalculator(45, 10)
            End Sub
        End Class
    End Namespace
```

Summary

In this chapter, you learned how to use the `System.CodeDom` namespace. You'll apply this knowledge to complete the AutomatedTest tool project in the upcoming chapters.

As a programmer, most of the time you will simply start Microsoft Visual Studio .NET and write the source code in the IDE. However, the `System.CodeDom` namespace in .NET provides many type classes to generate C#.NET or VB.NET code. When the CodeDom objects are initialized, the code to be generated is presented with the .NET types and implemented in memory. Finally, the object graph is committed to a physical code file. There are advantages to using the CodeDom namespace:

- The CodeDom namespace renders source code based on a single model. Therefore, source code could be generated for any language that supports the CodeDom specification.
- The CodeDom namespace writes code, compiles, and executes programs dynamically based on predefined software specification.
- The CodeDom provides a language-independent object mode representing the structure of source code in memory.

These are important features for generating test scripts for the AutomatedTest project. The test script generation is based on the information obtained using the Reflection namespace and the data store compositions at runtime, which were covered in previous chapters.

In the next chapters, you will use CodeDom techniques to enable the automatic code generation for the AutomatedTest project. Chapter 7 heavily involves the CodeDom methods in the AutomatedTest tool programming and generates a complete test script for general software test purposes.

In Chapter 8, the problems of testing parameters passed by objects and integration testing without the usual stubbing process will be solved. In Chapter 9, you will implement methods to generate test scripts for verification, validation, and presentation. In Chapter 10, you will add functions to complete all the automation configurations and put the last piece of the puzzle in the place. Chapter 11 will introduce a method on when and how to update the AutomatedTest project with new functions. And finally, in Chapter 12, you'll test the AutomatedTest tool.

Chapter 7

Generating Test Scripts

So far, this book has covered the basics of software testing, introduced some .NET fundamentals, and provided information on testing data storage. The rest of the book will be devoted to completing the AutomatedTest project.

By the end of Chapter 5, the AutomatedTest tool was capable of collecting information in detail from a given assembly. This has been a big task for test engineers when testing software manually and when using commercial testing tools. In Chapter 6, the `System.CodeDom` namespace was used to develop a program to write another program. In this chapter, we are going to make the process of generating the test scripts automatic as we have done for collecting testing information from an assembly.

Our code in this chapter will create CodeDom objects that write the actual testing program. When the code is added to the AutomatedTest tool, the project will be able to generate a test script for a given assembly. The test script will read an MS Excel worksheet with testing information stored, create a new Excel worksheet to store the test results, and then test each constructor, property, and method.

Restarting the AutomatedTest Project

As we have done before, we start this chapter by creating a folder, `C:\SourceCode\Chapter07`, and copying the AutomatedTest project to it. In this case, copy the AutomatedTest project from `C:\SourceCode\Chapter05` to the new folder. After adding a few more controls to the project and coding the project with the CodeDom namespace learned in Chapter 6, the AutomatedTest tool will be able to generate test scripts automatically by the end of this chapter.

Start the project from the new folder, activate the TestForm of the AutomatedTest project in the design editor, and add a new button control to the form. Give the button the following properties:

- Name: btnCreateScript
- Text: Create Script.

Since it doesn't take much, let's also add another button to terminate the application. Give the new button the following properties:

- Name: btnExit
- Text: Exit

After being built and run, the TestForm now looks like Figure 7.1.

FIGURE 7.1
The automated software test form with the new buttons

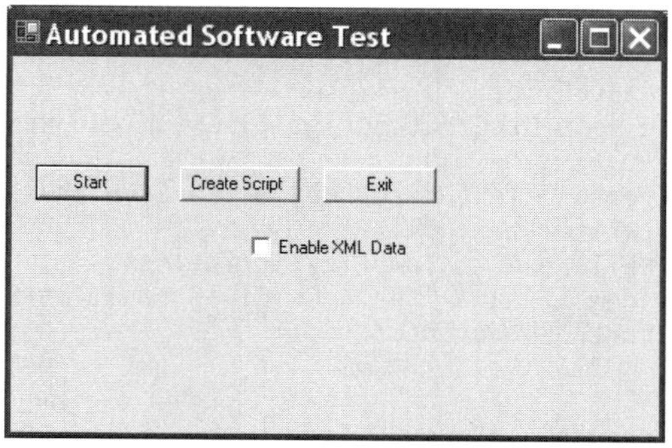

Not much has been changed for the TestForm since Chapter 5 except that it has two new buttons, one to create a test script and one to exit the application. It is easy to code the Exit button, so double-click the Exit button first and add one line of code at the cursor position to make the `btnExit_Click()` event handler look like Listing 7.1.

Listing 7.1 One Line of Code for the *btnExit_Click()* Event Handler to Terminate the AutomatedTest Application

```
private void btnExit_Click(object sender, System.EventArgs e)
{
   Application.Exit();
}
```

Next time you run the project and click the Exit button, you will exit the application. Now, if there are no `using` statements like the following in the `TestForm.cs` file, add them to the beginning of the file:

```
using System.CodeDom;
using System.CodeDom.Compiler;
```

Starting the Test Script Generation

At this point, with the TestForm open in the design editor, double-click the Create Script button. The TestForm.cs file opens in the code editor and your cursor is at the spot of the `btnCreateScript_Click()`event handler. You need to add C# code to create the script. All of the example source code in this book can be downloaded from `www.sybex.com` for your convenience. You can either copy or type the code segment to make the `btnCreateScript_Click()` event handler shown in Listing 7.2.

Listing 7.2 **Code for the *btnCreateScript_Click()* Event Handler**

```
string workFile;
private void btnCreateScript_Click(object sender, System.EventArgs e)
{
   //Create a TextWriter object to save the script
   TextWriter t = null;
   workFile = @"C:\Temp\TestScript.cs";
   t = new StreamWriter (new FileStream (workFile, FileMode.Create));
   //start generating script
   try
   {
      CreateTestCode(DUTAsm, t);
   }
   catch(Exception err)
   {
      MessageBox.Show(err.Message);
   }
   finally
   {
      t.Close();
   }
   //add code for CreateDataStoreCollection();
   //add code for StartDOTNETIDE();
   CloseExcelSheet();
}
```

The code segment in Listing 7.2 is readable. It first creates a `System.IO.TextWriter` object, `t`, to store the script to be generated. The filename is defined by the `workFile` string object. At this time, as in Chapter 5, the filenames are all fixed. However, in later chapters, you will program it to create names that are descriptive of testing different assemblies.In the `try-catch-finally` statement, it creates the script, or catches an error message, and closes the `TextWriter` object. At last, it closes the Excel application by calling the helper method `CloseExcelSheet()`, as shown in Listing 7.3. The Excel application was created for storing testing data by methods implemented in Chapter 5.

Before we code the other helper methods, this should be a good place for you to make a small modification for the `btnStart_Click()` event. Remember, you enabled the XML documentation for data store in Chapter 5. When XML documentation is available for testing data, there is no need for a pause for data editing. Once the Start button is clicked, the tester completes the tasks. The rest of the tasks are taken care of by the AutomatedTest tool. Thus, we need to add testing responsibilities to the Start button. The modification needs only one line of code to execute the `btnCreateScript_Click()` event at the end of the `btnStart_Click()` event. After this modification, the `btnStart_Click()` event looks similar to the following:

```
...
private void btnStart_Click(object sender, System.EventArgs e)
{
```

```
        GetAssemblyName();
        GetTypesOfAssemblyUnderTest();
        InitMethodInventory();
        if (chckXMLDataDoc.Checked)
        {
           MakeUseXMLDataStore();
           btnCreateScript_Click(sender, e);
        }
    }
    ...
```

The newly added line is bold. When the chckXMLDataDoc check box is checked, the AutomatedTest tool will compose the data store and obtain parameter values from the XML document to finish the test without a pause.

Then, you resume coding the helper methods for the btnCreateScript_Click() event. The code of the CloseExcelSheet() helper method is shown in Listing 7.3.

Listing 7.3 Code for the *CloseExcleSheet()* Method

```
private void CloseExcelSheet()
{
   xBook.Close(false, Missing.Value, false);
   xApp.Quit();
   xSheet = null;
   xBook = null;
   xApp = null;
}
```

The logic of the code in Listing 7.3 is straightforward; it closes an Excel application. At the beginning of the automatic test, it creates an Excel worksheet to provide testing data. After the data collection and test script generation, this method is executed to terminate the Excel application. First, it closes the Excel workbook. Then, it quits the Excel application. Finally, it sets all the Excel objects to null.

You learned about CodeDom in Chapter 6. But so far, you have not added any CodeDom code segments into the project. In the following sections, CodeDom will be heavily involved in the coding process. After you finish coding this chapter, you will be well versed in CodeDom.

Using CodeDom to Write Test Scripts

As a software test engineer, you are often informed that collecting information for a given assembly is important. Writing a meaningful test script is the final goal. After you finish coding the CreateTestCode() helper method for the AutomatedTest project, it will be able to generate test scripts, which have been considered tedious and time consuming for manual tests, and even for the commercial testing tools, which generate test scripts by reverse engineering or capture/replay methods. In this book, the AutomatedTest project will be enabled to generate a test script for an assembly or a class with full automation. One script tests an entire assembly or a class based on the preference of the tester. The advantage of one test script for testing a class is that after the test execution, this test script will return an object of the class under test. The returned object can then be reused for integration testing or for testing a method that passes a parameter by this object. Compared with using conventional stubbing or mock objects, testing an application against a real object provides deeper insight into the class under test and finds errors more effectively.

Next, you need to add the code in Listing 7.4 into the `TestForm.cs` file from the code editor. At first glance, you'll see that the code calls many methods to perform different tasks. Because many helper methods will be included in this method, their names should be descriptive to make sense when the code is reviewed.

Listing 7.4 Code of the *CreateTestCode()* Method Containing a Number of Fields and Helper Methods

```
//Declare fileds to access data store, create Type, Reflection
//and CodeDom objects needed by the CreateTestCode() method.
Excel.Range range;
string nameSpace;
string clsName = null;
Type typ = null;
Type[] types = null;;
CodeMemberMethod cm = null;
CodeDomProvider codeProvider = null;
ICodeGenerator cg = null;
CodeCompileUnit TestUnit;
CodeNamespace cnamespace;
CodeTypeDeclaration co;
CodePropertyReferenceExpression pState = null;
CodeExpression[] pCode = null;
CodeFieldReferenceExpression cLeft = null;
CodeFieldReferenceExpression cRight = null;

private void CreateTestCode(Assembly DUT, TextWriter t)
{
  //Call the CodeDom method to create the test script over headers
  StartCodeDom(DUT);
  AddNamespaceRefs(DUT);
  MakeFirstClassMethod();
  CreateExcelSheetCodes(cm);
  AddExcelHeaderCodes(cm);
  AddMoreMethodCodes(cm);
```

```
  //Information starts from row 2 of the Excel sheet
  int i=2;

  //Specify the first cell in the Excel worksheet
  range =xSheet.get_Range(TestUtility.ConvCHAR(1) + i,
➥TestUtility.ConvCHAR(1) + i);

  //Initiate an identifier to assure if a new class is under test
  string previousType = range.Value2.ToString();
  InitiateTypesUnderTest(i, ref previousType);

  int totalRows = CountSheetRows(xSheet);

  MethodInfo mi = null;
  ConstructorInfo ci = null; //added for constructor

  //Create a Type object for overloaded members
  Type[] AmbiguousOverLoad = null;
  string wholeCellText = null;
  string[] typeText = null;
  string strPar = null;
  string[] arrayPar = null;
  Excel.Range rng;
  Excel.Range rngCstr;

  //Start finding methods and parameters under tests
  for (i = 2; i < totalRows; i++)
  {
    //Make a counter for the column of a parameter
    int j = 3;

    DiscoverNewTypes(ref i, ref j, ref previousType);

    rng= xSheet.get_Range(TestUtility.ConvCHAR(j) + i,
➥TestUtility.ConvCHAR(j) + i);

    rngCstr = xSheet.get_Range(TestUtility.ConvCHAR(1) + i,
➥TestUtility.ConvCHAR(1) + i);

//check if the member is a constructor
    if (range.Value2.ToString() == rngCstr.Value2.ToString())
    {
      AddTestConstructorCodes(ref i, ref j, ref rng, ref wholeCellText,
➥ref typeText, ref strPar, ref arrayPar, ref AmbiguousOverLoad, ref ci);
    }
    else //the member is a method or a property
    {
      AddTestMethodCodeI(ref i, ref j, ref mi, ref rng, ref wholeCellText,
➥ref typeText, ref strPar, ref arrayPar, ref AmbiguousOverLoad);

      ParameterInfo[] ps = mi.GetParameters();
```

```
        string parStr="";

        //Use counter j to enumerate parameters
        CollectParametersForTest(ref i, ref j, ref rng, ref ps, ref parStr);

      //Code to write the name of method into the result report
        pState = new CodePropertyReferenceExpression(null, "obj" + typ.Name);
        pCode = new CodeExpression[]{new CodeFieldReferenceExpression(null,
➥parStr)};
        CodeStatement[] trySt = null;
        CodeExpression[] passPar = new CodeExpression[]{new
➥CodeFieldReferenceExpression(null, "xResult, shtRow, mName")};

        //Code the execution of the method under test
        AddInvokeTestMethodCallCode(ref i, ref parStr, ref mi, ref trySt,
➥ref passPar);

        //add log result code
        int colPosition = 0;
        LogParmResultAndReturnValue(ref i, colPosition, ps, ref mi);
      }
      range =xSheet.get_Range(TestUtility.ConvCHAR(1) + i,
➥TestUtility.ConvCHAR(1) + i);
    }

    //Add code to deal with the test report afterwards
    AddOtherCodesPartII(cm, clsName);

    if (objReturnStub == null)//add for COM test
      objReturnStub = new CodeSnippetExpression("null");

    //add a return statement return an object from the test script
    //for integration testing before the method is concluded
    cm.Statements.Add(new CodeMethodReturnStatement(objReturnStub));

    //Empty the returnObject for the next test
    objReturnStub = null;

    //Conclude the CodeDom coding by dump all the code into a pool
    AddUpClassesMethods();
    cg.GenerateCodeFromNamespace(cnamespace, t, null);
    //Add more code for further automation in later chapters
  }
```

In the Listing 7.4, the code at the beginning declares a series of private fields. The main purpose of these fields is to create various `System.CodeDom` objects. The `Excel.Range` object, `range`, is for the iteration of all the cells that contain the testing information on an MS Excel worksheet. The string fields, variables of `nameSpace` and `clsName`, are used to extrapolate a name for the namespace and a name for the class for testing the given assembly.

After the declaration of the fields, the `CreateTestCode()` method declaration takes two parameters. Of course, the first one must be the given assembly under test. The second one is the TextWriter object to help save the generated test script. The first part of this method calls other helper methods:

```
...
    StartCodeDom(DUT);
    AddNamespaceRefs(DUT);
    MakeFirstClassMethod();
    CreateExcelSheetCodes(cm);
    AddExcelHeaderCodes(cm);
    AddMoreMethodCodes(cm);
...
```

The first line calls the `StartCodeDom()` method to create the needed `System.CodeDom` objects. Then, the `AddNamespaceRefs()` method creates the required `using` statements. Finally, the code calls methods to create codes for a class, a method, an MS Excel worksheet, and so on. These methods will be coded and explained one by one in the rest of this chapter.

Next, within the `CreateTestCode()` method, some CodeDom methods are used to write more code. This happens within a `for` loop. The integer variable `i` is a counter which is initialized to be 2 in the `for`-loop. This initialization points to the first row in which the testing data is stored in the open MS Excel worksheet. Then, the `get_Range()` method of the worksheet accesses the name of the class under test from the MS Excel worksheet cell by cell in the first column (column A).

In case there is more than one type under test listed in column A, a `previousType` variable is declared. The `InitiateTypesUnderTest()` method will be implemented later to compare each value obtained by the `get_Range()` method with the preceding cell. The `totalRow` variable determines how many methods need to be tested in the MS Excel worksheet.

After the declaration of the `ConstructorInfo` and `MethodInfo` objects, the `AmbiguousOverload` Type object is declared to solve the problem of a method which is overloaded several times. Sometimes a class has more than one method carrying the same method name or more than one constructor that does the same thing but takes different parameters. This programming technique is termed overloading. A fully automated testing tool should be able to test the correct overloading method based on the testing data store. This has not been an issue for the available testing tools when the decision of testing which method is made manually by users. In Listing 7.4, the `AmbiguousOverload` is a `Type` array object. When the AutomatedTest tool loads a method to test from the data store, the data type information of the parameters required by this method is assigned as item values to the `AmbiguousOverload` array. Then, the tool searches the assembly under test for the method whose parameters match the types in the `AmbiguousOverload` array.

The string variables and string array variables declared are then able to help assign correct values to the AmbiguousOverload object.

All the code segments to test a method are written by an iteration of the for loop. The variable j is used to enumerate column by column in the same row i points to. The if statement determines whether this row is used to test a constructor or a method based on the text in the second column of the Excel test data store. Of course, the code to test a constructor is different from the code to test a method. Different constructors and methods will be handled by the methods called within the if-else decision maker.

During the execution of the CreateTestCode() method, a StartTest() method will be generated for each test script. The last statement of the StartTest() method is a return statement for a real and complete object of the class under test. The real object is stored in the objReturnStub field and is added to the StartTest() method by calling the cm.Statements.Add() method to pass a parameter of a new CodeMethodReturnStatement object.

After all the helper methods to generate the test script are called, the GenerateCodeFromNamespace() method saves the code with the help of TextWriter object, t. The rest of this chapter will proceed to the implementation for all of the helper methods.

Now, add the code for the StartCodeDom() method in Listing 7.5 into the project.

Listing 7.5 Code for the *StartCodeDom()* Helper Method

```
private void StartCodeDom(Assembly DUT)
{
  //Initiate CodeDom objects
  TestUnit = new CodeCompileUnit();
  types = DUT.GetTypes();
  codeProvider = new Microsoft.CSharp.CSharpCodeProvider();
  cg = codeProvider.CreateGenerator();

  //Use the namespace of the Type under to name the test script
  foreach (Type ty in types)
  {
    nameSpace = ty.Namespace + "Test";
  }
cnamespace = new CodeNamespace(nameSpace);

//Name the class of the test script
  clsName = "Test" + DUTAsm.FullName.Substring(0,
➥DUTAsm.FullName.IndexOf(", "));

  cg = codeProvider.CreateGenerator();
}
```

Armed with knowledge from the previous chapters, you should find the code in the `StartCodeDom()` method easy to read. First, the CodeDom objects are initialized. The `foreach` loop statement enumerates the type classes by using `System.Reflection` and finds out a proper name based on the given assembly for the `nameSpace` variable of the test script. The string variable `nameSpace` holds the name and initializes a `CodeNamespace` object, `cnamespace`. Next, it assigns a proper string value to the `clsName` variable. This name is to be used for the class name of the generated test script. Hereafter, objects of the Reflection namespace and Type class are used to investigate the assembly under test, and CodeDom objects are created and driven by the testing data store to write the test scripts.

Discovering Dependencies

When code of the .NET aware languages is compiled for the .NET Common Language Runtime (CLR), the .NET targeted compilers produce the metadata that describes all of the types contained in the executables (EXEs or DLLs). This metadata includes type information that you would typically find in a COM-type library and version dependency information. When executing or testing the application, the CLR looks to the assembly before loading to make sure that every dependency it needs to execute that code is available and proper. As you saw in the CodeDom examples in Chapter 6, you need to add references to these dependencies to a project and add `using`-statements for these references to the beginning of the C# source file. In order to fully automate the software testing process, these dependencies need to be discovered and the proper `using`-statements need to be added to the test script by the AutomatedTest tool. Thus, the topics introduced in Chapters 3 and 4 become useful. By using the Reflection namespace, the AutomatedTest project can discover the dependencies automatically. The next helper method adds dependencies into the test script by CodeDom to generate the respective `using` statement. Listing 7.6 lists the code for the `AddNamespaceRefs()` method.

Listing 7.6 Code to Import References to the Dependencies of the *AddNamespaceRefs()* Helper Method

```
private void AddNamespaceRefs(Assembly DUT)
{
  TestUnit.Namespaces.Add(cnamespace);
  cnamespace.Imports.Add(new CodeNamespaceImport("System"));
  cnamespace.Imports.Add(new CodeNamespaceImport("System.IO"));
  cnamespace.Imports.Add(new CodeNamespaceImport("Excel"));
  cnamespace.Imports.Add(new CodeNamespaceImport("System.Reflection"));


  AssemblyName[] asms = null;
  asms = DUT.GetReferencedAssemblies();

//the iteration finds all possible dependencies
```

```
    foreach (AssemblyName asm in asms)
    {
      if (asm.Name.ToString() != "mscorlib")
      {
        if (asm.Name.IndexOf(".")>0 && asm.Name != "")
          cnamespace.Imports.Add(new CodeNamespaceImport(asm.Name));
      }
    }
  }
```

Of the `AddNamespaceRefs()` method, the function of the first four lines calling for the `Imports.Add()` statements are obvious; they produce the following four `using` statements:

```
using System;
using System.IO;
using Excel;
using System.Reflection;
...
...
```

Every test script project needs these references, where the System namespace provides all the .NET basics. The `System.IO` namespace allows the test script to open and save files. The Excel namespace reads data from a test data store and saves testing results. The `System.Reflection` namespace will provide classes and methods for dynamical binding.

Then, an `Assembly.GetReferencedAssembly()` method is called to check what other namespaces the assembly under test has referred to. If it does refer to other namespaces, the `foreach` loop adds more `using` statements by namespace enumeration. But the `mscorlib.dll` file is not necessarily needed by the `using` statement, which is excluded by an `if` statement.

Next, you add a class and a method into the namespace object by coding the `MakeFirstClassMethod()` method (Listing 7.7).

NOTE The variables `co` and `cm` are the `CodeTypeDeclaration` and `CodeMemberMethod` objects. They will be initialized by the keyword `new` a few times when more classes and methods are needed for the test script to be generated.

Listing 7.7 Code of the *MakeFirstClassMethod()* to Generate a Class and a Method for the Test Script

```
private void MakeFirstClassMethod()
{
   //add class name
   co = new CodeTypeDeclaration(clsName);
   cnamespace.Types.Add(co);
   co.Attributes = MemberAttributes.Public;
```

```
        //add StartTest method
        cm = new CodeMemberMethod();
        cm.Name = "StartTest";

        //the StartTest method returns an object for the class under test
        //which can be used for integration test
        cm.ReturnType = new CodeTypeReference(typeof(object));

        //this is a public method
        cm.Attributes = MemberAttributes.Public | MemberAttributes.Final;
    }
```

In Listing 7.7, the `CodeTypeDeclaration` variable, `co`, makes a class with a name defined by the `clsName` string field. After the class declaration is added to the namespace declaration, the following line of code assigns a value `MemberAttributes.Public` as the attribute for this class. Then a `StartTest()` method is declared by the initialization of a `CodeMemberMethod` variable, `cm`. Its return type is an object. Returning an object of the class under test enables the AutomatedTest tool to test a higher-level module using this test script and test data stores. This approach avoids the stubbing procedures of the traditional testing processes and supplies a real object for integration testing. Finally, the attribute of the `StartTest()` method is defined as public to make it visible to other test script. Integration testing will be discussed in Chapter 8.

Programming the MS Excel Application

You wrote a program to create an Excel worksheet in Chapter 6. The strategy of initializing an Excel worksheet is to start an Excel application object from the highest hierarchy. Then, add a Workbook object and a Worksheet object into the application object. You can use a similar strategy to add the code segment for the `CreateExcelSheetCodes()` helper method in Listing 7.8 to the `TestForm.cs` file. This method generates the code for the test script to open an MS Excel worksheet for communicating with the saved data store and for recording the test result.

Listing 7.8 Adding the *CreateExcelSheetCodes()* Method to Generate Code for Starting an MS Excel Application

```
private void CreateExcelSheetCodes(CodeMemberMethod cm)
{
   //Initialize Excel objects for application, workbook and worksheet
   cm.Statements.Add(new CodeParameterDeclarationExpression(typeof(
➥Excel.Application), "xApp = new Excel.Application()"));

   //Open an existing Excel file
   cm.Statements.Add(new CodeParameterDeclarationExpression(typeof(
➥Excel.Workbook), "xBook = xApp.Workbooks.Open(fileName, 0, false, 1,
➥\"\", \"\", true, 1, 0, true, 1, 0, 0, 0, 0)"));

   //Make use of the active sheet
```

```
    cm.Statements.Add(new CodeParameterDeclarationExpression(typeof(
➥Excel.Worksheet), "xSheet = (Excel.Worksheet)xBook.ActiveSheet"));

    //Add a new workbook into the application to record test results
    cm.Statements.Add(new CodeParameterDeclarationExpression(typeof(
➥Excel.Workbook), "xBook2 = xApp.Workbooks.Add(1)"));

    //Create a new worksheet
    cm.Statements.Add(new CodeParameterDeclarationExpression(typeof(
➥Excel.Worksheet), "xResult = (Excel.Worksheet)xBook2.ActiveSheet"));
}
```

The name of the `CreateExcelSheetCode()` method makes sense. It is mainly a combination of the CodeDom and the Excel API programming. Each line of the code produces one line of code for an Excel property:

```
...
Excel.Application xApp = new Excel.Application();
Excel.Workbook xBook = xApp.Workbooks.Open(fileName, 0, false, 1, "",
➥"", true, 1, 0, true, 1, 0, 0, 0, 0);
Excel.Worksheet xSheet = (Excel.Worksheet)xBook.ActiveSheet;
Excel.Workbook xBook2 = xApp.Workbooks.Add(1);
Excel.Worksheet xResult = (Excel.Worksheet)xBook2.ActiveSheet;
...
```

NOTE This book assumes you have installed MS Excel XP in your system. The `Open()` method takes 15 parameters within the paratheses. If you have an earlier version of MS Excel (for example, MS Excel 2000) installed for your system, the `Open()`method takes only the first 13 parameters. Thus, you need to modify the corresponding code in Listing 7.8 to generate a line of code here: `Excel.Workbook xBook = xApp.Workbooks.Open(fileName, 0, false, 1, "", "", true, 1, 0, true, 1, 0, 0);`

After an Excel worksheet is open, information needs to be added. The `AddExcelHeaderCodes()` helper method (Listing 7.9) adds text for the header of the information collection. Add this method into the `TestForm.cs` file.

Listing 7.9 Adding the *AddExcelHeaderCodes()* Method

```
private void AddExcelHeaderCodes(CodeMemberMethod cm)
{
  //Make text headers for the result worksheet using one pattern
  CodePropertyReferenceExpression pState = null;
  CodeExpression[] pCode = null;

  pState =
    new CodePropertyReferenceExpression(null, "xResult");
  pCode = new CodeExpression[]{new CodeFieldReferenceExpression(null, "1, 1,
➥\"METHOD UNDER TEST\"")};
```

```
  cm.Statements.Add(new CodeMethodInvokeExpression(pState, "Cells.set_Item",
➥pCode));

  pCode = new CodeExpression[]{new CodeFieldReferenceExpression(null, "1, 2,
➥\"RESULT\"")};
  cm.Statements.Add(new CodeMethodInvokeExpression(pState, "Cells.set_Item",
➥pCode));

  pCode = new CodeExpression[]{new CodeFieldReferenceExpression(null, "1, 3,
➥\"ERROR MESSAGE\"")};
  cm.Statements.Add(new CodeMethodInvokeExpression(pState, "Cells.set_Item",
➥pCode));

  pCode = new CodeExpression[]{new CodeFieldReferenceExpression(null, "1, 4,
➥\"ACTUAL RETURN\"")};
  cm.Statements.Add(new CodeMethodInvokeExpression(pState, "Cells.set_Item",
➥pCode));

  pCode = new CodeExpression[]{new CodeFieldReferenceExpression(null, "1, 5,
➥\"EXPECTED RETURN\"")};
  cm.Statements.Add(new CodeMethodInvokeExpression(pState, "Cells.set_Item",
➥pCode));

  pCode = new CodeExpression[]{new CodeFieldReferenceExpression(null, "1, 6,
➥\"PARAMETERS AND VALUES\"")};
  cm.Statements.Add(new CodeMethodInvokeExpression(pState, "Cells.set_Item",
➥pCode));
}
```

This method does what its name implies by a series of coding patterns of the CodeDom statements. The `pCode` prepares a value for a pair of specified cell coordinates. For example, the value in the first `pCode` assignment is `"1, 1, \"METHOD UNDER TEST\""`. This assignment intends to generate a line of code to insert the text value `METHOD UNDER TEST` into row 1 and column 1 of the Excel worksheet. The `cm.Statements.Add()` method adds a similar statement to the test script. The code segment generated by this method is listed here:

```
...
xResult.Cells.set_Item(1, 1, "METHOD UNDER TEST");
xResult.Cells.set_Item(1, 2, "RESULT");
xResult.Cells.set_Item(1, 3, "ERROR MESSAGE");
xResult.Cells.set_Item(1, 4, "ACTUAL RETURN");
xResult.Cells.set_Item(1, 5, "EXPECTED RETURN");
xResult.Cells.set_Item(1, 6, "PARAMETERS AND VALUES");
...
```

In this code segment, within each `set_Item()` method, the first number indicates the row, the second number indicates the column of the result worksheet, and the text in the quotation marks is written into these cells.

The code in Listing 7.10, of the `AddMoreMethodCodes()` method, continues to add some more common code statements in the test script for any assemblies under test.

Listing 7.10 The *AddMoreMethodCodes()* Helper Method to Generate More Code

```
private void AddMoreMethodCodes(CodeMemberMethod cm)
{
  //Initiate related CodeDom objects
  CodePropertyReferenceExpression pState = null;
  CodeExpression[] pCode = null;
  CodeFieldReferenceExpression cLeft=null;
  CodeFieldReferenceExpression cRight=null;

  //Make the Excel application visible
  pCode=new CodeExpression[]{new CodeFieldReferenceExpression(null,
➥"xApp.Visible")};
  cLeft=new CodeFieldReferenceExpression(null, "xApp.Visible");
  cRight=new CodeFieldReferenceExpression(null, " true");

  cm.Statements.Add(new CodeAssignStatement(cLeft, cRight));

  //Make a range object for the first row of the worksheet
  //and change the color index and font
  cm.Statements.Add(new CodeParameterDeclarationExpression(typeof(
➥Excel.Range), "range"));
  cm.Statements.Add(new CodeParameterDeclarationExpression(typeof(
➥Excel.Range), "rangeCurr"));
  cLeft=new CodeFieldReferenceExpression(null, "range");
  cRight=new CodeFieldReferenceExpression(null, "xResult.get_Range(\"A1\",
➥\"H1\")");
  cm.Statements.Add(new CodeAssignStatement(cLeft, cRight));

  cLeft=new CodeFieldReferenceExpression(null, "range.Interior.ColorIndex");
  cRight=new CodeFieldReferenceExpression(null, "8");
  cm.Statements.Add(new CodeAssignStatement(cLeft, cRight));

  cLeft=new CodeFieldReferenceExpression(null, "range.Font.Bold");
  cRight=new CodeFieldReferenceExpression(null, " true");
  cm.Statements.Add(new CodeAssignStatement(cLeft, cRight));

  pState = new CodePropertyReferenceExpression(null, "range");
  cm.Statements.Add(new CodeMethodInvokeExpression(pState, "Columns.AutoFit"));

  //Declare a row counter to count the methods under test
  cm.Statements.Add(new CodeParameterDeclarationExpression(typeof(int),
➥"shtRow = 0"));

  //Declare a variable to get the name of the method
  cm.Statements.Add(new CodeParameterDeclarationExpression(typeof(string),
➥"mName = null"));

//Declare integer variable in case of passing array parameters
  cm.Statements.Add(new CodeParameterDeclarationExpression(typeof(int),
➥"tempArrayIndex = 0"));
}
```

Here is the output of this method:

```
...
xApp.Visible =  true;
Excel.Range range;
Excel.Range rangeCurr;
range = xResult.get_Range("A1", "H1");
range.Interior.ColorIndex = 8;
range.Font.Bold =  true;
range.Columns.AutoFit();
int shtRow = 0;
string mName = null;
int tempArrayIndex = 0;
...
```

These statements mainly assign values to the declared global variables of a test script, which are similar across different scripts for different assemblies under test. Starting from this point, the code segments generated later will be unique for each given assembly. The generated code won't be listed in the rest of the chapter. It's more important to understand the meaning of each line of code, therefore, the discussion will focus on the test logic instead of coding techniques.

Enumerating Type Information

Let's go back to Listing 7.4 and look at the code excerpt:

```
...
int i=2;

   range =xSheet.get_Range(TestUtility.ConvCHAR(1) + i,
➥TestUtility.ConvCHAR(1) + i);
   string previousType = range.Value2.ToString();
   InitiateTypesUnderTest(i, ref previousType);
...
```

The creation of the integer object `i` is to trace the methods under test by using a row index of the Excel data store. Whenever the `i` variable gets incremented by 1, the `range` object gets a new value. The `previousType` variable checks whether the type class under test changes and whether there are multiple types present in the Excel worksheet. After these are done, it calls the `InitiateTypesUnderTest()` method, which is coded as shown in Listing 7.11.

Listing 7.11 The *InitiateTypesUnderTest()* Helper Method to Discover Type Information

```
//initialize an object for the StartTest method to return an object
//in order to use a bottom up approach for integration testing.
CodeSnippetExpression objReturnStub;

private void InitiateTypesUnderTest(int i, ref string previousType)
{
  //Check if the class under test changes from the previous one
```

```
    foreach (Type ty in types)
    {
      if (ty.Name.ToString() == previousType)
      {
        typ = ty;
      }
    }

    //obtain the namespace of the type under test
    string nameSPLen = typ.Namespace;
    if (nameSPLen != null || typ.Namespace != null)
      cnamespace.Imports.Add(new CodeNamespaceImport(typ.Namespace));

    //This implementation tests only class types
    if (typ.IsClass)
    {
      //write a code to initiate a class type
      cm.Statements.Add(new CodeParameterDeclarationExpression(typ.Name,
➥"obj" + typ.Name + " = null"));
      //Catch the Type name under test
      objReturnStub = new CodeSnippetExpression("obj" + typ.Name);
    }

    //this implementation tests methods from interfaces
    else if (typ.IsInterface)
    {
      cm.Statements.Add(new CodeParameterDeclarationExpression(typ.Name,
➥"obj" + typ.Name + " = null"));
      foreach(Type ty in types)
      {
        if (ty.IsClass)
        {
          cm.Statements.Add(new CodeParameterDeclarationExpression(ty.Name,
➥"obj_" + i + ty.Name + " = new " + ty.Name + "()"));
          cLeft=new CodeFieldReferenceExpression(null, "obj" + typ.Name);
          cRight=new CodeFieldReferenceExpression(null, "(" + typ.Name + ")obj_" +
➥i + ty.Name);
          cm.Statements.Add(new CodeAssignStatement(cLeft, cRight));
        }
      }
    }
  }
```

The declaration of a `CodeSnippetExpression` field stores a piece of C# code, which will be used as the `return` statement of the `StartTest()` method for the test script. Making the `StartTest()` method return this object is using a bottom-up approach for the integration testing, which will be discussed in Chapter 8.

Within the `InitiateTypesUnderTest()` helper method, the first `foreach` loop completes the determination of whether a new type name is under test. Then, it uses an `if` statement to check whether the type under test needs any dependencies. The method writes a `using` statement for each dependency detected.

The following `if` statement checks whether the type under test is a class or an interface. It adds different variable declarations into the test script according to this check. If it is a class , the `objReturnStub` field catches the class name, which will be added at the end of the `StartTest()` method of the test script.

If it is an interface, the initialization of the interface is different from that of a class object. First, it declares the interface variable. Second, it obtains the interface reference to the class or structure which has implemted the abstract members of the interface.

In the future, you may add more logic to make this method aware of structures and enumerators.

The second `foreach` statement conducts exhaustive variable declarations for all types found in the given assembly and writes their respective code.

Enumerating Method Information

Next, we need to know the number of methods to be tested that are specified in the Excel data store. The `CountSheetRows()` method in Listing 7.12 helps achieve this purpose. This method simply counts the occupied cells in the first column of the Excel worksheet, and you don't need to use CodeDom objects to generate code for this method.

Listing 7.12 The *CountSheetRows()* Helper Method

```
private int CountSheetRows(Excel.Worksheet xSheet)
{
   Excel.Range range = null;
   int i = 1;
   range = xSheet.get_Range("A" + i, "A" + i);
   while (range.Value2 != null)
   {
      i++;
      range = xSheet.get_Range("A" + i, "A" + i);
   }
   return i;
}
```

The `CreateTestCode()` method in Listing 7.4 executes this method. After you add the code segment for the `CountSheetRows()` method into the `TestForm.cs` file, the following code statements from Listing 7.4 continues to declare variables:

```
...
   MethodInfo mi = null;
   ConstructorInfo ci = null;
```

```
    Type[] AmbiguousOverLoad = null;
    string wholeCellText = null;
    string[] typeText = null;
    string strPar = null;
    string[] arrayPar = null;
    Excel.Range rng;
    Excel.Range rngCstr;
   ...
```

Then, these declarations are followed by a for loop in Listing 7.4, which completes the test scripting process by calling a few more helper methods. The code iterates type classes, methods, and parameters in order. The following lists the excerpt of the for loop:

```
...
for (i = 2; i < totalRows; i++)
{
  int j = 3;

  DiscoverNewTypes(ref i, ref j, ref previousType);

  rng= xSheet.get_Range(TestUtility.ConvCHAR(j) + i,
➥TestUtility.ConvCHAR(j) + i);
  rngCstr = xSheet.get_Range(TestUtility.ConvCHAR(1) + i,
➥TestUtility.ConvCHAR(1) + i);

  if (range.Value2.ToString() == rngCstr.Value2.ToString())
//check if it is a constructor
  {
   AddTestConstructorCodes(ref i, ref j, ref rng, ref wholeCellText,
➥ref typeText, ref strPar, ref arrayPar, ref AmbiguousOverLoad, ref ci);
  }
  else
  {
  AddTestMethodCodeI(ref i, ref j, ref mi, ref rng, ref wholeCellText,
➥ref typeText, ref strPar, ref arrayPar, ref AmbiguousOverLoad);

    ParameterInfo[] ps = mi.GetParameters();
    string parStr="";

    CollectParametersForTest(ref i, ref j, ref rng, ref ps, ref parStr);

    pState = new CodePropertyReferenceExpression(null, "obj" + typ.Name);
    pCode = new CodeExpression[]{new CodeFieldReferenceExpression(null,
➥parStr)};
    CodeStatement[] trySt = null;
    CodeExpression[] passPar = new CodeExpression[]{new
➥CodeFieldReferenceExpression(null, "xResult, shtRow, mName")};
```

```
      AddInvokeTestMethodCallCode(ref i, ref parStr, ref mi, ref trySt,
➥ref passPar);

      //add log result code
      int colPosition = 0;
      LogParmResultAndReturnValue(ref i, colPosition, ps, ref mi);
    }
    range =xSheet.get_Range(TestUtility.ConvCHAR(1) + i,
➥TestUtility.ConvCHAR(1) + i);
  }
  ...
```

The `CreateTestCode()` method invokes a series of helper methods to discover the types, constructors, methods, and parameters:

- `DiscoverNewTypes()`
- `AddTestConstructorCodes()`
- `AddTestMethodCodeI()`
- `CollectParametersForTest()`
- `AddInvokeTestMethodCallCode()`
- `LogParmResultAndReturnValue()`

Listings 7.13–7.22 demonstrate these helper methods. Let's start by coding the `DiscoverNewTypes()` method for the `TestForm.cs` file. The code is in Listing 7.13.

Listing 7.13 The *DiscoverNewTypes()* Helper Method Generating Code to Discover More Type Information.

```
private void DiscoverNewTypes(ref int i, ref int j, ref string previousType)
{
  range =xSheet.get_Range(TestUtility.ConvCHAR(1) + i,
➥TestUtility.ConvCHAR(1) + i);
  string currentType = range.Value2.ToString();
  if (previousType != currentType)
  {
    foreach (Type ty in types)
    {
      if (ty.Name.ToString() == currentType)
      {
        typ = ty;
      }
    }
    previousType = currentType;
    //modified to add constructor
    cm.Statements.Add(new CodeParameterDeclarationExpression(typ.Name,
➥"obj" + typ.Name + " = null"));
  }
```

```
  range =xSheet.get_Range(TestUtility.ConvCHAR(2) + i,
➥TestUtility.ConvCHAR(2) + i);

  cLeft=new CodeFieldReferenceExpression(null, "shtRow");
  cRight=new CodeFieldReferenceExpression(null, "" + i);
  cm.Statements.Add(new CodeAssignStatement(cLeft, cRight));
}
```

As the name of the method implies, it continues to use differect approaches to discover whether a new type presents in the given assembly. Collecting all the needed dependencies for an assembly under test is the key to obtaining a fully automated test. The whole process of generating test scripts is to use `System.Reflection` and `System.CodeDom` namespaces alternatively throughout the `CreateTestCode()` method.

The following code will determine whether the target under test is a constructor, a method, or a property. Within the determination of these characteristics, it also enumerates the needed parameters. If the method under test has been overloaded more than one time, it will create tests to test all possible overloads with proper parameters. This is usually not implemented for the traditional software testing tools and their automation is limited.

Let's continue to add the code of the `AddTestConstructorCodes()` method, as shown in Listing 7.14.

Listing 7.14 The *AddTestConstructorCodes()*Generating Code to Test ConstructorsMethod.

```
 private void AddTestConstructorCodes(ref int i, ref int j,
➥                                     ref Excel.Range rng,
➥                                     ref string wholeCellText,
➥                                     ref string[] typeText,
➥                                     ref string strPar,
➥                                     ref string[] arrayPar,
➥                                     ref Type[] AmbiguousOverLoad,
➥                                     ref ConstructorInfo ci)
{
//Assign the member name to mName
  cLeft=new CodeFieldReferenceExpression(null, "mName");
  cRight=new CodeFieldReferenceExpression(null, "\"" + typ.Name + "\"");
  cm.Statements.Add(new CodeAssignStatement(cLeft, cRight));

strPar = ""; //Start a new variable

//Enumerate parameters one by one and concatenate them with a (,)
//from the Data store
  while (rng.Value2 != null)
  {
    wholeCellText = rng.Comment.Text("", 1, 0);
```

```
      typeText = wholeCellText.Split(' ');
      strPar = strPar + typeText[0] + ",";
      j++;
      rng= xSheet.get_Range(TestUtility.ConvCHAR(j) + i,
➥TestUtility.ConvCHAR(j) + i);
    }

    if (strPar != null) //When the constructor takes parameter(s)
    {
      //parse the comma separated string into an array
      strPar=strPar.Replace("Expect,", "");
      arrayPar = strPar.Split(',');

      //Assign the parameter types into a Type array object
      //for the possible overloaded methods
      AmbiguousOverLoad = new Type[arrayPar.Length-1];
      for (int parPos=0; parPos < arrayPar.Length - 1; parPos++)
      {
        TestUtility.ConvertStringToType(arrayPar[parPos],
➥ref AmbiguousOverLoad[parPos]);
      }

      //Get the correct constructor under test
      ci = typ.GetConstructor(AmbiguousOverLoad);
    }
    else //no parameters for the constructor
      //get the default constructor
      ci = typ.GetConstructor(new Type[0]);

    if (ci != null)
    {
      ParameterInfo[] pars = ci.GetParameters();
      //Enumerate parameters by Reflection to match the above
      foreach (ParameterInfo p in pars)
      {
        AddCstrParameterCode(p, cm, i);
      }

      AddConstructorCodes(typ, ci, cm, i);
    }
    pState = new CodePropertyReferenceExpression(null, "xResult");
    pCode = new CodeExpression[]{new CodeFieldReferenceExpression(null,
➥"shtRow, 4, \"Test Constructor\"")};
    cm.Statements.Add(new CodeMethodInvokeExpression(pState,
➥"Cells.set_Item", pCode));
  }
```

This method makes use of the information from the execution of the previous methods by passing parameters by references. The values of some parameters passed by references will be altered during the execution of this method. The first portion of the code obtains the class name using the Reflection namepace and Type methods. Then, it uses a `while` loop to find from the data store all the parameter types, which are for the constructor under test if it is not a default constructor. These parameter types are added to the `AmbiguousOverLoad` type array variable. The `Type.GetConstructor()` method uses the information in the `AmbiguousOverLoad` array to relocate the current constructor. If no parameter is found in the data store for this constructor, the default constructor is assigned to be tested.

To accomplish this task, the `AddTestConstructorCodes()` method calls a `TestUtility.ConvertStringToType()` method from the `TestUtility` class. You need to add the static `ConvertStringToType()` method in Listing 7.15 to the `TestUtility.cs` file.

Listing 7.15 The *ConvertStringToType()* Helper Method in the *TestUtility* Class

```
public static void ConvertStringToType(string parName, ref Type type)
{
  if (parName == "string")
    type =typeof(string);
  else if (parName == "int")
    type =typeof(int);
  else if (parName == "True" || parName =="False" || parName =="bool")
    type =typeof(bool);
  else if (parName == "double")
    type =typeof(double);
  else if (parName == "float")
    type =typeof(float);
  else if (parName == "object")
    type =typeof(object);
  else if (parName == "byte")
    type =typeof(byte);
  else if (parName == "sbyte")
    type =typeof(sbyte);
  else if (parName == "short")
    type =typeof(short);
  else if (parName == "ushort")
    type =typeof(ushort);
  else if (parName == "long")
    type =typeof(long);
  else if (parName == "uint")
    type =typeof(uint);
  else if (parName == "ulong")
    type =typeof(ulong);
  else if (parName == "char")
    type =typeof(char);
  else if (parName == "decimal")
    type =typeof(decimal);
  else if (parName == "bool")
    type =typeof(bool);
```

```
    else if (parName == "System.Text.StringBuilder")
      type =typeof(System.Text.StringBuilder);
    else if (parName == "System.IFormatProvider")
      type =typeof(System.IFormatProvider);
    else if (parName == "System.Array")
      type =typeof(System.Array);
    else if (parName == "System.AppDomain")
      type =typeof(System.AppDomain);
    else if (parName == "System.CharEnumerator")
      type =typeof(System.CharEnumerator);
    else if (parName == "System.Type")
      type =typeof(System.Type);
    else if (parName == "System.Runtime.Serialization.SerializationInfo")
      type =typeof(System.Runtime.Serialization.SerializationInfo);
    else if (parName == "VBIDE.CodePane")
      type =typeof(VBIDE.CodePane);
    else if (parName == "VBIDE.VBProject")
      type =typeof(VBIDE.VBProject);
    else if (parName == "VBIDE.vbext_WindowType")
      type =typeof(VBIDE.vbext_WindowType);
    else if (parName == "VBIDE.AddIn")
      type =typeof(VBIDE.AddIn);
    else if (parName == "VBIDE.Window")
      type =typeof(VBIDE.Window);
    else if (parName == "VBIDE.VBComponent")
      type =typeof(VBIDE.VBComponent);
    else if (parName == "VBIDE.Reference")
      type =typeof(VBIDE.Reference);
    else if (parName == "VBIDE._dispReferences_Events_ItemAddedEventHandler")
      type =typeof(VBIDE._dispReferences_Events_ItemAddedEventHandler);
    else if (parName == "VBIDE._dispReferences_Events_ItemRemovedEventHandler")
      type =typeof(VBIDE._dispReferences_Events_ItemRemovedEventHandler);
    else if (parName == "VBIDE._dispCommandBarControlEvents_ClickEventHandler")
      type =typeof(VBIDE._dispCommandBarControlEvents_ClickEventHandler);
    else if (parName == "VBIDE.VBComponent")
      type =typeof(VBIDE.VBComponent);
    else if (parName == "TESTTYPE")
      type =typeof(int);
  }
```

This method serves at lease three purposes:

- It helps write the test script correctly with accurate C# syntax.
- It helps to determine various overloads for the helper method discussed next.
- Today, some software projects include third-party components. It is hard for a commercial testing tool to complete a test involving third-party products. When you develop a tool by yourself, you can instruct your tool to use this helper method to recognize any third-party components. In this case, the `VBIDE.VBComponent` is one of the examples for testing a `VBComponent` interface that is within the `VBIDE` namespace as a third-party component.

After the correct constructor is located, the `AddTestConstructorCodes()` method uses the `ConstructorInfo` object to reflect the parameters and calls an `AddCstrParameterCode()` helper method to code the parameters correctly. Finally, it calls an `AddConstructorCodes()` method to complete the code to test the selected constructor. The code of these two methods is shown in Listing 7.16 and Listing 7.17 and needs to be added to the `TestForm.cs` file.

Listing 7.16 Code of the *AddCstrParamterCode()* Helper Methods

```
private void AddCstrParameterCode(ParameterInfo p, CodeMemberMethod cm, int i)
{
  //for passing parameter by object
  Excel.Range rng= xSheet.get_Range(TestUtility.ConvCHAR(p.Position+3) + i,
➥TestUtility.ConvCHAR(p.Position+3) + i);

  //get correct parameter from the data store
  CodeFieldReferenceExpression cLeft=new CodeFieldReferenceExpression(null,
➥"range");
  CodeFieldReferenceExpression cRight=new CodeFieldReferenceExpression(null,
➥"xSheet.get_Range(\"" + TestUtility.ConvCHAR(p.Position + 3) + i + "\", \"" +
➥TestUtility.ConvCHAR(p.Position + 3) + i + "\")");

  cm.Statements.Add(new CodeAssignStatement(cLeft, cRight));

  //declare a variable for a parameter using its name
  cLeft=new CodeFieldReferenceExpression(null, TestUtility.SysToCSPro(
➥p.ParameterType.ToString()) + " " + p.Name + "_" + i);

  //assign a value to a parameter based on its type by parsing
  if (p.ParameterType.ToString().StartsWith("System.String") ||
➥p.ParameterType.ToString().StartsWith("System.Object"))
  {
    cRight=new CodeFieldReferenceExpression(null, "range.Value2.ToString()");
  }
  else if (p.ParameterType.ToString().IndexOf("[]") > 0)
  {
    if (TestUtility.SysToCSPro(p.ParameterType.ToString().Replace("[]",""))
➥== "string")
    {
      cRight=new CodeFieldReferenceExpression(null,
➥"range.Value2.ToString().Split(',')");
    }
    else
    {
      cRight=new CodeFieldReferenceExpression(null, " null");

      cRight=new CodeFieldReferenceExpression(null, "new " +
➥TestUtility.SysToCSPro(p.ParameterType.ToString().Replace("[]","")) +
➥"[range.Value2.ToString().Split(',').Length]");
      cm.Statements.Add(new CodeAssignStatement(cLeft, cRight));
```

```
//make a simple for loop
      cLeft=new CodeFieldReferenceExpression(null,
➥"foreach (string z in range.Value2.ToString().Split(','))
➥{" + p.Name + "_" + i +"[tempArrayIndex]");

      cRight=new CodeFieldReferenceExpression(null,
TestUtility.SysToCSPro(p.ParameterType.ToString().Replace("[]","")) +
➥".Parse(z); tempArrayIndex++;}");
    }
  }
  else if (p.ParameterType.ToString().IndexOf("Text.StringBuilder") > 0)
  {
    cRight=new CodeFieldReferenceExpression(null,
➥"new System.Text.StringBuilder()");
  }
  else if (rng.Value2.ToString() == "new")
  {
    cRight=new CodeFieldReferenceExpression(null, "new " +
➥p.ParameterType.ToString() + "()");
  }
  else
  {
    cRight=new CodeFieldReferenceExpression(null,
➥TestUtility.SysToCSPro(p.ParameterType.ToString().Replace("[]","")) +
".Parse(range.Value2.ToString())");
  }
  cm.Statements.Add(new CodeAssignStatement(cLeft, cRight));

  //reduce the value of tempArrayIndex to 0 for a new array
  if (p.ParameterType.ToString().IndexOf("[]") >0)
  {
    cLeft=new CodeFieldReferenceExpression(null, "tempArrayIndex");
    cRight=new CodeFieldReferenceExpression(null, "0");
    cm.Statements.Add(new CodeAssignStatement(cLeft, cRight));
  }
}
```

Before the method deals with the parameters, it points to the correct spot in the data store. Because of the `if` statements for different data types of the parameters, the implementation of this method is lengthy. The context obtained for a parameter from the data store is regarded as a string, so each `if` statement solves the mystery of a parameter type to correctly parse the string. In the Listing 7.16, one of the `else-if` statements looks for the `[]` sign by an `IndexOf()` method to determine whether or not the parameter is passed by an array. If it is passed by an array, the CodeDom class generates code to parse an array from the testing data store with the data values separated by a comma. The last portion of the code assigns a value `0` to a new array parameter at this moment.

The code to test a constructor needs to declare a variable for the class in the first place. Then this variable needs to be initialized as a class instance with parameter values. The previous method has taken care of the parameters for a constructor. The next method, in Listing 7.17, makes code for the declaration and initialization of the constructor.

Listing 7.17 Code for *the AddConstructorCodes()* Helper Method

```
private void AddConstructorCodes(Type typ,
                                ConstructorInfo ci,
                                CodeMemberMethod cm,
                                int i)
{
  string pCodeStr = "";

  CodeStatement[] trySt;
  CodeExpression[] passPar = new CodeExpression[]{new
➥CodeFieldReferenceExpression(null, "xResult, shtRow, mName")};

  ParameterInfo[] pis = ci.GetParameters();
  foreach (ParameterInfo pi in pis)
  {
    pCodeStr += pi.Name + "_" + i + ", ";
  }
  if (pCodeStr.IndexOf(",")>0)
  {
    pCodeStr += "xxxx";
    pCodeStr = pCodeStr.Replace(", xxxx", "");
  }
  CodeExpression[] pCode = new CodeExpression[]{new
CodeFieldReferenceExpression(null, pCodeStr)};

  trySt = new CodeStatement[] {new CodeExpressionStatement(new
➥CodeMethodInvokeExpression(null, "obj" + typ.Name + " = new " + typ.Name,
➥pCode)), new CodeExpressionStatement(new CodeMethodInvokeExpression(null,
➥"TestPass", passPar)),
  };
  // add code to make a TestFail() method
  passPar = new CodeExpression[]{new CodeFieldReferenceExpression(null,
➥"xResult, shtRow, mName, err.Message")};
  CodeCatchClause catchCl = new CodeCatchClause("err", new
CodeTypeReference(typeof(Exception)), new CodeExpressionStatement(new
➥CodeMethodInvokeExpression(null, "TestFail", passPar)));

  CodeCatchClause[] catchSt = new CodeCatchClause[]{ catchCl
};
  cm.Statements.Add(new CodeTryCatchFinallyStatement(trySt, catchSt));
}
```

After the `AddConstructorCodes()` method is coded, the code for testing constructors is done. Next, the AutomatedTest tool starts to find methods and writes code to test the methods. Add the `AddTestMethodCodeI()` helper method in Listing 7.18 to the `TestForm.cs` file.

Listing 7.18 Code List of the *AddTestMethodCodeI()* Helper Method

```
private void AddTestMethodCodeI(ref int i, ref int j,
➥                                 ref MethodInfo mi,
➥                                 ref Excel.Range rng,
➥                                 ref string wholeCellText,
➥                                 ref string[] typeText,
➥                                 ref string strPar,
➥                                 ref string[] arrayPar,
➥                                 ref Type[] AmbiguousOverLoad)
{
  try
  {
    mi = typ.GetMethod(range.Value2.ToString());
  }
  catch(Exception err)
  {
    Console.WriteLine(err.Message);
    strPar = ""; //Start a new variable
    while (rng.Value2 != null)
    {
      wholeCellText = rng.Comment.Text("", 1, 0);
      typeText = wholeCellText.Split(' ');
      strPar = strPar + typeText[0] + ",";
      j++;
      rng= xSheet.get_Range(TestUtility.ConvCHAR(j) + i,
➥TestUtility.ConvCHAR(j) + i);
    }

    if (strPar == "Expect,")
      strPar = null;

    if (strPar != null)
    {
      strPar=strPar.Replace("Expect,", "");
      arrayPar = strPar.Split(',');
      AmbiguousOverLoad = new Type[arrayPar.Length-1];
      for (int parPos=0; parPos < arrayPar.Length-1; parPos++)
      {
         TestUtility.ConvertStringToType(arrayPar[parPos],
➥ref AmbiguousOverLoad[parPos]);
      }
      mi = typ.GetMethod(range.Value2.ToString(), AmbiguousOverLoad);
    }
    else //when (strPar == "")
```

```
        mi = typ.GetMethod(range.Value2.ToString(), new Type[0]);
    }
    cLeft=new CodeFieldReferenceExpression(null, "mName");
    cRight=new CodeFieldReferenceExpression(null, "\"" + mi.Name + "\"");
    cm.Statements.Add(new CodeAssignStatement(cLeft, cRight));
  }
```

By examining the code in the `AddTestMethodCodeI()`, you'll see that this method is meant mainly to collect the accurate information of the parameters in a given method and write the code to the test script. The approach of enumerating methods under test is similar to enumerating the constructors. I leave it to you to explore this method in more depth. The following sections discuss some unique aspects of testing a method with parameter variations and its return type.

Enumerating Parameter Information

Parameters are expressed by various data types. A method can pass a parameter by value or by reference. The behavior of an `out` parameter is different from that of a parameter passed by reference. Some methods integrate the objects of other classes. It is possible that a method may pass parameters using a combination of data types. An automated test script needs to address every detail of the parameter types with accuracy. Listing 7.19 is the code for a `CollectParametersForTest()` method. It uses a `for` loop to enumerate the parameters and a series of `if` statements to differentiate the situation of each parameter. For each parameter enumeration, it reassigns a `Range` object pointing at the correct cell of the data store reference. Then it uses the parameter data type and the parameter name to declare a variable for the parameter under the current cell reference as the L-value expression. Each `if` statement produces an appropriate R-value expression. This expression assigns a value to the L-value expression. Usually, an R-value expression consists of an Excel data store range reference and an unboxing expression. When all the possible situations are checked, it finally adds a line of code to the test script.

Listing 7.19 Code List for the *CollectParametersForTest()* Helper Method

```
private void CollectParametersForTest(ref int i, ref int j,
➥                                    ref Excel.Range rng,
➥                                    ref ParameterInfo[] ps,
➥                                    ref string parStr)
{
  foreach (ParameterInfo p in ps)
  {
    rng= xSheet.get_Range(TestUtility.ConvCHAR(p.Position+3) + i,
➥TestUtility.ConvCHAR(p.Position+3) + i); //added for pass parameter by object
    cLeft=new CodeFieldReferenceExpression(null, "range");
```

```
    cRight=new CodeFieldReferenceExpression(null, "xSheet.get_Range(\"" +
➥TestUtility.ConvCHAR(p.Position + 3) + i + "\", \"" +
➥TestUtility.ConvCHAR(p.Position + 3) + i + "\")");
    cm.Statements.Add(new CodeAssignStatement(cLeft, cRight));
    cLeft=new CodeFieldReferenceExpression(null,
➥TestUtility.SysToCSPro(p.ParameterType.ToString()) + " " + p.Name + "_" + i);
    if (p.ParameterType.ToString().StartsWith("System.String") ||
➥p.ParameterType.ToString().StartsWith("System.Object"))
    {
      cRight=new CodeFieldReferenceExpression(null, "range.Value2.ToString()");
    }
    else if (p.ParameterType.IsEnum)
    {
      cRight=new CodeFieldReferenceExpression(null,
➥p.ParameterType.ToString() + "." + rng.Value2);
    }
    else if (p.ParameterType.ToString().IndexOf("[]") > 0)
    {
      if (TestUtility.SysToCSPro(p.ParameterType.ToString().Replace("[]",""))
➥== "string")
      {
        cRight=new CodeFieldReferenceExpression(null,
➥"range.Value2.ToString().Split(',')");
      }
      else
      {
        cRight=new CodeFieldReferenceExpression(null, " null");
        cRight=new CodeFieldReferenceExpression(null, "new " +
➥TestUtility.SysToCSPro(p.ParameterType.ToString().Replace("[]","")) +
➥"[range.Value2.ToString().Split(',').Length]");
        cm.Statements.Add(new CodeAssignStatement(cLeft, cRight));
        cLeft=new CodeFieldReferenceExpression(null,
➥"foreach (string z in range.Value2.ToString().Split(',')){" +
➥p.Name + "_" + i +"[tempArrayIndex]");

        cRight=new CodeFieldReferenceExpression(null,
➥TestUtility.SysToCSPro(p.ParameterType.ToString().Replace("[]","")) +
➥".Parse(z); tempArrayIndex++;}");
      }
    }
    else if (p.ParameterType.ToString().IndexOf("Text.StringBuilder") > 0)
    {
      cRight=new CodeFieldReferenceExpression(null,
➥"new System.Text.StringBuilder()");
    }
    else if (rng.Value2.ToString() == "new")
    {
      //CreateObjectParameter(ref i, p);
    }
    else
    {
```

```
      cRight=new CodeFieldReferenceExpression(null,
➥TestUtility.SysToCSPro(p.ParameterType.ToString().Replace("[]","")) +
➥".Parse(range.Value2.ToString())");
    }

    //AddStubDecision(rng);
    if (p.ParameterType.ToString().IndexOf("[]") >0)
    {
      cLeft=new CodeFieldReferenceExpression(null, "tempArrayIndex");
      cRight=new CodeFieldReferenceExpression(null, "0");
      cm.Statements.Add(new CodeAssignStatement(cLeft, cRight));
    }

    if (p.ParameterType.ToString().IndexOf("Text.StringBuilder") > 0)
    {
      pCode = new CodeExpression[]{new CodeFieldReferenceExpression(null,
➥"range.Value2.ToString()")};
      cm.Statements.Add(new CodeMethodInvokeExpression(null,
➥p.Name.ToString() + "_" + i + ".Append", pCode));
    }

    if (p.Position != 0)
    {
      if (p.ParameterType.ToString().IndexOf("&") > 0)
      {
        if (!p.IsOut)
          parStr = parStr + ", ref " + p.Name + "_" + i;
        else
          parStr = parStr + ", out " + p.Name + "_" + i;
      }
      else
        parStr = parStr + ", " + p.Name + "_" + i;
    }
    else if (p.ParameterType.ToString().IndexOf("&") > 0)
    {
      if (!p.IsOut)
        parStr = parStr + "ref " + p.Name  + "_" + i;
      else
        parStr = parStr + "out " + p.Name  + "_" + i;
    }
    else
      parStr = parStr + p.Name  + "_" + i;
  }
}
```

NOTE In some code listings, some helper method invocations are commented out. This is done to provide a convenient way for you to locate them when you need them in later chapters.

All of the code in the `CollectParametersForTest()` method consists of CodeDom statements, which generate codes for the parameters of a method under test. Each branch of the `if` statement deals with a special case and a line of unique code. It makes code lines for strings, enumerators, various kinds of numeric data types, arrays, objects, references, `out` parameters, and so on. For example, one of the `else-if` statements looks for the `[]` markers to determine whether a parameter receives a value of an array. If the parameter is an array, the test script will be written to read an array from the data store and then parse the values into an array.

You have completed the part of the AutomatedTest tool that investigates parameters of a method under test and declares them in the test scripts. In order to test a method, you need to invoke it with the declared parameters. Then you expect the method to do what the software developers meant for it to do or what is specified in the software specification and design documentation. To accomplish this task, the AutomatedTest tool must generate code for the test scripts by calling the `AddInvokeTestMethodCallCode()` method in Listing 7.20.

Listing 7.20 The *AddInvokeTestMethodCallCode()* Generating Code to Test Methods

```
private void AddInvokeTestMethodCallCode(ref int i,
➥                                          ref string parStr,
➥                                          ref MethodInfo mi,
➥                                          ref CodeStatement[] trySt,
➥                                          ref CodeExpression[] passPar)
{
  if (mi.ReturnType.ToString() == "System.Void")
  {
    string propertySETname = "xxx" + mi.Name.ToString();
    if (propertySETname.Trim().StartsWith("xxxset_"))
    {
      trySt = new CodeStatement[] {new CodeExpressionStatement(new
➥CodeMethodInvokeExpression(null, "obj" + typ.Name + "." +
➥mi.Name.Replace("set_", "") + " = ", pCode)), new CodeExpressionStatement(new
➥CodeMethodInvokeExpression(null, "TestPass", passPar)),
      };
    }
    else
    {
      trySt = new CodeStatement[] {new CodeExpressionStatement(new
➥CodeMethodInvokeExpression(null, "obj" + typ.Name + "." + mi.Name, pCode)),
➥ new CodeExpressionStatement(new CodeMethodInvokeExpression(null,
➥"TestPass", passPar)),
      };
    }
  }
  else
  {
    string propertyname = "xxx" + mi.Name.ToString();
```

```
    if (propertyname.Trim().StartsWith("xxxget_"))
    {
      pCode= new CodeExpression[]{new CodeFieldReferenceExpression(null,
➥"" + i + ", " + 4 + ", obj" + typ.Name + "." + mi.Name.Replace("get_", ""))};
      trySt = new CodeStatement[] {new CodeExpressionStatement(new
➥CodeMethodInvokeExpression(null, "xResult.Cells.set_Item", pCode)),
➥new CodeExpressionStatement(new CodeMethodInvokeExpression(null,
➥"TestPass", passPar)),
      };
    }
    else
    {

      pCode= new CodeExpression[]{new CodeFieldReferenceExpression(null,
➥"" + i + ", " + 4 + ", obj" + typ.Name + "." + mi.Name + "(" + parStr + ")")};
      trySt = new CodeStatement[] {new CodeExpressionStatement(new
➥CodeMethodInvokeExpression(null, "xResult.Cells.set_Item", pCode)), new
➥CodeExpressionStatement(new CodeMethodInvokeExpression(null,
➥"TestPass", passPar)),
      };
    }
  }
  //CodeDom code to make code to invoke a TestFail() method
  passPar = new CodeExpression[]{new CodeFieldReferenceExpression(null,
➥"xResult, shtRow, mName, err.Message")};
➥  CodeCatchClause catchCl = new CodeCatchClause("err", new
➥CodeTypeReference(typeof(Exception)), new CodeExpressionStatement(new
➥CodeMethodInvokeExpression(null, "TestFail", passPar)));
  CodeCatchClause[] catchSt = new CodeCatchClause[]{ catchCl
                              };
  cm.Statements.Add(new CodeTryCatchFinallyStatement(trySt, catchSt));
}
```

Depending on the return type of a given method, the `AddInvokeTestMethodCallCode()` method generates corresponding types of code to test it. The code is nested in a `try-catch` statement. To present the test results, you need to program the AutomatedTest tool to insert a helper method in the test script to determine whether the test passes or fails. This will be covered in the next chapters.

By coding the script to invoke the method under test, you are approaching the completion of generating a test script. At this time, when the test script is executed, an exception will be caught if a method fails the test. When a method returns a value, you want to know whether it is the correct value. Thus, one more method is needed to generate code into the test script and set up a return value to test against. The code of the `LogParmResultAndReturnValue()` method is shown in Listing 7.21.

Listing 7.21 Generating Code to Test the Expected Return Value and Log the Test Results

```
private void LogParmResultAndReturnValue(ref int i, int colPosition,
                                   ➥ParameterInfo[] ps, ref MethodInfo mi)
{
  foreach (ParameterInfo p in ps)
  {
    colPosition = p.Position + 6;
    pCode = new CodeExpression[]{new CodeFieldReferenceExpression(null,
➥"shtRow" + ", " + colPosition + ", \"" + p.Name +" = \" + " +
➥p.Name + "_" + i)};
    cm.Statements.Add(new CodeMethodInvokeExpression(null,
➥"xResult.Cells.set_Item", pCode));
  }
  //added to transfer expected return to the result sheet
  if (mi.ReturnType.ToString() != "System.Void")
  {
    if (colPosition > 0)
      colPosition -= 6;
    else
      colPosition -= 1;

    AddMethodCodes(cm, colPosition, i);
  }
}
```

With the knowledge of the MS Excel application and CodeDom, this method is relatively easy to code. The last line of this method calls another helper method, `AddMethodCodes()`, as in Listing 7.22.

Listing 7.22 CodeDom Code to Add a Method to the Test Script

```
private void AddMethodCodes(CodeMemberMethod cm, int colPosition, int i)
{
  CodeExpression[] pCode = null;
  CodeFieldReferenceExpression cLeft=null;
  CodeFieldReferenceExpression cRight=null;

  cLeft=new CodeFieldReferenceExpression(null, "range");
  cRight=new CodeFieldReferenceExpression(null, "xSheet.get_Range(\"" +
➥TestUtility.ConvCHAR(colPosition+4) + i + "\", \"" +
➥TestUtility.ConvCHAR(colPosition + 4) + i + "\")");
  cm.Statements.Add(new CodeAssignStatement(cLeft, cRight));
  //Make code for reporting result
  pCode = new CodeExpression[]{new CodeFieldReferenceExpression(null,
➥"shtRow" + ", " + 5 + ", range.Value2.ToString()")};
  cm.Statements.Add(new CodeMethodInvokeExpression(null,
➥"if (range.Value2 != null) xResult.Cells.set_Item", pCode));
```

```
  cLeft=new CodeFieldReferenceExpression(null, "rangeCurr");
  cRight=new CodeFieldReferenceExpression(null, "xResult.get_Range(\"" +
➥TestUtility.ConvCHAR(4) + i + "\", \"" + TestUtility.ConvCHAR(4) + i + "\")");
  cm.Statements.Add(new CodeAssignStatement(cLeft, cRight));

  //Make code to alter color of an Excel range
  cLeft=new CodeFieldReferenceExpression(null,
➥"if (rangeCurr.Value2 != null) if (range.Value2 != null &&
➥rangeCurr.Value2.ToString() != range.Value2.ToString())
➥rangeCurr.Interior.ColorIndex");
  cRight=new CodeFieldReferenceExpression(null, "3");
  cm.Statements.Add(new CodeAssignStatement(cLeft, cRight));
  cLeft=new CodeFieldReferenceExpression(null,
➥"if (rangeCurr.Value2 != null) if (range.Value2 != null &&
➥rangeCurr.Value2.ToString() == range.Value2.ToString())
➥rangeCurr.Interior.ColorIndex");
  cRight=new CodeFieldReferenceExpression(null, "4");
  cm.Statements.Add(new CodeAssignStatement(cLeft, cRight));
}
```

Similar to other helper methods, code for this method is again overwhelmed with CodeDom statements. The main purpose of this method is to generate code for the test script to place the parameter values into a corresponding cell in the MS Excel worksheet. It also enables the test script to know whether the test passes or fails, using visual effects and text to inform the test engineers in the MS Excel report.

Closing the Test Script

After you code to test different methods, at the end of the test script, you need to declare some common statements to save the test results, close the opened file, and terminate the test session. The `AddOtherCodesPartII()` method in Listing 7.23 is coded for this purpose. You can now add it to the project.

Listing 7.23 Add Code to Save the Report and Close the MS Excel Worksheet

```
private void AddOtherCodesPartII(CodeMemberMethod cm, string clsName)
{
  CodeExpression[] pCode = null;
  CodeFieldReferenceExpression cLeft=null;
  CodeFieldReferenceExpression cRight=null;

  //record the date and time of the test
  cLeft=new CodeFieldReferenceExpression(null, "string datetime");
  cRight=new CodeFieldReferenceExpression(null,
➥"DateTime.Now.Date.ToShortDateString() + DateTime.Now.Hour.ToString()+
➥DateTime.Now.Minute.ToString() + DateTime.Now.Second.ToString()");
  cm.Statements.Add(new CodeAssignStatement(cLeft, cRight));
```

```
//targeting code: datetime = datetime.Replace("/", "");
  cLeft=new CodeFieldReferenceExpression(null, "datetime");
  cRight=new CodeFieldReferenceExpression(null,
➥"datetime.Replace(\"/\", \"\")");
  cm.Statements.Add(new CodeAssignStatement(cLeft, cRight));

//targeting code: datetime = datetime.Replace(":", "");
  cLeft=new CodeFieldReferenceExpression(null, "datetime");
  cRight=new CodeFieldReferenceExpression(null,
➥"datetime.Replace(\":\", \"\")");
  cm.Statements.Add(new CodeAssignStatement(cLeft, cRight));

  //make up a filename for the report
  cLeft=new CodeFieldReferenceExpression(null, "string resultFile");
  cRight=new CodeFieldReferenceExpression(null,
➥"System.IO.Path.Combine(\"" + XlsReportFilename + "\", \"" + clsName + "\" +
➥datetime + \".xls\")");
  cm.Statements.Add(new CodeAssignStatement(cLeft, cRight));

//targeting code: xBook2.SaveAs( ... );
  pCode = new CodeExpression[]{new CodeFieldReferenceExpression(null,
➥"resultFile, -4143, \"\", \"\", false, false, 0, \"\", 0, \"\", \"\", \"\"")};
  cm.Statements.Add(new CodeMethodInvokeExpression(null, "xBook2.SaveAs",
➥pCode));

  //Quit the excel application, worksheet and workbook
  //targeting code: xBook.Close(null, null, null);
  pCode = new CodeExpression[]{new CodeFieldReferenceExpression(null,
➥" false, null, false")};
  cm.Statements.Add(new CodeMethodInvokeExpression(null, "xBook.Close", pCode));

  //targeting code: xBook2.Close(null, null, null);
  cm.Statements.Add(new CodeMethodInvokeExpression(null, "xBook2.Close",
➥pCode));

  //targeting code: xApp.Quit();
  cm.Statements.Add(new CodeMethodInvokeExpression(null, "xApp.Quit"));

  //targeting code: xSheet = null;
  cLeft=new CodeFieldReferenceExpression(null, "xSheet");
  cRight=new CodeFieldReferenceExpression(null, " null");
  cm.Statements.Add(new CodeAssignStatement(cLeft, cRight));

  //targeting code: xResult = null;
  cLeft=new CodeFieldReferenceExpression(null, "xResult");
  cm.Statements.Add(new CodeAssignStatement(cLeft, cRight));

  //targeting code: xBook = null;
  cLeft=new CodeFieldReferenceExpression(null, "xBook");
  cm.Statements.Add(new CodeAssignStatement(cLeft, cRight));

  //targeting code: xBook2 = null;
  cLeft=new CodeFieldReferenceExpression(null, "xBook2");
```

```
        cm.Statements.Add(new CodeAssignStatement(cLeft, cRight));

        //targeting code: xApp = null;
        cLeft=new CodeFieldReferenceExpression(null, "xApp");
        cm.Statements.Add(new CodeAssignStatement(cLeft, cRight));
    }
```

It is easier to understand the CodeDom statements by comparing them with the generated code in the test scripts. Each `cm.Statement.Add()` of this method generates a respective line as shown here:

```
...
    string datetime = DateTime.Now.Date.ToShortDateString() +
➥DateTime.Now.Hour.ToString()+DateTime.Now.Minute.ToString() +
➥DateTime.Now.Second.ToString();
    datetime = datetime.Replace("/", "");
    datetime = datetime.Replace(":", "");
    string resultFile = System.IO.Path.Combine("C:/Temp",
➥"TestmyCalculator" + datetime + ".xls");
    xBook2.SaveAs(resultFile, -4143, "", "", false, false,
➥0, "", 0, "", "", "");
    xBook.Close( false, null, false);
    xBook2.Close( false, null, false);
    xApp.Quit();
    xSheet =  null;
    xResult =  null;
    xBook =  null;
    xBook2 =  null;
    xApp =  null;
...
```

NOTE This book assumes you have installed MS Excel XP in your system. The `SaveAs()` method takes 12 parameters within the paratheses. If you have an earlier version of MS Excel (for example, MS Excel 2000) installed for your system, the `SaveAs()`method takes only the first 11 parameters. Thus, you need to modify the corresponding code in Listing 7.23 to generate a line of code here: `Book2.SaveAs(resultFile, -4143, "", "", false, false, 0, "", 0, "", "");`

Thanks to these last code statements, the test script will automatically find the date and time when the test runs. Then, it combines the date, the time, and the name of the assembly under test to make a name for saving the test report. This naming convention will be of benefit for re-execution of the test script and for regression testing. For example, after the developers make modifications or fix defects of this assembly, the test script can be rerun. By comparing the test results marked by the time stamps, you can further automate the regression testing. Finally, the generated code closes the MS Excel application.

Executing Software Test Script

At this point, you have completed the code for testing constructors and methods. However, the test script still needs generating the code to execute the test. Compared with the previous tasks, this portion of coding is minor. The last method is named `AddUpClassesMethods()`; it adds up all the classes, fields, and methods into the test script. Thus, the CodeDom coding is concluded with the capability of generating test scripts for your future software test tasks. The code of the `AddUpClassesMethods()` is shown in Listing 7.24.

Listing 7.24 Completing the Previous Efforts by Adding the Class and Method to Start the Test

```
private void AddUpClassesMethods()
{
  co.Members.Add(cm);

  //Chapter 9 will complete these two methods
  //CreateTestPassMethod(cm, "TestPass");
  //CreateTestFailMethod(cm, "TestFail");

  //add a file name field
  AddFilenameField(co);
  //add a constructor
  AddCstorCodes(co);
  //add a class to start the Main method
  CodeTypeDeclaration eco = new CodeTypeDeclaration("Start" + clsName);
  eco.TypeAttributes = TypeAttributes.Public;
  cnamespace.Types.Add(eco);

  //add the Main method
  AddMainMethod(eco, clsName);
}
```

You can see that the `AddUpClassesMethods()` method continues to make use of a few CodeDom statements. The first statement, `co.Members.Add(cm)`, adds the method created by the previous efforts to the class object. Then, it calls a couple of helper methods to add a name field and a constructor. The `AddFilenameField()` method is in Listing 7.25.

Listing 7.25 Code to Generate a Filename Field Declaration

```
private void AddFilenameField(CodeTypeDeclaration co)
{
  CodeMemberField cf = new CodeMemberField();
  cf.Name = "fileName = \"" + xlsDataStoreFilename + "\"";
  cf.Attributes = MemberAttributes.Private | MemberAttributes.Final;
  cf.Type = new CodeTypeReference(typeof(string));
  co.Members.Add(cf);
}
```

The code in Listing 7.25 does nothing but add a private string `fileName` field as shown in the following line:

```
private string fileName = "C:/temp/SoftTestDataStore.xls";
```

Remember, you will not use a hard-coded name to save the data store in the next chapters. Instead, you are going to make this name reflect the assembly under test.

The `AddCstorCodes()` method is also simple and straightforward. The code generated adds a construct of the class to the test script. The code is shown in Listing 7.26.

Listing 7.26 Completing the Code of a Constructor

```
private void AddCstorCodes(CodeTypeDeclaration co)
{
  CodeFieldReferenceExpression cLeft=null;
  CodeFieldReferenceExpression cRight=null;

  //add a default test constructor
  CodeConstructor cc = new CodeConstructor();
  cc.Attributes = MemberAttributes.Public | MemberAttributes.Final;
  co.Members.Add(cc);

  //overload a constructor to load a data store file
  cc = new CodeConstructor();
cc.Attributes = MemberAttributes.Public | MemberAttributes.Final;
  cc.Parameters.Add(new CodeParameterDeclarationExpression(typeof(string),
➥"fileName"));
  cLeft=new CodeFieldReferenceExpression(null, "this.fileName");
  cRight=new CodeFieldReferenceExpression(null, "fileName");
  cc.Statements.Add(new CodeAssignStatement(cLeft, cRight));
  co.Members.Add(cc);
}
```

You may have checked the code in Listing 7.26 line by line and guessed the output. It generates a default constructor and overloads the constructor one time. The default constructor is generated for the test script in order to test a higher-level module with the integration of the class under test. The execution of a lower-level class test script is by means of late binding. (Integration testing will be discussed in Chapter 8.) The resulting default constructor has a public attribute and looks like this:

```
...
public TestXXXX() {
}
...
```

The postfixed `XXXX` is the name of the namespace under test. The overloaded constructor also has a public attribute, but it takes a filename of the test data as its parameter. This constructor is used by the test entry method to execute the test script immediately. Wherever a new filename is passed to this method, it conducts the test against a different set of testing cases. Thus, testing multiple test data stores is enabled. The generated code segment looks like this:

```
...
public TestXXXX(string fileName) {
     this.fileName = fileName;
}
...
```

The rest of the code in the `AddUpClassesMethods()` creates a test driver class and an entry point method. The following lines are from the `AddUpClassesMethods()`in Listing 7.24:

```
...
CodeTypeDeclaration eco = new CodeTypeDeclaration("Start" + clsName);
eco.TypeAttributes = TypeAttributes.Public;
cnamespace.Types.Add(eco);

//add the Main method
AddMainMethod(eco, clsName);
...
```

The three CodeDom statements add a class with the attribute `public <class name>`. Finally, you need to add the last helper method, `AddMainMethod()`, to the `TestForm.cs` file. The code for this class is shown in Listing 7.27.

Listing 7.27 Code to Generate an Entry Point Method for the Test Script

```
private void AddMainMethod(CodeTypeDeclaration eco, string clsName)
{
  CodeEntryPointMethod entryCM = new CodeEntryPointMethod();
  CodeFieldReferenceExpression cLeft=null;
  CodeFieldReferenceExpression cRight=null;

  //declare a string variable
  cLeft=new CodeFieldReferenceExpression(null, "string rootDir");
  cRight=new CodeFieldReferenceExpression(null, "Environment.CurrentDirectory");
  entryCM.Statements.Add(new CodeAssignStatement(cLeft, cRight));

  //add a string array;
  entryCM.Statements.Add(new CodeParameterDeclarationExpression(new
➥CodeTypeReference("System.String", 1), "fileArray = null"));

  //declare a StreamReader variable;
  cLeft=new CodeFieldReferenceExpression(null, "StreamReader sr");
  cRight=new CodeFieldReferenceExpression(null, "File.OpenText(
➥System.IO.Path.Combine(\"" + tempTestProjDir + "\", \"fileArray.txt\"))");
  entryCM.Statements.Add(new CodeAssignStatement(cLeft, cRight));

  //Targeting code: string input = null;
  cLeft=new CodeFieldReferenceExpression(null, "string input");
```

```
cRight=new CodeFieldReferenceExpression(null, " null");
entryCM.Statements.Add(new CodeAssignStatement(cLeft, cRight));

// Targeting code: string fStr;
cLeft=new CodeFieldReferenceExpression(null, "string fStr");
cRight=new CodeFieldReferenceExpression(null, " null");
entryCM.Statements.Add(new CodeAssignStatement(cLeft, cRight));

// Targeting at a while loop
cLeft=new CodeFieldReferenceExpression(null,
➥"while ((input = sr.ReadLine()) != null) fStr");
cRight=new CodeFieldReferenceExpression(null, "fStr + input + \",\"");
entryCM.Statements.Add(new CodeAssignStatement(cLeft, cRight));

//write code to invoke a method;
entryCM.Statements.Add(new CodeMethodInvokeExpression(null, "sr.Close"));
// write code to assign a value to a variable
cLeft=new CodeFieldReferenceExpression(null, "fStr");
cRight=new CodeFieldReferenceExpression(null,
➥"fStr.Replace(\"/\", \"\\\")");
entryCM.Statements.Add(new CodeAssignStatement(cLeft, cRight));

// write code to assign a value to a variable
cLeft=new CodeFieldReferenceExpression(null, "fileArray");
cRight=new CodeFieldReferenceExpression(null, "fStr.Split(\',\')");
entryCM.Statements.Add(new CodeAssignStatement(cLeft, cRight));

// write code to declare the test object;
cLeft=new CodeFieldReferenceExpression(null, clsName + " test");
cRight=new CodeFieldReferenceExpression(null, " null");
entryCM.Statements.Add(new CodeAssignStatement(cLeft, cRight));

// write code of a for loop
cLeft=new CodeFieldReferenceExpression(null, "test");
cRight=new CodeFieldReferenceExpression(null, "new " + clsName +
➥"(System.IO.Path.Combine(rootDir, fileArray[i]))");
CodeIterationStatement loop = new CodeIterationStatement(
  new CodeVariableDeclarationStatement("System.Int32", "i",
  new CodePrimitiveExpression(0)),
  new CodeBinaryOperatorExpression(
  new CodeFieldReferenceExpression(null, "i"),
  CodeBinaryOperatorType.LessThan,
  new CodeFieldReferenceExpression(
  new CodeFieldReferenceExpression(null, "fileArray"), "Length - 1")
  ),
  new CodeAssignStatement(
  new CodeFieldReferenceExpression(null, "i"),
  new CodeBinaryOperatorExpression(
  new CodeFieldReferenceExpression(null, "i"),
  CodeBinaryOperatorType.Add,
  new CodePrimitiveExpression(1))
```

```
        ),
        new CodeStatement[]
      {
    new CodeAssignStatement(cLeft, cRight),
    new CodeExpressionStatement(
    new CodeMethodInvokeExpression(null, "test.StartTest"))
      }
        );
      entryCM.Statements.Add(loop);
      eco.Members.Add(entryCM);
      //end
    }
```

With the code in Listing 7.27, the `AddMainMethod()` adds some statements in an entry point method, which is executed first when the program runs. For purpose of illustration, Listing 7.28 shows the code generated by the last helper method.

Listing 7.28 The Code Generated by the *AddMainMethod()* Method for the Entry Point Method of the Test Script

```
public class StartTestmyCalculator {
    public static void Main() {
        string rootDir = Environment.CurrentDirectory;
        string[] fileArray = null;
        StreamReader sr = File.OpenText(System.IO.Path.Combine("C:/Temp",
➥"fileArray.txt"));
        string input =  null;
        string fStr =  null;
        while ((input = sr.ReadLine()) != null) fStr = fStr + input + ",";
        sr.Close();
        fStr = fStr.Replace("/", "\\");
        fileArray = fStr.Split(',');
        TestmyCalculator test =  null;
        for (int i = 0; (i < fileArray.Length - 1); i = (i + 1)) {
            test = new TestmyCalculator(System.IO.Path.Combine(rootDir,
➥fileArray[i]));
            test.StartTest();
        }
    }
```

Not all lines of the code generated for different assemblies under test will be identical to the code in Listing 7.28. Some of the lines are assembly dependent. The `fileArray.txt` file stores a series of filenames of the MS Excel data stores. The `for` loop is used to invoke the test method with iteration based on how many MS Excel data stores are stored in the `fileArray.txt` file. Thus, it achieves the goal of testing an assembly against multiple test data stores with one test script.

Running the AutomatedTest

Note that in the AddUpClassesMethods() method, there are two other helper method calls, which are commented out at this moment:

```
//CreateTestPassMethod(cm, "TestPass");
//CreateTestFailMethod(cm, "TestFail");
```

We won't implement these two methods in this chapter. It is better and more appropriate to discuss the test results, the presentation of the test results, and verification of the results in the next chapters. However, you have finished coding the test script dynamically. Now you can build the AutomatedTest project and test-run it.

When the AutmatedTest.exe is executed, you'll see the Automated Software Test form, which looks similar to Figure 7.1. Then, perform these steps:

1. From the form, click the Start button. An open file dialog appears.
2. Navigate to the C:\SourceCode\Chapter04\LowLevelObj\bin\Debug\ folder, select the LowLeveObj.dll, and click the Open button. The AutomatedTest tool finds the names of the implemented types from the LowLevelObj assembly, as shown in Figure 7.2.

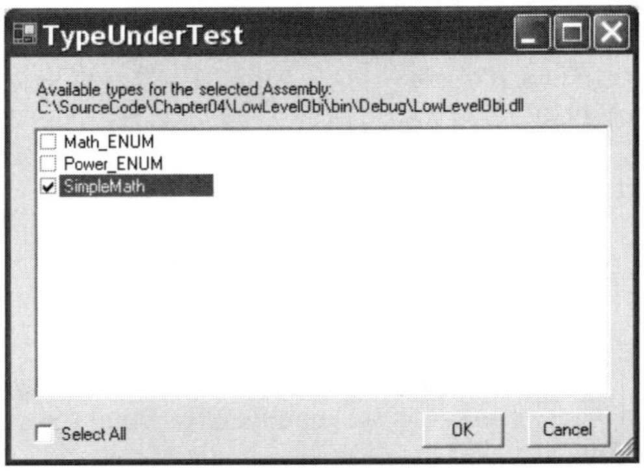

FIGURE 7.2
Select the SimpleMath classes of the assembly under test to test

3. All types of the LowLevelObj assembly are shown in the check list. However, the implemented AutomatedTest tool so far doesn't handle types of enumerators and structures. It is capable of testing only types of classes and interfaces. To generate a test script to test the SimpleMath class, select the check box beside SimpleMath and click the OK button. (You did this in Chapter 4 also.) An MS Excel application with the type information of the SimpleMath class opens (Figure 7.3). This is the third time you've tested this assembly. There might already be a SoftTestDataStor.xls file in the system created by previous testing. The MS Excel application will ask you to overwrite this file or save with a new filename. You can overwrite it. This time, the AutomatedTest tool is able to generate a test script.

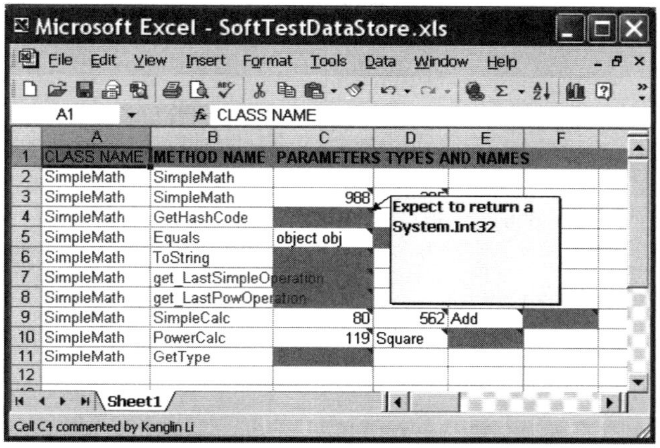

FIGURE 7.3
The MS Excel worksheet with testing information generated by the AutomatedTest Tool

4. Go back to the Automated Software Test window and click the Create Script button.
5. The AutomatedTest completes and generates a test script for testing the `SimpleMath` class. At this moment, the script is saved in the `C:\Temp` folder with a name `TestScript.cs`. You can open this file in a text editor.

Outcome of the AutomatedTest Project

You've reached the goal of generating the test script to test a given assembly. You must be excited to see the outcome of the dynamically generated code. This section lists the test script (Listing 7.29) and shows how to use this test script to complete a test. It also discusses some of the limitations of this script at this stage with regard to automation. In later chapters, we will conquer these limitations. Finally, this section concludes this chapter with a short discussion on the test script deployment and using the command line to compile the test script into a .NET assembly.

Listing 7.29 The Dynamically Generated *TestScript.cs* File for Testing the *LowLevelObj.dll* with the AutomatedTest Project

```
namespace LowLevelObjTest {
    using System;
    using System.IO;
    using Excel;
    using System.Reflection;
    using LowLevelObj;


    public class TestLowLeveObj {
```

```
        private string fileName = "C:/temp/SoftTestDataStore.xls";

        public TestLowLeveObj() {
        }

        public TestLowLeveObj(string fileName) {
            this.fileName = fileName;
        }

        public object StartTest() {
            Excel.Application xApp = new Excel.Application();
            Excel.Workbook xBook = xApp.Workbooks.Open(fileName, 0,
➥false, 1, "", "", true, 1, 0, true, 1, 0, 0, 0, 0);
            Excel.Worksheet xSheet = (Excel.Worksheet)xBook.ActiveSheet;
            Excel.Workbook xBook2 = xApp.Workbooks.Add(1);
            Excel.Worksheet xResult = (Excel.Worksheet)xBook2.ActiveSheet;
            xResult.Cells.set_Item(1, 1, "METHOD UNDER TEST");
            xResult.Cells.set_Item(1, 2, "RESULT");
            xResult.Cells.set_Item(1, 3, "ERROR MESSAGE");
            xResult.Cells.set_Item(1, 4, "ACTUAL RETURN");
            xResult.Cells.set_Item(1, 5, "EXPECTED RETURN");
            xResult.Cells.set_Item(1, 6, "PARAMETERS AND VALUES");
            xApp.Visible =  true;
            Excel.Range range;
            Excel.Range rangeCurr;
            range = xResult.get_Range("A1", "H1");
            range.Interior.ColorIndex = 8;
            range.Font.Bold =  true;
            range.Columns.AutoFit();
            int shtRow = 0;
            string mName = null;
            int tempArrayIndex = 0;
            SimpleMath objSimpleMath = null;
            shtRow = 2;
            mName = "SimpleMath";
            try {
                objSimpleMath = new SimpleMath();
                TestPass(xResult, shtRow, mName);
            }
            catch (System.Exception err) {
                TestFail(xResult, shtRow, mName, err.Message);
            }
            xResult.Cells.set_Item(shtRow, 4, "Test Constructor");
            shtRow = 3;
            mName = "SimpleMath";
            range = xSheet.get_Range("C3", "C3");
            int num1_3 = int.Parse(range.Value2.ToString());
            range = xSheet.get_Range("D3", "D3");
            int num2_3 = int.Parse(range.Value2.ToString());
            try {
                objSimpleMath = new SimpleMath(num1_3, num2_3);
```

```
    TestPass(xResult, shtRow, mName);
}
catch (System.Exception err) {
    TestFail(xResult, shtRow, mName, err.Message);
}
xResult.Cells.set_Item(shtRow, 4, "Test Constructor");
shtRow = 4;
mName = "GetHashCode";
try {
    xResult.Cells.set_Item(4, 4, objSimpleMath.GetHashCode());
    TestPass(xResult, shtRow, mName);
}
catch (System.Exception err) {
    TestFail(xResult, shtRow, mName, err.Message);
}
range = xSheet.get_Range("C4", "C4");
if (range.Value2 != null) {
    xResult.Cells.set_Item(shtRow, 5, range.Value2.ToString());
}
rangeCurr = xResult.get_Range("D4", "D4");
if (rangeCurr.Value2 != null)
   if (range.Value2 != null &&
   rangeCurr.Value2.ToString() != range.Value2.ToString())
      rangeCurr.Interior.ColorIndex = 3;
if (rangeCurr.Value2 != null)
  if (range.Value2 != null &&
  ➥rangeCurr.Value2.ToString() == range.Value2.ToString())
    rangeCurr.Interior.ColorIndex = 4;
shtRow = 5;
mName = "Equals";
range = xSheet.get_Range("C5", "C5");
object obj_5 = range.Value2.ToString();
try {
    xResult.Cells.set_Item(5, 4, objSimpleMath.Equals(obj_5));
    TestPass(xResult, shtRow, mName);
}
catch (System.Exception err) {
    TestFail(xResult, shtRow, mName, err.Message);
}
xResult.Cells.set_Item(shtRow, 6, "obj = " + obj_5);
range = xSheet.get_Range("D5", "D5");
if (range.Value2 != null) {
    xResult.Cells.set_Item(shtRow, 5, range.Value2.ToString());
}
rangeCurr = xResult.get_Range("D5", "D5");
if (rangeCurr.Value2 != null)
  if (range.Value2 != null &&
  rangeCurr.Value2.ToString() != range.Value2.ToString())
    ➥rangeCurr.Interior.ColorIndex = 3;
if (rangeCurr.Value2 != null)
  if (range.Value2 != null &&
```

```
  ➥rangeCurr.Value2.ToString() == range.Value2.ToString())
    rangeCurr.Interior.ColorIndex = 4;
shtRow = 6;
mName = "ToString";
try {
    xResult.Cells.set_Item(6, 4, objSimpleMath.ToString());
    TestPass(xResult, shtRow, mName);
}
catch (System.Exception err) {
    TestFail(xResult, shtRow, mName, err.Message);
}
range = xSheet.get_Range("C6", "C6");
if (range.Value2 != null) {
    xResult.Cells.set_Item(shtRow, 5, range.Value2.ToString());
}
rangeCurr = xResult.get_Range("D6", "D6");
if (rangeCurr.Value2 != null)
  if (range.Value2 != null &&
  ➥rangeCurr.Value2.ToString() != range.Value2.ToString())
    rangeCurr.Interior.ColorIndex = 3;
if (rangeCurr.Value2 != null)
  if (range.Value2 != null &&
  ➥rangeCurr.Value2.ToString() == range.Value2.ToString())
    rangeCurr.Interior.ColorIndex = 4;
shtRow = 7;
mName = "get_LastSimpleOperation";
try {
    xResult.Cells.set_Item(7, 4, objSimpleMath.LastSimpleOperation);
    TestPass(xResult, shtRow, mName);
}
catch (System.Exception err) {
    TestFail(xResult, shtRow, mName, err.Message);
}
range = xSheet.get_Range("C7", "C7");
if (range.Value2 != null) {
    xResult.Cells.set_Item(shtRow, 5, range.Value2.ToString());
}
rangeCurr = xResult.get_Range("D7", "D7");
if (rangeCurr.Value2 != null)
  if (range.Value2 != null &&
  ➥rangeCurr.Value2.ToString() != range.Value2.ToString())
    rangeCurr.Interior.ColorIndex = 3;
if (rangeCurr.Value2 != null)
  if (range.Value2 != null &&
  rangeCurr.Value2.ToString() == range.Value2.ToString())
    ➥rangeCurr.Interior.ColorIndex = 4;
shtRow = 8;
mName = "get_LastPowOperation";
try {
    xResult.Cells.set_Item(8, 4, objSimpleMath.LastPowOperation);
    TestPass(xResult, shtRow, mName);
```

```
}
catch (System.Exception err) {
    TestFail(xResult, shtRow, mName, err.Message);
}
range = xSheet.get_Range("C8", "C8");
if (range.Value2 != null) {
    xResult.Cells.set_Item(shtRow, 5, range.Value2.ToString());
}
rangeCurr = xResult.get_Range("D8", "D8");
if (rangeCurr.Value2 != null)
  if (range.Value2 != null &&
  ➥rangeCurr.Value2.ToString() != range.Value2.ToString())
    rangeCurr.Interior.ColorIndex = 3;
if (rangeCurr.Value2 != null)
  if (range.Value2 != null &&
  ➥rangeCurr.Value2.ToString() == range.Value2.ToString())
    rangeCurr.Interior.ColorIndex = 4;
shtRow = 9;
mName = "SimpleCalc";
range = xSheet.get_Range("C9", "C9");
int x_9 = int.Parse(range.Value2.ToString());
range = xSheet.get_Range("D9", "D9");
int y_9 = int.Parse(range.Value2.ToString());
range = xSheet.get_Range("E9", "E9");
LowLevelObj.Math_ENUM operation_9 = LowLevelObj.Math_ENUM.Add;
try {
    xResult.Cells.set_Item(9, 4,
➥objSimpleMath.SimpleCalc(x_9, y_9, operation_9));
    TestPass(xResult, shtRow, mName);
}
catch (System.Exception err) {
    TestFail(xResult, shtRow, mName, err.Message);
}
xResult.Cells.set_Item(shtRow, 6, "x = " + x_9);
xResult.Cells.set_Item(shtRow, 7, "y = " + y_9);
xResult.Cells.set_Item(shtRow, 8, "operation = " + operation_9);
range = xSheet.get_Range("F9", "F9");
if (range.Value2 != null) {
    xResult.Cells.set_Item(shtRow, 5, range.Value2.ToString());
}
rangeCurr = xResult.get_Range("D9", "D9");
if (rangeCurr.Value2 != null)
  if (range.Value2 != null &&
  ➥rangeCurr.Value2.ToString() != range.Value2.ToString())
    rangeCurr.Interior.ColorIndex = 3;
if (rangeCurr.Value2 != null)
  if (range.Value2 != null &&
    ➥rangeCurr.Value2.ToString() == range.Value2.ToString())
      rangeCurr.Interior.ColorIndex = 4;
shtRow = 10;
mName = "PowerCalc";
```

```
            range = xSheet.get_Range("C10", "C10");
            int x_10 = int.Parse(range.Value2.ToString());
            range = xSheet.get_Range("D10", "D10");
            LowLevelObj.Power_ENUM operation_10 = LowLevelObj.Power_ENUM.Square;
            try {
                xResult.Cells.set_Item(10, 4,
➥objSimpleMath.PowerCalc(x_10, operation_10));
                TestPass(xResult, shtRow, mName);
            }
            catch (System.Exception err) {
                TestFail(xResult, shtRow, mName, err.Message);
            }
            xResult.Cells.set_Item(shtRow, 6, "x = " + x_10);
            xResult.Cells.set_Item(shtRow, 7, "operation = " + operation_10);
            range = xSheet.get_Range("E10", "E10");
            if (range.Value2 != null) {
                xResult.Cells.set_Item(shtRow, 5, range.Value2.ToString());
            }
            rangeCurr = xResult.get_Range("D10", "D10");
            if (rangeCurr.Value2 != null)
              if (range.Value2 != null &&
              ➥rangeCurr.Value2.ToString() != range.Value2.ToString())
                rangeCurr.Interior.ColorIndex = 3;
            if (rangeCurr.Value2 != null)
              if (range.Value2 != null &&
              ➥rangeCurr.Value2.ToString() == range.Value2.ToString())
                rangeCurr.Interior.ColorIndex = 4;
            shtRow = 11;
            mName = "GetType";
            try {
                xResult.Cells.set_Item(11, 4, objSimpleMath.GetType());
                TestPass(xResult, shtRow, mName);
            }
            catch (System.Exception err) {
                TestFail(xResult, shtRow, mName, err.Message);
            }
            range = xSheet.get_Range("C11", "C11");
            if (range.Value2 != null) {
                xResult.Cells.set_Item(shtRow, 5, range.Value2.ToString());
            }
            rangeCurr = xResult.get_Range("D11", "D11");
            if (rangeCurr.Value2 != null)
              if (range.Value2 != null &&
              ➥rangeCurr.Value2.ToString() != range.Value2.ToString())
                rangeCurr.Interior.ColorIndex = 3;
            if (rangeCurr.Value2 != null)
              if (range.Value2 != null &&
              ➥rangeCurr.Value2.ToString() == range.Value2.ToString())
                rangeCurr.Interior.ColorIndex = 4;
            string datetime = DateTime.Now.Date.ToShortDateString() +
➥DateTime.Now.Hour.ToString()+DateTime.Now.Minute.ToString() +
```

```
➥DateTime.Now.Second.ToString();
            datetime = datetime.Replace("/", "");
            datetime = datetime.Replace(":", "");
            string resultFile = System.IO.Path.Combine("C:/Temp",
➥"TestLowLeveObj" + datetime + ".xls");
            xBook2.SaveAs(resultFile, -4143, "", "",
➥false, false, 0, "", 0, "", "", "");
            xBook.Close( false, null, false);
            xBook2.Close( false, null, false);
            xApp.Quit();
            xSheet =  null;
            xResult =  null;
            xBook =  null;
            xBook2 =  null;
            xApp =  null;
            return objSimpleMath;
        }
    }

    public class StartTestLowLeveObj {

        public static void Main() {
            string rootDir = Environment.CurrentDirectory;
            string[] fileArray = null;
            StreamReader sr = File.OpenText(System.IO.Path.Combine(
➥"C:/Temp", "fileArray.txt"));
            string input =  null;
            string fStr =  null;
            while ((input = sr.ReadLine()) != null) fStr = fStr + input + ",";
            sr.Close();
            fStr = fStr.Replace("/", "\\");
            fileArray = fStr.Split(',');
            TestLowLeveObj test =  null;
            for (int i = 0; (i < fileArray.Length - 1); i = (i + 1)) {
                test = new TestLowLeveObj(System.IO.Path.Combine(rootDir,
➥fileArray[i]));
                test.StartTest();
            }
        }
    }
}
```

The test script is generated by the AutomatedTest tool at this stage. There are two classes in it and each has one method. The code segment to test each individual method is unique based on the nature of the method. A `try-catch` statement is used to invoke the method under test. If the invocation executes successfully, a `TestPass()` method is invoked within the `try` statement. Otherwise, a `TestFail()` method is invoked within the `catch` statement. However, these two methods are not generated automatically at this stage. When you compile this test script, the compiler will complain about the missing methods, as in the following error message:

```
"TestScript.cs(47,17): error CS0103: The name 'TestPass' does not exist
➥in the class or namespace 'LowLevelObjTest.TestLowLevelObj'"
```

Although the test script generated by this chapter cannot be compiled directly at this point, you can add the required methods manually and make this test script compilable and executable. To make things simple, these two methods can be coded as follows:

```
private void TestPass(Excel.Worksheet xResult, int shtRow, string mName)
{
  Excel.Range range;
  xResult.Cells.set_Item(shtRow, 1, mName);
  xResult.Cells.set_Item(shtRow, 2, "PASS");
  xResult.Cells.set_Item(shtRow, 3, "NO ERROR");
  range = xResult.get_Range("B" + shtRow, "B" + shtRow);
  range.Interior.ColorIndex = 10;
  return;
}

private void TestFail(Excel.Worksheet xResult, int shtRow,
                      string mName, string errMsg)
{
  Excel.Range range;
  xResult.Cells.set_Item(shtRow, 1, mName);
  xResult.Cells.set_Item(shtRow, 2, "FAIL");
  xResult.Cells.set_Item(shtRow, 3, errMsg);
  range = xResult.get_Range("B" + shtRow, "B" + shtRow);
  range.Interior.ColorIndex = 3;
  return;
}
```

After you add the preceding code segment into the `TestLowLeveObj` class of the test script, navigate to `C:\Temp` and issue a `csc.exe` command from a Visual Studio .NET command prompt:

```
csc testscript.cs
➥/r:C:\SourceCode\Chapter07\AutomatedTest\Bin\Debug\Interop.Excel.dll
➥/r:C:\SourceCode\Chapter04\LowLevelObj\bin\debug\LowLevelObj.dll
```

This command is all one line. After issuing this command, you have an executable `TestScript.exe`. Before you execute the `TestScript.exe`, you need to deal with the .NET deployment following these steps:

1. Copy the `LowLevelObj.dll` into the directory where the `TestScript.exe` file is.
2. Also copy the `Interop.Excel.dll` into the directory where the `TestScript.exe` file is.

3. Finally, create a `fileArray.txt` file with one line of text in the directory where the `TestScript.exe` file is:

```
C:/TEMP/SoftTestDataStore.xls
```

NOTE The deployment process for the test script will not be needed when the project is completed. It is shown here to illustrate how much we have done manually in the past when an AutomatedTest tool was not available.

Now, you are ready to run the resulting `TestScript.exe`. There should be no errors. If you want assign different testing cases to the test data store, you can do so. Open the data store Excel worksheet and assign any numbers to the cells with regard to the parameters of `x` and `y`. Run the `TestScript.exe` again. You can continue this process until you find all the bugs. Alternatively, you can save the modified Excel data store with another name. Add this filename with its full path to the `fileArray.txt` file. Rerunning `TestScript.exe` will initialize testing against multiple test data stores.

As the test script is designed, the assembly can return an object of the class under test for integration test when a higher-level module requires a parameter passed by an object. Usually, a program looks for a DLL file to accomplish this. You can issue the following command with a `target: library` switch:

```
csc testscript.cs  /target:library
➥/r:C:\SourceCode\Chapter07\AutomatedTest\Bin\Debug\Interop.Excel.dll
➥/r:C:\SourceCode\Chapter04\LowLevelObj\Bin\Debug\LowLevelObj.dll
```

The execution of this command results in a DLL assembly. Make sure the DLL file is together with the EXE file in the same folder in order to load the dependencies properly. Then, this DLL assembly can be used to create an object of the LowLevelObj class. That object will be used in Chapter 8 when we test a higher level class with the integration of the LowLevelObj class.

Summary

The source code of this chapter can be downloaded from the website for this book at `www.sybex.com`. Although, we left the automatic generation of the `TestPass()` and `TestFail()` method for the next chapters, the AutomatedTest project is now able to generate real test scripts for any given assemblies.

The next chapter starts to cover testing methods which pass parameters by objects. When I worked in a software development team as a tester, I started to develop an automated tool. At the early stage of the tool development, my colleagues often asked me if the tool tested a method taking objects as parameters? In the beginning, my answer was no. I then began to think about it and decided to develop a tool capable of doing so.

It seems that testing parameters passed by objects is important and useful. In this chapter, you prepared the object for this purpose. In the next two chapters, we will discuss integration testing, how to verify the test results, and how to present the test results.

Chapter 8

Integration Testing

The AutomatedTest tool now has the capability of collecting test information and generating test scripts. This tool doesn't need to record any mouse clicking or keystrokes from a user to complete the code generation. It looks into the assembly for the members that need to be tested. Then, it generates a set of testing data to test each member. The generated data are finally used by the tool to drive the process of writing the test script. The test script then is compiled into an EXE or DLL assembly. This assembly can be used and reused for unit testing, integration testing and regression testing.

When a method under test requires parameters passed by values, the AutomatedTest tool is able to handle these testing cases well at this point. For example, the automatically generated MS Excel worksheet stores numbers for numeric parameters and texts for string parameters. In this chapter, I'll show you how to achieve automated integration testing and how to test methods with parameters passed by other class objects. In such cases, the commercial testing tools usually instruct the testers to make stubs or mock objects manually. In this chapter, you'll learn how to enable the AutomatedTest tool to create real objects as well as manual stubs for this purpose.

Testing Parameters Passed by Objects

Programming techniques have evolved from structured to object-oriented programming. There are many software development models in the industry today. The multitier programming model has been accepted throughout the software industry. In this model, presentation-tier (user) commands are passed to business-tier objects; business object commands are then passed to the data tier. When you test a method, which passes those parameters, you are testing whether the components from different tiers support one another.

An assembly tested successfully in isolation may not successfully integrate with other assemblies. Integration testing is used to verify the interaction between sets of classes. The sets are integrated for the next level of testing. The integration test is important to test the coordination between different assemblies. It involves testing all the assemblies that participate in the functionalities of a higher-lever assembly. There are usually three approaches to integration testing:

Big bang approach With this approach, each module is tested independently, followed by integration testing. All modules need to be coded completely. This strategy is time consuming, inefficient and prone to errors when traditional testing methods are used. But, in this chapter, you'll see how to implement a method to break through this bottleneck.

Top-down approach Today, organizations develop software product with multitier architectures; the lower levels contain the smaller modules of the program, and the higher modules incorporate and coordinate the lower-level modules. With regard to testing, there are two ways to use the top-down approach:

Depth-first The top-level module is tested first, and then the shortest path is used to reach the last level of the hierarchy. The focus is on checking the program design and its implementation. In addition, major functions are tested in small frames. This is an inefficient approach for incomplete hierarchies.

Breadth-first Again, the top-level module is tested first. Then, all the modules one level down are tested in order. The testing is then performed another level down.

Bottom-up approach With this approach, low-level modules are tested first. Then the integrated low-level modules that are one step higher in the hierarchy are tested. During the higher-level testing, the object created by the test script and testing cases, which are one level lower, is used.

The bottom-up approach is the most efficient among the three. Because the AutomatedTest tool generates one test script to test all the methods and properties of a class, it can initialize a complete and real object of a class. Other tools use reverse engineering or capture/replay to generate a test script to test only one method at a time. They usually employ stubbing or mock objects for the same purpose. The AutomatedTest tool generates a test script that always prepares an object of the class under test. When a higher-level class integrates an already tested class, the object returned from the low-level test script can be reused; that is, a basic class has to be tested before testing the classes that use the basic class. For example, if a higher-level module needs an object of the class tested in Chapter 7, the AutomatedTest tool can directly use the previously built assembly of the test script for the lower-level module object; that is, the `*.exe` file or `*.dll` file of the test script. The advantages of using this testing method include the following:

- It uses a complete object for integration testing to improve the inadequacy of stub framework which is popular within the current testing methods and tools.
- The higher-level test scripts access real objects of low-level classes rather than mock objects. Thus, the tester can gain valuable insight into a class as well as an application under test.
- It utilizes the test data store and eliminates any guesswork to initialize a class object. The testing becomes more effective and accurate.
- There is no need for reediting and debugging the test script, so a full automated testing is achieved.

Building a Higher-Level Module to Be Tested

In the previous chapters, we used the AutomatedTest tool under development to test the LowLevelObj assembly developed in Chapter 4. Now, to demonstrate the capabilities that will be implemented by the end of this chapter, you are going to build a higher-level module upon the LowLevelObj assembly with some new members. These new members will include constructor and overload methods. Some of the methods pass parameters by *reference* or have `out` parameters. One method passes a parameter by an object of the `LowLevelObj.SimpleMath` class. The purpose of these new implementations is to help ensure that testers can employ the AutomatedTest tool to test different aspects of this assembly created throughout this book.

Now, let's start the Microsoft Visual Studio .NET IDE and create the HighLevelObj project in the `C:\SourceCode\Chapter08` folder. The following steps describe how to do it:

1. Start Microsoft Visual Studio .NET IDE.
2. Choose File ➤ New ➤ Project. The New Project dialog box appears.
3. Select Visual C# Projects in the left pane and Class Library in the right.
4. In the name field, type **HighLevelObj**.
5. In the Location field, type **`C:\SourceCode\Chapter08`**.
6. Click the OK button. The C# program editor opens with some code skeleton.
7. Choose Project ➤ Add Reference ➤ Browser.
8. In the Open file dialog box, navigate to `C:\SourceCode\Chapter04\Bin\Debug`. Select the `LowLevelObj.dll` assembly.
9. Click the Open button and then the OK button.
10. Add the code shown in Listing 8.1 to the C# program editor.

Listing 8.1 Code of a New Class, *AdvancedCalc*, for the *HighLevelObj* Assembly

```
using System;
using System.Collections;

namespace HighLevelObj
{
  public class AdvancedCalc
  {
    public double LENGTH;
    public bool hasLength;

    public AdvancedCalc()
    {
    }
```

```
public AdvancedCalc(double length)
{
  this.LENGTH = length;
  hasLength = true;
}

//for areas of equilateral triangles
public double Triangle(double length)
{
  double height=Math.Sqrt(Math.Pow(length, 2)-Math.Pow(length/2,2));
  return (length * height)/2;
}

//for areas of isosceles triangles
public double Triangle(double length1, double length2)
{
  double height=Math.Sqrt(Math.Pow(length1, 2)-Math.Pow(length2/2, 2));
  return (length2 * height)/2;
}

//for areas of scalene triangles
public double Triangle(double length1, double length2, double length3)
{
  SortIT(ref length1, ref length2, ref length3);
  double len4 = GetTriangleHeight(length1,length2,ref length3);
  return length3*len4/2;
}

private void SortIT(ref double len1, ref double len2, ref double len3)
{
  ArrayList lengthArr = new ArrayList();
  lengthArr.Add(len1);
  lengthArr.Add(len2);
  lengthArr.Add(len3);
  lengthArr.Sort();
  len1 = (double)lengthArr[0];
  len2 = (double)lengthArr[1];
  len3 = (double)lengthArr[2];
}


public double GetTriangleHeight(double len1, double len2, ref double len3)
{
  SortIT(ref len1, ref len2, ref len3);
  double x=len1 * 0.75;
  bool isRight;
  isRightTriangle(len1,len2,ref len3, out isRight);
  if (isRight)
  {
    len3 = len1;
    return len2;
  }
```

```
        //Newton-Raphson Method
        while (Math.Abs(x*x - (len1*len1 -(len3-Math.Sqrt(len2*len2 - x*x))
          *(len3-Math.Sqrt(len2*len2 - x*x)))) > 0.00001)
        {
          x = x - (x*x - (len1*len1 -(len3-Math.Sqrt(len2*len2 - x*x))*
➥(len3-Math.Sqrt(len2*len2 - x*x))))/(4*x-len1*len1-len3*len3+2*len3*x/
➥(Math.Sqrt(len2*len2-x*x))-len2*len2);
        }

        return Math.Abs(x);
      }


      public void isRightTriangle(double len1, double len2,
➥                               ref double len3, out bool isRight)
      {
        if (len1*len1 + len2*len2 == len3*len3)
          isRight = true;
        else
          isRight = false;
      }

      public double Square(double length)
      {
         return length * length;
      }
      public double Circle(double Radius)
      {
        return Math.PI * Math.Pow(Radius, 2);
      }

      public void SimpleCalc(LowLevelObj.SimpleMath lvlMath,
➥LowLevelObj.Math_ENUM operation, out int Result)
      {
        Result = 0;
        switch (operation)
        {
          case LowLevelObj.Math_ENUM.Add:
            Result = lvlMath.FirstNum + lvlMath.SecondNum;
            break;
          case LowLevelObj.Math_ENUM.Subtract:
            Result = lvlMath.FirstNum - lvlMath.SecondNum;
            break;
          case LowLevelObj.Math_ENUM.Multiply:
            Result = lvlMath.FirstNum * lvlMath.SecondNum;
            break;
          case LowLevelObj.Math_ENUM.Divide:
            try
            {
              Result = lvlMath.FirstNum / lvlMath.SecondNum;
            }
            catch (Exception e)
```

```
          {
            throw e;
          }
          break;
      }
    }

    public double Sum(double[] anArray)
    {
      double sum=0;
      foreach (double arrItem in anArray)
      {
        sum += arrItem;
      }
      return sum;
    }
  }
}
```

By reviewing the code in Listing 8.1, you know that the constructor of the `AdvancedCalc` class has been overloaded two times. It has two public fields and nine public methods. The purposes of these methods are to calculate areas of different shapes and reuse the LowLevelObj assembly to include the simple math operations. Among them, the `Square()` method returns the area of a square and the `Circle()` method returns the area of a circle. The `Triangle()` method has been overloaded three times for computing the areas of an isosceles, an equilateral, and a scalene triangle, respectively. For example, the `Triangle()` method takes one parameter for the computation of the area of an equilateral triangle, two parameters for an isosceles, and three parameters for a scalene. These methods will be used to demonstrate the testing capability of the AutomatedTest tool for handling overloaded methods and constructors.

Then, a `SimpleCalc()` method is implemented to accept an object from the `LowLevelObj.SimpleMath` class and a `Math_ENUM` parameter and performs addition, subtraction, multiplication, or division for two given numbers. At the end of this chapter, this method will be used to verify the testing capabilities of the AutomatedTest tool for handling parameters passed by objects.

Finally, a `Sum()` method is implemented to receive a double array as its parameter and conduct a summation of the elements within the array. This method helps to test the capability of the AutomatedTest project for handling array parameters.

For the shapes, the area computations of a square and a circle are straightforward. The area for a circle is πr^2, where r is the radius. For a square, the area is a^2, where a is the side of a square. But the formulas for computing the areas of the three types of triangles with overloaded methods are a bit more involved, so a brief review is in order.

Basically, the calculations of the three kinds of triangles are all based on one equation, where *a* is the length of the base edge and *h* is the height of the triangle:

$$area = \frac{a \times h}{2}$$

Because the edges of a given triangle are always known, the key is to find value *h*, the height of a given triangle.

For an equilateral triangle, finding *h* is easy. Figure 8.1 shows an equilateral triangle with a given length, *a*. The relationship between *a* and *h* is shown here:

$$h = \sqrt{a^2 - (\frac{a}{2})^2}$$

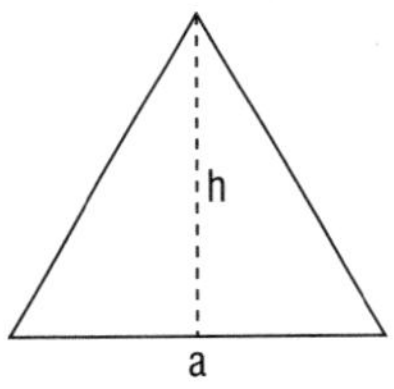

FIGURE 8.1
Finding the height (h) of an equilateral triangle

Figure 8.2 shows an isosceles triangle with two edges of length *b* and the other edge of length *a*. The relation between the *h*, *a*, and *b* is as follows:

$$h = \sqrt{b^2 - (\frac{a}{2})^2}$$

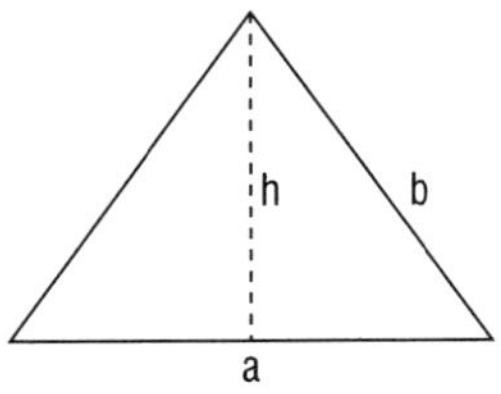

FIGURE 8.2
Finding the height of an isosceles triangle

For a triangle with sides of any length, a scalene triangle (Figure 8.3), you can find the height with the following assumptions:

- The triangle has sides of lengths *a*, *b*, and *c*. The overloaded method in Listing 8.1 requires these parameters be passed by values.

- a is always the base edge, that is, $b < c < a$. The private `SortIT()` method in Listing 8.1 achieves this.
- $a = b + c$.

With these assumptions, a typical scalene triangle looks like the one in Figure 8.3.

FIGURE 8.3
Finding the height of a scalene triangle

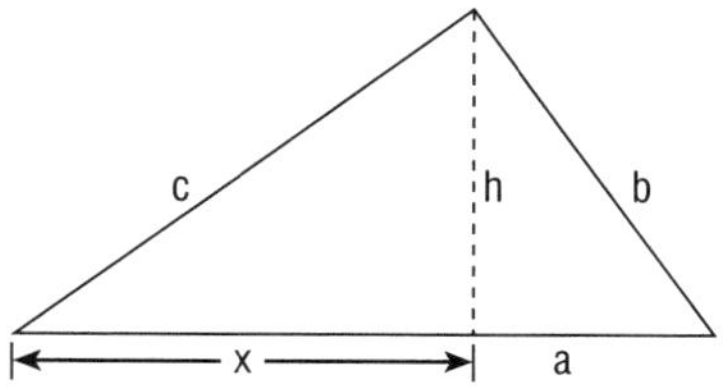

Making a line perpendicular to a from the intersection of b and c, the triangle is divided into two right triangles. Thus, the following equations can be created:

$$h^2 = c^2 - x^2$$
$$h^2 = b^2 - (a - x)^2$$

The height of the scalene triangle can be found by solving the preceding equations, substituting x with

$$\sqrt{c^2 - h^2}$$

as in the following:

$$h^2 - (b^2 - (a - \sqrt{c^2 - h^2})^2) = 0$$

The `GetTriangleHeight()` method in Listing 8.1 uses a Newton-Raphson iteration method to find the root of h, where $n > 1$ is the numbers of times the iteration takes place:

$$h_n = h_{n-1} - \frac{f\,(h_{n-1})}{f'\,(h_{n-1})}$$

The result of h by Newton-Raphson method is an approximation. The iteration will proceed until the root meets the tolerance of a particular application. Listing 8.1 specified the tolerance to be <0.00001 for this project. More detail information about the Newton-Raphson approximation method can be found in several references on numeric analysis listed in the bibliography at the end of this book.

There is one more special situation for solving a triangle problem. In the cases of isosceles and scalene, a given triangle could be a right triangle if the sum of the squares of two sides is the square of the third side. The `IsRightTriangle()` method in Listing 8.1 helps the `GetTriangleHeight()` find the height more easily and avoid using the Newton-Raphson approximation. Thus, the area of a given triangle is directly computed using

$$\frac{a \times h}{2}$$

After you finish typing in the code, save it and choose Build ➢ Build Solution in the Microsoft Visual Studio .NET IDE. A `HighLevelObj.dll` is generated, and to conclude the implementation of the HighLevelObj project, you can now use the AutomatedTest tool to test this assembly.

At this point, if you repeat the test process as described in Chapter 7 to generate a test script for the `HighLevelObj.dll` and to execute the test, you get an error. The error is caused by the object of the `LowLevelObj.SimpleMath` object, `lvlMath`, not being initialized by the test script or by a value read from the test data store. During the execution of the test, the script tries to fetch the value from the MS Excel worksheet for the object. Did you catch that? A value was not assigned to the `lvlMath` variable and it doesn't work. In the remainder of this chapter, I'll show you how to solve this problem and how to test methods that pass parameters by objects by using three scenarios.

- *The first is to implement a complete automation method, which is able to create a dummy instance for the class object in the test script.* This method is OK for simple classes that don't need to assign values to the properties or execute any methods to initialize an object.
- *The second allows the tester to specify a way to create an object for the class.* The tester can ask the AutomatedTest tool to assign values to the properties and invoke some methods before the object is passed to the method under test. This is similar to manual stubbing.
- *The third uses the bottom-up approach.* It creates a real object from the previously built test script for the lower-level module to test the higher-level module. This method breaks the bottleneck of the traditional stubbing and mock object processes.

Building a Form for Manual Stubbing

You now have enough background on why and how to test parameters passed by objects, which leads us to discuss integration testing. You have also built a `HighLevelObj.dll` assembly. One of the methods in the `HighLevelObj.dll` assembly requires a parameter that passes a `LowLevelObj.SimpleMath` object. In order for the AutomatedTest project to handle object parameters both manually and automatically, you will start to build a form as a dialog box for the AutomatedTest tool. This form will pop up when an object parameter is encountered during the process of test script generation and provide an interface so that the test engineers can build the object with convenience. To restart the implementation of the AutomatedTest tool, you need to copy the AutomatedTest project from `C:\SourceCode\Chapter07` to `C:\SourceCode\Chapter08` and start the project in Microsoft Visual Studio .NET IDE. To construct the form and code it, follow these steps:

1. In the Microsoft Visual Studio .NET IDE, choose Project ➤ Add Windows Form to add a Windows form with the name of StubForm.
2. Add the Windows form controls to the StubForm (see table below). After you populate the form with the controls, it will look similar to Figure 8.4.

Control	**Property**	**Value**
Label	Text	Available Constructor(s):
ListBox	Name	LstConstructors
	Modifiers	Public
Label	Text	Available Methods
ListBox	Name	LstMethods
	Modifiers	Public
Label	Text	Testing Constructor(s):
RichTextBox	Name	TxtConstructor
	Modifiers	Public
Label	Text	Testing Methods
RichTextBox	Name	TxtMethod
	Modifiers	Public
Button	Name	BtnAddConstructor
	Text	>
	Modifiers	Private
Button	Name	BtnRemoveConstructor
	Text	<
	Modifiers	Private
Button	Name	BtnAddMethod
	Text	>
	Modifiers	Private

Control	Property	Value
Button	Name	BtnRemovemethod
	Text	<
	Modifiers	Private
Button	Name	BtnOK
	Text	OK
	Modifiers	Private
OpenFileDialog	Name	opnFileDialog1
	Modifiers	Private
TextBox	Name	TxtDllToStub
	Text	“”
	Modifiers	Public
Button	Name	BtnBrowser
	Text	Browser
	Modifiers	Private

This form is used to show the information of the object the tester's interested in for the second scenario. The code of the `StubForm.cs` is mainly to define the actions taken when a corresponding button control is clicked. The list boxes on the left hold constructor information and method information, respectively. The user can add C# code from the list boxes on the left to the text boxes on the right in order to specify the behaviors of an object. Then, the code will be added to the test script when the OK button is clicked.

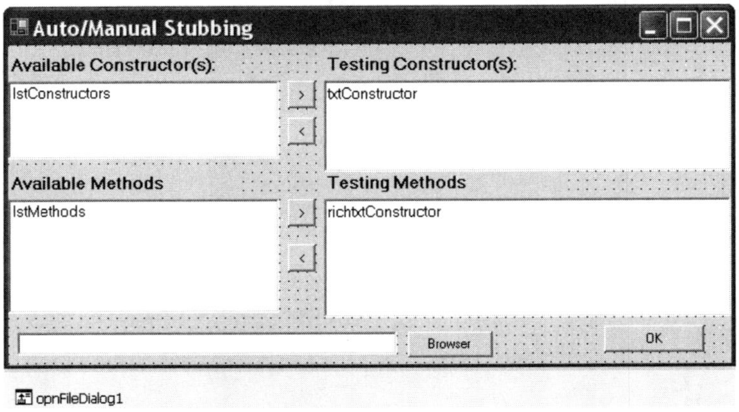

FIGURE 8.4
The StubForm after adding the controls

Now, I will explain how to add code for the button click events. Note that when programming a click event handler for a control in the Microsoft Visual Studio .NET IDE, double-clicking the control from the design editor will create an event handler delegate and lead the mouse pointer to where the code is needed. If the `btnAddConstructor` control is double-clicked, the Microsoft Visual Studio .NET IDE will generate a line of code for the event handler delegate, like here:

```
this.btnAddConstructor.Click += new System.EventHandler(
➥this.btnAddConstructor_Click);
```

The `this.btnAddConstructor_Click` within the parentheses refers to the event handler. You don't have to make change for this line of code. It also creates the starting and the ending curve brackets with respect to the event handler, such as:

```
private void btnAddConstructor_Click(object sender, System.EventArgs e)
{
}
```

You need to add code between the open and close curve brackets.

First, after you double-click the `btnAddConstructor`, it's the > button on the StubForm, add the code as it is in Listing 8.2.

Listing 8.2 Code for the *btnAddConstructor_Click()* Event Handler

```
private void btnAddConstructor_Click(object sender, System.EventArgs e)
{
  try
  {
    if (txtConstructor.Text!="")
    {
      string reasignCstor = lstConstructors.SelectedItem.ToString();
      reasignCstor = reasignCstor.Substring(reasignCstor.IndexOf(" "));
     txtConstructor.Text += "\n\n" + reasignCstor;

    }
    else
      txtConstructor.Text = lstConstructors.SelectedItem.ToString();

    lstConstructors.Items.RemoveAt(lstConstructors.SelectedIndex);
  }
  catch(Exception err)
  {
  MessageBox.Show(err.Message + "\nSelecte a constructor to add.",

➥"Error Reminder");
  }
}
```

The try-catch statement makes sure the selected item in the constructor information list on the left is added to the constructor's text box on the right. After the selected item is added to the right text box, the content of the text box is a line of correct C# code. Then, the event handler removes the selected item from the list in the left.

To appropriately initialize a constructor after the activities of the btnAddConstructor_Click() event handler, the users need to manually take care of the following matters:

- If the constructor requires parameters, the tester should specify them and assign values to them.
- If the tester wants to test more than one constructor, the tester needs to select the next constructor in sequence. The code of the event handler will reassign a new constructor to the created instance. The class name will be trimmed by the reasignCstor string variable.
- The tester needs to inspect the code in the text boxes of the right side. If errors are spotted in the coding or assignments, the tester needs to correct them. In the future, you may want the AutomatedTest program to detect code syntax errors.

When the OK button in the StubForm is clicked, the lines of code you just added will be incorporated into the test script exactly as they appear in the text box by a CodeSnippetStatement() method of the CodeDom namespace.

Next, double-click the btnAddMethod button from the StubForm design editor. Coding the btnAddMethod_Click() event handler is similar to adding code for the initialization of constructors. The code is in Listing 8.3.

Listing 8.3 Code for the *btnAddMethod_Click()* Event Handler

```
private void btnAddMethod_Click(object sender, System.EventArgs e)
{
  try
  {
    if (txtMethod.Text != "")
      txtMethod.Text += "\n\n" + lstMethods.SelectedItem.ToString();

    else
      txtMethod.Text = lstMethods.SelectedItem.ToString();

    lstMethods.Items.RemoveAt(lstMethods.SelectedIndex);
  }
  catch(Exception err)
  {
    MessageBox.Show(err.Message +"\nSelecte a method to add.",
➥"Error Reminder");
  }
}
```

This event handler adds a line of code by selecting a method from the method list on the left. If this method requires parameters, you have to type parameter values in the right text box based on testing requirements. Because this event handler is not implemented to check code errors, the contents must be correct C# code before the user clicks the OK button in the StubForm to add the code snippet to the test script. Otherwise, bugs will be introduced into the test script.

After coding the `btnAddConstructor_Click()` and `btnAddMethod_Click()` event handlers, use the same method to to add code to the `btnRemoveConstrutor_Click()` and `btnRemoveMethod_Click()` events. The code for `btnRemoveConstrutor_Click()` looks similar to Listing 8.4:

Listing 8.4 Code for the *btnRemove Constructor_Click()* Event Handler

```
private void btnRemoveConstructor_Click(object sender, System.EventArgs e)
{
  try
  {
    lstConstructors.Items.Add(txtConstructor.SelectedText.Replace("\n", ""));

    txtConstructor.Text =
ÂtxtConstructor.Text.Replace(txtConstructor.SelectedText, "").Trim();
  }
  catch(Exception err)
  {
    MessageBox.Show(err.Message + "\nSelecte a constructor to Remove.",

➥"Error Reminder");
  }
}
```

The rationale and coding techniques of the Remove (<) buttons are similar to those of the Add (>) buttons. The difference is the direction of the data flow. When the add constructor and method event handlers are executed, the selected items are removed from the left hand list boxes and added to the right hand text boxes. The Remove button click event removes the selected texts in the right text boxes and adds them back into the left list boxes for constructor code or method invocation code, respectively. Code for the `btnRemoveMethod_Click()` event handler is in Listing 8.5.

Listing 8.5 Code for the *btnRemoveMethod_Click()* Event Handler

```
private void btnRemoveMethod_Click(object sender, System.EventArgs e)
{
  try
  {
    lstMethods.Items.Add(txtMethod.SelectedText.Replace("\n", ""));"
```

```
      txtMethod.Text =
➥txtMethod.Text.Replace(txtMethod.SelectedText, "").Trim();
    }
    catch(Exception err)
    {
      MessageBox.Show(err.Message +
➥"\nSelecte a method to Remove.", "Error Reminder");

    }
  }
```

Because we want to test a higher-level module that makes use of an object of a lower-level module, the Browser button is placed to locate the previously built DLL assembly of a lower-level test script. When this button is clicked and a DLL assembly is selected, the code of the manual stubbing in the text boxes is ignored, and the needed object will be created by late binding from the selected test script assembly. To add code for the Browser button, double-click it in the design editor and code the `btnBrowser_Click()` event as in Listing 8.6:

Listing 8.6 Code for the *btnBrowser_Click()* Event Handler

```
private void btnBrowser_Click(object sender, System.EventArgs e)
{
  opnFileDialog1.Title = "Select a test script dll";
  opnFileDialog1.Filter = "Script Dlls (*.dll)|*.dll|All Files(*.*)|*.*";
  opnFileDialog1.Multiselect = false;

  if (opnFileDialog1.ShowDialog() == DialogResult.OK)
  {
    txtDllToStub.Text = opnFileDialog1.FileName;
  }
}
```

In the preceding code, after the event declaration, the first three lines set the `Title` and `Filter` properties of the `OpenFileDialog` control, `opnFileDialog1`. The `Filter` property allows `*.dll` files to appear in the open file dialog by default. The `Multiselect` property is set to false, which allows the tool to select only one test script assembly at a time to test a higher-level module. An `if` statement detects an OK button click. If the OK button is clicked, the DLL filename is stored in the `txtDllToStub.Text` property. The AutomatedTest tool creates the object using the DLL assembly and continues to generate the test script.

Next, one private field and one public property are created and coded to determine whether the DLL assembly contains a test script assembly. If the `TestClassFound` property is false, an error message should be programmed in the TestForm. The code is in Listing 8.7.

Listing 8.7 Code for the private field and the *TestClassFound* Property

```
private bool m_TestClassFound;
public bool TestClassFound
{
  get
  {
    Assembly stubAssm = Assembly.LoadFrom(txtDllToStub.Text);

    string typeName = "";

    foreach (Type type in stubAssm.GetTypes())
    {
      if (type.ToString().StartsWith("Test") ||
➥type.ToString().IndexOf("Test.Test")>-1)
      {
        typeName = type.ToString();
        m_TestClassFound = true;
        break;
      }
    }
    return m_TestClassFound;
  }
  set {m_TestClassFound = value;}
}
```

The code of this property uses the Assembly type from the Reflection namespace to load the specified DLL file. Then, the `foreach` loop enumerates the Type classes through the assembly. The enumeration looks for the class name starting with "Test" or containing "Test.Test" string by an `if` statement. When a test script assembly is found, the enumeration is stopped and returns a true. Otherwise, it returns a false.

Next, two public string fields and a `MakeNewObjOfStub()` helper method are created. This method is executed after the Browser button is clicked and creates a late binding to a low-level test script. The `MakeNewObjOfStub()` takes three parameters; one is the DLL filename, the others are the row number of the Excel worksheet and the object parameter information. Two segments of code are created based on the nature of the low-level test script DLL and are stored in `m_RealObject` and `m_CreateReference` string fields. The content in the first variable is for the test script C# code file. The second is for the modification of the C# project properties. Code for these fields and method is in Listing 8.8.

Listing 8.8 Code for the public fields and the *MakeNewObjofStub()* Helper Method

```
public string m_RealObject;
public string m_CreateReference;
public void MakeNewObjOfStub(string DllToStub, int shtRow, ParameterInfo p)
{
  string[] interpolNames = DllToStub.Split('\\);'
  string assmName = interpolNames[interpolNames.Length-1].Replace(".dll", "");
  Assembly stubAssm = Assembly.LoadFrom(DllToStub);

  string typeName = "";

  foreach (Type type in stubAssm.GetTypes())
  {
    if (type.ToString().StartsWith("Test") ||
➥type.ToString().IndexOf("Test.Test")>-1)
    {
      typeName = type.ToString();
      m_TestClassFound = true;
      break;
    }
  }

  m_RealObject   = "Assembly appDomain_" + shtRow;
  m_RealObject   += " = Assembly.LoadFrom(@\"" + DllToStub + "\");


  m_RealObject   += "Type TestClass_" + shtRow + " = appDomain_";
  m_RealObject   += shtRow + ".GetType(\"" + typeName + "\");


  m_RealObject   += "object objInst_" + shtRow;
  m_RealObject   += " = Activator.CreateInstance(TestClass_";
  m_RealObject   += shtRow + ");


  m_RealObject   += "MethodInfo mi_" + shtRow + " = TestClass_";
  m_RealObject   += shtRow +".GetMethod(\"StartTest\");


  m_RealObject   += "" + p.ParameterType.ToString() + " ";
  m_RealObject   += p.Name + "_" + shtRow + " =(";
  m_RealObject   += p.ParameterType.ToString() +") mi_" + shtRow;
  m_RealObject   += ".Invoke(objInst_" + shtRow + ", null);


  m_CreateReference = "<Reference\n";

  m_CreateReference += "Name = \"" + assmName + "\"\n";
```

```
    m_CreateReference += "AssemblyName = \"" + assmName + "\"\n";

    m_CreateReference += "HintPath = \"" + DllToStub + "\"\n";

    m_CreateReference += "/>\n";

    m_CreateReference += GetDependencies(stubAssm);
  }
```

In this code segment, after the `MakeNewObjOfStub()` helper method is declared, a string array and a string variable are created to prepare a proper name for the assembly. The assembly name requires only the first part of the name without the DLL extension. The `Split()` method of the string class converts the filename of the assembly into a string array using a backslash for separation. Then, the last element of the array is assigned to the `assmName` variable. The same code segment used for the `TestClassFound` property is used to ensure that this assembly creates the needed class object.

Finally, the `MakeNewObjOfStub()` helper method creates a segment of code for late binding to the specified DLL assembly and invokes the `StartTest()` method. Because this code is relatively stable, a string field, `CreateStub`, stores the code statements for late binding. There are five statements in total corresponding to the five `m_RealObject` clusters in the preceding code sample. The responsibilities of these five statements are:

- A statement to create an Assembly object to load the DLL assembly of the specified test script
- A statement to create a Type object to hold the test class information
- A statement that uses the Type object to create an activator object
- A statement that creates a `MethodInfo` object to hold the method information of the test method of the test script
- A statement that invokes the `Invoke()` method of the `MethodInfo` object, which returns an object of the lower-level module to the parameter passed by object. The object is unboxed with regard to the original type class.

Based on the preceding list, the code segment in the generated test scripts keeps a general pattern as shown here (where _xx are unique numbers for parameter differentiation):

```
Assembly appDomain_xx = Assembly.LoadFrom(DLLFilename);
Type TestClass_xx = appDomain_xx.GetType(ClassName);
object objInst_xx = Activator.CreateInstance(TestClass_xx);
MethodInfo mi_xx = TestClass_xx.GetMethod("StartTest");
ClassName objParam_xx = (ClassName) mi_xx.Invoke(objInst_xx, null);
```

The second string field, `m_CreateReference`, stores an XML tag for a dependency, which is needed by the `*.csproj` file. (This file will be discussed in Chapter 10.) The `MakeNewObjOfStub()` method first creates a `<Reference>` tag for the `m_CreateReference` field. Then, the method adds three attributes and closes the tag for the content of this field. For example, if the targeted assembly is the `LowLevelObj.dll`, this XML segment should look like the following:

```
<Reference
  Name = "LowLevelObj"
  AssemblyName = "LowLevelObj"
  HintPath = ""
\>
```

If the test script assembly depends on other lower-level modules, it appends the name(s) of the dependency(s) in the `m_CreateReference` field by calling another helper method, `GetDependencies()`, as coded in Listing 8.9. If the development and test strategy observe that a module only integrates modules one level lower, calling this method recursively can be avoided:

Listing 8.9 Code for the *GetDependencies()* Helper Method

```
private string GetDependencies(Assembly assmName)
{
  string refStr="";
  foreach (AssemblyName aRef in assmName.GetReferencedAssemblies())
  {
    if (aRef.FullName.IndexOf("mscorlib") < 0)
    {
      refStr += "<Reference\n";

      refStr += "Name = \"" + aRef.Name + "\"\n";

      refStr += "AssemblyName = \"" + aRef.Name + "\"\n";

      refStr += "HintPath = \"" + aRef.CodeBase + "\"\n" + "/>\n";

    }
  }
  return refStr;
}
```

The `GetDependencies()` helper method receives an assembly as the parameter. The `foreach` loop finds all the dependencies needed by this assembly and writes the XML code for the `*.csproj` file.

Finally, coding the OK button click event does nothing more than hide the StubForm. Its code is in Listing 8.10:

Listing 8.10 Code for the *GetDependencies()* Helper Method

```
private void btnOK_Click(object sender, System.EventArgs e)
{
  this.Hide();
}
```

Now, the StubForm is completely implemented. The coding for this form is straightforward. In order for you to check the code when you encounter compiling errors, Listing 8.11 has the code for each of the event handlers and helper methods. However, the .NET IDE–generated code segments are omitted. If you have downloaded the source code from the website, `www.sybex.com`, you can refer to it for the completed code.

Listing 8.11 The Full Code of the *StubForm.cs* File

```
using System;
using System.Drawing;
using System.Collections;
using System.ComponentModel;
using System.Windows.Forms;

namespace TestTools.AutomatedTest
{


  public class StubForm : System.Windows.Forms.Form
  {
    // Windows Form Designer generated code
    private void btnAddConstructor_Click(object sender, System.EventArgs e)
    {
      try
      {
        if (txtConstructor.Text!="")
        {
         string reasignCstor = lstConstructors.SelectedItem.ToString();
       reasignCstor = reasignCstor.Substring(reasignCstor.IndexOf(" "));

         txtConstructor.Text += "\n\n" + reasignCstor;

       }
       else
          txtConstructor.Text = lstConstructors.SelectedItem.ToString();

        lstConstructors.Items.RemoveAt(lstConstructors.SelectedIndex);
```

```
      }
      catch(Exception err)
      {
        MessageBox.Show(err.Message + "\nSelecte a constructor to add.",
➥"Error Reminder");
      }
    }

    private void btnAddMethod_Click(object sender, System.EventArgs e)
    {
      try
      {
        if (txtMethod.Text != "")
          txtMethod.Text += "\n\n" + lstMethods.SelectedItem.ToString();

        else
          txtMethod.Text = lstMethods.SelectedItem.ToString();

        lstMethods.Items.RemoveAt(lstMethods.SelectedIndex);
      }
      catch(Exception err)
      {
        MessageBox.Show(err.Message +"\nSelecte a method to add.",
➥"Error Reminder");
      }
    }

    private void btnRemoveConstructor_Click(object sender, System.EventArgs e)
    {
      try
      {
        lstConstructors.Items.Add(
➥txtConstructor.SelectedText.Replace("\n", ""));

        txtConstructor.Text =
➥txtConstructor.Text.Replace(txtConstructor.SelectedText, "").Trim();
      }
      catch(Exception err)
      {
        MessageBox.Show(err.Message + "\nSelecte a constructor to Remove.",
➥"Error Reminder");
      }
    }

    private void btnRemoveMethod_Click(object sender, System.EventArgs e)
    {
      try
```

```
        {
          lstMethods.Items.Add(txtMethod.SelectedText.Replace("\n", ""));

          txtMethod.Text =
➥txtMethod.Text.Replace(txtMethod.SelectedText, "").Trim();
        }
        catch(Exception err)
        {
          MessageBox.Show(err.Message + \nSelecte a method to Remove.", "Error
➥Reminder");"

        }
      }

      private void btnBrowser_Click(object sender, System.EventArgs e)
      {

        opnFileDialog1.Title = "Select a test script dll";
        opnFileDialog1.Filter = "Script Dlls (*.dll)|*.dll|All Files(*.*)|*.*";
        opnFileDialog1.Multiselect = false;

        if (opnFileDialog1.ShowDialog() == DialogResult.OK)
        {
          txtDllToStub.Text = opnFileDialog1.FileName;
        }
      }


      private bool m_TestClassFound;
      public bool TestClassFound
      {

        get
        {
          Assembly stubAssm = Assembly.LoadFrom(txtDllToStub.Text);

          string typeName = "";

          foreach (Type type in stubAssm.GetTypes())
          {
            if (type.ToString().StartsWith("Test") ||
➥type.ToString().IndexOf("Test.Test")>-1)
            {
              typeName = type.ToString();
              m_TestClassFound = true;
              break;
            }
          }
          return m_TestClassFound;
```

```
      }
      set {m_TestClassFound = value;}
    }


    public string m_RealObject;
    public string m_CreateReference;

    public void MakeNewObjOfStub(string DllToStub, int shtRow, ParameterInfo p)
    {
      string[] interpolNames = DllToStub.Split('\\);'
      string assmName =
➥interpolNames[interpolNames.Length-1].Replace(".dll", "");
      Assembly stubAssm = Assembly.LoadFrom(DllToStub);

      string typeName = "";

      foreach (Type type in stubAssm.GetTypes())
      {
        if (type.ToString().StartsWith("Test") ||
➥type.ToString().IndexOf("Test.Test")>-1)
        {
          typeName = type.ToString();
          m_TestClassFound = true;
          break;
        }
      }

m_RealObject   = "Assembly appDomain_" + shtRow;
m_RealObject   += " = Assembly.LoadFrom(@\"" + DllToStub + "\");


m_RealObject   += "Type TestClass_" + shtRow + " = appDomain_";
m_RealObject   += shtRow + ".GetType(\"" + typeName + "\");


m_RealObject   += "object objInst_" + shtRow;
m_RealObject   += " = Activator.CreateInstance(TestClass_";
m_RealObject   += shtRow + ");


m_RealObject   += "MethodInfo mi_" + shtRow + " = TestClass_";
m_RealObject   += shtRow +".GetMethod(\"StartTest\");


m_RealObject   += "" + p.ParameterType.ToString() + " ";
m_RealObject   += p.Name + "_" + shtRow + " =(";
m_RealObject   += p.ParameterType.ToString() +") mi_" + shtRow;
```

```
m_RealObject   += ".Invoke(objInst_" + shtRow + ", null);

m_CreateReference = "<Reference\n";

m_CreateReference += "Name = \"" + assmName + "\"\n";

m_CreateReference += "AssemblyName = \"" + assmName + "\"\n";

m_CreateReference += "HintPath = \"" + DllToStub + "\"\n";

m_CreateReference += "/>\n";

m_CreateReference += GetDependencies(stubAssm);
}

    private string GetDependencies(Assembly assmName)
    {
      string refStr="";
      foreach (AssemblyName aRef in assmName.GetReferencedAssemblies())
      {
        if (aRef.FullName.IndexOf("mscorlib") < 0)
        {
         refStr += "<Reference\n

          refStr += "Name = \"" + aRef.Name + "\"\n";

          refStr += "AssemblyName = \"" + aRef.Name + "\"\n";

          refStr += "HintPath = \"" + aRef.CodeBase + "\"\n" + "/>\n";

        }
      }
      return refStr;
    }

    private void btnOK_Click(object sender, System.EventArgs e)
    {
      this.Hide();
    }

  }
}
```

The form construction and coding are completed. But you have not done anything directly related to testing the parameter objects. As usual, the testing code will be implemented in the `TestForm.cs` file. Remember to save the code before you begin the next tasks.

Code for Testing Parameters Passed by Objects

The previous section implemented a StubForm to allows the users to specify the behavior of an object used to test a higher level module. After the specification, the resulting code should be returned to the main TestForm class in order to be incorporated into the generated test script. This section resumes updating and coding the TestForm by completing the following steps:

1. Open the TestForm in the design editor.
2. Add a CheckBox control to the TestForm with the following properties:
   - Name: chckManualStub
   - Text: Manual Stub

The addition of this check box is to allow the test engineer to decide whether to test the object parameters by generating a dummy object of the low-level module by the tool or to interface with StubForm to specify an object.

Now you are ready to add more code to the `TestForm.cs` file to deal with parameters passed by objects. With the `TestForm.cs` file open in the code editor, navigate to the `CollectParametersForTest()` method. Then find the location of the following `else-if` statement containing a commented `CreateObjectParameter()` method call. I assume you have coded your project exactly as it was coded in Chapter 7. Otherwise, you can locate the position with the logic of the parameter types:

```
...
else if (rng.Value2.ToString() == "new")
{
   //CreateObjectParameter(ref i, p);
}
...
```

The commented `CreateObjectParameter()` method is the first method you will code for this section. You can remove the two slashes to activate the method calling. After the slashes are removed, the code looks like this with activated code line in bold:

```
...
else if (rng.Value2.ToString() == "new")
{
   CreateObjectParameter(ref i, p);
}
...
```

Move to another location outside the `CollectParametersForTest()` method and start declaring the `CreateObjectParameter()` method. The code segment of the `CreateObjectParameter()` method is shown in Listing 8.12.

Listing 8.12 The Code for the First Helper Method, *CreateObjectParameter()*

```
private void CreateObjectParameter(ref int i, ParameterInfo p)
{
  if (chckManualStub.Checked)
  {
    Excel.Range stubRang = xSheet.get_Range(TestUtility.ConvCHAR(p.Position+3)
➥ + i, TestUtility.ConvCHAR(p.Position+3) + i);
    string[] stubType = stubRang.Comment.Text("", 1, 0).Split(' ');
    OBJStub(stubType[0], p.Name, i);
    if (stubForm.txtDllToStub.Text.Length > 0)//added for integration
    {
       stubForm.MakeNewObjOfStub(stubForm.txtDllToStub.Text, i, p);
    }
    if (stubForm.m_RealObject != "" || stubForm.m_RealObject != null)
    {

      cm.Statements.Add(new CodeSnippetStatement(stubForm.m_RealObject  ));
      stubForm.m_RealObject  ="";
      stubForm.txtDllToStub.Text = "";
    }
    if (stubForm.textBox1.Text.Trim() != "")
    {
      cm.Statements.Add(new CodeSnippetStatement(stubForm.textBox1.Text));
    }
    if (stubForm.textBox2.Text.Trim() != "")
    {
      cm.Statements.Add(new CodeSnippetStatement(stubForm.textBox2.Text));
    }
  }
  else
  {
    cRight=new CodeFieldReferenceExpression(null, "new " +
➥p.ParameterType.ToString() + "()");
  }
}
```

Not bad—this method has fewer than 20 lines of code. The names of classes and methods of the CodeDom namespace are lengthy. The action is to grab the parameter information from the MS Excel worksheet to initialize a call for the `OBJStub()` method. The `stubType` string array is to extrapolate the parameter type from the Excel comments. The `OBJStub()` method prepares the `StubForm` object. Then it copies the composed code from the `StubForm` object to the test scripts by calling the CodeDom method `CodeSnippetStatement()`.

Note that the `CodeSnippetStatement()` method of `System.CodeDom` directly adds a specific code segment to the test script. Thus, it enables the tester to add a code stub and specify the behavior of the object to be passed. The coding logic is easy enough to follow. The first `if` statement determines whether the manual stub check box is checked or not. If it is checked, the CodeDom method adds the code specified by the StubForm to the test script based on the nested `if` statement logic. If it is not checked, the test script uses its default method to create an instance for the parameter under test. The nested `if` statements include three possible approaches to creating a code segment and initializing an object for testing:

- *If the manual stub check box is not checked, the object stubbing is totally automatic and a simple dummy object is created.* The last `else` statement handles this by reassigning the `cRight` object. For example, the `HighLevelObj.dll` assembly has a method that requires a parameter of the `LowLevelObj.Simplemath` object. This approach enables the AutomatedTest tool to produce the following line of code:

```
LowLevelObj.SimpleMath lvlMath_x = new LowLevelObj.SimpleMath();
```

- *A manual stub is created when there are code segments in the text areas of the StubForm.* These code segments are specified by the tester. If the tester has a good knowledge of the assembly under test, this stub creation will be accurate. Otherwise, some guesswork is needed.
- *When the Browser button is clicked from the StubForm, the AutomatedTest tool invokes the StartTest() method of the specified test script assembly generated for a lower-level module by late binding.* This invocation creates a real object of the lower-level module to complete this test. Thus, software engineers will find this approach most useful and desirable.

Now let's proceed with the AutomatedTest project by coding the `OBJStub()` method.

Making Code Stubs with a Given Assembly

The `OBJStub()` method calls two simple helper methods before it continues to process the parameter information. Let's make these two methods first. The `InitiateStubForm()` and `RelocateObjectAssembly()` methods are shown in Listing 8.13.

Listing 8.13 Code for the *InitiateStubForm()* and *RelocateObjectAssembly()* Helper Methods

```
private void InitiateStubForm(string typeStr)
{
  stubForm.Text = typeStr + " Stub";
  stubForm.txtConstructor.Text = "";
  stubForm.txtMethod.Text = "";
  stubForm.lstConstructors.Items.Clear();
  stubForm.lstMethods.Items.Clear();
  stubForm.ControlBox = false;
}

private void RelocateObjectAssembly(out string PathStr, string typeStr)
{
```

```
    PathStr = null;
    openFileDialog1.Title = "Locate the " + typeStr;
    openFileDialog1.Filter = "DLL Files(*.dll)|*.dll|All Files|*.*";
    if (openFileDialog1.ShowDialog() == DialogResult.OK)
      PathStr = openFileDialog1.FileName;
  }
```

As Listing 8.13 shows, before you code the method, you need to declare a `StubForm` object field. Then you code the two helper methods. The first helper method initiates the `StubForm` object. The second method helps the AutomatedTest tool with an open file dialog to locate the assembly where the parameter object comes from. The code in these two methods is fundamental.

Enumerating Assembly Information

Next, you can make your code for the `OBJStub()` method look like Listing 8.14.

Listing 8.14 Code for the *OBJStub()* Method

```
  private StubForm stubForm = new StubForm();
  private void OBJStub(string typeStr, string pName, int i)
  {
    InitiateStubForm(typeStr);

    string PathStr = null;

    RelocateObjectAssembly(out PathStr, typeStr);
    try //added for integration test
    {
      Assembly asm = Assembly.LoadFrom(PathStr);

      Type type = asm.GetType(typeStr);

      string list1Str = "";
      ConstructorInfo[] cis = type.GetConstructors();
      foreach (ConstructorInfo ci in cis)
      {
        list1Str += type.Name + "(";
        ParameterInfo[] ps = ci.GetParameters();
        foreach (ParameterInfo p in ps)
        {
          list1Str += p.ParameterType +" "+ p.Name + ", ";
        }
        if (list1Str.IndexOf(",")>0)
        {
          list1Str += "Xtra";
          list1Str = list1Str.Replace(", Xtra", ")");
        }
        if (list1Str.EndsWith("("))
```

```
        list1Str += ")";
      list1Str = type.Name.ToString() + " " + pName + "_" + i +
➥" = new " + list1Str + ";";
          stubForm.lstConstructors.Items.Add(list1Str);
      list1Str = "";
    }
    MethodInfo[] mis = type.GetMethods();
    foreach (MethodInfo mi in mis)
    {
      list1Str += mi.Name + "(";
      ParameterInfo[] ps = mi.GetParameters();
      foreach (ParameterInfo p in ps)
      {
        list1Str += p.ParameterType + " " + p.Name + ", ";
      }
      if (list1Str.EndsWith(", "))
      {
        list1Str += "Xtra";
        list1Str = list1Str.Replace(", Xtra", ")");
      }
      if (list1Str.Trim().EndsWith("("))
        list1Str += ")";
      if (list1Str.Trim().StartsWith("set_"))
      {
        list1Str = list1Str.Replace("set_", "");
        list1Str = list1Str.Replace("(", " = ");
        list1Str = list1Str.Replace(")","");
      }
      list1Str = pName + "_" + i + "." + list1Str + ";";
      stubForm.lstMethods.Items.Add(list1Str);
      list1Str = "";
    }
    stubForm.ShowDialog(this);
  } //added for integration test
  catch //added for integration test
  {
    stubForm.txtDllToStub.Text = PathStr;

    if (!stubForm.TestClassFound)
    {
      stubForm.txtDllToStub.Text = "";
      MessageBox.Show("Test method is not found in this assembly.",
➥"Wrong Stubbing Information", MessageBoxButtons.OK,
➥MessageBoxIcon.Information);
      stubForm.ShowDialog();
    }
    stubForm.TestClassFound = false;
  }
}
```

When the two helper methods, `InitiateStubForm()` and `RelocateObjectAssembly()`, are called, the `OBJStub()` method initializes the `StubForm` object and gets the location of the assembly where the parameter object belongs. Then, a `try-catch` segment accomplishes the entire object creation. The `try` statement starts with code to invoke methods from the `System.Reflection` namespace and the Type class. The first `foreach` loop with a nested `foreach` loop enumerates the constructor information and its parameters. The second `foreach` loop with the nested `foreach` loop enumerates the method information and its parameters within an assembly. After these enumerations are done, information about the constructors and methods are planted in the list boxes of the StubForm and the `StubForm` object appears as a modal form by calling the `ShowDialog()` method. At runtime, if the manual stub check box is checked, the AutomatedTest tool hands the torch to the test engineer. The test engineer is able to specify how to build the parameter object by a few mouse clicks and some keystrokes. Entering code into the StubForm creates an object stub, or clicking the Browser button in the StubForm reuses an object from an exiting test script. After the OK button is clicked, the process is automatic again.

If the assembly selected by clicking the Browser button is not a properly built assembly from a test script, the `catch` statement reports an error to alert the user.

Finally, you need to navigate to the `CollectParametersForTest()` method and locate the lines with a CodeDom statement and a comment:

```
cm.Statements.Add(new CodeAssignStatement(cLeft, cRight));
//AddStubDecision(rng);
```

You should alter these lines of code simply by switching the slashes (//) from the `AddStubDecision()` method to the `cm.Statement.Add()` method. After the slashes are switched, these two lines look like this:

```
//cm.Statements.Add(new CodeAssignStatement(cLeft, cRight));
AddStubDecision(rng);
```

Then you code the `AddStubDecision()` method. The `AddStubDecision()` method is very simple, as you can see in Listing 8.15.

Listing 8.15 Code for the *AddStubDecision()* Method

```
private void AddStubDecision(Excel.Range rng)
{
   if (!(rng.Value2.ToString() == "new" && chckManualStub.Checked))
   {
      cm.Statements.Add(new CodeAssignStatement(cLeft, cRight));
   }
}
```

You have seen a few decision makers based on the value "new" originated from the MS Excel worksheet. The AutomatedTest tool is capable of assigning values to primitive data type parameters while gathering information from a given assembly. When the parameter is an object, the test engineer must give new as the value of the object. Thus, when the execution of the AutomatedTest tool finds a value new in a cell in the MS Excel worksheet, it recognizes that this parameter is passed by object. The word new is the only reserved keyword for the AutomatedTest tool for editing testing data.

Finishing Testing Parameters Passed by Objects

Now the code for generating a script to test the parameters passed by objects has been completed. You can build the project and test-run it with the newly added code to see how it tests the `HighLevelObj.dll` assembly, which was created at the beginning of this chapter. One of the methods of the HighLevelObj assembly takes an object of the `LowLevelObj.dll` assembly from Chapter 4. When you start running the AutomatedTest tool, the TestForm looks similar to Figure 8.5.

FIGURE 8.5
The new appearance of the TestForm with the addition of a Manual Stub check box

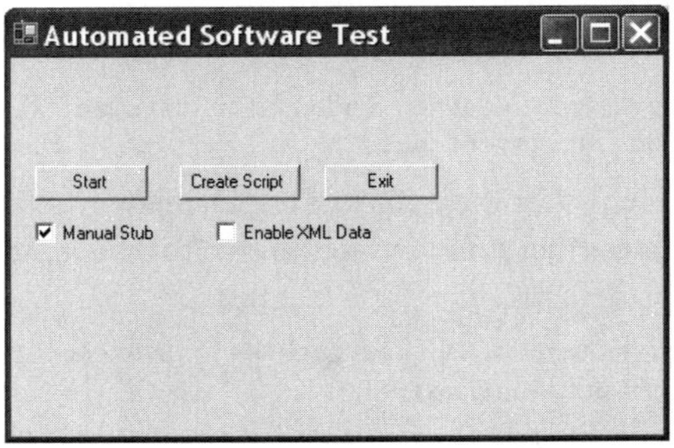

Follow these steps to create a test script to test the `HighLevelObj.dll`:

1. Click the Start button to open the Open file dialog box.
2. Navigate to `C:\SourceCode\Chapter08\HighLevelObj\bin\Debug` and select the `HighLevelObj.dll` file.
3. Click the Open button from the Open file dialog box to open the TypeUnderTest form.
4. Check the `AdvancedCalc` class in the check list box.
5. Click the OK button.

6. An MS Excel worksheet opens (Figure 8.6). In the Excel worksheet, the constructor(s) and methods in the `AdvancedCalc` class are listed. You may be interested to test all of them at this point. The AutomatedTest tool has assigned values to all the numeric and Boolean parameters. This is a powerful feature to make this testing method efficient. For this test , the only editing you need to do is for the `SimpleCalc()` method. This method takes a `LowLevelObj.SimpleMath` object as a parameter. Type in **new** into cell C14 as the value for the parameter `lvlMath`. Leave all others intact.

   Remember to save the MS Excel worksheet before you proceed, but don't exit the worksheet.

FIGURE 8.6
The data for testing all the methods and properties of the Advanced-Math class generated by the AutomatedTest tool

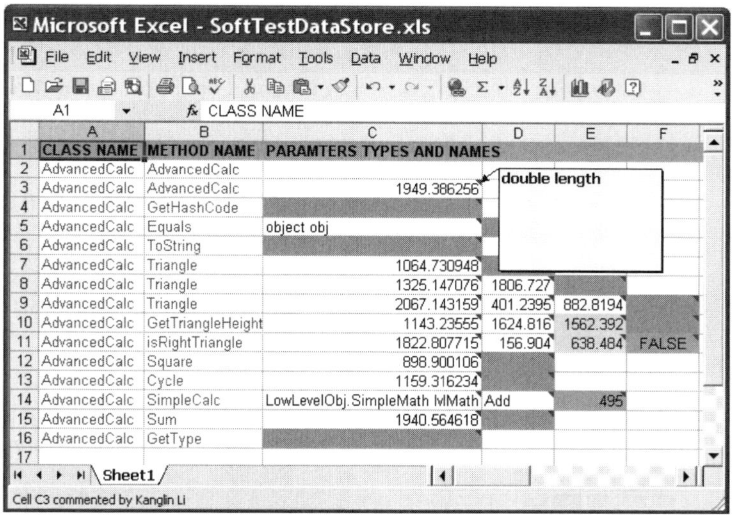

7. Switch to the Automated Software Test form.
8. Make sure the Manual Stub check box is checked. (If you do not check this check box, it is OK. The AutomatedTest tool will generate a dummy object for the test script without human interaction, which works only when the initialization of the object doesn't require specific set-ups of its properties and methods.)
9. Click the Create Script button. It starts to generate the test script until it encounters the value `"new"` for the parameter of `LowLevelObj.SimpleMath`. A StubForm form opens.
10. Click the Browser button on the StubForm. An open file dialog box opens for you to tell the AutomatedTest tool where to find the assembly from which the `SimpleMath` object should be created. In Chapter 7, you used the AutomatedTest tool to generate the test script `TestScript.cs` for the `LowLevelObj.dll` assembly. When you built a `TestScript.exe`

assembly, you might also have built a TestScript.dll assembly for it. Select either the TestScript.exe or the TestScript.dll assembly to create the LowLevelObj.SimpleMath object for this test by navigating to the location where you saved the TestLowLevelObj.dll. If your code is identical to the sample code, the TestScript.exe or TestScript.dll is created in C:\Temp at this point.

11. Click the Open button. The test script is completed. It is still saved as C:\Temp\TestScript.cs because it overwrites the previous test script at this stage.

12. Open this file in a text editor. Examine the file and find the following code segment:

```
...
Assembly appDomain_14 = Assembly.LoadFrom(@"C:\Temp\ TestScript.dll");

Type TestClass_14 = appDomain_14.GetType("LowLevelObjTest.TestLowLeveObj");

object objInst_14 = Activator.CreateInstance(TestClass_14);

MethodInfo mi_14 = TestClass_14.GetMethod("StartTest");

LowLevelObj.SimpleMath lvlMath_14 =(LowLevelObj.SimpleMath)
➥ mi_14.Invoke(objInst_14, null);
...
```

This piece of code reuses the previously built test script by using late binding. The advantages of this method over the stubbing method or mock objects are reiterated by the programming and testing:

- It reuses a previously built test script assembly and provides a real object, which refines the practice of higher-level unit testing by ensuring totally independent operation of the code under test.
- It avoids manual stubbing or mock objects by utilizing the previously built object setup. Manual stubbing for certain application always requires time for learning, is time consuming, and guesswork is sometimes required.
- It improves code design of the test script. An isolated object from a lower-level unit testing script improves the code by preserving encapsulation, enhancing reusability, reducing global dependencies, and clarifying the interactions between classes.

Now, the AutomatedTest tool is able to test parameters passed by objects, which was the desired goal at the beginning of this chapter. The example demonstrates only one of the three approaches implemented, the bottom-up approach. The other two methods will be covered in Chapter 12 of the book.

At this point, the TestPass() and TestFail() methods are still missing from the generated test script. If you want to build an assembly from the generated test script now, add the

TestPass() and TestFail() methods as was done in Chapter 7. Then open a DOS command window and type the following command all on one line:

```
C:\WINDOWS\Microsoft.NET\Framework\v1.0.3705\csc testscript.cs
➥/r:C:\SourceCode\Chapter08\AutomatedTest\Bin\Debug\Interop.Excel.dll
➥/r:C:\SourceCode\Chapter08\HighLevelObj\bin\debug\HighLevelObj.dll
➥/r:C:\SourceCode\Chapter04\LowLevelObj\bin\debug\LowLevelObj.dll
```

This time, you need to add the LowLevelObj.dll in the command as a reference in order to compile this test script. Make sure the TestScript.exe executable and the reference DLLs are in the same folder. Use a text editor to create a fileArray.txt file that includes the line: C:/Temp/SoftTestDataStore.xls.

Run the executable and check the results.

In the next chapter, I will discuss the implementation of test verification and validation. When the script generation programming is completed in Chapter 9, the TestPass() and TestFail() methods will be automatically added to the test scripts.

Summary

This chapter ended with the successful automatic test script generation and execution. The AutomatedTest project has improved with the introduction of the System.Reflection and System.CodeDom namespaces, the Type class, the XML documentation, and the Excel API programming. Enabling the reusability of the lower-level test scripts eliminated the need to make stub or mock objects. Integration testing uses real objects.

You now have an understanding of how the test process is automated. In the next chapters, we will finish the last part of generating the test script. Then, we will wrap up the project by adding string variables to replace the fixed naming conventions and improving its GUI and its usability.

Chapter 9

Verification, Validation, and Presentation

The focus of this book is on building an AutomatedTest project. Although not much of the text is devoted to discussing theories of software testing, you understand the importance of the software testing process in producing a quality product. I strongly believe that a successful business owes its reputation to a skillful testing team. The quality of its software products adds value to a company in the competitive market.

At this point, you have enabled the AutomatedTest tool to complete the portions of the testing process from collecting test information to generating test scripts. In this chapter, I'll discuss the following topics:

- How the test scripts use the test results to verify the execution of the assembly under test
- How the test scripts validate the test results
- Finally, how the test scripts present the test results

Conventional verification involves reviewing and evaluating code logic. In this chapter, validation involves actual testing and takes place after verification is completed. The verification is completed by the interface between the computer hardware and software and the execution of the test scripts. It determines the following:

- Whether the members of a class under test execute as they are expected
- Whether the execution is compatible with the specified configuration of the hardware and software
- Whether the execution catches exceptions
- Whether the execution generates an error message

Eventually, the verification answers the question of whether the code executes correctly under a set of predefined conditions.

Validation can be defined as the process of evaluating the software product at the end of the test to ensure the correct outcome and compliance with the software requirements. This chapter serves as a summary of the previous implementations with regard to these purposes.

Finally, the test report presents the test results of the verification and validation. In this chapter, you will code the AutomatedTest project to enable the result presentation.

Automated Verification

An automated testing tool is a software product. It generates code based on the architecture of a product for testing purpose. It is not designed to evaluate documents, schedules, and specifications in writing in place of a human tester. The generated test process is automated and capable of ensuring that the system logically operates according to the code by executing the functions through a series of testing cases. With the AutomatedTest tool, you can expect the test script to conduct the verification processes and return results that verify whether the product under test meets the code logic. Thus, the capabilities of the AutomatedTest tool reflect the testing requirements of an organization and the knowledge of the engineers. In order to increase the verification capability, as a tool developer, you need to have a good understanding of the software requirements with regard to the following criteria:

- Programming objectives specified by the requirement documents
- Metrics to measure the accuracy of the verification
- Actions the specified hardware and software perform in order to accomplish the programming objectives

Verification by the Test Scripts

In the previous chapters, you have implemented the AutomatedTest tool to test constructors, methods, and properties. To understand how the verification is conducted, you need to examine the generated test scripts. For example, to test the default constructor of the `AdvancedCalc` class in Chapter 8, the AutomatedTest tool generates a code segment as shown in Listing 9.1.

Listing 9.1 An Automated Code Segment to Test the *AdvancedCalc* Class Constructor of the *HighLevelObj.dll* Assembly

```
...
AdvancedCalc objAdvancedCalc = null;
shtRow = 2;
mName = "AdvancedCalc";
try {
   objAdvancedCalc = new AdvancedCalc();
   TestPass(xResult, shtRow, mName);
}
catch (System.Exception err) {
   TestFail(xResult, shtRow, mName, err.Message);
}
...
```

The code in Listing 9.1 first declares a null object for the `objAdvancedCalc` class. Then it assigns the name of the class to the `mName` string variable. The code inside the `try` statement initializes the `objAdvancedCalc` object. If the initialization is successful, a `TestPass()` method is invoked, which ensures that there is no logic error from the code execution. If the execution fails inside the `try` statement, the code inside the `catch` statement reports the cause of this failure. Thus, the `try-catch` statement invokes the critical testing actions.

To verify the successful execution of a method, the test script also uses a `try-catch` statement to invoke the `TestPass()` method. For example, the code segment to test the `Triangle()` method is shown in Listing 9.2.

Listing 9.2 **An Automated Code Segment for Testing the *Triangle()* Method of the *AdvancedCalc* Class**

```
...
shtRow = 8;
mName = "Triangle";
range = xSheet.get_Range("C8", "C8");
double length1_8 = double.Parse(range.Value2.ToString());
range = xSheet.get_Range("D8", "D8");
double length2_8 = double.Parse(range.Value2.ToString());
try {
   xResult.Cells.set_Item(8, 4, objAdvancedCalc.Triangle(length1_8, length2_8));
   TestPass(xResult, shtRow, mName);
}
catch (System.Exception err) {
   TestFail(xResult, shtRow, mName, err.Message);
}
xResult.Cells.set_Item(shtRow, 6, "length1 = " + length1_8);
xResult.Cells.set_Item(shtRow, 7, "length2 = " + length2_8);
range = xSheet.get_Range("E8", "E8");
if (range.Value2 != null) {
   xResult.Cells.set_Item(shtRow, 5, range.Value2.ToString());
}
rangeCurr = xResult.get_Range("D8", "D8");
if (rangeCurr.Value2 != null) if (range.Value2 != null &&
➥rangeCurr.Value2.ToString() != range.Value2.ToString())
   rangeCurr.Interior.ColorIndex = 3;
if (rangeCurr.Value2 != null) if (range.Value2 != null &&
➥rangeCurr.Value2.ToString() == range.Value2.ToString())
   rangeCurr.Interior.ColorIndex = 4;

...
```

The code in Listing 9.2 first assigns a value to the `shtRow` variable, pointing at the location where the method and the testing data are in the MS Excel worksheet. Then it retrieves the values for the required parameters of the method in sequence. The code within the `try` statement determines whether the execution of this method is a success or a failure. If it is successful, the `TestPass()` method reports a successful verification. If it fails, the `catch` statement invokes the `TestFail()` method to report the reason for the failure.

To test a property, the AutomatedTest tool generates two segments of code in the test script. One is to test the `set` method of a property, the other, the `get` method of a property:

- The `set` property method has a void return type.
- The `get` property method returns a value.

Some properties are read-only. For example, to test the `get_LastSimpleOperation()` method for the `LastSimpleOperation` property, the generated code segment looks like Listing 9.3.

Listing 9.3 An Automated Code Segment for Testing a Property, *LastSimpleOperation*

```
...
shtRow = 6;
mName = "get_LastSimpleOperation";
try {
   xResult.Cells.set_Item(6, 4, objmyCalculator.LastSimpleOperation);
   TestPass(xResult, shtRow, mName);
}
catch (System.Exception err) {
   TestFail(xResult, shtRow, mName, err.Message);
}
...
```

As in the previous test cases, the `shtRow` variable tells the test script which row in the Excel worksheet stores the value of the testing data. Then it assigns the name of the method under test to the `nName` variable. The first line of code inside the `try` statement invokes the method under test and retrieves the value of this property. After all the critical actions, if the invocation of this extraction is successful, it reports the test pass result. Otherwise, it reports the test fail result within the `catch` statement.

After the verification, the `catch` statements are capable of finding bugs. Thus, this test serves the following purposes:

- Providing data on product quality and execution efficiency
- Informing the developers of the defects
- Increasing the effectiveness of software testing
- Raising the standard of excellence for software engineers.

The responsibility of a test engineer is to find defects but not to fix them. With the previous code extracted from the generated test script, the AutomatedTest tool accomplishes the task of finding problems. Eventually, the verification information can be used by the developers to fix the defects with accuracy.

Verification Decision

A test engineer usually follows a procedure to decide whether a problem found is a defect. However, the AutomatedTest tool makes decisions based on the invocation of the methods. During the invocation, it detects errors and defects. In the previous chapter, you tested the `LowLevelObj.dll` a few times. You probably noticed that the `Divide()` method does not implement any mechanism to handle errors. When a number is divided by 0, an error is reported. Thus, the AutomatedTest tool makes an effort to remind the developers of the importance of adopting a good error handling technique.

But, can the AutomatedTest tool verify that all testing tasks have been performed? The answer is based on the requirements of your organization and on the architecture of the software project. The implementation of this AutomatedTest tool is for general testing purposes. You can apply the fundamentals of these methods to the development of the tool to address all the needs of your institution.

Based on the nature of the general testing requirements, this AutomatedTest tool is capable of performing the following testing tasks at this stage:

Unit testing Developers and testers can use this tool as a test driver or a test harness to generate test code for all components within an assembly.

Integration testing You have enabled the test tool to accept objects as parameters for a method. It can test the combined modules of an application.

White box and black box testing With the help of the .NET Reflection namespace, the tool itself performs a white box test of the methods of an assembly. On the other hand, the generated test scripts can be executed on client computer systems. To the user of this tool at this time, it is a black box test.

Compatibility testing The tool can determine how well an application performs in a given hardware and software environment.

Incremental regression testing The AutomatedTest tool is capable of generating test scripts at any stage of the software development life cycle. When new functionalities are added, it reruns the previously generated test script or generates a new test script to address the change in the modified designs. It is usually a difficult task for the traditional testing methods to decide how much retesting is needed. This tool is useful for retesting a product after defects are fixed or after the application and the testing environment are modified. Each test of a higher-level module is regression testing for the involved lower-level modules. Thus, immediately after the final line of code is added to the product, all the code should have been tested at least one time.

Automated Validation

The mission of a test engineer is to find as many bugs as possible and as early as possible. Then the developers should fix the bugs based on the test reports. Although this testing/fixing process happens continuously for a software development project, nobody has guaranteed that their software does not have bugs. The known difficulties are obvious. For example, when we test a method that accepts integer values as parameters, it is impossible to test all the valid integers mathematically and test all the combinations of this integer parameter working under various conditions. Plus, the processor uses other modules to manipulate the integers that are out of the control of the testing code. The AutomatedTest uses the same boundary condition strategy to handle these problems. To use the boundary condition strategy in the Automated Test tool, the test engineers need to do the following:

- Thoroughly review the generated data store and have a good understanding of every piece of information.
- Assign to the Excel data store values that have a high probability of detecting an undiscovered defect, not values that show that the program works correctly.
- Assign valid data to the Excel data store as well as invalid data to test whether the method under test returns expected results or error messages.
- Make use of the expected return value to validate the test results.
- Use other test methods to perform the same testing cases.
- Be critical and aggressive in finding fault with the quality of a product.

Validation Scope of the Automated Test

The objective of the AutomatedTest tool is to find bugs in data and algorithms in a software product. With regard to unit testing, the AutomatedTest tool validates the test based on data retrieved from the Excel data store. On the other hand, this tool can be used for regression testing by rerunning the generated test script on a scheduled basis. The result of the regression testing will determine whether the execution of the application still meets all the requirements after changes and modifications are made. In addition, the tests can be conducted continuously without the attention of a human engineer. Engineers will be informed of the results in a timely manner when a defect is found. This feature of the AutomatedTest tool is useful and makes regression testing management easier.

The programming you completed in Chapter 8 gave the AutomatedTest tool the capability to test parameters passed by objects. The scope of the validation includes the following:

- Whether modules can adversely affect each other
- Whether a method returns the desired outcome by integrating other types of classes as parameters
- Whether passing parameters by object affects the accuracy and precision of the execution

During a software development project, it requires a skillful manager to keep track and make sure that all the necessary tests are performed. This is usually a difficult task for a big and complex project. The use of the AutomatedTest tool will significantly reduce the degree of difficulty and ensure that the following criteria have been satisfied:

- All test scripts have been executed.
- All errors and defects found have been logged and satisfactorily resolved (fixed, deferred to a later release, declared as not a bug, etc.) by rerunning the test script.
- All changes made have been retested on time.

The AutomatedTest tool guarantees that there is a complete copy of the test results with evidence that all the methods of the assembly have been tested. It is also stamped with date and time. The results clearly report which methods pass the test and which methods fail the test. Test conditions are listed. The date and time stamps report the effects of the evolution based on the automatic regression testing.

Finally, the result of this test will reveal whether the logic, business, and presentation tiers are integrated correctly.

Creating Early Phase Test Scripts

By definition of the extreme programming (XP) practice, software engineers often reprioritize aspects of a project, such as changing requirements or modifying specifications. In this section of the chapter, I'll discuss using the AutomatedTest tool for early stage testing in conjunction with XP practices. You can execute the test script throughout the development cycle, and a new test script can be easily regenerated when modifications occur to the project.

Much of the literature has emphasized that software testing should be done early in the software development process. It saves money to fix a defect in the early stage. The AutomatedTest tool is able to generate test scripts in parallel to the project development.

For example, a software organization starts a project to develop an application for a scientific instrument that takes automatic measurements. The development team plans to implement the measurement modules in C#. The instrument is connected to a computer system via an RS-232 interface. The measurement modules must be compatible with COM class modules that at a minimum implements the standards across this organization. The entire application has a multitier architecture. Objects of the classes can only be referenced by the objects of the classes that are one level higher.

For illustration purposes, one of the classes for this system is named `XYZDriver` and it represent an instrument used to take measurements. The class has the following requirements:

- It has functions that are adaptable in that they can be used for the organization's other instruments.

- It has functions that are specific to the hardware for which it's designed.
- The design is consistent across the organization with regard to software development strategy and hardware manufacturing.
- The complete module should be able to operate the instrument independently.
- Other applications can reuse or integrate this module when this instrument is in the assembly of a different measurement system.
- It must meet the ISO industrial standard.

Based on these requirements, a specification document is drafted and inspected by the software engineers and the users. The team coins a namespace as `XYZInstrumentDrivers` and a class name as `XYZDriver`. Then, the R&D personnel construct a detailed design for this module, which has the methods in Listing 9.4.

Listing 9.4 A Typical Design for the *XYZDriver* Class

```
public int Init(string resourceName, bool idQuery, bool reset)
public void ErrorQuery(ref int errorCode, ref string errorMessage)
public void ErrorMessage(int statusCode, ref string message)
public void RevisionQuery(ref string instrumentDriverRevision,
➥ref string firmwareRevision)
public void Reset()
public void SelfTest(ref short selfTestResult, ref string selfTestMessage)
public void TimeOut(int setTimeOut)
public void Dcl()
public void exec(string sendStringCommand)
public void SetPaddlePosition(int paddle, int positionSelector,
➥short optionalPosition)
public void SetScanRate(int scanSelector, int optionalScanRate)
public void PaddlePosition(int paddle, short position)
public void InitiateScan()
public void AbortScan()
public void ScanRate(int rate)
public void MaxScanRate()
public void MinScanRate()
public void ScanRateQ(ref short rateResult)
public void MaxScanRateQ(ref short maxRateResult)
public void MinScanRateQ(ref short minRateResult)
public void ClearScanTimer()
public void ScanTimerQ(ref int timerResult)
public void Preset()
public void ScanQ(ref short status)
public void PaddleQ(ref short status)
public void SaveState(int saveLoc)
public void RecallState(int saveLoc)
```

The descriptions of the members in Listing 9.4 are explained in the XML comments of the code. Once a detailed design is available, it is easy for the programmers to code a skeleton and the comments of this class, shown in Listing 9.5.

Listing 9.5 A Code Skeleton for the *XYZDriver* Class and *XYZInstrumentDrivers* Namespace

```
using System;
using System.Runtime.InteropServices;
using System.Text;

namespace XYZInstrumentDrivers
{
  /// <summary>
  /// XYZ measurement system driver
  /// </summary>
  [
  Guid("C5EA5B79-0C08-4f88-A3EF-FAEF56C44040"),
  ClassInterface (ClassInterfaceType.AutoDual)
  ]

  public class XYZDriver
  {
    /// <summary>
    /// Default constructor
    /// </summary>
    public XYZDriver()
    {
    }


    /// <summary>
    ///  initialization
    /// </summary>
    /// <param name="resourceName">[INPUT PARAMETER], e.g., XYZ
➥Instrument</param>
    /// <param name="idQuery">[INPUT PARAMETER], e.g., true</param>
    /// <param name="reset">[INPUT PARAMETER], e.g., false</param>
    /// <returns>
    /// [OUTPUT PARAMETER] succeed: return 0, e.g., 0
    /// </returns>

    public int Init(string resourceName, bool idQuery, bool reset)
    {
      return 0;
    }
    /// <summary>
    /// This function returns the error numbers and corresponding error messages
    /// in the error queue of an instrument.  See the manual for a listing of
    /// the instrument error numbers and messages.
    ///
```

```
    /// Instrument errors may occur when a user attempts to place the instrument
    /// in an invalid state such as sending an invalid sequence of coupled
➥commands.
    ///
    /// Instrument errors can be detected by polling.  Automatic polling can be
    /// accomplished by using the XYZ_errorQueryDetect() function.
    /// </summary>
    /// <param name="errorCode">
    /// [INPUT PARAMETER]
    /// Instrument&apos;s error code.
    /// </param>
    /// <param name="errorMessage">
    /// [OUTPUT PARAMETER]
    /// Instrument&apos;s error message.  This is limited to 256 characters.
    /// </param>
    public void ErrorQuery(ref int errorCode, ref string errorMessage)
    {
      return;
    }
    /// <summary>
    /// This function translates the error value returned from an instrument
    /// driver function to a user-readable string.
    /// </summary>
    /// <param name="statusCode">
    /// [INPUT PARAMETER]
    /// The error return value from an instrument driver function.
    /// </param>
    /// <param name="message">
    /// [OUTPUT PARAMETER]
    /// Error message string.  This is limited to 256 characters.
    /// </param>
    public void ErrorMessage(int statusCode, ref string message)
    {
      return;
    }
    /// <summary>
    /// This function returns the revision of the instrument driver and the
    /// firmware of the instrument being used.
    /// </summary>
    /// <param name="instrumentDriverRevision">
    /// [OUTPUT PARAMETER]
    /// Instrument driver revision.  This is limited to 256 characters.
    /// </param>
    /// <param name="firmwareRevision">
    /// [OUTPUT PARAMETER]
    /// Instrument firmware revision.  This is limited to 256 characters.
    /// </param>
    public void RevisionQuery(ref string instrumentDriverRevision,
➥ref string firmwareRevision)
    {
      return;
```

```
}
/// <summary>
/// The reset function places the instrument in a default state.
/// Before issuing this function, it may be necessary to send a
/// device clear to ensure that the instrument can execute a reset.
/// A device clear can be issued by invoking XYZ_dcl().
///
/// For the states affected by the reset command, see the instrument
➥manual.
///
/// Reset does not affect the status system or clear any errors.
/// </summary>
public void Reset()
{
  return;
}
/// <summary>
/// The self-test function causes the instrument to perform a self-test
///  and returns the result of that self-test.  This is used to verify
///  that an instrument is operating properly.  A failure may indicate
///  a potential hardware problem.
///
///  For a list of possible self-test errors, consult the instrument
➥manual
/// </summary>
/// <param name="selfTestResult">
/// [OUTPUT PARAMETER]
/// Numeric result from self-test operation.
/// 0 = no error ( test passed), e.g., 3
/// </param>
/// <param name="selfTestMessage">
/// [OUTPUT PARAMETER]
/// Self-test status message.  This is limited to 256 characters,
➥e.g., previous message
/// </param>
public void SelfTest(ref short selfTestResult, ref string selfTestMessage)
{
  return;
}


/// <summary>
/// The timeout function sets the timeout value for driver I/O
/// transactions in milliseconds. The timeout period may vary on
/// computer platforms.
///
/// The default timeout period varies by implementation.  For
/// XYZ standard, it is 2 seconds...
/// </summary>
/// <param name="setTimeOut">
/// [INPUT PARAMETER]
```

```
///
/// This value sets the I/O timeout for all functions in the driver.
/// It is specified in milliseconds.
///
/// MAX = XYZInstrument_TIMEOUT_MAX   2147483647
/// MIN = XYZInstrument_TIMEOUT_MIN   0, e.g., 6
/// </param>
public void TimeOut(int setTimeOut)
{
  return;
}


/// <summary>
/// This function sends a device clear (DCL) to the instrument.
///
/// A device clear will abort the current operation and enable the
/// instrument to accept a new command or query.
///
/// This is particularly useful in situations where it is not
/// possible to determine the instrument state...
/// </summary>
public void Dcl()
{
  return;
}

/// <summary>
/// This function passes an instrument command to the instrument.
/// The function does not expect any response.
/// </summary>
/// <param name="sendStringCommand">
/// [INPUT PARAMETER]
/// The instrument command.  It must be a NULL termianted C string
/// and may not exceed 256 bytes in length, e.g., command string
/// </param>
public void exec(string sendStringCommand)
{
  return;
}

/// <summary>
/// Set the selected paddle position to the specified value, or to
/// the minimum or maximum value.
/// </summary>
/// <param name="paddle">
/// Select which of the four panels will have their position altered.
/// Value from 1 to 4, e.g., 0
/// </param>
/// <param name="positionSelector">
/// Select whether the paddle position is set from the optional
```

```
    /// value, to the maximum position or to the minimum position.
    /// Value from 0 to 2, e.g., 3
    /// </param>
    /// <param name="optionalPosition">
    /// Optional paddle position value. The selector must be set to
    /// Value for this parameter to be examined.
    /// Value from 0 to 999, e.g., 500
    /// </param>
    public void SetPaddlePosition(int paddle, int positionSelector,
➥short optionalPosition)
    {
      return;
    }

    /// <summary>
    /// No function help available from driver file
    /// </summary>
    /// <param name="scanSelector">
    /// Select whether the scan rate is set from the Scan Rate slider,
    /// to the maximum position or to the minimum position.
    /// Value from 0 - 2, e.g., 0
    /// </param>
    /// <param name="optionalScanRate">
    /// Enumeration of the eight (8) scan rates available on the
    /// instrument.
    /// Value from 1 - 8, e.g., 4
    /// </param>
    public void SetScanRate(int scanSelector, int optionalScanRate)
    {
      return;
    }

    /// <summary>
    /// No function help available from driver file
    /// </summary>
    /// <param name="paddle">
    /// Select which of the four panels will have their position altered.
    /// Value from 1 to 4, e.g., 4
    /// </param>
    /// <param name="position">
    ///Paddle postion from 0 to 999, e.g., 500
    /// </param>
    public void PaddlePosition(int paddle, short position)
    {
      return;
    }

    /// <summary>
    /// No function help available from driver file
    /// </summary>
    public void InitiateScan()
```

```
{
  return;
}
/// <summary>
/// No function help available from driver file
/// </summary>
public void AbortScan()
{
  return;
}
/// <summary>
/// Scan Rate selector.
/// </summary>
/// <param name="rate">
/// Enumeration of the eight (8) scan rates available on the
/// instrument, e.g., 1
/// </param>
public void ScanRate(int rate)
{
  return;
}
/// <summary>
/// No function help available from driver file
/// </summary>
public void MaxScanRate()
{
  return;
}
/// <summary>
/// No function help available from driver file
/// </summary>
public void MinScanRate()
{
  return;
}
/// <summary>
/// No function help available from driver file
/// </summary>
/// <param name="rateResult">
/// No parameter help available from driver file, e.g., 35
/// </param>
public void ScanRateQ(ref short rateResult)
{
  return;
}
/// <summary>
/// No function help available from driver file
/// </summary>
/// <param name="maxRateResult">
/// No parameter help available from driver file, e.g., 400
/// </param>
```

```
public void MaxScanRateQ(ref short maxRateResult)
{
  return;
}
/// <summary>
/// No function help available from driver file
/// </summary>
/// <param name="minRateResult">
/// No parameter help available from driver file, e.g., 400
/// </param>
public void MinScanRateQ(ref short minRateResult)
{
  return;
}
/// <summary>
/// No function help available from driver file
/// </summary>
public void ClearScanTimer()
{
  return;
}

/// <summary>
/// No function help available from driver file
/// </summary>
/// <param name="timerResult">
/// No parameter help available from driver file, e.g., 4
/// </param>
public void ScanTimerQ(ref int timerResult)
{
  return;
}
/// <summary>
/// No function help available from driver file
/// </summary>
public void Preset()
{
  return;
}
/// <summary>
/// Return the state of the scan:
///
/// 0 - Manual Mode
/// 1 - Scan Mode
/// </summary>
/// <param name="status">
/// No parameter help available from driver file, e.g., 4
/// </param>
public void ScanQ(ref short status)
{
  return;
```

```
        }
        /// <summary>
        /// No function help available from driver file
        /// </summary>
        /// <param name="status">
        /// No parameter help available from driver file, e.g., 5
        /// </param>
        public void PaddleQ(ref short status)
        {
          return;
        }
        /// <summary>
        /// No function help available from driver file
        /// </summary>
        /// <param name="saveLoc">
        /// No parameter help available from driver file, e.g., 5
        /// </param>
        public void SaveState(int saveLoc)
        {
          return;
        }
        /// <summary>
        /// No function help available from driver file
        /// </summary>
        /// <param name="saveLoc">
        /// No parameter help available from driver file, e.g., 6
        /// </param>
        public void RecallState(int saveLoc)
        {
          return;
        }

    }  //end of class
  }  //end of namespace
```

In Listing 9.5, the code skeleton includes the XML comments. The XML comments describe the nature of the class and methods under development. It also has testing data values attached. If you are interested in developing plug-and-play drivers for instruments, you may find that this design complies with today's industrial standards. Although most of the methods have void return types, it is good programming practice to add a return statement for each of them. At this point, the developers can compile the skeleton code to build an assembly and an XML document.

Today, software organizations often use one of the Unified Modeling Language (UML) packages for documenting requirements, specifications, and designs. Once a detailed design is available, the UML package is capable of generating a code skeleton similar to Listing 9.5.

When this AutomatedTest method is incorporated with a UML development tool, a test script for this project can be generated at the same time a code skeleton is completed.

Although the assembly could not do anything because the methods are not implemented, it could be fed to the AutomatedTest tool to generate a precise test script. If the Enable XML Data check box is checked, the parameter values in the XML comments will be used as testing cases for the test script. As long as the design remains unchanged, this test script can be reused throughout the development life cycle. After the skeleton code is built into a `XYZDriver.dll` assembly and an `XYZDriver.xml` document, you can run the `AutomatedTest.exe` from the `C:\SourceCode\Chapter08\AutomatedTest\bin\Debug` folder and complete the following steps to generate a reusable test script:

1. Make the Enable XML Data check box be checked on the Automated Software Test form.
2. Click the Start button to open the Open file dialog box.
3. Navigate to `C:\SourceCode\Chapter09\xyzDriver\bin\Debug` folder and select the `XYZDriver.dll` file.
4. Click the Open button from the Open file dialog box to open the TypeUnderTest form.
5. Check the `XYZDriver` class in the check list box.
6. Click the OK button. You can see an Excel worksheet opens and extracts data from the `XYZDriver.xml` document. If the Microsoft Excel pops up a message to ask you whether to replace the existing `C:\Temp\SoftwareTestDataStore.xls`, you can click the Yes button. Then, the data continues to drive the generation of the test script. The Excel worksheet closes when the script generation is completed. At this point, the generated test script is still saved as C:\Temp\TestScript.cs. You can open and review this script in a text editor and see the code similar to Listing 9.6.

Listing 9.6 Test Script Generated at the Early Stage for Testing a Product Throughout the Development Cycle

```
namespace XYZInstrumentDriversTest {
  using System;
  using System.IO;
  using Excel;
  using System.Reflection;
  using XYZInstrumentDrivers;


  public class TestXYZDriver {

    private string fileName = "C:/temp/SoftTestDataStore.xls";
```

```
public TestXYZDriver() {
}

public TestXYZDriver(string fileName) {
  this.fileName = fileName;
}

public object StartTest() {
  Excel.Application xApp = new Excel.Application();
  Excel.Workbook xBook = xApp.Workbooks.Open(fileName, 0, false, 1,
➥"", "", true, 1, 0, true, 1, 0, 0, 0, 0);
  Excel.Worksheet xSheet = (Excel.Worksheet)xBook.ActiveSheet;
  Excel.Workbook xBook2 = xApp.Workbooks.Add(1);
  Excel.Worksheet xResult = (Excel.Worksheet)xBook2.ActiveSheet;
  xResult.Cells.set_Item(1, 1, "METHOD UNDER TEST");
  xResult.Cells.set_Item(1, 2, "RESULT");
  xResult.Cells.set_Item(1, 3, "ERROR MESSAGE");
  xResult.Cells.set_Item(1, 4, "ACTUAL RETURN");
  xResult.Cells.set_Item(1, 5, "EXPECTED RETURN");
  xResult.Cells.set_Item(1, 6, "PARAMETERS AND VALUES");
  xApp.Visible =  true;
  Excel.Range range;
  Excel.Range rangeCurr;
  range = xResult.get_Range("A1", "H1");
  range.Interior.ColorIndex = 8;
  range.Font.Bold =  true;
  range.Columns.AutoFit();
  int shtRow = 0;
  string mName = null;
  int tempArrayIndex = 0;
  XYZDriver objXYZDriver = null;
  shtRow = 2;
  mName = "XYZDriver";
  try {
    objXYZDriver = new XYZDriver();
    TestPass(xResult, shtRow, mName);
  }
  catch (System.Exception err) {
    TestFail(xResult, shtRow, mName, err.Message);
  }
  xResult.Cells.set_Item(shtRow, 4, "Test Constructor");
  shtRow = 3;
  mName = "GetHashCode";
  try {
    xResult.Cells.set_Item(3, 4, objXYZDriver.GetHashCode());
    TestPass(xResult, shtRow, mName);
  }
  catch (System.Exception err) {
    TestFail(xResult, shtRow, mName, err.Message);
  }
  range = xSheet.get_Range("C3", "C3");
```

```
if (range.Value2 != null) {
  xResult.Cells.set_Item(shtRow, 5, range.Value2.ToString());
}
rangeCurr = xResult.get_Range("D3", "D3");
if (rangeCurr.Value2 != null)
  if (range.Value2 != null &&
  ➥rangeCurr.Value2.ToString() != range.Value2.ToString())
    rangeCurr.Interior.ColorIndex = 3;
if (rangeCurr.Value2 != null)
  if (range.Value2 != null &&
  ➥rangeCurr.Value2.ToString() == range.Value2.ToString())
    rangeCurr.Interior.ColorIndex = 4;
shtRow = 4;
mName = "Equals";
range = xSheet.get_Range("C4", "C4");
object obj_4 = range.Value2.ToString();
try {
  xResult.Cells.set_Item(4, 4, objXYZDriver.Equals(obj_4));
  TestPass(xResult, shtRow, mName);
}
catch (System.Exception err) {
  TestFail(xResult, shtRow, mName, err.Message);
}
xResult.Cells.set_Item(shtRow, 6, "obj = " + obj_4);
range = xSheet.get_Range("D4", "D4");
if (range.Value2 != null) {
  xResult.Cells.set_Item(shtRow, 5, range.Value2.ToString());
}
rangeCurr = xResult.get_Range("D4", "D4");
if (rangeCurr.Value2 != null)
  if (range.Value2 != null &&
  ➥rangeCurr.Value2.ToString() != range.Value2.ToString())
    rangeCurr.Interior.ColorIndex = 3;
if (rangeCurr.Value2 != null)
  if (range.Value2 != null &&
➥rangeCurr.Value2.ToString() == range.Value2.ToString())
    rangeCurr.Interior.ColorIndex = 4;
shtRow = 5;
mName = "ToString";
try {
  xResult.Cells.set_Item(5, 4, objXYZDriver.ToString());
  TestPass(xResult, shtRow, mName);
}
catch (System.Exception err) {
  TestFail(xResult, shtRow, mName, err.Message);
}
range = xSheet.get_Range("C5", "C5");
if (range.Value2 != null) {
  xResult.Cells.set_Item(shtRow, 5, range.Value2.ToString());
}
rangeCurr = xResult.get_Range("D5", "D5");
```

```
      if (rangeCurr.Value2 != null)
        if (range.Value2 != null &&
➥rangeCurr.Value2.ToString() != range.Value2.ToString())
          rangeCurr.Interior.ColorIndex = 3;
      if (rangeCurr.Value2 != null)
if (range.Value2 != null &&
➥rangeCurr.Value2.ToString() == range.Value2.ToString())
        rangeCurr.Interior.ColorIndex = 4;
      shtRow = 6;
      mName = "Init";
      range = xSheet.get_Range("C6", "C6");
      string resourceName_6 = range.Value2.ToString();
      range = xSheet.get_Range("D6", "D6");
      bool idQuery_6 = bool.Parse(range.Value2.ToString());
      range = xSheet.get_Range("E6", "E6");
      bool reset_6 = bool.Parse(range.Value2.ToString());
      try {
        xResult.Cells.set_Item(6, 4, objXYZDriver.Init(resourceName_6,
➥idQuery_6, reset_6));
        TestPass(xResult, shtRow, mName);
      }
      catch (System.Exception err) {
        TestFail(xResult, shtRow, mName, err.Message);
      }
      xResult.Cells.set_Item(shtRow, 6, "resourceName = " + resourceName_6);
      xResult.Cells.set_Item(shtRow, 7, "idQuery = " + idQuery_6);
      xResult.Cells.set_Item(shtRow, 8, "reset = " + reset_6);
      range = xSheet.get_Range("F6", "F6");
      if (range.Value2 != null) {
        xResult.Cells.set_Item(shtRow, 5, range.Value2.ToString());
      }
      rangeCurr = xResult.get_Range("D6", "D6");
      if (rangeCurr.Value2 != null)
        ➥if (range.Value2 != null &&
        ➥rangeCurr.Value2.ToString() != range.Value2.ToString())
          rangeCurr.Interior.ColorIndex = 3;
      if (rangeCurr.Value2 != null)
        if (range.Value2 != null &&
        ➥rangeCurr.Value2.ToString() == range.Value2.ToString())
          rangeCurr.Interior.ColorIndex = 4;
      shtRow = 7;
      mName = "ErrorQuery";
      range = xSheet.get_Range("C7", "C7");
      int errorCode_7 = int.Parse(range.Value2.ToString());
      range = xSheet.get_Range("D7", "D7");
      string errorMessage_7 = range.Value2.ToString();
      try {
        objXYZDriver.ErrorQuery(ref errorCode_7, ref errorMessage_7);
        TestPass(xResult, shtRow, mName);
      }
      catch (System.Exception err) {
```

```
      TestFail(xResult, shtRow, mName, err.Message);
    }
    xResult.Cells.set_Item(shtRow, 6, "errorCode = " + errorCode_7);
    xResult.Cells.set_Item(shtRow, 7, "errorMessage = " + errorMessage_7);
    shtRow = 8;
    mName = "ErrorMessage";
    range = xSheet.get_Range("C8", "C8");
    int statusCode_8 = int.Parse(range.Value2.ToString());
    range = xSheet.get_Range("D8", "D8");
    string message_8 = range.Value2.ToString();
    try {
      objXYZDriver.ErrorMessage(statusCode_8, ref message_8);
      TestPass(xResult, shtRow, mName);
    }
    catch (System.Exception err) {
      TestFail(xResult, shtRow, mName, err.Message);
    }
    xResult.Cells.set_Item(shtRow, 6, "statusCode = " + statusCode_8);
    xResult.Cells.set_Item(shtRow, 7, "message = " + message_8);
    shtRow = 9;
    mName = "RevisionQuery";
    range = xSheet.get_Range("C9", "C9");
    string instrumentDriverRevision_9 = range.Value2.ToString();
    range = xSheet.get_Range("D9", "D9");
    string firmwareRevision_9 = range.Value2.ToString();
    try {
      objXYZDriver.RevisionQuery(ref instrumentDriverRevision_9,
➥ref firmwareRevision_9);
      TestPass(xResult, shtRow, mName);
    }
    catch (System.Exception err) {
      TestFail(xResult, shtRow, mName, err.Message);
    }
    xResult.Cells.set_Item(shtRow, 6, "instrumentDriverRevision = " +
➥instrumentDriverRevision_9);
    xResult.Cells.set_Item(shtRow, 7, "firmwareRevision = " +
➥firmwareRevision_9);
    shtRow = 10;
    mName = "Reset";
    try {
      objXYZDriver.Reset();
      TestPass(xResult, shtRow, mName);
    }
    catch (System.Exception err) {
      TestFail(xResult, shtRow, mName, err.Message);
    }
    shtRow = 11;
    mName = "SelfTest";
    range = xSheet.get_Range("C11", "C11");
    short selfTestResult_11 = short.Parse(range.Value2.ToString());
    range = xSheet.get_Range("D11", "D11");
```

```
string selfTestMessage_11 = range.Value2.ToString();
try {
  objXYZDriver.SelfTest(ref selfTestResult_11, ref selfTestMessage_11);
  TestPass(xResult, shtRow, mName);
}
catch (System.Exception err) {
  TestFail(xResult, shtRow, mName, err.Message);
}
xResult.Cells.set_Item(shtRow, 6, "selfTestResult = " +
➥selfTestResult_11);
xResult.Cells.set_Item(shtRow, 7, "selfTestMessage = " +
➥selfTestMessage_11);
shtRow = 12;
mName = "TimeOut";
range = xSheet.get_Range("C12", "C12");
int setTimeOut_12 = int.Parse(range.Value2.ToString());
try {
  objXYZDriver.TimeOut(setTimeOut_12);
  TestPass(xResult, shtRow, mName);
}
catch (System.Exception err) {
  TestFail(xResult, shtRow, mName, err.Message);
}
xResult.Cells.set_Item(shtRow, 6, "setTimeOut = " + setTimeOut_12);
shtRow = 13;
mName = "Dcl";
try {
  objXYZDriver.Dcl();
  TestPass(xResult, shtRow, mName);
}
catch (System.Exception err) {
  TestFail(xResult, shtRow, mName, err.Message);
}
shtRow = 14;
mName = "exec";
range = xSheet.get_Range("C14", "C14");
string sendStringCommand_14 = range.Value2.ToString();
try {
  objXYZDriver.exec(sendStringCommand_14);
  TestPass(xResult, shtRow, mName);
}
catch (System.Exception err) {
  TestFail(xResult, shtRow, mName, err.Message);
}
xResult.Cells.set_Item(shtRow, 6, "sendStringCommand = " +
➥sendStringCommand_14);
shtRow = 15;
mName = "SetPaddlePosition";
range = xSheet.get_Range("C15", "C15");
int paddle_15 = int.Parse(range.Value2.ToString());
range = xSheet.get_Range("D15", "D15");
```

```
        int positionSelector_15 = int.Parse(range.Value2.ToString());
        range = xSheet.get_Range("E15", "E15");
        short optionalPosition_15 = short.Parse(range.Value2.ToString());
        try {
          objXYZDriver.SetPaddlePosition(paddle_15, positionSelector_15,
➥optionalPosition_15);
          TestPass(xResult, shtRow, mName);
        }
        catch (System.Exception err) {
          TestFail(xResult, shtRow, mName, err.Message);
        }
        xResult.Cells.set_Item(shtRow, 6, "paddle = " + paddle_15);
        xResult.Cells.set_Item(shtRow, 7, "positionSelector = " +
➥positionSelector_15);
        xResult.Cells.set_Item(shtRow, 8, "optionalPosition = " +
➥optionalPosition_15);
        shtRow = 16;
        mName = "SetScanRate";
        range = xSheet.get_Range("C16", "C16");
        int scanSelector_16 = int.Parse(range.Value2.ToString());
        range = xSheet.get_Range("D16", "D16");
        int optionalScanRate_16 = int.Parse(range.Value2.ToString());
        try {
          objXYZDriver.SetScanRate(scanSelector_16, optionalScanRate_16);
          TestPass(xResult, shtRow, mName);
        }
        catch (System.Exception err) {
          TestFail(xResult, shtRow, mName, err.Message);
        }
        xResult.Cells.set_Item(shtRow, 6, "scanSelector = " + scanSelector_16);
        xResult.Cells.set_Item(shtRow, 7, "optionalScanRate = " +
➥optionalScanRate_16);
        shtRow = 17;
        mName = "PaddlePosition";
        range = xSheet.get_Range("C17", "C17");
        int paddle_17 = int.Parse(range.Value2.ToString());
        range = xSheet.get_Range("D17", "D17");
        short position_17 = short.Parse(range.Value2.ToString());
        try {
          objXYZDriver.PaddlePosition(paddle_17, position_17);
          TestPass(xResult, shtRow, mName);
        }
        catch (System.Exception err) {
          TestFail(xResult, shtRow, mName, err.Message);
        }
        xResult.Cells.set_Item(shtRow, 6, "paddle = " + paddle_17);
        xResult.Cells.set_Item(shtRow, 7, "position = " + position_17);
        shtRow = 18;
        mName = "InitiateScan";
        try {
          objXYZDriver.InitiateScan();
```

```
  TestPass(xResult, shtRow, mName);
}
catch (System.Exception err) {
  TestFail(xResult, shtRow, mName, err.Message);
}
shtRow = 19;
mName = "AbortScan";
try {
  objXYZDriver.AbortScan();
  TestPass(xResult, shtRow, mName);
}
catch (System.Exception err) {
  TestFail(xResult, shtRow, mName, err.Message);
}
shtRow = 20;
mName = "ScanRate";
range = xSheet.get_Range("C20", "C20");
int rate_20 = int.Parse(range.Value2.ToString());
try {
  objXYZDriver.ScanRate(rate_20);
  TestPass(xResult, shtRow, mName);
}
catch (System.Exception err) {
  TestFail(xResult, shtRow, mName, err.Message);
}
xResult.Cells.set_Item(shtRow, 6, "rate = " + rate_20);
shtRow = 21;
mName = "MaxScanRate";
try {
  objXYZDriver.MaxScanRate();
  TestPass(xResult, shtRow, mName);
}
catch (System.Exception err) {
  TestFail(xResult, shtRow, mName, err.Message);
}
shtRow = 22;
mName = "MinScanRate";
try {
  objXYZDriver.MinScanRate();
  TestPass(xResult, shtRow, mName);
}
catch (System.Exception err) {
  TestFail(xResult, shtRow, mName, err.Message);
}
shtRow = 23;
mName = "ScanRateQ";
range = xSheet.get_Range("C23", "C23");
short rateResult_23 = short.Parse(range.Value2.ToString());
try {
  objXYZDriver.ScanRateQ(ref rateResult_23);
  TestPass(xResult, shtRow, mName);
```

```
}
catch (System.Exception err) {
  TestFail(xResult, shtRow, mName, err.Message);
}
xResult.Cells.set_Item(shtRow, 6, "rateResult = " + rateResult_23);
shtRow = 24;
mName = "MaxScanRateQ";
range = xSheet.get_Range("C24", "C24");
short maxRateResult_24 = short.Parse(range.Value2.ToString());
try {
  objXYZDriver.MaxScanRateQ(ref maxRateResult_24);
  TestPass(xResult, shtRow, mName);
}
catch (System.Exception err) {
  TestFail(xResult, shtRow, mName, err.Message);
}
xResult.Cells.set_Item(shtRow, 6, "maxRateResult = " + maxRateResult_24);
shtRow = 25;
mName = "MinScanRateQ";
range = xSheet.get_Range("C25", "C25");
short minRateResult_25 = short.Parse(range.Value2.ToString());
try {
  objXYZDriver.MinScanRateQ(ref minRateResult_25);
  TestPass(xResult, shtRow, mName);
}
catch (System.Exception err) {
  TestFail(xResult, shtRow, mName, err.Message);
}
xResult.Cells.set_Item(shtRow, 6, "minRateResult = " + minRateResult_25);
shtRow = 26;
mName = "ClearScanTimer";
try {
  objXYZDriver.ClearScanTimer();
  TestPass(xResult, shtRow, mName);
}
catch (System.Exception err) {
  TestFail(xResult, shtRow, mName, err.Message);
}
shtRow = 27;
mName = "ScanTimerQ";
range = xSheet.get_Range("C27", "C27");
int timerResult_27 = int.Parse(range.Value2.ToString());
try {
  objXYZDriver.ScanTimerQ(ref timerResult_27);
  TestPass(xResult, shtRow, mName);
}
catch (System.Exception err) {
  TestFail(xResult, shtRow, mName, err.Message);
}
xResult.Cells.set_Item(shtRow, 6, "timerResult = " + timerResult_27);
shtRow = 28;
```

```
mName = "Preset";
try {
  objXYZDriver.Preset();
  TestPass(xResult, shtRow, mName);
}
catch (System.Exception err) {
  TestFail(xResult, shtRow, mName, err.Message);
}
shtRow = 29;
mName = "ScanQ";
range = xSheet.get_Range("C29", "C29");
short status_29 = short.Parse(range.Value2.ToString());
try {
  objXYZDriver.ScanQ(ref status_29);
  TestPass(xResult, shtRow, mName);
}
catch (System.Exception err) {
  TestFail(xResult, shtRow, mName, err.Message);
}
xResult.Cells.set_Item(shtRow, 6, "status = " + status_29);
shtRow = 30;
mName = "PaddleQ";
range = xSheet.get_Range("C30", "C30");
short status_30 = short.Parse(range.Value2.ToString());
try {
  objXYZDriver.PaddleQ(ref status_30);
  TestPass(xResult, shtRow, mName);
}
catch (System.Exception err) {
  TestFail(xResult, shtRow, mName, err.Message);
}
xResult.Cells.set_Item(shtRow, 6, "status = " + status_30);
shtRow = 31;
mName = "SaveState";
range = xSheet.get_Range("C31", "C31");
int saveLoc_31 = int.Parse(range.Value2.ToString());
try {
  objXYZDriver.SaveState(saveLoc_31);
  TestPass(xResult, shtRow, mName);
}
catch (System.Exception err) {
  TestFail(xResult, shtRow, mName, err.Message);
}
xResult.Cells.set_Item(shtRow, 6, "saveLoc = " + saveLoc_31);
shtRow = 32;
mName = "RecallState";
range = xSheet.get_Range("C32", "C32");
int saveLoc_32 = int.Parse(range.Value2.ToString());
try {
  objXYZDriver.RecallState(saveLoc_32);
  TestPass(xResult, shtRow, mName);
```

```
      }
      catch (System.Exception err) {
        TestFail(xResult, shtRow, mName, err.Message);
      }
      xResult.Cells.set_Item(shtRow, 6, "saveLoc = " + saveLoc_32);
      shtRow = 33;
      mName = "GetType";
      try {
        xResult.Cells.set_Item(33, 4, objXYZDriver.GetType());
        TestPass(xResult, shtRow, mName);
      }
      catch (System.Exception err) {
        TestFail(xResult, shtRow, mName, err.Message);
      }
      range = xSheet.get_Range("C33", "C33");
      if (range.Value2 != null) {
        xResult.Cells.set_Item(shtRow, 5, range.Value2.ToString());
      }
      rangeCurr = xResult.get_Range("D33", "D33");
      if (rangeCurr.Value2 != null)
        if (range.Value2 != null &&
        ➥rangeCurr.Value2.ToString() != range.Value2.ToString())
          rangeCurr.Interior.ColorIndex = 3;
      if (rangeCurr.Value2 != null)
        if (range.Value2 != null &&
       ➥ rangeCurr.Value2.ToString() == range.Value2.ToString())
          rangeCurr.Interior.ColorIndex = 4;
      string datetime = DateTime.Now.Date.ToShortDateString() +
➥DateTime.Now.Hour.ToString()+DateTime.Now.Minute.ToString() +
➥DateTime.Now.Second.ToString();
      datetime = datetime.Replace("/", "");
      datetime = datetime.Replace(":", "");
      string resultFile = System.IO.Path.Combine("C:/Temp",
➥"TestXYZDriver" + datetime + ".xls");
      xBook2.SaveAs(resultFile, -4143, "", "", false, false, 0,
➥"", 0, "", "", "");
      xBook.Close( false, null, false);
      xBook2.Close( false, null, false);
      xApp.Quit();
      xSheet =  null;
      xResult =  null;
      xBook =  null;
      xBook2 =  null;
      xApp =  null;
      return objXYZDriver;
    }
  }

  public class StartTestXYZDriver {

    public static void Main() {
```

```
            string rootDir = Environment.CurrentDirectory;
            string[] fileArray = null;
            StreamReader sr = File.OpenText(System.IO.Path.Combine("C:/Temp",
➥"fileArray.txt"));
            string input =  null;
            string fStr =  null;
            while ((input = sr.ReadLine()) != null) fStr = fStr + input + ",";
            sr.Close();
            fStr = fStr.Replace("/", "\\");
            fileArray = fStr.Split(',');
            TestXYZDriver test =  null;
            for (int i = 0; (i < fileArray.Length - 1); i = (i + 1)) {
              test = new TestXYZDriver(System.IO.Path.Combine(rootDir, fileArray[i]));
              test.StartTest();
            }
          }
        }
      }
```

This generated test script can be reused throughout the project life cycle and repeatedly test the newly implemented code toward its maturity. Thus, the AutomatedTest tool provides the following advantages:

- It provides an opportunity to test a product in the early stage of the software development life cycle.
- It provides early feedback about the most recently developed code, which is consistent with the XP philosophy of coding a little and testing a little.
- When coding is completed, all the test script should have been executed at least once, thereby increasing confidence that the software meets the requirements.
- If there is a need to change the design details, the AutomatedTest tool can easily regenerate a new test script addressing all the modifications and continue testing while the developers are coding.
- It provides unbiased testing evaluations. The metrics will be observed for all the testing cases.

These features are useful for software development projects. It is especially important for projects in which XP practices are used. XP is known as a software development approach for a team on risk-prone projects with unstable requirements. There is no detailed requirements documentation. The projects are frequently rescheduled, reestimated, and reprioritized. Early and frequent testing is a core aspect of extreme programming. Developers and testers are expected to write unit and functional test scripts before the application is developed. The test script is checked-in in the source code control as a part of the project code. Customers are also an integral part of the project team and help develop scenarios for acceptance and black box testing. When the AutomatedTest tool is used, the test scripts for these practices are automatically generated or modified and rerun for each of the frequent development iterations. In order to ensure code quality, this tool achieves the principle of coding a little and testing a little to the extreme. For example, developers write code during the day. Testing can be done after working hours without human attention. Thus, quality assurance and software testing are fully automated, which can play a critical role in the success of the project.

Presentation of the Test Results

The previous sections have summarized the validation and verification capabilities of the AutomatedTest project. This section shows you how the testing results will be presented and provides information for developers to fix defects.

During the implementation of the AutomatedTest tool in the previous chapters, you inserted two kinds of the test results in the Excel report by the execution of the test script. One of them reports whether the execution of the test is successful. The other tests whether the actual return value of the execution matches an expected return value. These are handled by the `TestPass()` and `TestFail()` methods in the test script. The rest of this chapter will be devoted to adding an automatic method to complete these tasks.

If you have manually added the `TestPass()` and `TestFail()` methods into the generated `TestScrip.cs` file and compiled and run it, you have seen the MS Excel report. The MS Excel report includes the following test results:

- The first column lists the names of the methods tested, which are inherited from the test data store.
- The second column reports whether the test passes or fails, which is the result of the method invocation.
- The third column gives the error messages, if the test fails, that tell the cause of the failure. These messages are from different computing resources.
- The forth column lists the actual return of the method after the testing, which checks whether there is a specified expected return value. This functionality was implemented as early as Chapter 5 for the `TestForm.cs`, in which you coded a method `AddExpectedValue()`. This method is called by the `InitMethodInventory()` method. The code of this method makes a space to hold the expected value.
- The fifth column prints the expected return value from the Excel data store specified by the tester. Sometimes, the method may execute successfully with a pass in the second column, which leads to the execution of the `TestPass()` method. But the actual return may not be a value as expected. Based on the match between the actual return and the specified expected return, the `TestPass()` method reports a test result of pass or fail.

- Starting from the sixth column, the test reports list the current value of all the parameters after a method execution. Thus, the engineers can examine the conditions that yield the actual return. This feature is especially useful to test the final status of the parameters that are passed by reference or are *out* parameters.

NOTE After implementing the AutomatedTest project in this chapter, Figure 9.2, later in this chapter, shows an example of a test result. You may refer to it when you read this section.

Passing a Test

Previously, you copied the AutomatedTest project to a folder for a new chapter from its previous chapter folder and continued adding more methods to reach the full automation. Now you need to add the methods to the AutomatedTest tool in order to generate a complete test script, including the `TestPass()` and `TestFail()` methods. First you need to copy the project again:

1. Make a copy of the AutomatedTest project from `C:\ScourceCode\Chapter08` and copy it to `C:\ScourceCode\Chapter09`.
2. Start the Microsoft Visual Studio .NET IDE and load the AutomatedTest project from the `C:\ScourceCode\Chapter09` folder.
3. Navigate to the `TestForm.cs` editor.
4. Add code as shown in Listing 9.7 to complete the `CreateTestPassMethod()`.

Listing 9.7 The *CreateTestPassMethod()* to Generate a *TestPass()* Method into the Test Script Programmatically

```
private void CreateTestPassMethod(CodeMemberMethod cm, string MethodName)
{
   cm = new CodeMemberMethod();

   CodeExpression[] pCode = null;
   CodeFieldReferenceExpression cLeft=null;
   CodeFieldReferenceExpression cRight=null;

   cm.Name = MethodName;//"TestPass";
   cm.ReturnType = new CodeTypeReference(typeof(void));

   cm.Attributes = MemberAttributes.Private | MemberAttributes.Final;
   cm.Parameters.Add(new
➥CodeParameterDeclarationExpression("Excel.Worksheet", "xResult"));
   cm.Parameters.Add(new
➥CodeParameterDeclarationExpression("System.Int32", "shtRow"));
   cm.Parameters.Add(new
➥CodeParameterDeclarationExpression("System.String", "mName"));
```

```
    CodeExpression[] pCode = null;
    CodeFieldReferenceExpression cLeft=null;
    CodeFieldReferenceExpression cRight=null;

    cm.Statements.Add(new
➥CodeParameterDeclarationExpression(typeof(Excel.Range), "range"));

    pCode = new CodeExpression[]{new
➥CodeFieldReferenceExpression(null, "shtRow, 1, mName")};
    cm.Statements.Add(new CodeMethodInvokeExpression(null,
➥"xResult.Cells.set_Item", pCode));

    pCode = new CodeExpression[]{new
➥CodeFieldReferenceExpression(null, "shtRow, 2, \"PASS\"")};
    cm.Statements.Add(new CodeMethodInvokeExpression(null,
➥"xResult.Cells.set_Item", pCode));

    pCode = new CodeExpression[]{new
➥CodeFieldReferenceExpression(null, "shtRow, 3, \"NO ERROR\"")};
    cm.Statements.Add(new CodeMethodInvokeExpression(null,
➥"xResult.Cells.set_Item", pCode));

    cLeft=new CodeFieldReferenceExpression(null, "range");
    cRight=new CodeFieldReferenceExpression(null,
➥"xResult.get_Range(\"B\" + shtRow, \"B\" + shtRow)");
    cm.Statements.Add(new CodeAssignStatement(cLeft, cRight));

    cLeft=new CodeFieldReferenceExpression(null, "range.Interior.ColorIndex");
    cRight=new CodeFieldReferenceExpression(null, "10");
    cm.Statements.Add(new CodeAssignStatement(cLeft, cRight));
    co.Members.Add(cm);
}
```

In Listing 9.7, the first statement makes a new `CodeDom.CodeMemberMethod()` object. The lines of the code immediately following assign a name to the method, define its attributes, and make parameters for it. Then it uses the following CodeDom objects repeatedly to generate the code for the `TestPass()` method:

```
CodeExpression[] pCode;
CodeFieldReferenceExpression cLeft;
CodeFieldReferenceExpression cRight;
cm.Statements.Add(new CodeMethodInvokeExpression(null,
➥"xResult.Cells.set_Item", pCode));
```

or

```
cm.Statements.Add(new CodeAssignStatement(cLeft, cRight));
```

At last, this adds the newly created method into the test script:

```
co.Members.Add(cm);
```

When you apply CodeDom objects, this repeated pattern makes the code easy to understand. After execution, this `TestPass()` method will generate a method for the test script as shown in Listing 9.8.

Listing 9.8 The Automatically Generated *TestPass()* Method, Which Is a Part of the Test Script

```
private void TestPass(Excel.Worksheet xResult, int shtRow, string mName) {
    Excel.Range range;
    xResult.Cells.set_Item(shtRow, 1, mName);
    xResult.Cells.set_Item(shtRow, 2, "PASS");
    xResult.Cells.set_Item(shtRow, 3, "NO ERROR");
    range = xResult.get_Range("B" + shtRow, "B" + shtRow);
    range.Interior.ColorIndex = 10;
}
```

NOTE In the `TestPass()` method, the integer variable `shtRow` indicates the row where the testing result of a method will be populated in a worksheet. The literal numbers 1, 2, and 3 indicate columns A, B, and C of the worksheet, respectively. However, when the `get_Range()` method is used to point at a worksheet cell, a letter is used to indicate the column. For example, letter B points at column B.

As we have discussed in the previous section, this method plugs the name of the method in the first column of the MS Excel worksheet, a PASS in the second column, and a NO ERROR in the third column. The color index assigns a green background color of the current cell, indicating that a test passes.

Failing a Test

After the generation of the `TestPass()` method, add the method in Listing 9.9 to the `TestForm.cs` file to generate the `TestFail()` method.

Listing 9.9 The *CreateTestFailMethod()* to Generates a *TestFail()* Method for the Test Script

```
private void CreateTestFailMethod(CodeMemberMethod cm, string MethodName)
{

   CodeExpression[] pCode = null;
   CodeFieldReferenceExpression cLeft=null;
   CodeFieldReferenceExpression cRight=null;

  cm = new CodeMemberMethod();
```

```
    cm.Name = MethodName;//"TestFail";
    cm.ReturnType = new CodeTypeReference(typeof(void));
    cm.Attributes = MemberAttributes.Private |MemberAttributes.Final;
    cm.Parameters.Add(new
➥CodeParameterDeclarationExpression("Excel.Worksheet", "xResult"));
    cm.Parameters.Add(new
➥CodeParameterDeclarationExpression("System.Int32", "shtRow"));
    cm.Parameters.Add(new
➥CodeParameterDeclarationExpression("System.String", "mName"));
    cm.Parameters.Add(new
➥CodeParameterDeclarationExpression("System.String", "errMsg"));

    cm.Statements.Add(new
➥CodeParameterDeclarationExpression(typeof(Excel.Range), "range"));

    CodeExpression[] pCode = null;
    CodeFieldReferenceExpression cLeft=null;
    CodeFieldReferenceExpression cRight=null;

    pCode = new CodeExpression[]{new
➥CodeFieldReferenceExpression(null, "shtRow, 1, mName")};
    cm.Statements.Add(new CodeMethodInvokeExpression(null,
➥"xResult.Cells.set_Item", pCode));

    pCode = new CodeExpression[]{new
➥CodeFieldReferenceExpression(null, "shtRow, 2, \"FAIL\"")};
    cm.Statements.Add(new
➥CodeMethodInvokeExpression(null, "xResult.Cells.set_Item", pCode));

    pCode = new CodeExpression[]{new
➥CodeFieldReferenceExpression(null, "shtRow, 3, errMsg")};
    cm.Statements.Add(new
➥CodeMethodInvokeExpression(null, "xResult.Cells.set_Item", pCode));

    cLeft=new CodeFieldReferenceExpression(null, "range");
    cRight=new CodeFieldReferenceExpression(null,
➥"xResult.get_Range(\"B\" + shtRow, \"B\" + shtRow)");
    cm.Statements.Add(new CodeAssignStatement(cLeft, cRight));

    cLeft=new CodeFieldReferenceExpression(null, "range.Interior.ColorIndex");
    cRight=new CodeFieldReferenceExpression(null, "3");
    cm.Statements.Add(new CodeAssignStatement(cLeft, cRight));
    co.Members.Add(cm);

}
```

The techniques and rationale of the `CreateTestFailMethod()` are similar to those of the `CreateTestPassMethod()`. After the execution of this method, it will generate a `TestFail()` method for the test script, such as in Listing 9.10.

Listing 9.10 The Automatically Generated *TestFail()* Method for a Test Script

```
private void TestFail(Excel.Worksheet xResult,
➥int shtRow, string mName, string errMsg) {
    Excel.Range range;
    xResult.Cells.set_Item(shtRow, 1, mName);
    xResult.Cells.set_Item(shtRow, 2, "FAIL");
    xResult.Cells.set_Item(shtRow, 3, errMsg);
    range = xResult.get_Range("B" + shtRow, "B" + shtRow);
    range.Interior.ColorIndex = 3;
}
```

This method will be called inside a `catch` statements of a test script. Similar to what has been done by the `TestPass()` method, the `TestFail()` method also plugs the name of the method being tested in the first column of the MS Excel worksheet. But it reports a FAIL in the second column. In the third column, it reports the exact cause of the failure so that the developers can use this report to fix the defects. Finally, the color index assignment makes a red background, indicating a test failure.

After the implementation, you need to enable the calling of these two methods in your AutomatedTest project. To do this, locate the `AddUpClassesMethods()` declaration in the `TestForm.cs` editor and add the two method calls immediately below the first line of the code (`co.Members.Add(cm);`):

```
CreateTestPassMethod(cm, "TestPass");
CreateTestFailMethod(cm, "TestFail");
```

Listing 9.11 shows the modified `AddUpClassesMethods()` method with the newly added lines of code in bold.

Listing 9.11 Enabling the *TestPass()* and *TestFail()* Methods for the AutomatedTest Project within the *AddUpClassesMethods()* Method

```
...
private void AddUpClassesMethods()
{
      co.Members.Add(cm);

      CreateTestPassMethod(cm, "TestPass");
      CreateTestFailMethod(cm, "TestFail");

      //add a file name field
      AddFilenameField(co);
      //add a constructor
      AddCstorCodes(co);
```

```
        //add a class to start the Main method
        CodeTypeDeclaration eco = new CodeTypeDeclaration("Start" + clsName);
        eco.TypeAttributes = TypeAttributes.Public;
        cnamespace.Types.Add(eco);

        //add the Main method

        AddMainMethod(eco, clsName);

}
...
```

Now you have finished the implementation to create a fully functional test script. You can build the AutomatedTest project and execute it by pressing F5 again. Then follow these steps to experiment with the new functions:

1. Click Start. An Open file dialog box appears.
2. Navigate to `C:\SourceCode\Chapter08\HighLevelObj\bin\Debug` and select the `HighLevelObj.dll` assembly.
3. Click the Open button. The TypeUnderTest form appears with the `AdvancedCalc` class name.
4. Select the check box beside the `AdvancedCalc` class.
5. Click the OK button. An MS Excel application opens with the names of methods and parameters and other information (Figure 9.1).

FIGURE 9.1
Edit the Excel data store for the first complete test script (SoftTestDataStore.xls)

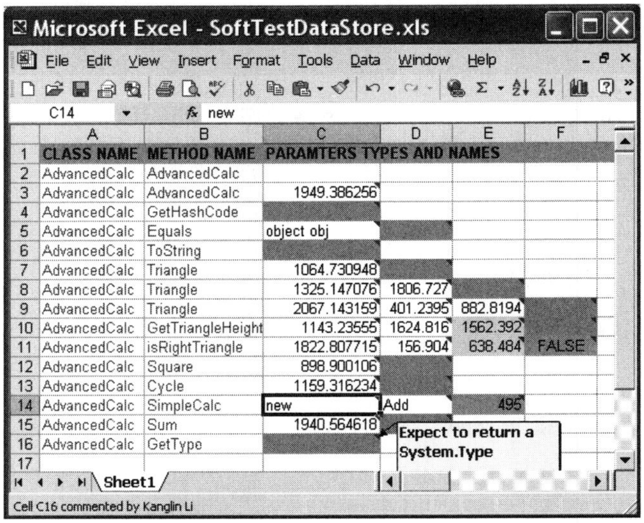

6. The values are all assigned by the AutomatedTest tool for the parameters to test a method. If you want to alter some numbers, you can do it now or later, but you need to always assign a value `new` to a parameter passed by object. Right now, point your cursor to activate Cell C14 and change the value of it to `new` for the `HighLevelObj.AdvancedCalc` object `lvlMath`. Leave all the others values intact because they are assigned properly by the AutomatedTest tool.
7. Save the change and switch back to the AutomatedTest tool.
8. Leave the Manual Stub check box unchecked. Click the Create Script button.
9. Within a second or two, the automatic test script generation is complete. Now you can compile it using the `csc.exe` command and run it. The `csc.exe` command is listed here:

```
C:\WINDOWS\Microsoft.NET\Framework\v1.0.3705\csc testscript.cs
➥/r:C:\SourceCode\Chapter09\AutomatedTest\Bin\Debug\Interop.Excel.dll
➥/r:C:\SourceCode\Chapter08\HighLevelObj\bin\debug\HighLevelObj.dll
➥/r:C:\SourceCode\Chapter04\lowLevelObj\bin\debug\LowLevelObj.dll
```

10. Execute the `TestScript.exe`. The test result looks similar to Figure 9.2.

NOTE You need the references of the `HighLevelObj.dll` and `LowLevelObj.dll` in `C:\SourceCode\Chapter08` and `C:\SourceCode\Chapter04` to successfully compile this test assembly. Type this entire command in one line in the Command Console window.

FIGURE 9.2 The test result report by the first fully automated software test script

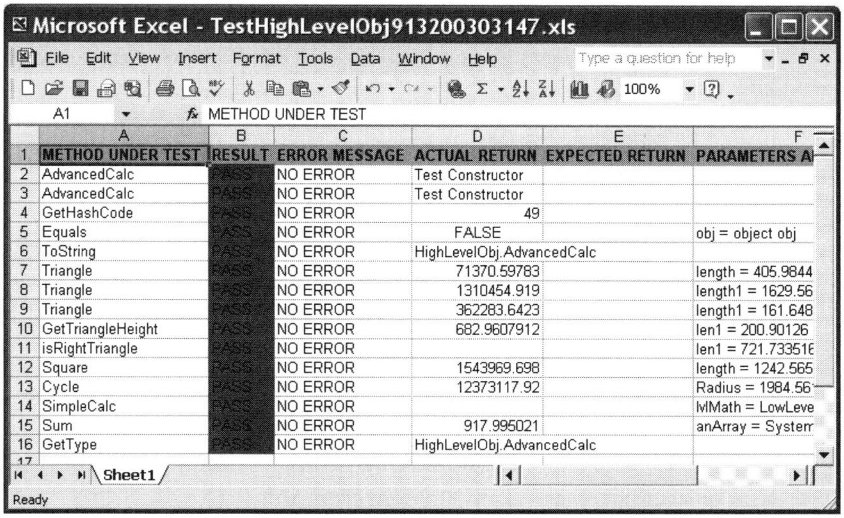

Microsoft Excel - TestHighLevelObj913200303147.xls

	METHOD UNDER TEST	RESULT	ERROR MESSAGE	ACTUAL RETURN	EXPECTED RETURN	PARAMETERS A
2	AdvancedCalc	PASS	NO ERROR	Test Constructor		
3	AdvancedCalc	PASS	NO ERROR	Test Constructor		
4	GetHashCode	PASS	NO ERROR	49		
5	Equals	PASS	NO ERROR	FALSE		obj = object obj
6	ToString	PASS	NO ERROR	HighLevelObj.AdvancedCalc		
7	Triangle	PASS	NO ERROR	71370.59783		length = 405.9844
8	Triangle	PASS	NO ERROR	1310454.919		length1 = 1629.56
9	Triangle	PASS	NO ERROR	362283.6423		length1 = 161.648
10	GetTriangleHeight	PASS	NO ERROR	682.9607912		len1 = 200.90126
11	isRightTriangle	PASS	NO ERROR			len1 = 721.73351
12	Square	PASS	NO ERROR	1543969.698		length = 1242.565
13	Cycle	PASS	NO ERROR	12373117.92		Radius = 1984.56
14	SimpleCalc	PASS	NO ERROR			lvlMath = LowLeve
15	Sum	PASS	NO ERROR	917.995021		anArray = System
16	GetType	PASS	NO ERROR	HighLevelObj.AdvancedCalc		

NOTE At this stage, in order to successfully execute the test, the references should be manually moved into the same folder with the executable test assembly, which are `Interop.Excel.dll`, `LowLevelObj.dll`, and `HighLevelObj.dll`. You also need to check whether `C:\Temp` contains the `fileArray.txt` and `SoftTestDataStore.xls` files. However, this is a temporary solution. The problem will be solved after Chapter 10.

In the report, the first two methods tested by the test script are the two `AdvancedCalc` constructors. They are followed by thirteen other methods. Among them, nine methods are from the implementation in the previous chapters. The other four methods are inherited from the .NET base class, that is, `GetHashCode()`, `Equals()`, `ToString()`, and `GetType()`.

All the methods passed the tests in this report. As it is generated by the AutomatedTest tool, the `TestPass()` method lists the names of the tested methods in column A and reports the PASSes in column B with green color indication. There are no error messages for failure in column C. Column D lists the actual return value for each method invocation.

WARNING Each time you run an MS Excel application programmatically, the `Excel.exe` residue accumulates in your system. This doesn't stop you from executing a new test with the AutomatedTest tool. The residue will disappear after a while. However, if you want to run a new session of MS Excel through a normal procedure with the residue still in the system, the Excel worksheet becomes invisible. A resolution to this is to clean the residue using the Windows Task Manager by pressing the Delete key while holding Ctrl+Alt and then clicking the Task Manager button. Then, from the Windows Task Manager, you activate the Processes tab and highlight the `Excel.exe` processes one by one. Clean each one by clicking the End Process button.

Summary

In this chapter, I discussed how the AutomatedTest tool generates test script that have the capability for result verification, validation, and presentation. The discussions in this chapter also served as a summary of the capabilities of the AutomatedTest tool that have been implemented since the beginning of this book.

In the discussion of automated verification, you saw how many testing tasks this automated tool can perform. These tasks are time consuming with traditional testing methods. The AutomatedTest tool is perfect for testing projects developed with XP methods. The quality of an XP project will significantly benefit from this tool.

With the verification and validation methods, this tool can report defects. The developers can use the report to fix the defects. This follows the working pattern of a traditional testing team, in which the testers find bugs and the developers fix them.

Finally, you implemented two methods by using CodeDom objects in this chapter to add the `TestPass()` and `TestFail()` methods to the test script. These additions conveniently enable a real automated test script process. Thus, the AutomatedTest tool can generate a flawless test script with an example. After the execution of the example test script, the test script demonstrates the capability to test all of the classes, methods, and properties of a given assembly. This is difficult when traditional testing methods are used and when the assembly under test contains hundreds of such members.

However, after generating the test script, the AutomatedTest tool still lacks the power to invoke the test script automatically. You need to manually compile it through the `csc.exe` line command and pool the dependencies into one folder. In the next chapter, you will make the test process totally automated by adding some more helper methods.

Chapter 10

Finalizing the AutomatedTest Tool

Technically, after Chapter 9, "Verification, Validation, and Presentation," you have enabled the AutomatedTest project to generate the test scripts for any given assembly. The process is totally automatic after an assembly is fed. This avoids cumbersome human interaction and debugging efforts required by the current commercial testing tools.

The test script generated by the AutomatedTest tool has the functions to test the code logic and to take care of error handling. Testing cases are automatically stored in XML documents or MS Excel worksheets. It also creates complete and real objects for integration testing. The test scripts can be scheduled to conduct continuous regression testing and find defects for newly added code.

The objectives of this chapter are to reconstruct the GUI interface of the TestForm, to add functions that deploy the test script executable, and to achieve a fully automated testing tool, from test script generation to test result presentation and defect reporting.

Improving the Appearance of the AutomatedTest Project

This section describes the process of adding more GUI controls to the AutomatedTest form so it will perform the software test with full automation.

To proceed with this section and the next sections, copy the AutomatedTest project from `C:\SourceCode\Chapter09` to `C:\SourceCode\Chapter10`. Then, start the Microsoft Visual Studio .NET IDE and load the newly copied project. Click the TestForm design editor.

From the previous chapters, the TestForm has accumulated three buttons and two check box controls. The buttons have been implemented to perform the following actions:

- Clicking the Start button, you can feed the AutomatedTest tool an assembly in need of testing. It also stores testing information into a data store.
- Clicking the Create Script button generates a test script. The entire process of generating the testing cases and the test script completes within seconds.
- Finally, clicking the Exit button terminates the session.

With the check boxes, you can turn on/off the manual stub and the XML data store capabilities. When the manual stubbing is off, the AutomatedTest tool initiates a class instance automatically.

Now we need to add a few more text boxes for the specification of the paths and names that the generated test script can use. And we need to add a few labels to identify the text boxes.

Finally, we need to add two more buttons to enable the multiple data store functions. The additions and properties of these new controls are listed below.

Control	Property	Value
Label	Text	Project Target Folder
Label	Text	Result Target Folder
Label	Text	.NET IDE Location
TextBox	Text	C:\Temp
	Name	txtTargetProj
TextBox	Text	C:\Temp
	Name	txtCurrDir
TextBox	Name	txtDOTNETLocation
Panel	Name	panel1
Button	Text	Add Data Store
	Name	btnAddDataStore
Button	Text	Save Data Store
	Name	btnSaveDataStore
RichTextBox	Name	txtDataStore

Instead of using the default icon provided by the Microsoft Visual Studio .NET IDE, a new icon image is also created and saved in the AutomatedTest project folder. This icon appears in the upper-left corner of the AutomatedTest tool. However, you can use the default icon or choose an icon for your organization. To enable an icon, follow these steps:

1. You can right-click the TestForm from the design editor.
2. Choose Properties from the pop-up menu.
3. In the property page, locate the Icon property and click the eclipsed button on the right. A file open dialog box appears.
4. Navigate to your icon file, and click to select the filename.
5. Finally, click the Open button. The icon is changed on the TestForm.

After the TestForm is populated with the new controls and the icon, it looks like Figure 10.1. The form is ready for further programming now.

FIGURE 10.1
The final look of the AutomatedTest form

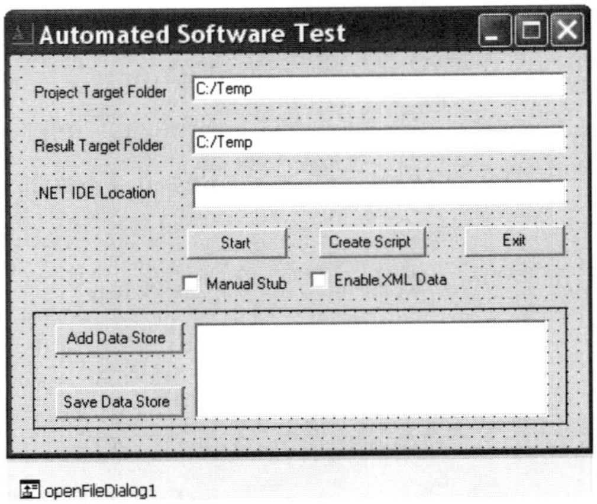

Automatically Generating .NET Project Components

In previous chapters, we discussed the late binding technique. Using late binding will execute the test scripts dynamically. The test engineer will not need to review the test script and debug it. This chapter adds another automatic mechanism by creating other components of a C# project based on the C# .NET IDE specification. Thus, test script can be loaded and built by the Microsoft Visual Studio .NET IDE. With the test script opened as a C# project, the test engineers can execute the test or review the test scripts. This adds more flexibility to the tool.

In order for the Microsoft Visual Studio .NET IDE to load the test script as a C# project, you need to enable the tool to create the following helper files:

- A test script file with a `.cs` file extension. This file is generated by the AutomatedTest tool and the filename is extrapolated from the name of the assembly under test.
- A test script project file with a `.csproj` file extension. This file is modified by the AutomatedTest tool and the filename is also extrapolated from the name of the assembly under test.
- The `AssemblyInfo.cs` file, which is relatively constant across projects
- The `App.ico` file, which is an icon file

At this moment, the AutomatedTest tool is able to generate the test script file, which is the most important file in the project. This section illustrates how to make the others.

The *App.ico* and *AssemblyInfo.cs* Files

`App.ico` is simply an icon image for the test script to be generated. The Microsoft Visual Studio .NET IDE generates a default icon file for every .NET project. In the AutomatedTest project, you may want to add your own icon file for the test script. Or you may just want to use an existing icon file. Either way is fine. At this moment, you need to save your favorite icon file with a name `TestApp.ico` in the `C:\SourceCode\Chapter10\AutomatedTest\bin\Debug` folder, where the sample code made a copy of the icon created for the TestForm in the previous section.

The `AssemblyInfo.cs` file contains all of the information about the assembly. Typically, it has the content in Listing 10.1. For the AutomatedTest project, you do not need to alter this file.

Listing 10.1 The *AssemblyInfo.cs* File Generated by the Microsoft Visual Studio .NET IDE

```
using System.Reflection;
using System.Runtime.CompilerServices;

//
// General Information about an assembly is controlled through the following
// set of attributes. Change these attribute values to modify the information
// associated with an assembly.
//
 [assembly: AssemblyTitle("Automated Software Tester")]
[assembly: AssemblyDescription("")]
[assembly: AssemblyConfiguration("")]
[assembly: AssemblyCompany("")]
[assembly: AssemblyProduct("Automated Software Tester")]
[assembly: AssemblyCopyright("2003")]
[assembly: AssemblyTrademark("")]
[assembly: AssemblyCulture("")]

//
// Version information for an assembly consists of the following four values:
//
//      Major Version
//      Minor Version
//      Build Number
//      Revision
//
// You can specify all the values or you can default the Revision and
➥Build Numbers
// by using the '*' as shown below:

[assembly: AssemblyVersion("1.0.0.0")]

//
// In order to sign your assembly you must specify a key to use. Refer to the
// Microsoft .NET Framework documentation for more information on
➥assembly signing.
//
// Use the attributes below to control which key is used for signing.
//
// Notes:
//   (*) If no key is specified, the assembly is not signed.
```

```
//   (*) KeyName refers to a key that has been installed in the Crypto Service
//       Provider (CSP) on your machine. KeyFile refers to a file which contains
//       a key.
//   (*) If the KeyFile and the KeyName values are both specified, the
//       following processing occurs:
//       (1) If the KeyName can be found in the CSP, that key is used.
//       (2) If the KeyName does not exist and the KeyFile does exist, the key
//           in the KeyFile is installed into the CSP and used.
//   (*) In order to create a KeyFile, you can use the sn.exe
➥(Strong Name) utility.
//       When specifying the KeyFile, the location of the KeyFile should be
//       relative to the project output directory which is
//       %Project Directory%\obj\<configuration>. For example,
➥if your KeyFile is
//       located in the project directory, you would specify the AssemblyKeyFile
//       attribute as [assembly: AssemblyKeyFile("..\..\mykey.snk")]
//   (*) Delay Signing is an advanced option - see the Microsoft .NET Framework
//       documentation for more information on this.
//
[assembly: AssemblyDelaySign(false)]
[assembly: AssemblyKeyFile("")]
[assembly: AssemblyKeyName("")]
```

The `AssemblyInfo.cs` file contains quite a few attributes, which identify your company and your product. A big portion of this file is comments. You don't need to make a new `AssemblyInfo.cs` file by typing. The Microsoft Visual Studio .NET IDE generates this file when you open a new project. For the AutomatedTest project, you need to save a copy of this file in the folder `C:\SourceCode\Chapter10\AutomatedTest\Bin\Debug` and rename it `TestAssemblyInfo.cs`.

When it is time to generate a new test script, the `testApp.ico` and the `TestAssemblyInfo.cs` are copied and renamed back to `App.ico` and `AssemblyInfo.cs`, respectively.

After you understand the necessity of these two files, you are ready to add a `MakeFileCopy()` method into the `TestForm.cs` file. The code segment of this method is shown in Listing 10.2. Navigate to your `TestForm.cs` editor in the opened project and add this method into it.

Listing 10.2 Code for the *MakeFileCopy()* Method

```
string rootDir = Environment.CurrentDirectory;
private void MakeFileCopy(string fileKind)
{
  FileInfo f = null;
  if (fileKind == "ico")
  {
    f = new FileInfo(rootDir + "/testApp.ico");
    try
    {
```

```
        FileInfo AppF = f.CopyTo(AppIconFilename, true);
      }
      catch(Exception err){MessageBox.Show(err.Message);}
    }
    else
    {
      f = new FileInfo(rootDir + "/TestAssemblyInfo.cs");
      try
      {
        FileInfo AppF = f.CopyTo(AsmInfoFilename, true);
      }
      catch(Exception err){MessageBox.Show(err.Message);}
    }
  }
```

Before the declaration of this method, a `rootDir` string field is added. This field is always assigned with a string of the location where the `AutomatedTest.exe` file is saved.

Within the method declaration, a `FileInfo` object is declared. Then the `FileInfo` instance is initialized based on the `fileKind` argument. The rest of the code all evolves around the `FileInfo` object. The only purpose of this method is to invoke the `FileInfo.CopyTo()` method. The `FileInfo.CopyTo()` method takes two parameters: the first string parameter gives a new name to the file, the second is a Boolean for overwrite, which is set to be true. When the value of the `fileKind` argument is `"ico"`, it copies the `TestApp.ico`. Otherwise, it copies the `TestAssemblyInfo.cs`. All these actions occur inside a `try` statement.

After this implementation, locate the end of the `btnCreateScript_Click()` event handler and add two lines of code for the invocation of the `MakeFileCopy()` method twice with different arguments. After the new lines are added, the method becomes like Listing 10.3, where the newly added lines are bold.

Listing 10.3 The Modified *btnCreateScript_Click()* Event Handler with New Code in Bold

```
private void btnCreateScript_Click(object sender, System.EventArgs e)
{
  btnStart.Focus();
  if (dirName == null || xApp == null)
  {
    MessageBox.Show("Click the Start button to collect test information
➥first.");
    return;
  }
      //Create a TextWriter object to save the script
  TextWriter t = null;

  t = new StreamWriter (new FileStream (TestScriptCSFilename, FileMode.Create));
      //start generating script
```

```
    try
    {
      CreateTestCode(DUTAsm, t);
    }
    catch(Exception err)
    {MessageBox.Show(err.Message);}
    finally
    {
      t.Close();
    }
    CreateDataStoreCollection(xlsDataStoreFilename);
    CloseExcelSheet();

    MakeFileCopy("ico");
    MakeFileCopy("cs");

  }
```

This takes care of the `AssemblyInfo.cs` and `App.ico` files for the test script project to be generated automatically.

The .NET **.csproj*

Microsoft Visual Studio .NET IDE uses information from this file to build a .NET project. The information includes versioning and self-described entities, building configuration, and locations of the source code and dependent references needed to build the assembly. The Microsoft Visual Studio .NET IDE generates an initial `*.csproj` file with the project name. Then, this file continues to be updated during the process of coding a project as references are added and other configuration parameters are altered. The default content of this file at project initialization is shown in Listing 10.4. A plain text editor is able to open this file. In order to enable the AutomatedTest tool, the implementation of a `makeCSPROJFile()` method in Listing 10.5 modifies the initial `*.csproj` file, assigns filename and adds needed dependencies according to the assembly under test.

Listing 10.4 The Context of the **.csproj* File for the AutomatedTest Project at the Initial State

```
<VisualStudioProject>
    <CSHARP
        ProjectType = "Local"
        ProductVersion = "7.10.3077"
        SchemaVersion = "2.0"
        ProjectGuid = "{656354BC-2A2F-4915-ACC0-73FEC812695B}"
    >
        <Build>
            <Settings
                ApplicationIcon = "App.ico"
                AssemblyKeyContainerName = ""
```

```
        AssemblyName = "OATLStest"
        AssemblyOriginatorKeyFile = ""
        DefaultClientScript = "JScript"
        DefaultHTMLPageLayout = "Grid"
        DefaultTargetSchema = "IE50"
        DelaySign = "false"
        OutputType = "Exe"
        PreBuildEvent = ""
        PostBuildEvent = ""
        RootNamespace = "OATLStest"
        RunPostBuildEvent = "OnBuildSuccess"
        StartupObject = ""
    >
        <Config
            Name = "Debug"
            AllowUnsafeBlocks = "false"
            BaseAddress = "285212672"
            CheckForOverflowUnderflow = "false"
            ConfigurationOverrideFile = ""
            DefineConstants = "DEBUG;TRACE"
            DocumentationFile = ""
            DebugSymbols = "true"
            FileAlignment = "4096"
            IncrementalBuild = "true"
            NoStdLib = "false"
            NoWarn = ""
            Optimize = "false"
            OutputPath = "bin\Debug\"
            RegisterForComInterop = "false"
            RemoveIntegerChecks = "false"
            TreatWarningsAsErrors = "false"
            WarningLevel = "4"
        />
        <Config
            Name = "Release"
            AllowUnsafeBlocks = "false"
            BaseAddress = "285212672"
            CheckForOverflowUnderflow = "false"
            ConfigurationOverrideFile = ""
            DefineConstants = "TRACE"
            DocumentationFile = ""
            DebugSymbols = "false"
            FileAlignment = "4096"
            IncrementalBuild = "false"
            NoStdLib = "false"
            NoWarn = ""
            Optimize = "true"
            OutputPath = "bin\Release\"
            RegisterForComInterop = "false"
            RemoveIntegerChecks = "false"
            TreatWarningsAsErrors = "false"
            WarningLevel = "4"
        />
```

```
            </Settings>
            <References>
                <Reference
                    Name = "System"
                    AssemblyName = "System"
                    HintPath =
"C:\WINNT\Microsoft.NET\Framework\v1.0.3705\System.dll"
                />
                <Reference
                    Name = "System.Data"
                    AssemblyName = "System.Data"
                    HintPath =
"C:\WINNT\Microsoft.NET\Framework\v1.0.3705\System.Data.dll"
                />
                <Reference
                    Name = "System.XML"
                    AssemblyName = "System.Xml"
                    HintPath =
"C:\WINNT\Microsoft.NET\Framework\v1.0.3705\System.XML.dll"
                />
                <Reference
                    Name = "VBIDE"
                    Guid = "{0002E157-0000-0000-C000-000000000046}"
                    VersionMajor = "5"
                    VersionMinor = "3"
                    Lcid = "0"
                    WrapperTool = "tlbimp"
                />
                <Reference
                    Name = "Office"
                    Guid = "{2DF8D04C-5BFA-101B-BDE5-00AA0044DE52}"
                    VersionMajor = "2"
                    VersionMinor = "1"
                    Lcid = "0"
                    WrapperTool = "tlbimp"
                />
                <Reference
                    Name = "stdole"
                    Guid = "{00020430-0000-0000-C000-000000000046}"
                    VersionMajor = "2"
                    VersionMinor = "0"
                    Lcid = "0"
                    WrapperTool = "primary"
                />
                <Reference
                    Name = "Excel"
                    Guid = "{00020813-0000-0000-C000-000000000046}"
                    VersionMajor = "1"
                    VersionMinor = "4"
                    Lcid = "0"
                    WrapperTool = "tlbimp"
                />
```

```
            </References>
        </Build>
        <Files>
            <Include>
                <File
                    RelPath = "App.ico"
                    BuildAction = "Content"
                />
                <File
                    RelPath = "AssemblyInfo.cs"
                    SubType = "Code"
                    BuildAction = "Compile"
                />
                <File
                    RelPath = "OATLS1TESTRep.cs"
                    SubType = "Code"
                    BuildAction = "Compile"
                />
            </Include>
        </Files>
    </CSHARP>
</VisualStudioProject>
```

This is an XML document that contains the product version of the current Microsoft Visual Studio .NET IDE, GUID, settings, build configurations, references, and locations to look for the needed files. Although this book doesn't discuss this file in further detail, there are several references to books on .NET project in the bibliography. To make this file available for AutomatedTest project to create a `.csproj` file for each test script, you need to open a text editor, type in the content, and save it to the following folder with the name `OATestProj.csproj`:

```
C:\SourceCode\Chater10\AutomatedTest\Bin\Debug
```

The name is randomly selected and doesn't have any special meaning.

The forth and fifth lines of the `OATestProj.csproj` document specify the current product version and schema version of the Microsoft Visual Studio .NET IDE installed on a system. At this point, their values are:

```
ProductVersion = "7.10.3077"
SchemaVersion = "2.0"
```

These values are specific for the Microsoft Visual Studio .NET IDE 2003. If you use a different version of the Microsoft Visual Studio .NET IDE, you can find the correct values by opening your Microsoft Visual Studio .NET IDE and click About Microsoft Development Environment from the Help menu. For example, the values for the Microsoft Visual Studio .NET IDE 2002 should be:

```
ProductVersion = "7.0.9466"
SchemaVersion = "1.0"
```

If you have earlier versions of MS Excel

This book assumes you have installed MS Excel XP in your system. In Listing 10.4, the Excel reference fragment assigns value 1 to the major version of the MS Excel, and value 4 to the minor version. If you have an earlier version of MS Excel (for example, MS Excel 2000) installed for your system, you need to locate the XML segment of the Excel reference in Listing 10.4:

```
<Reference
        Name = "Excel"
        Guid = "{00020813-0000-0000-C000-000000000046}"
        VersionMajor = "1"
        VersionMinor = "4"
        Lcid = "0"
        WrapperTool = "tlbimp"
/>
```

Then, modify the value of the minor version. After the modification, the XML segment for the Excel reference should be:

```
<Reference
        Name = "Excel"
        Guid = "{00020813-0000-0000-C000-000000000046}"
        VersionMajor = "1"
        VersionMinor = "3"
        Lcid = "0"
        WrapperTool = "tlbimp"
/>
```

You have enabled the AutomatedTest to have a seed of the `OATestProj.csproj` file. With the `OATestProj.csproj` file, the AutomatedTest project will be capable of generating a file that will be modified to fit the test script of a given assembly. Your next task is to program the AutomatedTest project to add this file to the test script project. The implementation of a `MakeCSPROJFile()` method is in Listing 10.5 and should be located in the `TestForm.cs` file.

Listing 10.5 Code for the *MakeCSPROJFile()* Method

```
private void MakeCSPROJFile(string clsName, Assembly asm)
{
  StreamReader sr = File.OpenText(rootDir + "/OATestProj.csproj");
  string input = null;
  string output = null;
  string refStr = "";
  string relPath = TestScriptCSFilename;
  string[] RelPath = relPath.Split('/');
  relPath = RelPath[RelPath.Length-1];

  while (null != (input = sr.ReadLine()))
  {

    if (input.IndexOf("OATLStest") > 0)
    {
      input = input.Replace("OATLStest", clsName);
    }
    if (input.IndexOf("</References>") > 0)
    {
      AssemblyName[] asmRefs = asm.GetReferencedAssemblies();

      foreach (AssemblyName aRef in asmRefs)
      {
        if (aRef.FullName.IndexOf("mscorlib") < 0)
        {
          refStr = refStr + "<Reference\n";
          refStr = refStr + "Name = \"" + aRef.Name + "\"\n";
          refStr = refStr + "AssemblyName = \"" + aRef.Name + "\"\n";
          refStr = refStr + "HintPath = \"" + aRef.CodeBase + "\"\n" + "/>\n";
        }
      }

refStr = refStr + "<Reference\n" +
 "Name = \"" + asm.FullName.Substring(0,
➥asm.FullName.IndexOf(", "))  + "\"\n" +
➥"AssemblyName = \"" + asm.FullName.Substring(0,
➥asm.FullName.IndexOf(", ")) + "\"\n" +
➥"HintPath = \"" + asm.CodeBase + "\"\n" +
➥"/>\n";

//Add lower level module dependencies
if (stubForm.m_CreateReference != "")
      {
        refStr += stubForm.m_CreateReference;
        stubForm.m_CreateReference = "";
```

```
          }

          refStr = refStr.Replace("file:///", "");
          refStr = refStr.Replace("/", "\\");
          input = refStr + input + "

        }

        if (input.IndexOf("RelPath = \"OATLS1TESTRep.cs\"") > 0)
        {
          input=input.Replace("OATLS1TESTRep.cs", relPath);
        }
        output = output + input + "\n";

      }
      FileInfo f = new FileInfo(CSProjFilename);
      StreamWriter write = f.CreateText();
      write.Write(output);
      write.Close();
      sr.Close();
    }
```

The actions performed by this method are mainly to read the predefined `*.csproj` file and alter references and file locations according to the assembly under test. When the predefined `*.csproj` file is modified, a `FileInfo` object creates and saves a new `*.csproj` file for the test script. Finally, it closes the opened files.

After coding this method, you need to invoke it in the `TestForm.cs`. Because this method makes changes to the `.csproj` file with regard to the assembly given for the test, it is appropriate to be called in the `CreateTestCode()` method. Locate the `CreateTestCode()` method and add a line calling the `MakeCSPROJFile()` method at the end of it. After the addition, the `CreateTestCode()` method implementation looks like Listing 10.6, with the first portion of the code segment omitted and the addition in bold.

Listing 10.6 The New Look of the *CreateTestCode()* Method

```
  ...
  private void CreateTestCode(Assembly DUT, TextWriter t)
  {
    StartCodeDom(DUT);

    ...
    ...
    ...
```

```
    AddUpClassesMethods();
    cg.GenerateCodeFromNamespace(cnamespace, t, null);
    MakeCSPROJFile(clsName, DUTAsm);
}
...
```

At this point, if you want to compile the project, and run it, it will generate four files for the test script project (`TestScript.cs`, `App.ico`, `AssemblyInfo.cs`, and `TestScript.csproj`). In the next section, you will implement methods to define a naming convention and file folders for the test script and put all the files with the test script in the same location.

Test Script Naming Convention

You may have noticed the inconvenience of copying EXE, DLL, and data store files into a folder in the previous chapters. In this section, I'll show you how to solve this problem by adding some string fields and a method to initiate the strings. These fields will be used as names and locations for the test script project. The names and locations directly reflect the assembly under test.

After the naming convention for the files and folders is defined, you need to add a method to create folders and subfolders so that you can store all the test project files in proper folders for respective assemblies.

Conversion from old versions to new versions.

Usually newer versions of Microsoft Visual Studio .NET can automatically convert C# projects developed on an older version of Microsoft Visual Studio .NET. But the conversion from newer to older version is not true. The OATestProj.csproj file of this book is developed based on the Microsoft Visual Studio .NET 2003. If you only have Microsoft Visual Studio .NET 2002 or older for your system, you can refer to the ReadMe.txt file in the downloaded source code (www.sybex.com) and copy the older OATestProj.csproj to the C:\SourceCode\Chapter10\AutomatedTest\Bin\Debug folder. Make sure the major and minor versions of the Microsoft Visual Studio .NET and Excel match your system configuration.

Another way to convert the generated test script project to an older Microsoft Visual Studio .NET version is to open a new project for it. The steps are:

1. Start your version of Microsoft Visual Studio .NET IDE.
2. Create a C# console project.
3. Remove the Microsoft Visual Studio .NET IDE generated C# file.
4. Add the AutomatedTest tool generated test script into the new project.
5. Add respective references to the new project.

First, let's look at the `InitConstString()` method; the code for this is shown in Listing 10.7.

Listing 10.7 Code for the *InitConstString()* Method and Its Related Fields

```
string dirName;
string AssemblyNameUT;
string testResultStr;
string TestScriptCSFilename;
string CSProjFilename;
string AsmInfoFilename;
string AppIconFilename;

private void InitConstStrings()
{
   try
   {
      dirName = openFileDialog1.FileName;
      dirName = dirName.Replace("\\", "/");
      string[] DirName = dirName.Split('/');
      dirName = DirName[DirName.Length-1];
      dirName = dirName.Replace(".dll", "");
   }
   catch (Exception err)
   {
      MessageBox.Show("Select a DLL file\n" + err.Message,
➥"XOA Software Tester");
   }

   if (txtTargetProj.Text == "textBox8")
   {
      txtTargetProj.Text="C:/Temp";
   }
   tempTestProjDir = txtTargetProj.Text.Replace("\\", "/");

   AssemblyNameUT = openFileDialog1.FileName;
   xlsDataStoreFilename = tempTestProjDir + "/" + dirName +
➥"/Bin/Debug/test" + dirName + "Data.xls";
   testResultStr = tempTestProjDir + "/" + dirName + "/TestResult.xls";
   TestScriptCSFilename = tempTestProjDir + "/" + dirName +
➥"/test" + dirName + ".cs";
   CSProjFilename = tempTestProjDir + "/" + dirName + "/Test" +
➥dirName + ".csproj";
   AsmInfoFilename= tempTestProjDir + "/" + dirName + "/AssemblyInfo.cs";
   AppIconFilename = tempTestProjDir + "/" + dirName + "/App.ico";

   if (txtCurrDir.Text == "Current Directory")
      txtCurrDir.Text= txtTargetProj.Text;
   XlsReportFilename = txtCurrDir.Text.Replace("\\", "/");
}
```

This method uses the assembly filename as the reference. It mainly invokes some string function to manipulate the assembly name. Then it assigns each string field a value with respect to the name of the assembly file. These string fields are filenames for the test script, the test project, and the test results. Thus, the filenames of the entire test project are consistent.

The second method is the `CreateTestDirectory()` method. It also uses the name of the Assembly under test to create a test directory. Then, a `bin` and a `debug` subdirectory are created inside the test project directory. Listing 10.8 lists the code for the `CreateTestDirectory()` method.

Listing 10.8 Code for the *CreateTestDirectory()* Method

```
private void CreateTestDirectory()
{
  DirectoryInfo dir = new DirectoryInfo(tempTestProjDir);
  try
  {
    if (dirName != null)
      dir.CreateSubdirectory(dirName);
  }
  catch(IOException err){MessageBox.Show(err.Message);}
  dir = new DirectoryInfo(tempTestProjDir + "/" + dirName);
  try
  {
    dir.CreateSubdirectory("Bin");
  }
  catch(IOException err){MessageBox.Show(err.Message);}
  dir = new DirectoryInfo(tempTestProjDir + "/" + dirName + "/Bin");
  try
  {
    dir.CreateSubdirectory("Debug");
  }
  catch(IOException err){MessageBox.Show(err.Message);}
}
```

Similar to the file manipulation, this method uses the `DirectoryInfo` class to create these directories. The `try-catch` statements are used to handle errors when the directories already exist. If a directory exists, the `try` statement will not create another one and the method can continue to proceed to the next code line. After coding these two methods, locate the `btnStart_Click()` event. Add two lines of code:

```
InitConstStrings();
CreateTestDirectory();
```

Now the `btnStart_Click()` event handler looks similar to Listing 10.9, with the new lines of code in bold.

Listing 10.9 The Updated *btnStart_Click()* Event handler with the New Lines in Boldface

```
...
private void btnStart_Click(object sender, System.EventArgs e)
{
  GetAssemblyName();
  InitConstStrings();
  CreateTestDirectory();
  GetTypesOfAssemblyUnderTest();

  InitMethodInventory();

  if (chckXMLDataDoc.Checked)
  {
    MakeUseXMLDataStore();
    btnCreateScript_Click(sender, e);
  }

  btnCreateScript.Focus();
}
...
```

These two methods create a naming convention for each assembly under test. The combined efforts solve the problem of creating directories and naming files.

You may remember that you hard-coded some strings to save the generated files as a temporary measure. After the naming algorithm is created, you can locate those hard-coded names and delete the assignment. But keep the field declarations.

In the previous chapters, the test script has always been saved with the path and name as `C:\Temp\TestScript.cs`. After this implementation, a `TestScriptCSFilename` field is created. You can delete the `workFile` variable declaration and replace the occurrences of the `workFile` variable with the `TestScriptCSFilename` variable. Please see the affected code in Listing 10.11.

Building Multiple Data Stores

The test script can be rerun. For each run, the test engineer can use the same data store or use a different one. Very often, the test engineer wants to run the test script with more than one Excel data store within one execution. Thus, the AutomatedTest project builds a data store with a collection of multiple Excel files. The code in Listing 10.10 for the `CreateDataStoreCollection()` method is also to create and close a text file. The content of this text file is the path and names of the Excel data stores contained by the `xlsDataStoreFilename` variable.

Listing 10.10 Code for the *CreateDataStoreCollection()* Method

```
private void CreateDataStoreCollection(string Content)
{
   FileInfo f = new FileInfo(System.IO.Path.Combine(tempTestProjDir +
➥"/" + dirName + "/Bin/Debug", "fileArray.txt"));
   StreamWriter sw = f.CreateText();
   sw.Write(Content);
   sw.Close();
}
```

After coding this method in the `TestForm.cs` file, add the following code lines to the end of the `btnCreateScript_Click()` event handler:

```
CreateDataStoreCollection(xlsDataStoreFilename);
txtDataStore.Text = xlsDataStoreFilename;
```

This is the second time that the `btnCreateScript_Click()` event handler is updated in this chapter (see Listing 10.3 for the first updating). Listing 10.11 shows the location where the new code is placed. The unchanged code of the first portion is omitted. The new code is in bold and the `workFile` variable is replaced with the `TestScriptCSFilename` variable.

Listing 10.11 The Second Modification of the *btnCreateScript_Click()* Event Handler

```
...
private void btnCreateScript_Click(object sender, System.EventArgs e)
{
  btnStart.Focus();

  ...

  t = new StreamWriter (new FileStream (TestScriptCSFilename, FileMode.Create));

  ...


  CloseExcelSheet();

  MakeFileCopy("ico");
  MakeFileCopy("cs");

  CreateDataStoreCollection(xlsDataStoreFilename);
  txtDataStore.Text = xlsDataStoreFilename;
}
...
```

This addition of the code in Listing 10.11 creates a file with a name of `fileArray.txt` in the `..\bin\debug` folder for each assembly under test.

After this is done, you need to make a corresponding change for the test script to be generated. Locate the AddMainMethod() declaration and find the line of code that looks like this:

```
cRight=new CodeFieldReferenceExpression(null,
➥"File.OpenText(System.IO.Path.Combine(\"" + tempTestProjDir /*+
➥"/" + dirName + "/Bin/Debug"*/ + "\", \"fileArray.txt\"))");
```

A portion of this line is in bold. You need to remove the comment markers (/* and */ in bold) from this line. After the modification, the line of this code looks like the following:

```
cRight=new CodeFieldReferenceExpression(null,
➥"File.OpenText(System.IO.Path.Combine(\"" + tempTestProjDir +
➥"/" + dirName + "/Bin/Debug" + "\", \"fileArray.txt\"))");
```

At this point, this line of code creates a value for the test script to open a text file which contains information about multiple testing data stores. After a test script is generated, the AutomatedTest tool adds only one data store filename to the fileArray.txt file. When the test engineer needs to add or remove data stores from the fileArray.txt file, they can use a text editor or other word processor to do it. However, the AutomatedTest project has prepared controls for this implementation. To enable the controls, from the AutomatedTest design editor, double-click the Add Data Store button. The cursor is at the btnAddDataStore_Click() event definition. Add the code in Listing 10.12 to this event.

Listing 10.12 Code for the *btnAddDataStore_Click()* Event Definition

```
private void btnAddDataStore_Click(object sender, System.EventArgs e)
{
   if (dirName == null)
   {
      MessageBox.Show("Please click Start button,
➥then Create Script button to generate a test script first.");
      return;
   }
   openFileDialog1.Title = "Add more data store";
   openFileDialog1.Filter = "Excel Files (*.xls)|*.xls";
   openFileDialog1.Multiselect = true;
   if (openFileDialog1.ShowDialog() == DialogResult.OK)
   {
      foreach (string fn in openFileDialog1.FileNames)
      {
         txtDataStore.Text +="\n" + fn;

      }
   }
}
```

Reviewing the code in Listing 10.12, the action will open a file dialog box that allows the user to select a data store filename. The dialog's Multiselect property is enabled to be true. When the OK button is clicked, the selected filenames are appended to the `txtDataStore.Text` property one after another by the `foreach` loop.

Click the design form to go to the TestForm design editor again. Double-click the Save Data Store button. Add two lines of code in the `btnSaveDataStore_Click()` event definition. The `btnSaveDataStore_Click()` event has the code listed in Listing 10.13.

Listing 10.13 Code for the *btnSaveDataStore_Click()* Event

```
private void btnSaveDataStore_Click(object sender, System.EventArgs e)
{
   if (txtDataStore.Text.Trim() == "")
      return;

   CreateDataStoreCollection(txtDataStore.Text);
}
```

The execution of this button click checks whether or not there are any filenames in the RichTextBox object. If yes, it calls the `CreateDataStoreCollection()` method to save the content of the RichTextBox object.

Auto-Execution of the Test Script Project

As described previously, the AutomatedTest project will open the test script after its generation into the Microsoft Visual Studio .NET IDE. In order to do this, one more .NET namespace is needed, `System.Diagnostics`. The `System.Diagnostics` namespace provides numerous type classes and methods— for example, `PerformanceCounter`, `Process`, `Trace`, `TraceListner`, and so on. You can consult with the references listed in the bibliography for more information on these type classes. The test project will only make use of a few functions of the `Process` class.

To enable the AutomatedTest tool to open the generated test script into a Microsoft Visual Studio .NET IDE, first add a `using` statement at the beginning of the `TestForm.cs` file like this:

```
using System.Diagnostics;
```

Then add the `StartDOTNETIDE()` method to the `TestForm.cs` file. The code for this method is shown in Listing 10.14.

Listing 10.14 Code for the *StartDOTNETIDE()* Method

```
private void StartDOTNETIDE(string fileName, string args)
{
   Process shell = new Process();
   shell.StartInfo.FileName = fileName;
   shell.StartInfo.Arguments = args;
   shell.Start();
}
```

This method initializes a `Process` object, `shell`, to collect the executable name, `fileName`, of the Microsoft Visual Studio .NET IDE and the test project name referenced by `args`. You can also use this method to start other programs.

During the execution of the code in Listing 10.14, it passes the paths and names of the Microsoft Visual Studio .NET IDE and the test script project as parameters. The Microsoft Visual Studio .NET IDE starts and loads the test script just generated. If you want to open the test script project manually, you can issue the same command through the DOS command window. For example, when you test the `LowLevelObj.dll` assembly, the path and name of the test script project will be generated as `C:/Temp/LowLeveObj/TestLowLeveObj.csproj`. The executable file name of the Microsoft Visual Studio .NET IDE is always `devenv.exe`. Thus, the DOS command to open the test script project in the Microsoft Visual Studio.NET IDE is as follows:

```
C:\devenv.exe C:/Temp/LowLeveObj/TestLowLeveObj.csproj
```

At this point, you can review and debug the test script, which you often need to do with other test methods. The capability of reviewing and debugging a generated test script may also be helpful during the process of developing an automated testing tool at an earlier stage.

The `devenv.exe` executable can not only open a test script project, it can also compile the project. When using the `devenv.exe` to compile a project, it locates the references stored in the `csproj` document. The syntax of the `devenv.exe` command doesn't need the reference switches as the `csc.exe` command does. To automate the compiling test script for the AutomatedTest tool, you can alter the `StartDOTNETIDE()` helper method to execute the Microsoft Visual Studio .NET IDE with a `/build debug` switch. The `debug` configuration builds a debug version of the test script. The alternative is `release`. For software testing purposes, the `debug` option is more appropriate. When this option is implemented, the `StartDOTNETIDE()` method will build a test script project behind the scenes.

To add code to the AutomatedTest Tool and build the test script automatically, navigate to the code of the `StartDOTNETIDE()` method and change the value of the `StartInfo.Arguments` property from

```
shell.StartInfo.Arguments = args;
```

to

```
shell.StartInfo.Arguments = args + " /build debug";
```

Automatic invocation of the `StartDOTNETIDE()` method occurs at the end of the `btnCreateScript_Click()` event handler again. This is the third time in this chapter we've updated the `btnCreateScript_Click()` event handler. The update adds the bold line of code in Listing 10.15.

Listing 10.15 The Third Modification of the *btnCreateScript_Click()* Event Handler with the New Code in Bold

```
...
private void btnCreateScript_Click(object sender, System.EventArgs e)
{
  btnStart.Focus();

  ...
  ...


  MakeFileCopy("ico");
  MakeFileCopy("cs");

  CreateDataStoreCollection(xlsDataStoreFilename);
  txtDataStore.Text = xlsDataStoreFilename;

  StartDOTNETIDE(txtDotNETLocation.Text, CSProjFilename);
}
...
```

So far in this chapter, you have added five lines of code to this event handler, and this is the last modification needed for this event.

You have solved many problems relating to automating the C# project process. The last problem is for a special situation. You need to enable a process to locate the path for the Microsoft Visual Studio .NET IDE dynamically in case it is not added to the environment variables of a system. This will ensure that the AutomatedTest project can invoke the Microsoft Visual Studio .NET IDE. This can be achieved with the following approach:

1. Double-click the TestForm from the design editor. The IDE adds a `TestForm_Load()` event handler for the `TestForm.cs` file.
2. Between the curve brackets, add the code. The code for the `TestForm_Load()` event is in Listing 10.16.

Listing 10.16 The Code for the TestForm_Load() Event

```
private void TestForm_Load(object sender, System.EventArgs e)
{
  try
  {
    string DevenvPath = Environment.ExpandEnvironmentVariables(
➥@"%VSCOMNTOOLS%devenv.exe").Replace(@"Tools", "IDE").Replace("\"", "");

    if (!File.Exists(DevenvPath)) //for VS .NET 2003
```

```
      {
        DevenvPath = Environment.ExpandEnvironmentVariables(
➥@"%VS71COMNTOOLS%devenv.exe").Replace(@"Tools", "IDE");
      }

      txtDotNETLocation.Text = DevenvPath;
    }
    catch
    {
    }

    btnStart.Focus();

  }
```

The `TestForm_Load()` event will be the first visual event to occur when the AutomatedTest tool is started. The `Environment.ExpandEnvironmentVariables()` static method is used to assign a value to the `DevenvPath` variable. The installation of the Microsoft Visual Studio .NET IDE 2002 created an environmental variable, `VSCOMNTOOLS`, to store the Visual Studio common tools. This variable is the closest neighbor to the path where the `Devenv.exe` is installed. Thus, the AutomatedTest tool first looks for the value of the `VSCOMNTOOLS` variable. Because the actual return of the variable is similar to `C:\Program Files\Microsoft Visual Studio .NET 2003\Common7\Tools\`, a `Replace()` method is used to replace the `..\Tools` folder with the `..\IDE` folder. However, the installation of Microsoft Visual Studio .NET IDE 2003 creates a `VS71COMNTOOLS` environmental variable. The `if` statement is used to check whether the first call of the `Environment.ExpandEnvironmentVariables()` method finds the correct file path. If it doesn't, it calls the `Environment.ExpandEnvironmentVariables()` static method the second time with an argument pointing at the environment variable of the Microsoft Visual Studio .NET IDE 2003. Finally, the value of `DevenvPath` is assigned to the `txtDotNETLocation.Text` field. This task can also be performed by retrieving information from the Windows Registry system. The next chapter will introduce techniques for accessing and mutating the values in the Windows Registry programmatically.

The last statement, `btnStart.Focus()`, makes the Start button be focused. After the program runs, pressing the Enter key will start a test session just as clicking the Start button will, which is a usability issue.

Achieving Full Test Automation

Now the AutomatedTest tool is completed. The last step is to build the project into an assembly and then execute `AutomatedTest.exe` for your software testing tasks. When it is executed, the AutomatedTest tool looks like Figure 10.2.

The steps for AutomatedTest tool to conduct a software test are the same as demonstrated in the previous chapters. Click the Start button to specify an assembly and modify the generated MS Excel worksheet. Then click the Create Script button. At this moment, a new Microsoft Visual Studio .NET IDE opens with the newly generated test script project loaded. Within the Microsoft Visual Studio .NET IDE, press F5 to build and run the test script. The IDE might ask you to save a Text Solution File (*.sln). Always click the Save button to save it with the default filename. The test script is compiled and executed. The time needed for the execution depends on the complexity of the assembly under test and the number of methods under test. The test results are saved into the location you specified on the form with corresponding folders and filenames. Thus, you achieved the goal of automatic software testing.

At this point, by checking against descriptions in *The Economic Impacts of Inadequate Infrastructure for Software Testing* by Gregory Tassey (National Institute of Standards and Technology, 2002), the AutomatedTest tool has addressed the areas of inadequacy in the current test infrastructure:

- Integration testing is automated by the test script returning a complete and real object of the class under test.
- The generated test script is ready to be executed without debugging.
- The automatically generated data stores and the use of the XML documents for testing cases save a lot of the frustration and time involved when the commercial testing tools and methods are used.
- It tests all the methods, properties, and constructors within a class, including those inherited from bass classes and those in lower-level modules of the hierarchy.

FIGURE 10.2
The final appearance of the AutomatedTest tool while running

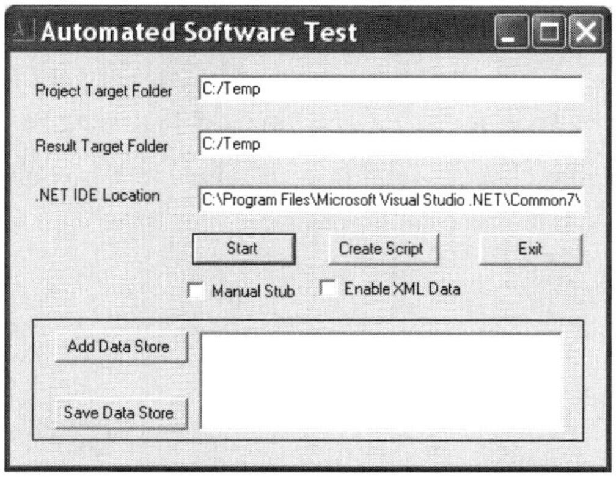

Summary

In this chapter, you become familiar with the files of a C# project. The `App.ico`, `AssemblyInfo.cs`, test script `*.cs`, and test script `*.csproj` files are automatically generated and modified based on the assembly under test. However, I did not discuss these files in detail. Additional knowledge of these files is not required to complete this project. The bibliography at the end of this book contains a number of references that I have found helpful.

After the project files are generated, the AutomatedTest tool creates a fileArray.txt document. The fileArray.txt document can contain multiple file names of the Excel data stores so that the test script can test an assembly against as many data stores as it is specified. This set of data stores and the generated test script can be rerun for regression testing. Later, if you decide to use different testing cases for this test script, you can edit the data stores in the MS Excel worksheet. Thus, the software test is fully automated.

At this point, you can use this AutomatedTest tool with full automation; that is, you feed the tool with an assembly to be tested and collect the test result after the test execution. There is no need for data composing and debugging. The test script assembly can be reused later for regression testing and integration testing. In general, the generated test scripts have the following advantages:

- There are no testability hooks coded for the test script. Testability implementation by other testing tools may introduce bugs into the software under test.
- The generation of the test script is data driven, which eliminates hard-coded testing data values and makes multiple data stores possible. The testing cases are stored with a spreadsheet or an XML document.
- The test scripts are modular based and conduct white box testing. The complete object of a module after the test execution improves the integration testing.
- A reusable library of the test scripts is built parallel to the software development life cycle. The regression testing becomes easily manageable.

In Chapter 11, you'll see how to upgrade this tool to test new requirements.

Chapter 11

Updating the Automated Test Tool for Testing the Windows Registry

In the previous chapters, you have given the AutomatedTest tool the capability to test methods, properties, and various kinds of parameters. In addition, it now has validation, verification, and presentation capabilities. It is already a fully functional tool designed to meet general needs at this point.

You may have noticed that third-party software testing tools often lack some components that are necessary to test your products. You make phone calls for technical support only to find out that the particular capability you need is in development and will be available for the next release.

Would you rather conduct testing within your time frame using conventional methods or wait for the new release? If your organization has specific testing requirements, you may need to incorporate additional special testing features into this tool, and this chapter will show you how.

Software developers often use the Windows Registry to make their software more portable. To obtain this portability, the software registers some properties and their values into the Windows Registry when a software product is installed or run. This chapter uses a Windows Registry example to add more functions to your AutomatedTest tool.

Windows Registry

As a software test engineer, you often need to access information about application installation settings, COM registrations, options, and other statistics from the Windows system registry.

Using the analogy of a disk drive, which has the hierarchical structure of directories, subdirectories and files, the Windows Registry has hives, subhives, keys, and values. The most common hives include HKEY_CLASSES_ROOT, HKEY_CURRENT_USER, HKEY_LOCAL_MACHINE, and HKEY_CURRENT_CONFIG. Each of the hives contains information in a specific category.

The HKEY_CLASSES_ROOT hive contains information about both object linking and embedding (OLE) and various file associations. OLE is a way to transfer and share information between applications by pasting information created in one application into a document created in another application, such as a spreadsheet or a word processing file. The purpose of HKEY_CLASSES_ROOT is to provide for compatibility with the existing Windows 3.*x* Registry.

The HKEY_CURRENT_CONFIG key contains information about the system's current configuration.

The HKEY_CURRENT_USER manages specific information about the user who is currently logged on. The information determines the appearance of the user's desktop, connections to network devices (such as printers and shared disk resources), desktop program items, application preferences, screen colors, personal preferences, security rights, and other environment settings.

The HKEY_LOCAL_MACHINE hive contains information about the current hardware configuration of the local computer. The information stored in this hive is updated using Control Panel, hardware and software installation programs, administrative tools, and some other properties automatically updated by the Windows operating system.

Installing or running a software product sometimes affects the keys and values of the Windows Registry. The purpose of this chapter is to enable the AutomatedTest tool to verify whether these keys and values behave as expected.

Accessing the Windows Registry

MS Windows stores its configuration information in a database called the Windows Registry. In most cases, the Registry contains profiles for each user of a computer and information about system hardware, installed programs, and property settings. If your software project requires information from the Registry, you need to enable the AutomatedTest tool to test against the Windows Registry.

Usually, a Registry editor is available that enables you to inspect and modify the Registry. The Registry editor that ships with Windows is `RegEdit.exe`. When you set up environmental variables, you also make modifications to the Windows Registry. To help you understand and test the Registry, the following sections will discuss how to manipulate it using means provided by the Windows system and how to programmatically read, change, and test the keys and values in the Registry.

RegEdit

The tool most often used to access to the Windows Registry is `RegEdit.exe`, which provides a quick user interface, easy-to-understand options, and a clean, uncluttered look for the users. Perform the following steps to use the `RegEdit.exe` tool:

1. Choose Start ➤ Run.
2. Type **RegEdit** in the Open text box.
3. Click the OK button. RegEdit displays the Windows Registry (see Figure 11.1). You see the five base hives.
4. Navigate to HKEY_LOCAL_MACHINE\SYSTEM\ControlSet001\Control\Session Manager\Environment. The environment variables and their values are listed in the right pane, as shown in Figure 11.2.

If you have had a chance to set up environment variables for a system, you should be familiar with these values. At this point, you can add new environment variables or delete some of them.

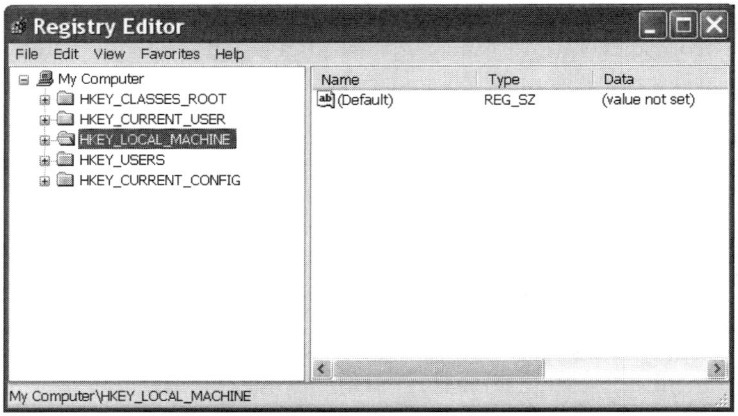

FIGURE 11.1
The Microsoft Windows Registry Editor with five base hives

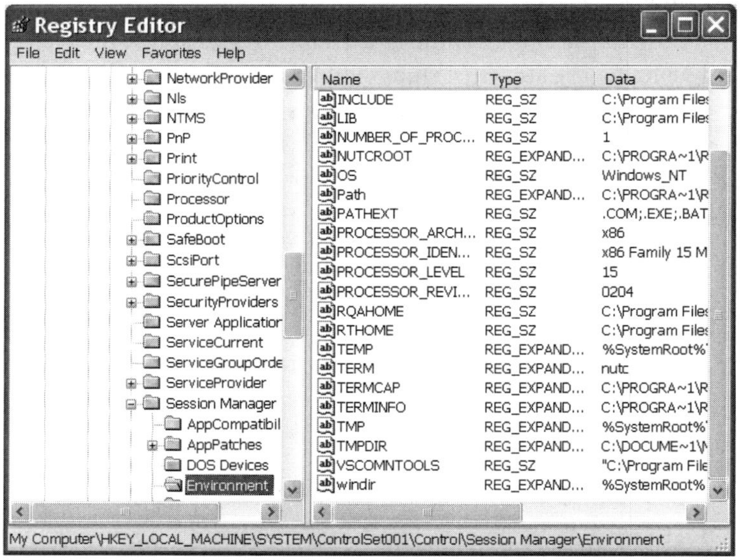

FIGURE 11.2
The Registry Editor with the environment variables listed

WARNING Deleting or modifying Registry entries or their values may prevent your computer from running properly. Be very sure you know exactly what effects your actions will have before you proceed.

Usually, experimentally adding a key and value is safer than deleting an existing one. Let's add a new environment variable, `AutomatedTestPath`.

1. Right-click on an empty area in the right pane.
2. From the pop up menu, select New ➤ String Value.
3. Rename it from New Value #1 to AutomatedTestPath.
4. Double-click on the name. The Edit String dialog box appears (Figure 11.3).

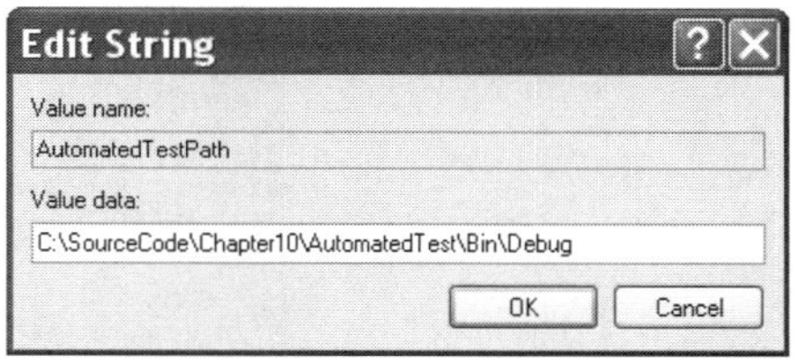

FIGURE 11.3 The Edit String dialog box for the Windows Registry

5. Type **C:\SourceCode\Chapter10\AutomatedTest\Bin\Debug** in the Value Data area.

NOTE Because the Chapter11 folder is not created at this point, Chapter10 is used.

6. Click the OK button.

An AutomatedTestPath variable is added to your Windows Registry.

System Properties

Here is another way to add an environment variable and then to see whether it takes effect:

1. Right-click the My Computer icon on your desktop. If your operating system is Windows XP, the My Computer icon is not installed on the desktop by default. In that case, left-click the Start button and right-click the My Computer item on the Start menu.
2. Choose Properties from the pop-up menu. The System Properties dialog box appears, shown in Figure 11.4.
3. Click the Environment Variables button on the Advanced tab. A form with user variables and system variables appears (Figure 11.5). You can add new variables, edit the values of the existing variables, and delete useless variables from here.
4. Make sure `AutomatedTestPath` variable is listed. As you can see, it is in the list of the system variables.

FIGURE 11.4
The Advanced tab of the My Computer System Properties dialog box

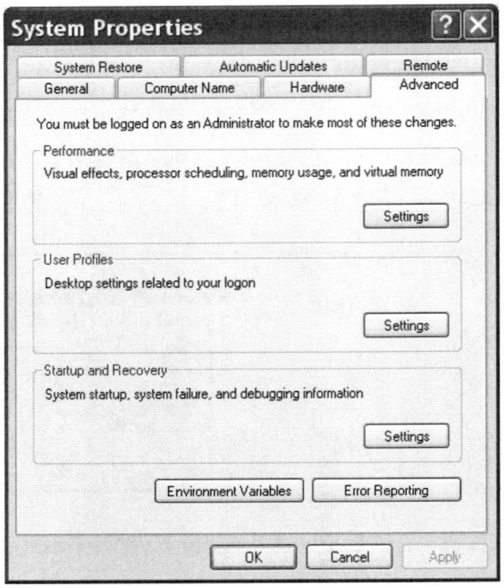

FIGURE 11.5
The Environment Variables dialog box

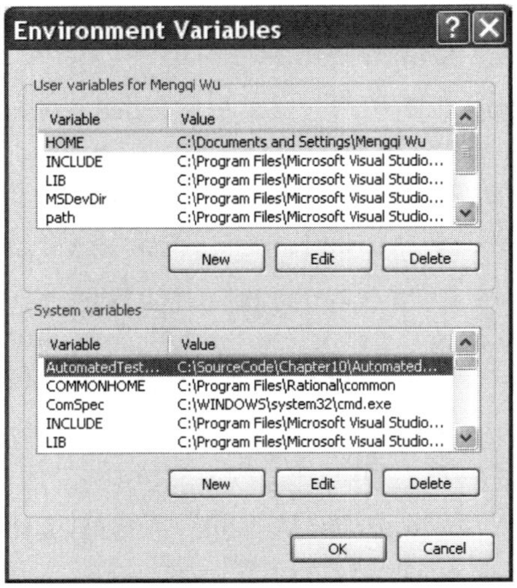

You can easily modify environment variables this way. But `RegEdit.exe` provides information about the entire Registry, not just the environment variables.

Command Prompt Window

Another way to check the status of the environment variables is to use the Command Console window. You can do so by following these steps:

1. Choose Start ➢ Run. Or look for the Visual Studio .NET command prompt on the Start menu and go to step 4.
2. Type **cmd** in the Open text box.
3. Click the OK button.
4. After the prompt, type **`set AutomatedTestPath`**.
5. Press Enter. The Visual Studio .NET Command Prompt window looks like Figure 11.6.

FIGURE 11.6 The set command in the Visual Studio .NET Command Prompt window

You can also alter the values of an environment variable from the console screen by typing the following code:

"**`set AutomatedTestPath= C:\SourceCode\Chapter10\AutomatedTest\Bin\Debug`**".

However, this alteration will hold only for this login session.

Issuing the command `set AutomatedTestPath` allows you to view the current value of this variable.

Or, you can issue the command `set` to view the entire list of environment variables.

Windows Registry Programming

The three methods all provide you with interfaces to access and modify the Windows Registry properties, specifically the environment variables. However, as a tester, you would probably prefer to write a program to access and modify the Registry automatically. In this section, you begin to create a C# console application to accomplish that. The final product will meet the following specifications:

- It is an executable (`.exe`) application.
- It prompts the user with a menu to decide whether to create or delete a variable.
- If the user chooses to create a variable, it automatically creates an `AutomatedTestPath` variable and assigns `C:\SourceCode\Chapter10\AutomatedTest\Bin\Debug` as its value.

- If the user chooses to delete a variable, it automatically deletes the `AutomatedTestPath` variable from the system.
- After the action (to create or delete), the application terminates.

The implementation is completed with the following steps:

1. Create a new C# console application project from the Microsoft Visual Studio .NET IDE.
2. Name this project AddAutoTestPath in a new folder, `C:\SourceCode\Chapter11`.
3. Type in the C# code in Listing 11.1.

Listing 11.1 **Code of the *AddAutoTestPath.cs* File**

```
using System;
using Microsoft.Win32;

namespace AddAutoTestPath
{

  public class SetEnvironmentVariable
  {
    public void SetSystemEnvironmentVariable(bool CreateVar, string newVal)
    {
      try
      {
        RegistryKey key = Registry.LocalMachine;
        key = key.OpenSubKey(
➥@"SYSTEM\ControlSet001\Control\Session Manager\Environment", true);
        if (CreateVar)
        {
          try
          {
            key.SetValue("AutomatedTestPath", newVal);
            Console.WriteLine("AutomatedTestPath = " +
➥key.GetValue("AutomatedTestPath"));
          }
          catch{}
        }
        else
        {
          try
          {
            key.DeleteValue("AutomatedTestPath");
            Console.WriteLine("An environment variable is deleted.");
          }
          catch{}
        }
      }
      catch (Exception ec)
```

```
        {
          Console.WriteLine(ec.Message);
        }
      }


      public void EditAutoTestPath(string newVal)
      {
        RegistryKey key = Registry.LocalMachine;
        key = key.OpenSubKey(
➥@"SYSTEM\ControlSet001\Control\Session Manager\Environment", true);
        key.SetValue("AutomatedTestPath", newVal);
      }


      public void ReadAutoTestPath(ref object keyVal)
      {
        RegistryKey key = Registry.LocalMachine;
        key = key.OpenSubKey(
➥@"SYSTEM\ControlSet001\Control\Session Manager\Environment", true);
        keyVal = key.GetValue("AutomatedTestPath");
      }
    }

    class AddTestPathAPP
    {
      [STAThread]
      static void Main(string[] args)
      {
        Console.WriteLine("What do you what to do?");
        Console.WriteLine("1: Create an environment variable");
        Console.WriteLine("2: Delete an environment variable");
        Console.Write("

        string action = Console.ReadLine();
        SetEnvironmentVariable setENV = new SetEnvironmentVariable();
        if (action == "1")
          setENV.SetSystemEnvironmentVariable(true,
➥@"C:\SourceCode\Chapter10\AutomatedTest\Bin\Debug");
        else
          setENV.SetSystemEnvironmentVariable(false, "");
        Console.WriteLine("

        Console.Read();
      }
    }
  }
```

This program completes the same work you used in the `RegEdit.exe` program in the previous section. The entire application consists of two classes: `AddAutoTestPath` and `AddTestPathAPP`.

In the AddAutoTestPath class, there are three public methods: SetEnvironmentVariable(), EditAutoTestPath(), and ReadAutoTestPath().

The SetSystemEnvironmentVariable() method creates or deletes an AutomatedTestPath key, which takes two parameters: a Boolean parameter (true to create a variable, false to delete a variable) and a string parameter as the value of the AutomatedTestPath variable to be created. Logically, the SetSystemEnvironmentVariable() method performs the following actions:

1. Creates a RegistryKey object, key, which belongs to the Microsoft.Win32 namespace.
2. Uses the key object to navigate through HKEY_LOCAL_MACHINE\SYSTEM\ControlSet001\Control\Session Manager\Environment.
3. Uses the SetValue() or the DeleteValue() method to create the specified environment variable or delete it.
4. Uses the GetValue() method to return the value of an existing variable.

The second method is EditAutoTestPath(), which takes one parameter and assigns the value of the parameter to the existing AutomatedTestPath key. The following actions occur within the EditAutoTestPath()method:

1. The OpenSubKey() method of RegistryKey class navigates to the specified hive and subhives.
2. The SetValue() method sets a specified value to the AutomatedTestPath key.

The third method, ReadAutoTestPath(), is similar to the second method. The difference is that it navigates to the hive and subhives and then gets the existing value of the AutomatedTestPath key instead of assigning a value to it. The other difference is that this method takes a parameter passed by reference. Thus, when the value of the AutomatedTestPath key is obtained, it assigns this value to the parameter.

The second class, AddTestPathAPP, has only an entry point method. The first few Console.WriteLine() statements print an instruction. The Console.ReadLine() method allows the user to enter a number to select an action. Then the initialization of the SetEnvironmentVariable class creates a setENV object. At last, an if-else statement is used to perform the requested action. If the user types 1 after the instruction, the entry point method invokes the SetEnvironmentVariable() method with a value true from the first parameter to create an AutomatedTestPath key to the Windows Registry, and assigns a value, C:\SourceCode\Chapter10\AutomatedTest\Bin\Debug, to the created key. Otherwise, it invokes the same method with a value false of the first parameter to delete the AutomatedTestPath key from the Windows Registry

The other two methods are not called in this application and will be used for testing the new updated AutomatedTest tool when this chapter is completed.

When you test-run this program, you will see that it does exactly what the `RegEdit.exe` tool or modifying the environment variables does. The `RegistryKey` class makes this task very easy. The following lists include the useful properties and the methods of the `RegistryKey` class (based on Microsoft Visual Studio .NET IDE documents).

Here are the properties:

`Name` Retrieves the name of the registry key.

`SubKeyCount` Retrieves the count of subkeys at the base level for the current key.

`ValueCount` Retrieves the count of values in the key.

Here are the methods:

`Close` Closes the key and flushes it to disk if the contents have been modified.

`CreateSubKey` Creates a `RegistryKey` object to represent a new subkey or opens an existing subkey. The `subKey` string is not case sensitive.

`DeleteSubKeyTree` Deletes a subkey and any child subkeys recursively. The string `subKey` is not case sensitive.

`DeleteValue` Overloaded. Deletes the specified value from this key. The string `subKey` is not case sensitive.

`Flush` Writes all the attributes of the specified open Registry key into the Registry.

`GetSubKeyNames` Retrieves an array of strings that contains all the subkey names.

`GetValue` Overloaded. Retrieves the specified value.

`GetValueNames` Retrieves an array of strings that contain all the value names associated with this key.

`OpenRemoteBaseKey` Creates a new `RegistryKey` object that represents the requested key on a foreign machine.

`OpenSubKey` Overloaded. Creates a `RegistryKey` object to represent a specified subkey that specifies whether the value of the key is writable after it is open.

`SetValue` Sets the specified value. The string `subKey` is not case sensitive.

We have completed the discussion of how to access the Windows Registry through the tools Microsoft provides and through a C# program. The rest of this chapter will cover how to enable the AutomatedTest tool to test against the Windows Registry.

Creating a Test Script to Test Software against the Windows Registry

To test against a value read from the Windows Registry, you need to add two helper methods into the test script. These methods will be called only when a value from the Windows Registry needs to be read. First, let's have a look at the target code of an `AccessRegKey()` method as shown in Listing 11.2, which will be generated and inserted into an automatically generated test script at the end of this chapter.

Listing 11.2 **Code of the *AccessRegKey()* Method Needed by the Final Test Script**

```
private void AccessRegKey(string locHive, ref RegistryKey key)
{
  if (locHive == "HKEY_CLASSES_ROOT")
    key = Registry.ClassesRoot;
  if (locHive == "HKEY_CURRENT_USER")
    key = Registry.CurrentUser;
  if (locHive == "HKEY_LOCAL_MACHINE")
    key = Registry.LocalMachine;
  if (locHive == "HKEY_USERS")
    key = Registry.Users;
  if (locHive == "HKEY_CURRENT_CONFIG")
    key = Registry.CurrentConfig;
}
```

This method takes two parameters:

- The first is the string value of a Registry base hive specified by a tester (to look for the appropriate hive to test). The specified hive can be any of the five base hives. The correct Registry key is going to be determined by the five `if` statements.
- The second parameter is a reference RegistryKey object. When the first parameter is located by one of the `if` statements, the value of the second parameter is altered.

A second `GetWinRegValue()` helper method targeted for the test script makes use of the `AccessRegKey()` method, which uses the hive obtained by the first method and the specified subhives to find the value of the specified Registry variable. The final code of the `GetWinRegValue()` method is shown in Listing 11.3, which will also be generated and inserted into the test script by the AutomatedTest tool at the end of this chapter.

Listing 11.3 **Code for the *GetWinRegValue()* Method Needed by the Final Test Script**

```
public string GetWinRegValue(string WinRegKey)
{
  WinRegKey = WinRegKey.ToUpper().Replace("WINREG:", "");
  string[] HiveSubs = WinRegKey.Split('\\);'
  WinRegKey = WinRegKey.Replace(HiveSubs[0]+@"\",
```

```
"").Replace(@"\"+HiveSubs[HiveSubs.Length-1], "");

  RegistryKey key=null;
  string WinRegVal = "";

  AccessRegKey(HiveSubs[0], ref key);
  key=key.OpenSubKey(WinRegKey);
  WinRegVal = (string)key.GetValue(HiveSubs[HiveSubs.Length-1]);
  key.Close();

  return WinRegVal;
}
```

When the `RegistryKey` class is used in the test script, the code in Listing 11.3 is easy to comprehend. This method takes a string parameter that is read from a testing case and required for accessing the Windows Registry. After the method declaration, the first three statements analyze the `WinRegKey` string.

Note that the first statement discards the text *WinReg* which is added to the Excel worksheet by the tester.Then the `split()` method from the `string` class determines a correct structure of the hierarchical hive, subhives and the key of interest.

After that, it creates a RegistryKey object, `key`, to look for the hive and subhives, and a string variable, `WinRegVal`, to hold the value found. Then the RegistryKey object explores the hive and subhives in a hierarchical order and then assigns the value to the `WinRegVal` variable.

These two methods are simple and straightforward. However, for the AutomatedTest tool, you are not going to write these two methods into the test scripts every time you test your software against the Windows Registry. Your next task is to update the AutomatedTest project by giving it the capability of coding these two methods automatically. Therefore, you need to use some CodeDom methods for the AutomatedTest tool project.

Adding CodeDom Methods to Update the AutomatedTest Tool

As you have done in previous chapters, you need to perform the following steps:

1. Copy the AutomatedTest project from `C:\SourceCode\Chapter10` to `C:\SourceCode\Chapter11`.
2. Open a Microsoft Visual Studio .NET IDE to load the AutomateTest project from `C:\SourceCode\Chapter11`.
3. From the Solution Explorer in the Microsoft Visual Studio .NET IDE, navigate to the code view of the `TestForm.cs`.
4. At the very end of the `TestForm` class, add a Boolean field:

   ```
   bool NeedWinReg;
   ```

This field will tell the program whether the tester is interested in testing against the Windows Registry. If the value of `NeedWinReg` is `true`, the following methods you'll add next will be executed.

First, declare a `MakeIfStatementForAccessRegKey()` method immediately after the new field declaration with the code in Listing 11.4.

Listing 11.4 The code for the New Field *NeedWinReg* and the *MakeIfStatementForAccessRegKey()* Method

```
...
bool NeedWinReg;

private void MakeIfStatementForAccessRegKey(CodeMemberMethod cm,
➥string strCondition, string strLeft, string strRight)
{
  CodeFieldReferenceExpression cLeft=null;
  CodeFieldReferenceExpression cRight=null;
  cLeft=new CodeFieldReferenceExpression(null, strLeft);
  cRight=new CodeFieldReferenceExpression(null, strRight);
  CodeConditionStatement ifState = new CodeConditionStatement(
➥new CodeSnippetExpression(strCondition),
➥new  CodeAssignStatement(cLeft, cRight));
  cm.Statements.Add(ifState);
}
```

This method makes a single `if` statement by taking a condition and a left and right expression for writing the `AccessRgKey()` method in the test script. It will be called by the next method, `CreateAccessRegKeyMethod()`.

Add the `CreateAccessRegKeyMethod()` method to complete writing the `AccessRegKey()` method for the test script in Listing 11.2. The code for the method is in Listing 11.5.

Listing 11.5 Code for the *CreateAccessRegKeyMethod()* Method

```
private void CreateAccessRegKeyMethod(CodeMemberMethod cm, string MethodName)
{
  cm = new CodeMemberMethod();

  cm.Name = MethodName;
  cm.ReturnType = new CodeTypeReference(typeof(void));
  cm.Attributes = MemberAttributes.Private |MemberAttributes.Final;

  cm.Parameters.Add(new
➥CodeParameterDeclarationExpression("System.String", "locHive"));
  cm.Parameters.Add(new
➥CodeParameterDeclarationExpression("ref RegistryKey", "key"));
```

```
    CodeFieldReferenceExpression cLeft=null;
    CodeFieldReferenceExpression cRight=null;

    cLeft=new CodeFieldReferenceExpression(null, "locHive");
    cRight=new CodeFieldReferenceExpression(null, "locHive.Trim()");
    cm.Statements.Add(new CodeAssignStatement(cLeft, cRight));

    MakeIfStatementForAccessRegKey(cm, "locHive == \"HKEY_CURRENT_CONFIG\"",
➥"key", "Registry.CurrentConfig");
    MakeIfStatementForAccessRegKey(cm, "locHive == \"HKEY_LOCAL_MACHINE\"",
➥"key", "Registry.LocalMachine");
    MakeIfStatementForAccessRegKey(cm, "locHive == \"HKEY_CURRENT_USER\"",
➥"key", "Registry.CurrentUser");
    MakeIfStatementForAccessRegKey(cm, "locHive == \"HKEY_CLASSES_ROOT\"",
➥"key", "Registry.ClassesRoot");
    MakeIfStatementForAccessRegKey(cm, "locHive == \"HKEY_USERS\"",
➥"key", "Registry.Users");

    co.Members.Add(cm);
  }
```

This method first defines the name, the return type, the attribute, and the parameters for the `AccessRegKey()` method. Then it uses a `cLeft` and a `cRight` `CodeFieldReferenceExpression` object to write a statement to trim the hive text read from the data store. And last, it makes use of the method `MakeIfStatementForAccessRegKey()`, corresponding to the five `if` statements in Listing 11.2. The last statement, `co.Members.Add()`, incorporates the code of this method into the test class of the script.

Now you need to add a method to write the second method for the test script in Listing 11.3. This method is declared as `CreateGetWinRegValueMethod()`, and its code is in Listing 11.6.

Listing 11.6 Code for the *CreateGetWinRegValueMethod()* Method

```
private void CreateGetWinRegValueMethod(CodeMemberMethod cm, string MethodName)
{
  cm = new CodeMemberMethod();

  cm.Name = MethodName;
  cm.ReturnType = new CodeTypeReference(typeof(object));
  cm.Attributes = MemberAttributes.Private |MemberAttributes.Final;

  cm.Parameters.Add(new CodeParameterDeclarationExpression("System.String",
➥"WinRegKey"));

  CodeFieldReferenceExpression cLeft=null;
  CodeFieldReferenceExpression cRight=null;

  cLeft=new CodeFieldReferenceExpression(null, "WinRegKey");
```

```
  cRight=new CodeFieldReferenceExpression(null,
➥"WinRegKey.ToUpper().Replace(\"WINREG:\", \"\")");
  cm.Statements.Add(new CodeAssignStatement(cLeft, cRight));

  cm.Statements.Add(new ➥
CodeParameterDeclarationExpression(typeof(Microsoft.Win32.RegistryKey),
➥"key = null"));

  cm.Statements.Add(new
➥CodeParameterDeclarationExpression(typeof(object), "WinRegVal = \"\""));

  cLeft=new CodeFieldReferenceExpression(null, "string[] HiveSubs");
  cRight=new CodeFieldReferenceExpression(null, "WinRegKey.Split('\\\')");
  cm.Statements.Add(new CodeAssignStatement(cLeft, cRight));

  cLeft=new CodeFieldReferenceExpression(null, "WinRegKey");
  cRight=new CodeFieldReferenceExpression(null,
➥"WinRegKey.Replace(HiveSubs[0]+@\"\\",
➥\"\").Replace(@\"\\"+HiveSubs[HiveSubs.Length-1], \"\")");
  cm.Statements.Add(new CodeAssignStatement(cLeft, cRight));


  pCode = new CodeExpression[]{new
➥CodeFieldReferenceExpression(null, "HiveSubs[0], ref key")};
  cm.Statements.Add(new
➥CodeMethodInvokeExpression(null, "AccessRegKey", pCode));

  cLeft=new CodeFieldReferenceExpression(null, "key");
  cRight=new CodeFieldReferenceExpression(null, "key.OpenSubKey(WinRegKey)");
  cm.Statements.Add(new CodeAssignStatement(cLeft, cRight));


  cLeft=new CodeFieldReferenceExpression(null, "WinRegVal");
  cRight=new CodeFieldReferenceExpression(null,
➥"key.GetValue(HiveSubs[HiveSubs.Length-1])");
  cm.Statements.Add(new CodeAssignStatement(cLeft, cRight));


  pCode = new CodeExpression[]{new CodeFieldReferenceExpression(null, null)};
  cm.Statements.Add(new CodeMethodInvokeExpression(null, "key.Close", pCode));


  cm.Statements.Add(new CodeMethodReturnStatement(new
➥CodeSnippetExpression("WinRegVal")));
  co.Members.Add(cm);
}
```

Similarly, this method first defines the name, the return type, the attribute, and the parameters for the `GetWinRegValue()` method (Listing 11.3). Then it uses a `cLeft` and a `cRight` object and a few other CodeDom methods to write the code in Listing 11.3. Because there is a detailed discussion in Chapter 6 of the CodeDom namespace, it should be easy for you to understand the code in Listing 11.6 by comparing its CodeDom statements with the code in Listing 11.3.

Locate the `AddUpClassesMethods()` method in the `TestForm.cs` file. Add an `if` statement to determine whether the Windows Registry is in need of testing. If the determination is true, the actions are taken inside the `if` statement. Listing 11.7 shows the newly added code in bold and some other code omitted.

Listing 11.7 Adding New Statements into the *AddUpClassesMethods()* Method

```
...
private void AddUpClassesMethods()
{
      co.Members.Add(cm);

      CreateTestPassMethod(cm, "TestPass");
      CreateTestFailMethod(cm, "TestFail");

      if (NeedWinReg)
      {
        cnamespace.Imports.Add(new CodeNamespaceImport("Microsoft.Win32"));
        CreateAccessRegKeyMethod(cm, "AccessRegKey");
        CreateGetWinRegValueMethod(cm, "GetWinRegValue");
        NeedWinReg = false;
      }

      //add a file name field
      AddFilenameField(co);
      //add a constructor
      ...
      ...
    }
...
```

The added `if` statement checks whether the tester defines a testing case in the Excel data store to test against the Windows Registry. If the value of `NeedWinReg` is `true`, it first adds a statement:

```
using Microsoft.Win32;
```

Then it calls the `CreateAccessRegKeyMethod()` and `CreateGetWinRegValueMethod()` methods to write an `AccessRegKey()` method and a `GetWinRegValue()` method, respectively. Finally, it resets the `NeedWinReg` flag to `false`.

Locate the `CollectParametersForTest()` method inside the `TestForm.cs` file and navigate to the first `if` statement. Add the bold lines of the code in Listing 11.8 before the old `if` statement and change this `if` statement to an `else-if` statement.

Listing 11.8 New Lines of Code Added into the *CollectParametersForTest()* Method

```
...
private void CollectParametersForTest(ref int i, ref int j,
➥ref Excel.Range rng, ref ParameterInfo[] ps, ref string parStr)
{
  foreach (ParameterInfo p in ps)
  {
        ...
        ...

    if (rng.Value2.ToString().ToUpper().StartsWith("WINREG"))
    {
      NeedWinReg = true;
      if (p.ParameterType==typeof(string) ||
➥p.ParameterType.ToString()=="System.String&")
      {
        cRight=new CodeFieldReferenceExpression(null,
➥"(string)GetWinRegValue(range.Value2.ToString())");
      }
      else if (p.ParameterType==typeof(bool) ||
➥p.ParameterType.ToString()=="System.Boolean&")
      {
        cRight=new CodeFieldReferenceExpression(null,
➥"(bool)GetWinRegValue(range.Value2.ToString())");
      }
      else if (p.ParameterType==typeof(object) ||
➥p.ParameterType.ToString()=="System.Object&")
      {
        cRight=new CodeFieldReferenceExpression(null,
➥"GetWinRegValue(range.Value2.ToString())");
      }
      else
      {
        cRight=new CodeFieldReferenceExpression(null,
➥"(int)GetWinRegValue(range.Value2.ToString())");
      }
    }
    else if (p.ParameterType.ToString().StartsWith("System.String") ||
➥p.ParameterType.ToString().StartsWith("System.Object"))
    {
      cRight=new CodeFieldReferenceExpression(null, "range.Value2.ToString()");
    }
    ...
    ...
  }
}

...
```

The outermost `if` statement checks a reading from the Excel data store. The text *WinReg* is the identifier for requesting the AutomatedTest tool to test against the Windows Registry. When this identifier is found by the AutomatedTest tool, it writes a single line of code similar to the following to retrieve the value of the specified variable:

```
string newVal_x = (string)GetWinRegValue(range.Value2.ToString());
```

By checking this code segment carefully, you find out that the `if` statement only writes the right side of this statement based on various cases of the parameters. For example, if the parameter type is an integer, the right side of the statement should become this:

```
(int)GetWinRegValue(range.Value2.ToString()).
```

The purpose of this statement is to explicitly convert the object value returned from the calling of `GetWinRegValue(range.Value2.ToString()` into an integer by unboxing.

After you finish the coding, build the AutomatedTest project and run it.

Testing the AddAutoTestPath Project against the Windows Registry

In the beginning of this chapter, you defined a project to add an environment variable to the Windows Registry. In this section, you'll test this variable in the Windows Registry using the updated AutomatedTest tool. First perform the following steps:

1. Run the `AutomatedTest.exe`. The user interface of the `AutomatedTest.exe` appears. The default project target folder and result target folder were defined in the previous chapter. You can alter the value at your convenience. The purpose of these two folders is to hold the generated test script projects and the result reports.

NOTE In the previous chapter, we also enabled the AutomatedTest tool to look for the .NET IDE location based on the setting of the environment variables of a computer system. You don't need to modify the text for this field.

2. Leave the Manual Stub check box unchecked. In Chapter 8, you enabled the test tool to cope with testing parameters passed by objects. Leaving this check box unchecked will enable the default functions of the test tool to test parameters passed by objects. Otherwise, there will be some interactions needed from a human tester.
3. Click the Start button. An open file dialog box appears. This dialog box has a file filter for the `*.dll` and `*.exe` files; that is, the AutomatedTest tool is capable of testing DLL and EXE assemblies.

4. From the open file dialog box, navigate to `C:\SourceCode\Chapter11\AddAutoTestPath\Bin\Debug`, select `*.exe` from the Files of type, and select the `AddAutoTestPath.exe` from the file list.
5. Click the Open button. The available types of the assembly are listed in a pop-up form (Figure 11.7). A check box at the bottom left allows you to make a decision and to test all of the available class types of the assembly. For this demonstration, check the check box beside the `SetEnvironmentVar` type.
6. Click the OK button. An MS Excel worksheet opens (Figure 11.8).
7. Switch to the MS Excel worksheet. Insert an empty row after row 6 (Figure 11.9).

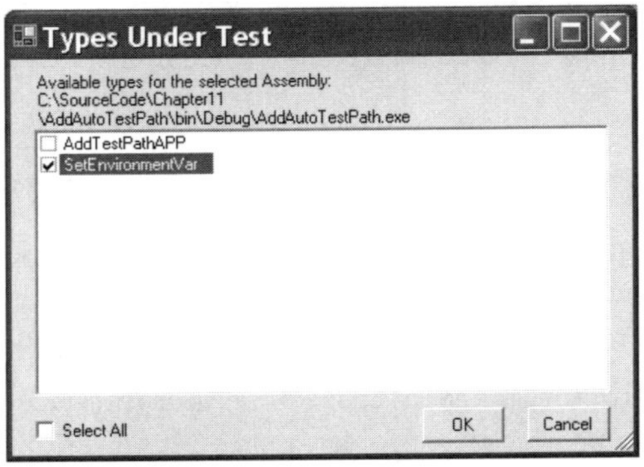

FIGURE 11.7 Available types of the AddAutoTestPath.exe assembly

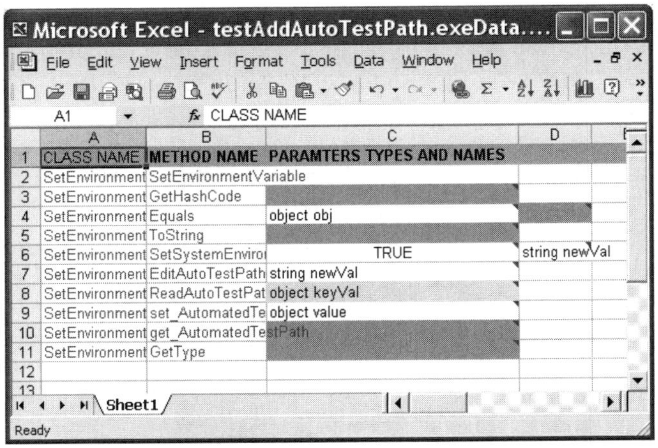

FIGURE 11.8 The methods from the SetEnvironmentVar class in need of testing

FIGURE 11.9
Inserting an empty row for adding more methods to test

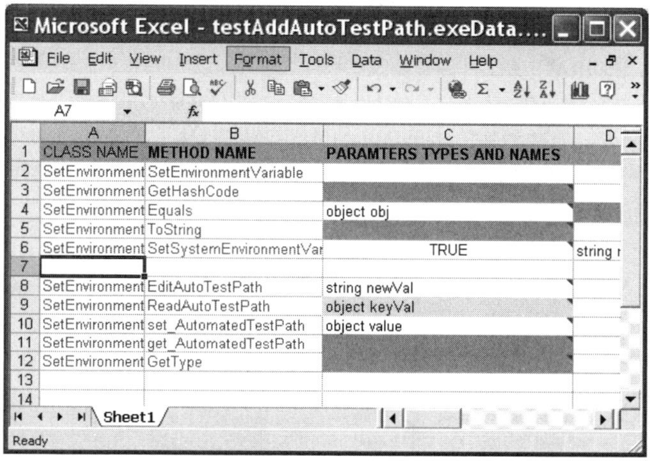

8. Copy the entire contents of row 9 (with the `ReadAutoTestPath()` method) to row 7.
9. Click cell D6 in the worksheet and enter the following value:

   `C:\SourceCode\Chapter11\AddAutoTestPath\Bin\Debug`

10. Choose Start ➢ Run and type **RegEdit** in the Open text box. Click the OK button and the Windows Registry Editor opens (see Figure 11.2). You are going to use this method as an easy way to copy and paste the complex hive, subhives, and keys to the MS Excel worksheet instead of having to type them in.
11. Navigate to HKEY_LOCAL_MACHINE\SYSTEM\ControlSet001\Control\Session Manager\Environment. Let the mouse pointer hover over the Environment key and right-click the Environment key.
12. Choose Copy Key Name from the pop-up menu.
13. Switch back to the MS Excel worksheet. Click cell C7, where the `ReadAutoTestPath()` method asks for a parameter.
14. Press Ctrl+V to paste the key name to this location. Modify the value to include the `WingReg:` identifier. The new value is as follows:

```
WinReg:HKEY_LOCAL_MACHINE\SYSTEM\ControlSet001\Control\
➥Session Manager\Environment\AutomatedTestPath
```

NOTE The bold characters need to be typed. `WinReg` is needed to instruct the AutomatedTest tool to look for a variable in the Windows Registry.

15. Copy the value in cell C7 to cell C9 of the worksheet.
16. Click cell C8, where the `EditAutoPath()` method asks for a parameter. Press Ctrl+V to paste the key name to this cell. But this time, modify the text value to look like this:

```
WinReg:HKEY_LOCAL_MACHINE\SYSTEM\ControlSet001\Control\
➥Session Manager\Environment\TEMP
```

Now the MS Excel worksheet looks similar to Figure 11.10.

FIGURE 11.10
The MS Excel worksheet after the editing. The bold WinReg: is for emphasis. Users don't have to do this.

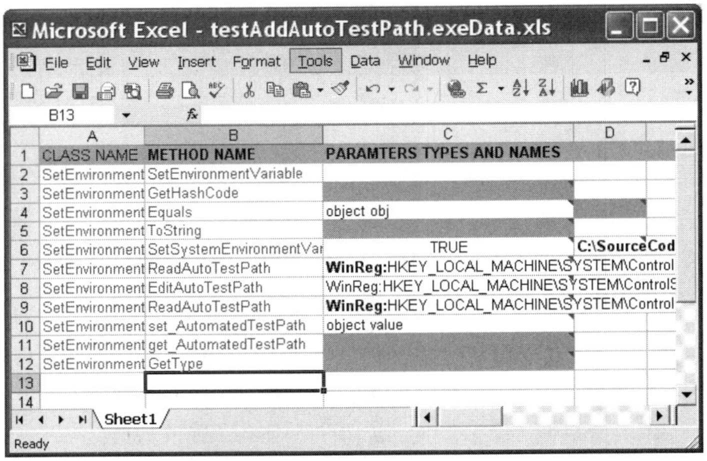

17. Save the MS Excel worksheet.
18. Switch to the Automated Software Test window and click the Create Script button. A new window of the Microsoft Visual Studio .NET IDE opens with the newly written test script.
19. Press F5. Upon the prompt to save a TestAddAutoTestPath.sln file, click the Save button. The test project completes testing the AddAutoTestPath assembly within a wink.
20. Open Windows Explorer and navigate to the `C:\Temp` folder.
21. Look for the file with a name similar to `TestAddAutoTestPath213200301330.xls`. The numeric part of the filename reflects the time and date the test is performed
22. Double-click this filename to open the file into a new MS Excel worksheet. You will see the results similar to Figure 11.11.

NOTE MS Excel often leaves some object residue in the system when an Excel application has been executed programmatically. If this happens, the test result will not be visible in the MS Excel application. You can make it visible by pressing Ctrl+Alt+Del to bring the Task Manager onto the screen. Click the Processes tab. Select all the Excel residue objects and click the End Process button to clear them. Then return to Windows Explorer and double click the result report. The report is now visible.

FIGURE 11.11
Test results for the AddAutoTestPath assembly

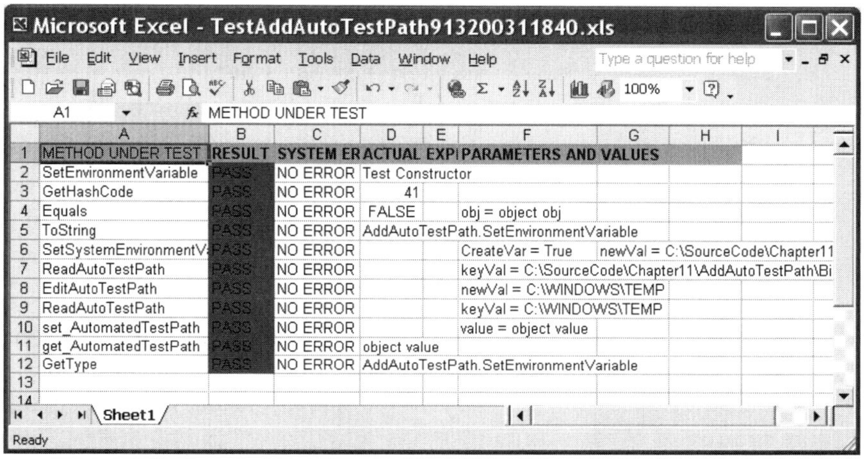

The MS Excel worksheet presents the test results of the `AddAutoPath` assembly. It tested nine methods in total; four methods are inherited from the .NET system base classes, and three methods in rows 6 through 9 are implemented for the assembly under test. The `ReadAutoTestPath()` method was tested two times. The `SetSystemEnvrionmentVariable()` method creates a new environment variable and sets a value for the variable in the Windows system (row 6). The `ReadAutoTestPath()` retrieves the value of the `AutomatedTestPath` variable (cell F7) from the Windows Registry. The `EditAutoTestPath()` method modifies the value of the `AutomatedTestPath` variable to `C:\Windows\Temp`, which was retrieved from HKEY_LOCAL_MACHINE\SYSTEM\ControlSet001\Control\Session Manager\Environment\TEMP in the Windows Registry (cell F8). To verify the modification, the method `ReadAutoTestPath()` was tested the second time in row 9. It simply retrieves the newly modified value of the `AutomatedTestPath` in cell F9, which was the value just as you expected it to be. This is a successful test. Rows 10 and 11 treat the `AutomatedTestPath` property as two methods, `set_AutomatedTestPath()` and `get_AutomatedTestPath()`. The former assigns the property value. The latter reads the value.

The updated AutomatedTest tool can now test a software product that has the capability of modifying values in the Windows system Registry.

At this point, the auto value assignment is not enabled for testing the Windows Registry. Many of the preceding steps are for data editing for the Registry values. The Excel data store provides great flexibilities for users to manipulate testing cases with ease. The script generation and the test deployment and execution are fully automated.

Summary

Testing against the Windows Registry is important because it contains the information about whether software under test is correctly installed, whether the component is registered, whether the environment variables are updated as expected, and so on.

You can access the Windows Registry via the MS `RegEdit.exe` tool, the environment variable properties of the computer system, the Command Prompt console, and C# programming using the `Microsoft.Win32.RegistryKey` class. By using the .NET CodeDom methods, you enabled the AutomatedTest project to write code to access Registry hives, open subhives and keys, and retrieve values of variables to test with.

More important, by adding the capability of testing software against the Windows Registry, this chapter demonstrates the flexibility of the AutomatedTest tool. As your software product becomes more complex, you can continue to enhance it to meet your other testing needs in the future.

The next chapter will conclude the book by testing the functions of the AutomatedTest project so that you can experience its advantages. However, as you have seen in this chapter, the software test automation is not limited by what you have done. Engineers and project managers have many good ideas. I encourage you to add your ideas to this tool and make it more capable for your organization and for the future projects of software development.

CHAPTER 12

Testing the AutomatedTest Tool

In the previous chapters, you applied the .NET fundamentals for the development of the AutomatedTest project. You used the `System.Reflection` namespace to provide testing information during the tool development process and the `System.CodeDom` namespace to write the test scripts. You used the `Type` class with these namespaces to complete the project throughout the book. You also used XML programming and the MS Excel API programming for testing data stores and testing result presentations.

You completed the Automated Test project in Chapter 10 and updated the tool with more capabilities in Chapter 11. The AutomatedTest tool has demonstrated some testing capabilities that many of the commercial tools don't have. This chapter will provide more explanation of features implemented in other chapters but not demonstrated with examples. The strategy is to feed the previously built assemblies to this tool. Thus, the AutomatedTest tool will test different areas of these assemblies automatically. Conversely, the assemblies under test will test the AutomatedTest project manually.

So that the explanation is straightforward, the assemblies under test contain healthy code. This chapter will also serve as a brief review and a user's guide for the AutomatedTest tool.

Starting the Automated Test Tool

The ultimate goal of this book is to introduce some new testing tactics to address the inadequacies of the current test infrastructures. After following along in the previous chapters and completing the project, you should now have an `AutomatedTest.exe` executable file. Otherwise, the source code can be downloaded from the `www.sybex.com`. To develop and run the program, your system needs to meet the following requirements:

- Windows NT/2000/XP
- Microsoft Visual Studio .NET Framework
- Microsoft Visual Studio .NET IDE 2003
- Microsoft Excel 2000/XP

After you prepare the source code for the AutomatedTest project, you can build the project with a debug configuration or a release configuration. After you build the project, there will be at a minimum the following files in the respective `..Bin\Debug` or `..Bin\Release` folder:

`AutomatedTest.exe` The executable file created from building the project. It is the dynamic representation of the AutomatedTest code.

`AutomatedTest.pdb` A program database (PDB) file built together with the `Automated-Test.exe` when the build configuration of the Microsoft Visual Studio .NET IDE is set for Debug (the alternative is Release). This file was generated as the static representation of the

AutomatedTest tool. It provides meaningful information about the classes, variables, and methods of the assembly during the debugging process.

`Interop.Excel.dll` A file converted from an `Excel.dll` COM to a .NET managed assembly after a reference is added to the project. The DOS command to execute the `tlbimp.exe` can accomplish this task as well. In case you need to test a COM component developed by the earlier development platforms (MS ATL, VB 6.0, etc.), you can convert this COM component into a managed library and submit the managed library to this tool.

`Interop.VBIDE.dll` The VBIDE is also a COM component. The creation of this file is similar to the creation of the `Interop.Excel.dll` file.

`OATestProj.csproj` A seed file to produce a C# project for the assembly under test. It contains information about the project configuration, sources of the references, and locations of the source code files. This file helps in building the test script project.

`testApp.ico` A seed file of the icon to reproduce icons for the test projects.

`TestAssemblyInfo.cs` This file is always identical for all the test projects in this book. In order to avoid system conflicts, an advanced test tool should make necessary modifications in this file because it contains some GUID information.

You can make a shortcut of the `AutomatedTest.exe` on your desktop in order to access the project quickly. After you run it, the AutomatedTest form will appear as shown in Figure 12.1, which illustrates that some parameters are assigned to the GUI components by default. The following sections explain these GUI components and their significance for the testing.

NOTE Although some of the figures in this chapter also appear in the other chapters, they are shown here for your convenience.

FIGURE 12.1
A snapshot of the Automated Software Test tool

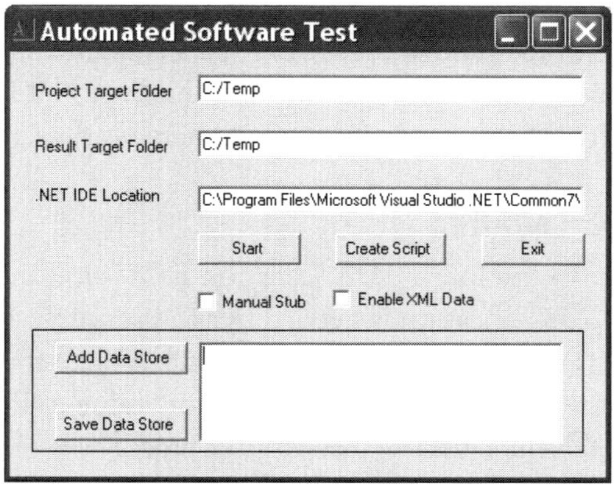

Project Target Folder

When you start a test, you need to think about where to save the test script project. The value for the Project Target Folder field is where the test directory dwells. The default setting is `C:\Temp`. For example, if you test the `HighLevelObj.dll` assembly developed in Chapter 8, the corresponding folders are going to be created under `C:\Temp` after the Start button is clicked. The following are the newly created directories:

- `C:\Temp\HighLevelObj`
- `C:\Temp\HighLevelObj\Bin\Debug`

All of the test script project files generated by the tool are saved into the `C:\Temp\HighLevelObj` folder, including the following files:

- `App.ico`
- `AssemblyInfo.cs`
- `TestHighLevelObj.cs`
- `TestHighLevelObj.csproj`

Then, a `testHighLevelObjData.xls` file and a `fileArray.txt` file are saved into the `C:\Temp\HighLevelObj\Bin\Debug` folder. The `testHighLevelObjData.xls` file is the MS Excel data store. The `fileArray.txt` file stores multiple filenames of the Excel data stores. The default `fileArray.txt` stores only the `testHighLevelObjData.xls` file, which instructs the test script to run once using testing cases in this file.

Result Target Folder

The result target folder is used to store the test result report, and the default is `C:\Temp`. In the case of testing the `HighLevelObj.dll`, a file named similar to `TestHighLevelObj9132003112752.xls` is saved directly under the `C:\Temp` folder after the test script is run. The filename is made up of three parts. The first part, `Test`, is given by the AutomatedTest tool. The `HighLevelObj` part is the name of the assembly tested. Finally, the number `9132003112752` indicates the date and time, 9/13/2003 11:27:52, when the test was conducted. This format of the report name is designed to help regression testing.

.NET IDE Location

The value of the .NET IDE Location field is located by the AutomatedTest tool itself, and usually no modification is needed by the user, unless you are sure the automatic detection is wrong or the detection returns no results. When the AutomatedTest tool finishes the generation of the test script project, it uses this value to find and start the Microsoft Visual Studio .NET IDE and loads the test script project.

The automatic mechanism to detect this path was implemented for the `TestForm_Load()` event in Chapter 10. Another way to edit this value is to set the path where `Devenv.exe` dwells to the path environment variable. Then type in **`devenv.exe`** for this field. Chapter 11 introduced how to set up an environment variable.

After these three values are set, the other controls are used to specifically test an assembly.

Testing the *LowLevelObj.dll* Assembly

Throughout the book, you have developed a `LowLevelObj.dll`, a `HighLevelObj.dll`, and an `AddAutoTestPath.dll` for the purpose of being tested by and testing the AutomatedTest tool. In this section, you will do a thorough test on this assembly in different areas with regard to software quality. The previous testing cases will not be repeated. For demonstration purposes, you don't have to change the Project Target Folder and the Result Target Folder fields. But you need to make sure a `C:\Temp` folder exists on your system.

Assuming the AutomatedTest tool has been started, perform the following steps:

1. From the Automated Software Test form (Figure 12.1), click the Start button. The open file dialog box appears.
2. Navigate to the `C:\SourceCode\Chapter04\LowLevelObj\Bin\Debug` folder. Select the `LowLevelObj.dll` assembly file.
3. Click the Open button. The names of the available type classes appear in the Types Under Test form, shown in Figure 12.2.
4. Check the check box beside the `SimpleMath` class. Click the OK button. An MS Excel worksheet opens. The AutomatedTest tool starts to collect information from the `SimpleMath` class. After it completes the collection, the MS Excel worksheet looks like the worksheet in Figure 12.3.

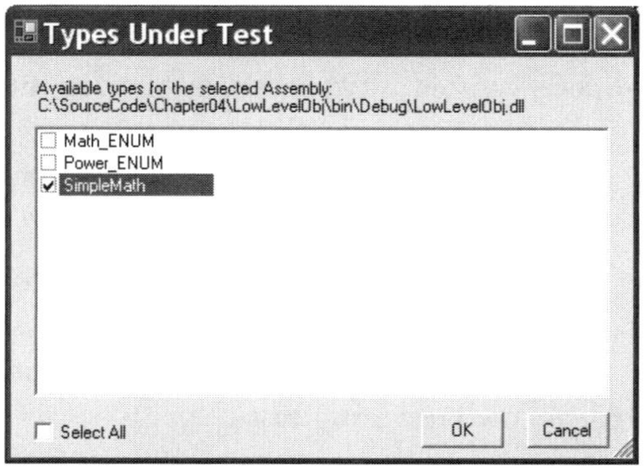

FIGURE 12.2 Available type classes of the LowLevelObj assembly found by the Automated Test tool

FIGURE 12.3
Information collected from the SimpleMath class testing the Low-LevelObj.dll assembly

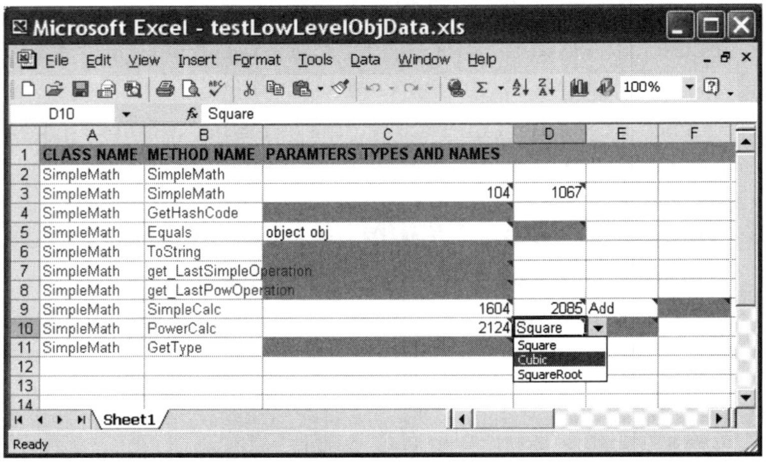

This Excel worksheet contains many pieces of information that is needed to write and run the test script. Test engineers can access this information at any time. The following section explains how to use this information.

Editing theData Store

Let's examine the Excel worksheet (see Figure 12.3). The first column lists the class names. Because you selected to test only one type class, `SimpleMath`, there is only one class name in the first column for all the rows.

The second column of the MS Excel worksheet lists the names of the constructor(s), properties, and methods extracted from the `SimpleMath` class. From here you can decide which methods and how many occurrences of the methods you want to test by copying, pasting, or deleting. The constructor of the class is always listed at the beginning. You have to test at least one constructor if it is overloaded more than one time.

Each property is listed as two methods, the `set_` method and the `get_` method. For example, the `LastSimpleOperation` and the `LastPowOperation` properties are read-only properties, and the methods listed for these properties are `get_LastSimpleOperation()` and `get_LastPowOperation()`.

Starting with the third column and thereafter, it lists the parameters, if the methods take any. When a nonnumeric parameter is listed, the value is set as the parameter type followed by the parameter name. The presentation is consistent with C# code syntax. This is where you can modify, add, and delete testing cases.

When the parameter has a numeric type, a random number is assigned as its value by the AutomatedTest tool. However, if this value is not desirable, you can modify it at any time.

The MS Excel worksheet has a validation property that can be used to list possible values. This property is shown in Figure 12.3. The `PowerCalc()` method in the `SimpleMath` class requires an enumeration parameter, which is `Power_ENUM`. The `Power_ENUM` type has three possible values: `Square`, `Cubic` and `SquareRoot`. In order to activate this property, you simply click the worksheet cell. In this case, it is D10. A gray arrow appears to the right of this cell. Click the arrow and a list of the possible values of the enumeration type appears. You can choose a desired math operator from this list. The tool has assigned a value `Square` to this parameter by default. Thus, you can see that when the parameter type is an enumeration type, the MS Excel worksheet creates a drop-down list of all the values to choose from. Using this feature, the testers will not enter invalid values by mistake. When there is a long list of the possible values for an enumeration type, this feature is tremendously useful in editing the data stores. However, if the tester wants to test this method against an invalid value, they can enter anything into this worksheet cell.

Notice the red triangle at the upper-right corner of each parameter cell. Move the mouse pointer over a parameter cell. A small form pops up showing the parameter type and the parameter name. This is the Comment property of the MS Excel worksheet. This feature helps you enter correct parameter types in case you need modify the data sheet again in the future (see Figure 12.4).

When a parameter is passed by a value, you can change the value for your testing purpose if the default assigned value doesn't serve the purpose. If it is a numeric data type, do not enter letters in the cell. Otherwise, the test tool will generate an error message. However, you may want to do this on purpose to test how the product's error handlers deal with invalid entries. If it is a string, you can decide whether to leave it as it is or give it an appropriate text value.

When a parameter is an object of another class, you must type a value `new` in the cell. The AutomatedTest tool will use this value to initialize an object for the test script automatically or manually. The user decides whether this process is automatic or manual.

FIGURE 12.4
The comment form for the operation parameter

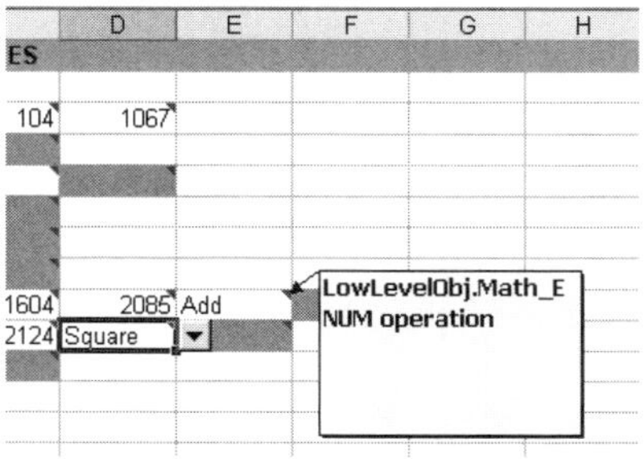

For a Boolean type parameter, the value of this parameter is set to be `true` when it is passed by value. It is set to be `false` when it is passed by reference or it is an `out` parameter.

Some visual effects are implemented for quick examinations. For example, a parameter passed by value is in a cell with a white background. When a method takes a parameter passed by reference, the background turns yellow, and an `out` parameter is magenta. When a method returns a value (i.e., not a void return method), the last cell appears as shown Figure 12.5, with a greenish background.

FIGURE 12.5
The comment form for the expected return value cell

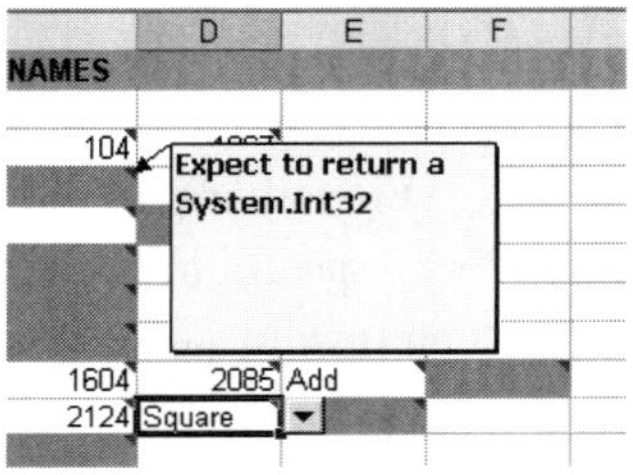

The comment reminds the test engineer that this is a cell for entering an expected return value. The cell is empty by default with a comment containing the return type. For example, the text "Expect to return a System.Int32" is prompting you to enter an integer for this cell. If an expected return is entered, the AutomatedTest tool will compare its actual return with the specified expected return. If they are different, the test fails.

If you want to test a method more than once with different parameter values, or test cases, you can copy the row in which the method appears, paste it into as many rows as desired, and enter different values for the parameters. You may delete an entire row if you are not interested in testing a certain method. It is important to remember not to leave any empty rows between the methods for the test. The AutomatedTest tool will stop at the first empty row it comes across.

The other way to test a method more than once is to save more copies of the Excel worksheet with other filenames. Then, in each worksheet, you can assign different values to the parameters, but the rows of the methods must be identical. This will be discussed further in the section "Testing with Multiple Sets of Data Stores" later in this chapter.

Remember to save the modified data sheet but don't exit it because the Create Script button needs to use it and will close the sheet without saving the changes.

Based on the preceding explanation, Figure 12.6 shows the Excel worksheet after the modification.

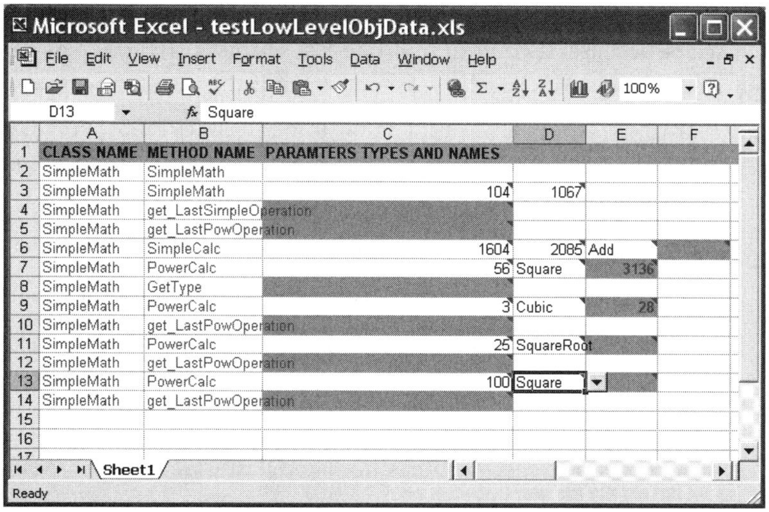

FIGURE 12.6 The data sheet after assigning values to some parameters and adding and removing some methods to test

Note that three of the methods—`Equals()`, `GetHashCode()`, and `ToString()`, which are inherited from the .NET base classes—have been removed. The `PowerCalc()` method and the `get_LastPowOperation()` method are copied and pasted four times in total. For the first `PowerCalc()` method in row number 7, you expect $56^2 = 3136$. Based on the testing results of the previous chapters, the code of the LowLevelObj class handles the `PowerCalc()` method correctly. In order to demonstrate how the generated test script reports a testing failure, Figure 12.6 deliberately assigns a wrong expected return value in row 9 that expects the result of $3^3 = 28$ for testing the invocation of the `PowerCalc(3, cubic)` method. But, you don't have to assign expected return values for testing a method if you don't wish to. There are other methods—for example, `get_LastPowOperation()`, `get_LastSimpleOperation()`, and `GetType()`—that are expected to return results. But this data store did not assign the values you would expect for these methods.

Reviewing Test Results

After you save the changes to the Excel worksheet, switch to the Automated Software Test form. Make sure the Manual Stub check box is unchecked. Then click the Create Script button. The test script is generated, and the Microsoft Visual Studio .NET IDE starts with the generated test script project, `TestLowLevelObj.csproj`.

Press F5 in the Microsoft Visual Studio .NET IDE to build and run the test script. If the IDE prompts you to save a `TestLowLevelObj.sln` file, you always click the Save button to save it. A console screen appears, and then an Excel worksheet appears. The test results are filling the

Excel worksheet. For this test, the process is fast. When it is finished, the Excel worksheet and the console screen are closed. The MS Excel worksheet is closed after the completion of a test script because, if you run multiple test scripts within one test harness in the future, there will be too many MS Excel worksheets open if the result reports are not closed.

At this point, you will find a new folder, `LowLevelObj`, created by the AutomatedTest tool under the project target folder, `C:\Temp`. The new folder, `C:\Temp\LowLevelObj`, includes the following files:

`App.ico` Created by the AutomatedTest tool.

`AssemblyInfo.cs` Created by the AutomatedTest tool.

`TestLowLevelObj.cs` The test script in C# code, created by the AutomatedTest tool. In previous chapters, this file was saved as `C:\Temp\TestScript.exe`.

`TestLowLevelObj.csproj` Contains information of reference, compiling configurations and others; created by the AutomatedTest tool.

`TestLowLevelObj.csproj.user` Created after pressing F5 (Build and Run) in Microsoft Visual Studio .NET IDE.

`TestLowLevelObj.sln` Also created after pressing F5 (Build and Run) in Microsoft Visual Studio .NET IDE. When you build the test project the first time, Microsoft Visual Studio .NET IDE will ask you to save this file. Click the OK button to save it.

The test folder also includes two subfolders:

`Bin` Used to hold the executable files copied from the `Obj` folder.

`Obj` Used to hold the files created when the program is compiled.

Under the subfolder `Bin`, another subfolder, `Debug`, has been created and includes the following files:

`fileArray.txt` Holds the filenames for multiple test data stores. The test script looks in this file for the filename(s) of the Excel data stores.

`Interop.Excel.dll` Converted from the `Excel.dll` COM based on information contained in `TestLowLevelObj.csproj`.

`Interop.Microsoft.Office.Core.dll` Converted from the `Microsoft.Office.Core.dll` COM based on information contained in `TestLowLevelObj.csproj`.

`Interop.VBIDE.dll` Converted from the `VBIDE.dll` COM based on information contained in `TestLowLevelObj.csproj`.

`LowLevelObj.dll` Copied from `C:\SourceCode\Chapter04\LowLevelObj\bin\Debug`.

`LowLevelObj.pdb` Also copied from `C:\SourceCode\Chapter04\LowLevelObj\bin\Debug`.

`TestLowLevelObj.exe` Generated by the Microsoft Visual Studio .NET IDE when you press F5. You may remember that you used `csc.exe` to compile the test script and generate this file before Chapter 10.

`TestLowLevelObj.pdb` Generated at the same time the `TestLowLevelObj.exe` file is generated because the build configuration of the test project is set to Debug. This file contains the debugging information.

`testLowLevelObjData.xls` Contains data of the testing cases. You can make copies of this file and modify the values in the future.

Because the main purpose of the tool is for software testing, the debug configuration for the test script is appropriate; the release configuration will not be used. You can execute the `TestLowLevelObj.exe` at any time in the future to rerun this test.

At this point, test results have been saved in the designated result target folder, `C:\Temp` in this case. You can view the results by navigating to this folder. The name of the file is similar to `TestLowLevelObj913200315433.xls`. As we have discussed, the numbers in the name indicate the date and time the test was run, in this case 9/13/2003 15:4:33. This name format is designed for the later regression testing. Open the test result with MS Excel. It looks similar to Figure 12.7.

FIGURE 12.7 The test report in the Excel worksheet

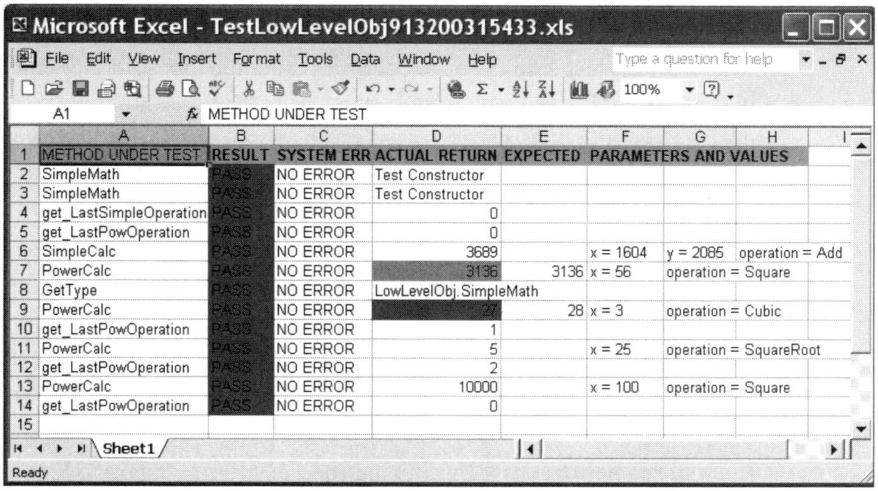

	A	B	C	D	E	F	G	H
1	METHOD UNDER TEST	RESULT	SYSTEM ERR	ACTUAL RETURN	EXPECTED	PARAMETERS AND VALUES		
2	SimpleMath	PASS	NO ERROR	Test Constructor				
3	SimpleMath	PASS	NO ERROR	Test Constructor				
4	get_LastSimpleOperation	PASS	NO ERROR	0				
5	get_LastPowOperation	PASS	NO ERROR	0				
6	SimpleCalc	PASS	NO ERROR	3689		x = 1604	y = 2085	operation = Add
7	PowerCalc	PASS	NO ERROR	3136	3136	x = 56	operation = Square	
8	GetType	PASS	NO ERROR	LowLevelObj.SimpleMath				
9	PowerCalc	PASS	NO ERROR	27	28	x = 3	operation = Cubic	
10	get_LastPowOperation	PASS	NO ERROR	1				
11	PowerCalc	PASS	NO ERROR	5		x = 25	operation = SquareRoot	
12	get_LastPowOperation	PASS	NO ERROR	2				
13	PowerCalc	PASS	NO ERROR	10000		x = 100	operation = Square	
14	get_LastPowOperation	PASS	NO ERROR	0				
15								

In the report, the first column lists the names of the methods tested. The second column lists the test results for verification purpose, with the value Pass or Fail. The third column reports an error message to tell the cause of the failure, if the second column reports a Fail. The fourth column lists the actual return value if the method returns a value. The fifth column is the expected return value the test engineer specified.

In the result report shown in Figure 12.7, the second column indicates that all the methods under test passed. There are no system errors. However, in column 4 (D), a cell with a red background indicates a test failure. When the data store was edited in the previous section, an expected return value in row 9 of $3^3 = 28$ was specified, and it doesn't match the actual return value, $3^3 = 27$. A tester has the right to ask for $3^3 = 28$. The AutomatedTest tool supports the tester's judgment. When the actual result was $3^3 = 27$, the AutomatedTest tool indicated that the test fails the `PowerCalc(3, Cubic)` invocation.

In another testing case, an expected return value was specified for method `PowerCalc(56, Square)` in row 7 for $56^2 = 3136$, which matches the actual return value. A green background in that cell indicates they match.

Columns holding values after column E are current values of the respective parameters after the calling of the method, which are used to test reference and `out` parameters.

At this point, the test is done. You have the test script project with its executable files. You can rerun this test with different testing cases in the future at any time and on other systems. You may want to change the value in row 9 from 28 to 27.

Testing Parameters Passed by Objects

In the previous test cases, the `LowLevelObj` assembly does not depend on any other lower-level modules. You left the Manual Stub check box unchecked before you clicked the Create Script button. This time, you are going to test the `HighLevelObj.dll` assembly, which has a dependency on the `LowLevelObj.dll` assembly. One example was given in Chapter 8 using a real object from the previously built test script to test a higher-level module.

When testing the `HighLevelObj.dll`, if the `LowLevelObj.dll` test script is not available, you have to pursue other alternatives. If you assign a value `new` to the object in the data store and leave the Manual Stub check box unchecked, the AutomatedTest tool can create a new dummy object by using the default constructor. This is OK to test a simple class. When the object initialization requires alteration of the properties or invocation of the methods, the AutomatedTest tool allows you to write a manual stub for it.

Let's start a new test case by clicking the Start button again to locate the assembly under test.

The `HighLevelObj.dll` assembly is located in `C:\SourceCode\Chapter08\HighLevelObj\bin\Debug\HighLevelObj.dll`. Specify this assembly and choose the `AdvancedCalc` class for testing. After collecting the test information in the MS Excel worksheet, you can edit it as you desire. But remember the following:

- At least one constructor is preceding all the members to be tested.
- You have assigned a value `new` in row 14 and column C to the `lvlMath` parameter of the `SimpleCalc()` method.
- Save the worksheet as you did before.
- Make sure the Manual Stub check box is checked. In this case, the Automated Software Test form should look like Figure 12.8.

FIGURE 12.8 The Automated Software Test form with the Manual Stub check box checked

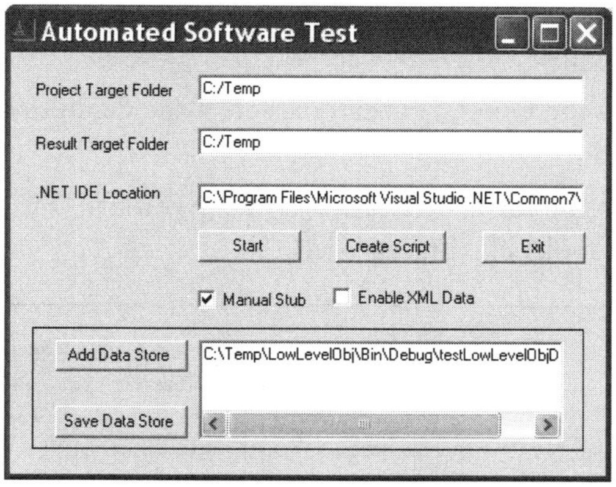

Complete this test by following these steps:

1. Click the Create Script button. When the AutomatedTest tool proceeds to row 14 for the value of the `lvlMath` parameter, an open file dialog box appears. It asks you where the assembly is located for the creation of a `SimpleMath` object.
2. In this case, the `SimpleMath` is a class of the `LowLevelObj` assembly residing in the `C:\SourceCode\Chapter04\LowLevelObj\bin\Debug` folder. Navigate to this folder and click the mouse button to select the `LowLevelObj.dll file`.
3. Click the Open button. The stub form opens (Figure 12.9). This form has all the possible members and their parameters of the class in the left.
4. Select the desired code to insert into the test script by clicking the > buttons. The selected code appears in the right text boxes.

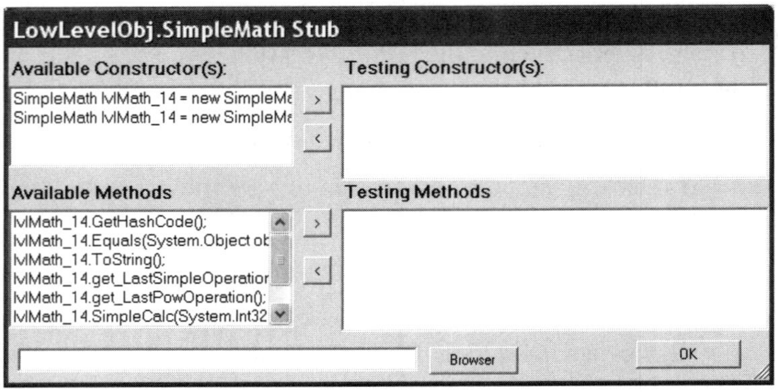

FIGURE 12.9
The initial form of the LowLevelObj.SimpleMath stub with constructors and methods on the left

The text boxes on the right of this form provide test engineers with a space to write C# code segments.

5. From the upper-left textbox, select the default constructor declaration and click the > button.
6. From the lower-left textbox, select `lvlMath_14.ToString()` and click the > button. The form looks like Figure 12.10.

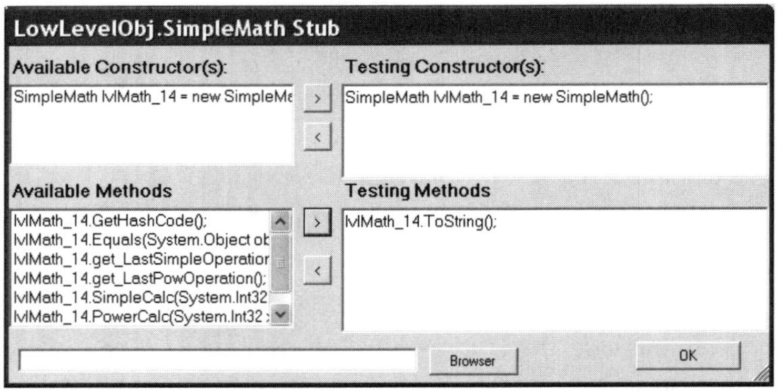

FIGURE 12.10
The LowLevelObj.SimpleMath stub form after editing

7. Click the OK button. Your test script auto-generation resumes. The Microsoft Visual Studio .NET IDE starts with the test script loaded.

With the Microsoft Visual Studio .NET IDE opened, you are ready to press F5 (Build and Run) and collect the test results. You can navigate to the designated folder and view the results as you have done in the previous test cases. If you have used the traditional stubbing method or the Mock Objects method of the Cactus integration testing for Java programming, you should find that this method resembles them except this one is easier. However, when comparing with the testing example in Chapter 8, you can see the disadvantage of this method:

- Efforts to design and implement the stubbing are required. It is hard to write the accurate code in the first place. Modifications and debugging may be required after the test script generation.
- Test engineers find it difficult to make the stub represent types in a complex external library.
- The most difficult task of this method is usually the assignment of appropriate values to the parameters to initialize the object. There are no clues as to what the valid and invalid values should be.

Another way you can test a parameter passed by objects is to create a dummy object of the class. For this particular test, you can uncheck the Manual Stub check box. Click the Start button, and then the Create Script button to generate a new test project. You can try it and compare the difference between the test scripts.

Testing with Multiple Sets of Data Stores

At this time, instead of copying a method within the same data store to test it with various parameter values, you can use an existing script to test multiple testing cases. Suppose you have just finished building a test script for the `LowLevelObj.dll` assembly and you are going to make multiple data stores. To do so, follow these steps:

1. Open Windows Explorer. Navigate to the `C:\Temp\LowLevelObj\Bin\Debug` folder.
2. Make a few copies of the `testLowLevelObjData.xls` with different filenames.
3. Open the copies in an MS Excel worksheet, and assign different values to the parameters.
4. Save the modifications.
5. Switch to the Automated Software Test form.
6. Click the Add Data Store button. An open file dialog box appears.
7. Navigate to the folder where you made the copies of the data stores (e.g., `C:\Temp\LowLevelObj\Bin\debug`). Select the data store files.
8. Click the Open button. The text box at the bottom of the Automated Software Test form now looks similar to the way it looks in Figure 12.11.
9. From the Automated Software Test form, click the Save Data Store button. The contents in the text box are saved within the following path and filename:

   `C:\Temp\LowLevelObj\Bin\Debug\fileArray.txt.`

FIGURE 12.11
More than one Excel worksheet is added to the automated test

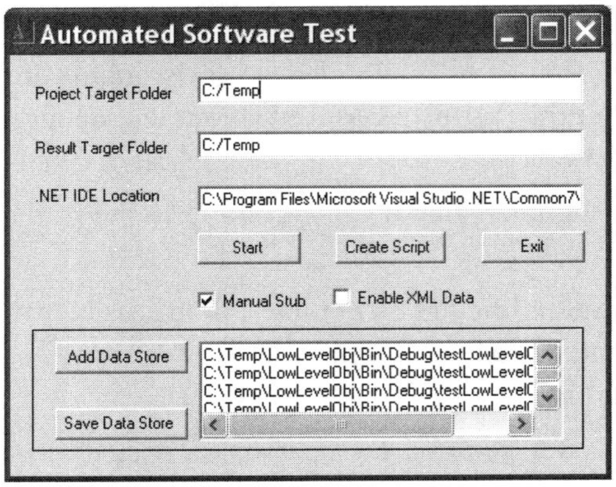

If you open the `fileArray.txt` file with your text editor (e.g., Notepad), you see that the text of this file consists of the paths and filenames of the test data stores:

```
C:\Temp\LowLevelObj\Bin\DebugestLowLevelObjData.xls
C:\Temp\LowLevelObj\Bin\DebugestLowLevelObjData1.xls
C:\Temp\LowLevelObj\Bin\DebugestLowLevelObjData2.xls
C:\Temp\LowLevelObj\Bin\DebugestLowLevelObjData3.xls
```

Now you can navigate to the `C:\Temp\LowLevelObj\Bin\Debug` folder and double-click the `testLowLevelObj.exe` to rerun the test script. It runs four times with the specified data stores this time and produces four MS Excel reports, respectively.

Testing Overloaded Methods

Some methods within a class are often overloaded a few times in order to solve the same problem in different situations and increase the flexibility of a software product. In many a case, finding the overloading information has always been a manual process. Because of the ambiguous parameters, it is hard to know which method to use for a test. Fortunately, you solved this problem by improving the AutomatedTest tool in the previous chapters. Now, let's test an assembly that has methods overloaded.

You might remember the implementation of three `Triangle()` methods within the `AdvancedCalc` class in Chapter 8. These three `Triangle()` methods compute areas for isosceles, equilateral, or scalene triangles, respectively. The constructor of the `AdvancedCalc` class is also overloaded two times. You can follow these steps for a new test:

1. Start the test by clicking the Start button as usual. Navigate to the `C:\SourceCode\Chapter08\HighLevelObj\bin\Debug` folder and select the `HighLevelObj.dll` assembly to open it.

2. This time, you'll select the `AdvancedCalc` class to test. Then you'll see a new Excel worksheet with the names of the class constructors, properties, and methods. Figure 12.12 shows the Excel worksheet for this testing case.
3. There are two constructors. One of them (in row 2) takes no parameter. The other (in row 3) takes one parameter. There are three `Triangle()` methods. The method in row 7 takes one parameter, which calculates the area of an equilateral triangle. The one in row 8 takes two parameters for isosceles, and the one in row 9 takes three parameters for a scalene triangle. Assign values to all the double parameters. In the worksheet, you can modify the values in C9, D9, E9, and F9 to 40, 50, 20, and 379.9671038, respectively, to test an expected return against an actual return. Then, you have to assign a value `new` to C14 for the `lvlMath` object to test the `SimpleCalc()` method. The other values are all left intact as they are assigned by the AutomatedTest tool. And finally, remember to save the modifications.

NOTE Reference parameter values are assigned to yellowish cells. The magenta-colored cells are `out` parameters. In many cases, you can accept the values generated by the AutomatedTest tool. For the triangles, the lengths should be greater than 0 and one side cannot be longer than the sum of the other two sides in order to form a triangle. However, if you intend to test methods with invalid parameter values, you should assign values = 0 to these parameters or let one side be longer than the sum of the other two sides.

4. Save the Excel worksheet.

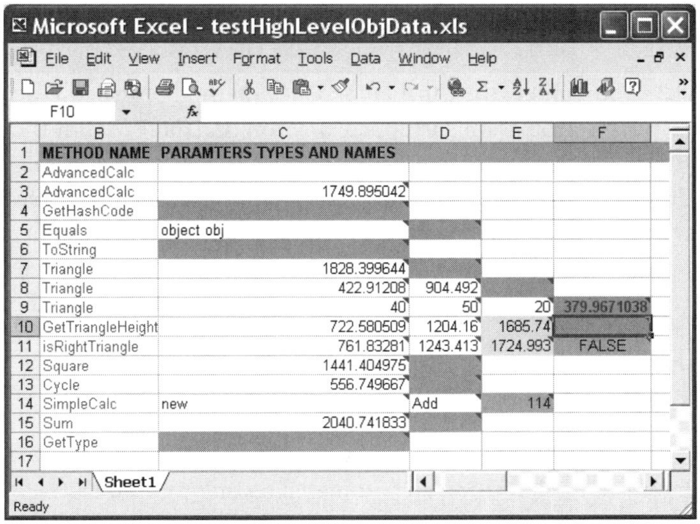

	B	C	D	E	F
1	METHOD NAME	PARAMTERS TYPES AND NAMES			
2	AdvancedCalc				
3	AdvancedCalc	1749.895042			
4	GetHashCode				
5	Equals	object obj			
6	ToString				
7	Triangle	1828.399644			
8	Triangle	422.91208	904.492		
9	Triangle	40	50	20	379.9671038
10	GetTriangleHeight	722.580509	1204.16	1685.74	
11	isRightTriangle	761.83281	1243.413	1724.993	FALSE
12	Square	1441.404975			
13	Cycle	556.749667			
14	SimpleCalc	new	Add	114	
15	Sum	2040.741833			
16	GetType				
17					

FIGURE 12.12 The Excel worksheet with overloaded methods under test

5. Switch to the Automated Software Test form.
6. Leave the Manual Stub check box unchecked.
7. Click the Create Script button to generate the test script project. A new Microsoft Visual Studio .NET IDE opens with the test script loaded.
8. Click F5 (Build and Run) from the Microsoft Visual Studio .NET IDE to conduct the test. The test results should look similar to Figure 12.13.

FIGURE 12.13
Test results with overloaded methods and constructors

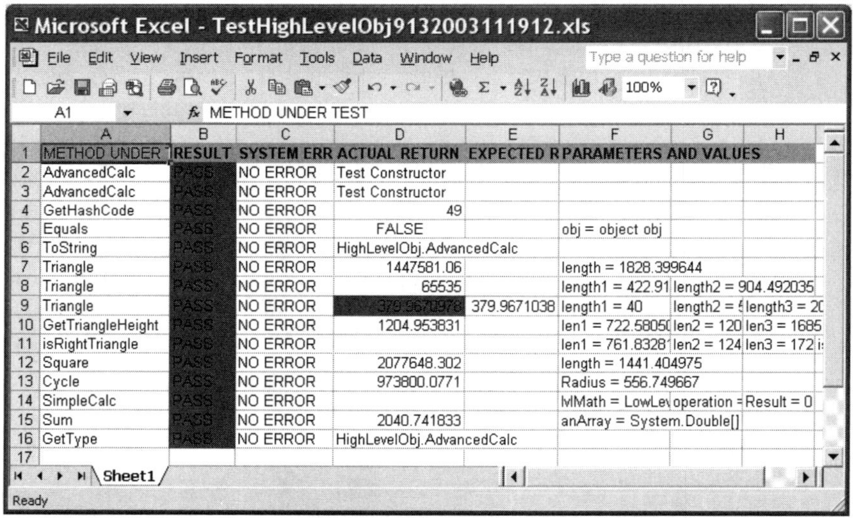

As you can see, the third `Triangle()` method returns an incorrect value for this test case due to the Newton-Raphson approximation (Chapter 8). But the expected return and the actual return are very close to each other. The difference is less than 0.00001. The tolerance for this difference between the actual return and the expected return depends on the requirements of the application under test. Based on my personal interest, I regard this test as a success. To be on the safe side, you may want to use other test cases to test this method and find out the circumstances under which it calculates the area precisely and calculates the area approximately.

Testing Parameters Passed by Arrays

The method to compose array values for this tool is a convenient feature that test engineers are interested in having in an automated testing tool. In the past, when a method under test receives arrays as parameters, test engineers usually needed to play some tricks with the commercial testing tools. But the AutomatedTest tool provides a simpler approach.

In Chapter 8, you programmed a `Sum()` method, which receives a parameter passed by an array. The data type of the array is double. The `Sum()` method adds up all the values of the array elements and returns the summation. In order to complete this test, you can follow these steps to do another test project:

1. Execute the AutomatedTest system.
2. Click the Start button as usual.
3. Point to the `HighLevelObj.dll` assembly created in Chapter 8.
4. Click the Open button on the open file dialog box.
5. Check the check box beside the `AdvancedCalc` class.
6. Click the OK button.
7. The Excel worksheet appears. If a dialog box appears asking you to save the data sheet, click Yes.
8. Now you can modify the test cases. You can leave only one constructor and the `Sum()` method in the worksheet and delete all the other methods. Make three more copies of the `Sum()` method and assign some values to the arrays. Figure 12.14 shows the data sheet after the modification. After saving the data sheet, switch to the Automated Software Test form.

NOTE The values within the arrays are separated by commas. The `Sum()` method is tested four times with different array values.

9. Leave the Manual Stub check box unchecked.
10. Click the Create Script button. Microsoft Visual Studio .NET IDE opens with the TesHighLevelObj project loaded. Press F5 when the Microsoft Visual Studio .NET IDE is active. The test script is executing. Figure 12.15 shows the test results.

FIGURE 12.14 Arrays to test the Sum() method

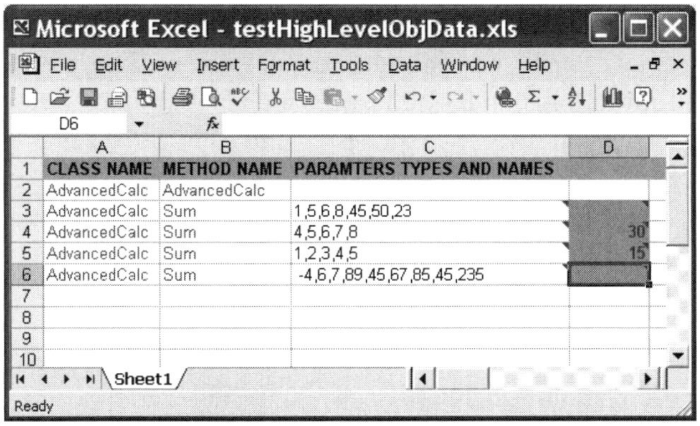

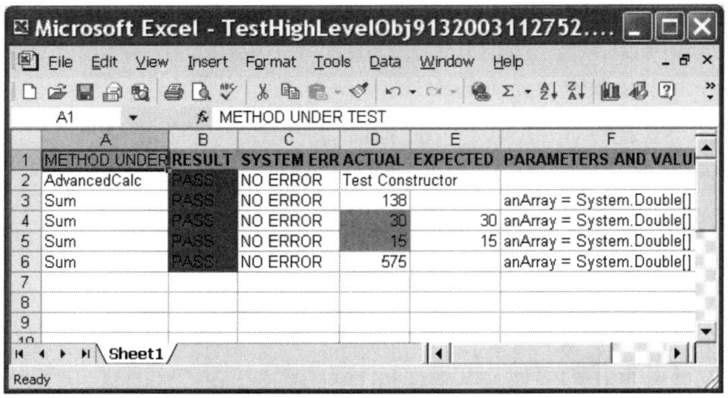

FIGURE 12.15
Testing results of the Sum() method receiving an array as the parameter

Summary

This chapter demonstrated testing capabilities for which there were no examples in other chapters. It began by listing the system requirements necessary to develop and run the AutomatedTest project. Then we tested the `LowLevelObj.dll` and `HighLevelObj.dll` assemblies automatically. These assemblies also test the AutomatedTest tool manually. The worksheet provides various features that make it easy for the test engineers to edit and modify test cases. Many parameter values are assigned by the AutomatedTest tool. The test results verify whether the execution of a method is successful or an error message is reported. It also determines whether the return value of the execution is expected or is invalid. When an error occurs during the execution, the test result tells you what causes the error, which is helpful for developers so they can fix defects the test finds.

Testing examples in the previous chapters emphasized many other testing features of this tool. Using a script that can test all members of a class is the only way to return a complete and real object of this class, which can be reused for integration testing. The complete and real object is the opposite of a stub and mock object. The test script generation has been data driven and fully automated by Reflection and CodeDom techniques. This helps test engineers avoid the traditional reverse-engineering and capture/replay processes. Thus, the testing values are not hard-coded. The full automation is achieved by programming and creating a Microsoft Visual Studio .NET C# project for each test script. This automation can be furthered by late binding because the C# project is a memory image for the CodeDom namespace. Alternatives for automation were also discussed.

You saw how to add more testing requirements to the AutomatedTest project and tested software against the Windows system registry. The AutomatedTest tool demonstrates testing capabilities for processes that are tedious and time consuming when other testing methods are used. By using the methods in this book, you can ensure that your AutomatedTest tool meets specific testing requirements for your organization and is always updated as technology advancements are introduced. It can benefit your development and test project in many ways:

Reduced testing time This tool needs minimal human intervention to collect the testing information, compose the testing cases, generate the test script, execute the test, and present the test results.

Reduced quality assurance cost It is difficult to meet the testing requirements of a company with third-party testing tools because of rapid technology advancements and increasing complexity of the projects. Today, experts urge software developers to develop their tools to automate their software testing projects. This tool can be used for many projects. The testing capabilities are accumulated as projects progress, and this tool is capable of testing new areas the commercial testing tools may not be aware of.

Improved testing effectiveness Because testing is automated, it can be performed day and night, reducing the chance of missing a deadline. More testing is conducted within a short period of time, and more bugs are detected earlier and corrected on time.

Consistent testing metrics Manual testing is conducted by different individuals. Although an organization requires testers to observe a set of standards, individuals tend to make their own judgments. A testing tool can incorporate a set of testing standard and metrics. Therefore, the quality of a software product becomes more measurable.

Improved overall product quality The ultimate result is the improved quality of a final product. A fully automated testing tool saves engineers' time so they can devote more time to the areas that cannot be automated. The product under test will have healthy source code and high-quality supporting materials as well.

NOTE How about GUI testing? Is this automated testing tool capable of testing GUI interfaces? The answer is *no* at this time. GUI testing requires different techniques. I have developed a VB 6.0 version of the AutomatedTest tool. Using this tool, you do not record a test scenario or macro. The tool looks for all GUI components to test by itself. This is a topic for a separate book, however.

Ultimately, this chapter serves as a user's guide for the AutomatedTest tool and concludes the book. I wish you good luck in automating the software testing projects for your organization.

Selected Bibliography

Astels, David. *Test Driven Development: A Practical Guide, 1st Edition.* Upper Saddle River, New Jersey: Prentice Hall PTR, 2003.

Beck, Kent. *Extreme Programming Explained.* Boston, Mass.: Addison-Wesley, 2000.

Beuzer, B. *Software Testing Techniques.* Boston: International Thompson Computer Press, 1990.

Burden, R. L., and J. D. Faires. *Numerical Analysis, 4th Edition.* Boston, Mass.: PWS-Kent, 1989.

Davis, Harold. Visual. *C#™ .NET Programming*. Alameda, Calif.: Sybex, 2002.

Dustin, Elfriede, Jeff Rashka, and John Paul. *Automated Software Testing: Introduction, Management, and Performance*. Boston, Mass.: Addison-Wesley, 1999.

Dustin, Elfriede. *Effective Software Testing: 50 Specific Ways to Improve Your Testing.* Boston, Mass.: Addison-Wesley, 2002.

Graham, Dorothy, and Mark Fewster. *Software Test Automation: Effective Use of Test Execution Tools.* Boston, Mass.: Addison-Wesley, 2000.

ITToolbox. ITToolbox Knowledge Bank Forums. RE: SAP 4.5B Test Scripts. 1999 [cited 1999]. Available from World Wide Web @ `www.sapassist.com/forum/`

Kit, E. *Software Testing in the Real World: Improving the Process.* Boston, Mass.: ACM Press Addison-Wesley Longman, Inc., 1995.

Koomen, Time, and Martin Pol. *Test Process Improvement: A practical step-by-step guide to structured testing.* Boston, Mass.: Addison-Wesley, 1999.

Marick, Brian. "When Should a Test Be Automated?" 1998 [cited 22 December 2003]. Available from World Wide Web @ `www.visualtest.com` Mueller, John Paul. *Visual C#™ .NET Developer's Handbook*™. Alameda, Calif.: Sybex, 2003

Perry, William E. *Effective Methods for Software Testing.* New York City: John Wiley & Sons, 2000.

Petroutsos, Evangelos, and M. Ridgeway. *Visual Basic .NET Developer's Handbook.* Alameda, Calif.: Sybex, 2003.

Petroutsos, Evangelos, and Richard Mansfield. *Visual Basic .NET Power Tools.* Alameda, Calif.: Sybex, 2004.

Pohl , Ira. *C# by Dissection: The Essentials of C# Programming*. Boston, Mass.: Addison-Wesley, 2002.

Price, Jason, and Mike Gunderloy. *Mastering™ Visual C#™ .NET*. Alameda, Calif.: Sybex, 2002.

Shea, Billie. "Software Testing Gets New Respect." In InformationWeek [online magazine]. July 2000 [cited 23 December 2003]. Available from World Wide Web @ `www.informationweek.com/`

Sweeney, Mary Romero. *Visual Basic for Testers*. Berkeley, Calif.: Apress, 2001.

Tassey, Gregory, ed.. *The Economic Impacts of Inadequate Infrastructure for Software Testing*. Collingdale, PA: DIANE Publishing Co, 2003.

Troelson, Andrew. *C# and the .NET Platform*. Berkeley, Calif.: Apress, 2001.

Index

Note to the Reader: Throughout this index **boldfaced** page numbers indicate primary discussions of a topic. *Italicized* page numbers indicate illustrations.

A

B

C

D

E

F

G

H

I

N

O

S

T

W

X